Negro Slavery in Arkansas

Negro Slavery in Arkansas

Orville W. Taylor

Introduction by Carl H. Moneyhon

The University of Arkansas Press
Fayetteville
2000

Originally published in 1958 by Duke University Press.
The University of Arkansas Press edition, 2000.

04   03   02   01   00   5   4   3   2   1

☉ The paper used in this publication meets the minimum requirements of the American National Standard for Permanence of Paper for Printed Library Materials Z39.48-1984.

Library of Congress Cataloging-in-Publication Data

Taylor, Orville W. (Orville Walters), 1917–
    Negro slavery in Arkansas / Orville W. Taylor ; introduction by
    Carl H. Moneyhon.
        p. cm. — (Arkansas classics)
    Originally published: Durham, N.C. : Duke University Press, 1958.
    Includes bibliographical references and index.
    ISBN 1-55728-613-2 (pbk. : alk. paper)
        1. Slavery—Arkansas—History. 2. Afro-Americans—Arkansas—
    History. I. Title. II. Series.
    E445.A8 T3 2000
    973'.0496—dc21

                                                        00-044307

To my wife, Evelyn Bonham
"I can no other answer make but thanks, and thanks, and ever thanks—"
Shakespeare, *Twelfth Night*

Contents

ILLUSTRATIONS

Preface to the Arkansas Classics Edition

MORE THAN FORTY YEARS ago I finished final revisions of the text of this book in my hot mud-walled office at Baptist College in back-country Iwo, Nigeria. A few weeks later, back in the United States on leave from our work as educational missionaries, my wife Evelyn and I burned the midnight oil in Little Rock as we completed the index and sent it to Duke University Press. I am happy that this Arkansas Classics edition is being presented under more comfortable and less-hurried circumstances.

In the months and years after its appearance the book was reviewed widely in scholarly journals and newspapers in the United States and abroad; several years later it was even reviewed in French in a Belgian journal. Most reviewers treated the book kindly, but a few were critical of some portions. I cited the wealth of James Sheppard of Waterford Plantation near Pine Bluff, which grew from a $3,035 legacy in 1847 to more than $161,000 in 1863, as an example of the profitability of slavery. A reviewer felt that I minimized the importance of the legacy and also the low rate of hire of some of the slaves from his father in accounting for the great growth of Sheppard's wealth.

Other reviewers believed I overstated the importance of slavery in a state in which only 3.5 percent of the population owned slaves, paying little attention to my conclusion that, actually, when the families of slave-owners and the slaves themselves are added, at least 42.5 percent of the population was directly involved in slavery. And this does not include the thousands of overseers and their families, merchants, craftsmen, shippers, bankers, and others who were at least partially economically dependent upon slavery.

One reviewer even called me a racist for using my great-great-grandfather's 1857 county tax assessment to demonstrate the high value of slaves compared to other types of property. Despite these criticisms and others, I still hold to my original conclusions.

That other historians and writers have valued the book has been shown by the many hundreds of citations and quotations in dozens of books and articles (sometimes perhaps from lack of other sources!). One now-departed writer even devoted most of five pages to it—with minimum credit. Probably the most gratifying to me is that several historians of slavery used statements from this book to reinforce major conclusions in their own.

In addition to the thanks expressed in the original preface I want to acknowledge many people who have shown continuing interest in slavery in Arkansas by inviting me to read papers or appear otherwise on programs, review books on slavery, and by publishing my articles in journals and encyclopedias or as portions of books.

I especially want to thank the University of Arkansas Press, and in particular Kevin Brock, acquisitions editor, for bringing this book back into print as a volume in the new Arkansas Classics series. I have never considered myself or the book as a "classic," but I am pleased to be in the company of such immortal chroniclers of Arkansas as Thomas Nuttall and Henry Rowe Schoolcraft. I also want to thank Duke University for relinquishing the copyright to me.

Finally, thanks again to my wife, who is still as energetic and helpful as in those long-ago nights of the midnight oil.

Jacksonville, Florida   ORVILLE W. TAYLOR
October 1. 1999

Preface to the 1958 Edition

IN A REAPPRAISAL of historical literature on Negro slavery before a gathering of Southern historians several years ago, Professor Chase C. Mooney of Indiana University called attention to "glaring voids" in the literature on Florida, South Carolina, Texas, and Arkansas. This book has been written in an attempt to fill the Arkansas portion of that void. My primary purpose has been to trace the growth of and describe the institution of slavery as it existed in Arkansas prior to abolition nearly a hundred years ago, but I hope that the book will also help to provide more adequate background for an understanding of racial problems in Arkansas and the South today.

I should like here to acknowledge gratefully the assistance of many people, organizations, and institutions in research, writing, and publication of the book. Duke University generously awarded me several financial grants. The staffs of the following libraries were helpful in my search for materials: Library of Congress, National Archives, Howard University, Duke University, University of North Carolina, Louisiana State University, New Orleans Public Library, Tulane University, Cossit Library (Memphis, Tennessee), University of Chicago, Northwestern University, University of Arkansas, Hendrix College, Arkansas State Teachers College, Ouachita College, Little Rock University, Arkansas History Commission, Arkansas Supreme Court Library, Little Rock Public Library, and many other public libraries in Arkansas.

These individuals rendered various services: Professor Robert H. Woody and the late Professor Charles S. Sydnor, both of the Department of History of Duke University; Mr. Ashbel G. Brice of Duke University Press; Mr. Ted R. Worley, executive secretary of the Arkansas History Commission; Mr. Howard Stebbins, Jr., Mr. Owen Lyon, Mr. John K. Shamburger, the Reverend W. O. Taylor, my father, and Mrs. Glenn H. Packer, my sister, all of Little Rock; Mr. R. C. Stuart of Columbus; Professor Walter J. Lemke of the University of Arkansas; several former colleagues at Little Rock University; a number of fellow-members of the Arkansas Historical Association not otherwise named; and numerous state, county, and city officials. Other people and institutions who permitted me to use collections of manuscripts or other materials are indicated in the book.

Finally, I want to express my deepest appreciation to my wife, Evelyn Bonham Taylor, whose interest, encouragement, and hard work have spanned the book from inception to completion.

Baptist College   ORVILLE W. TAYLOR
Iwo, Nigeria, West Africa
July 15, 1958

Introduction by Carl H. Moneyhon

Orville Taylor's Negro Slavery in Arkansas *and the Study of American Slavery*

WHEN ORVILLE TAYLOR'S *Negro Slavery in Arkansas* appeared in 1958, it was the first scholarly examination of slavery in that state, and over forty years later it remains the only comprehensive study that has been produced. Taylor's work endures as the most thorough investigation of existing primary sources that has been attempted. His observations and conclusions lie at the foundation of subsequent studies of Arkansas's early nineteenth-century history. The book also was an important addition to the revisionist literature of its time. Since the appearance of *Negro Slavery in Arkansas* scholars have changed their approaches to the subject, developed new sources, and explored a wide variety of topics that Taylor did not deal with. Still, his work offers valuable information on and insights into local slavery and is the necessary starting point for any future study of slavery in Arkansas.

Negro Slavery in Arkansas was part of the new scholarship appearing in the middle of the twentieth century that challenged the pervasive interpretation of slavery that had been developed by Ulrich Bonnell Phillips. Phillip's characterization of slavery had been formed at the beginning of the century and, supported by the work of his students, dominated the field for decades. To understand Taylor's work and the new directions that it took, it is important to be aware of the work that he challenged. Phillips was a native Georgian trained in the new "scientific history" while studying at Columbia under the direction of William A. Dunning. Most of his ideas were brought together in his 1918 study *American Negro Slavery,* the first comprehensive modern historical assessment of that institution. In this work, Phillips drew upon a vast array of previously unused primary sources to address what he stated to be his principal concerns: the "rise, nature and influence in the regions of its concentration" of Negro slavery.[1]

Phillips's interpretation of the overall character of slavery in the United States touched on a wide variety of topics and offered numerous insights. Because of its implications for other aspects of his study, however, his determination that slavery was not profitable may be considered the central idea of this work. Examining the development of slavery from the colonial period to its end, Phillips concluded that the institution may have been profitable initially. He also understood that many planters believed it continued to be profitable up to the end. He considered that the expanding cultivation of cash crops into new territories reflected this view. Applying an accounting model to the data gathered from plantation records for the 1850s, however, he found that, especially given the increasing price of slaves as the cotton frontier moved westward, income could not justify the cost of slaves. He concluded that by the 1850s "no slaveholders but those few whose plantations lay in the most advantageous parts of the cotton and sugar districts and whose managerial ability was exceptionally great were earning anything beyond what would cover their [the slave's] maintenance and carrying charges."[2]

Although he did not apply a statistical analysis to the problem, Phillips believed that slavery was equally unprofitable for the South as a whole and, indeed, an economic burden. Phillips drew heavily on the insights of contemporary southerners to catalog the ills produced by slavery. He concluded that investment in slaves produced a scarcity of money, low land values, a failure to develop the natural resources of the southern countryside, and the lack of success in creating industries. In addition, he saw slavery producing economic problems with social implications. Slavery

[1] Ulrich B. Phillips, *American Negro Slavery: A Survey of the Supply, Employment and Control of Negro Labor As Determined by the Plantation Regime* (New York: D. Appleton and Company, 1918), i; for a discussion of Phillips in the broader context of American historiography see Harvey Wish, *The American Historian: A Social-Intellectual History of the Writing of the American Past* (New York: Oxford University Press, 1960), 236–64.

[2] Phillips, *American Negro Slavery,* 211, 359–60, 391–92 (quote).

restricted economic opportunity, led to the steady monopolization of land and slaves by planters, and brought about the segregation of planters and farmers into different regions. While he recognized the prevalence of small farmers and small slaveholders in the production of cotton, nonetheless he believed that the "plantation system" and the planter came to dominate the society. Such problems limited white immigration, restricted overall population growth, and contributed to a sparse, un-urbanized population. Overall, Phillips concluded, "[p]lantation slavery had in strictly business aspects at least as many drawbacks as it had attractions."[3]

The obvious question raised by Phillips's economic assessment of slavery was why Southerners held on to it if it was not profitable. Phillips believed that this happened in part because slavery had evolved into something more than an economic institution. Southerners continued to purchase slaves because of social reasons. He wrote that since "the scale of slaveholdings was in some degree a measure of social rank, . . . men were accordingly tempted by uneconomic motives to increase their trains of retainers." In addition to the social status acquired through the ownership of slaves, Phillips thought that slavery persisted because it kept the main body of labor under control. It maintained necessary order and a degree of harmony in a society that included, as Phillips perceived them, an uncivilized component in its African American laborers. Phillips concluded that "in the large it was less a business than a life; it made fewer fortunes than it made men."[4]

Phillips's appraisal of the profitability of slavery and its broader social role provided the framework for the most controversial aspects of his study, his characterization of slavery itself. Phillips assessed the slave system as one of relative moderation and benignity. Concerning the operations of plantations, Phillips concluded that in most cases, for a combination of economic and social reasons, slaveowners provided their slaves with adequate housing, food, and clothing. The owners also encouraged the development of slave families. They attended to the health of their

---

[3] Ibid., 226, 401 (quote).
[4] Ibid., 394 (first quote), 401 (second quote).

slaves. Because of the value of their slave investments, slave-owners generally did not overwork their slaves. Neither was their punishment severe. While he admitted some slaves were whipped, he found this to be atypical of the system that sought to secure labor through encouraging loyalty and pride and the use of some rewards. As to the controversial charge that planters bred their slaves, he found no evidence that it existed. "The theory of rigid coercion and complete exploitation was as strange to the bulk of the planters as the doctrine and practice of moderation was to those who viewed the regime from afar and with the mind's eye," he wrote.[5]

Phillips went so far as to assert that slavery was a critical means for transforming an uncivilized people into a civilized one. His assumptions concerning the character of the African people and their culture underlay this view. In the first chapter of the book he examined the background of slaves and concluded that the African environment conspired over generations to create physically healthy peoples unable to perform "mental effort of severe or sustained character." Further, it had given Africans a peculiar personality, characterized by Phillips as "[i]mpulsive and inconstant, sociable and amorous, voluble, dilatory, and negligent, but robust, amiable, obedient, and contented." He viewed their social development as rudimentary and concluded that even what little they had had been lost in the Atlantic passage.[6]

Given these considerations, Phillips saw the plantations as schools to raise up a backward peoples. "On the whole," he wrote, "the plantations were the best schools yet invented for the mass training of that sort of inert and backward people which the bulk of the American negroes represented." When he wrote of education, Phillips saw it largely as a process in which whites taught the slaves western customs and values, although he recognized, but did not fully develop, the idea that slaves had some impact on

---

[5] Ibid., see chapter 14, (quote), 293.

[6] Ibid., 4, 8; Eugene D. Genovese has judged this chapter to have been "foolish and incompetent" and "embarrassing." Eugene D. Genovese, introduction to *American Negro Slavery* by U. B. Phillips(Baton Rouge: Louisiana State University Press, 1966), viii.

whites. The process of acculturating Africans was patently one-sided. Planters and their families provided African American slaves with patterns to emulate. The plantation taught the slaves orderly and well-bred conduct, including a work discipline. Paraphrasing an old plantation saying, Phillips agreed that within limits "a negro was what a white man made him."[7]

Since Phillips believed that North American slavery was comparatively mild when compared with the institution elsewhere, he concluded that most slaves became comfortable and relatively happy under the slave regime. Some slaves even secured a degree of autonomy within the system. Phillips observed in the interaction of masters and slaves a certain amount of bargaining and reasoned that running away was more a mechanism for negotiating better working conditions than a reflection of a desire to escape to freedom. While noting the resistance of some slaves to the system, he did not believe that such behavior was typical. Rebellions were few, and he went so far as to suggest that the major impact of this and other slave "crime" was to "restrain that progress of liberalism which the consideration of economic interests, the doctrines of human rights and the spirit of kindness all tended to promote." As a general rule slaves were complacent; and, he suggested, the submissiveness of the slave encouraged the planter in his "paternalism" and the avoidance of the use of more repressive means of controlling the slaves.[8]

Phillips's view of slavery dominated professional history for four decades and raised questions that scholars have addressed since. Initially, case studies of slavery in Alabama, Georgia, Kentucky, Mississippi, and North Carolina appeared that reinforced his basic point of view. In fact, these works often appeared to be little more than the acquiring and cataloging of more details that were fitted within the Phillips thesis. The dominance of Phillips and his ideas in studies published in 1933 by Ralph B. Flanders and Charles S. Sydnor led E. Merton Coulter to refer to their studies uncharitably as "ponderous footnotes" to the master's work. In fact, Sydnor in particular contributed significantly to the

---

[7] Phillips, *American Negro Slavery,* 343 (first quote), 291 (second quote).
[8] Ibid., 488 (first quote), 303, 341–42 (second quote).

xx   *Introduction*

development of the literature on slavery because he attempted in his work to evaluate empirically the question of slave profitability. Still, his conclusions did support those of the "master."[9]

Despite this consensus among many white historians, Phillips's was not the only interpretation of slavery that existed, and soon after the publication of *American Negro Slavery,* contrary voices challenged the work and provided alternative ideas for future scholars to consider. Among the most strident of these other views were those of African American historians. In a review of Phillips in the *Mississippi Valley Historical Review,* Carter G. Woodson, the son of freedmen who had received a Ph.D. from Harvard and then devoted the rest of his life to the study of African American history, found the book "far from being the last word on the subject." His central criticism of Phillips was that he had failed to consider the slaves themselves in this study, instead treating them as "goods and chattels in the cold-blooded fashion that their masters bartered them away." Woodson refused to believe that any slaves were satisfied with slavery or that in any way it could be defended for its moderation.[10]

Woodson and scholars who contributed to his *Journal of Negro History* worked to undermine Phillips's views on the character of African culture and the process of slave acculturation with articles on Africa and slave life published in the 1920s and 1930s, but much of their work was ignored by white historians. The work of prominent anthropologist Melville J. Herskovits could not be brushed aside as easily, however. Herskovits's attack on Phillips's view began in his 1935 article entitled "What Has Africa Given America?" He concluded that in a variety of forms African culture survived in the face of American slavery. In his *The Myth of the*

---

[9] E. M. Coulter review in *The Mississippi Valley Historical Review* 11 (June 1934): 96 (quote); Rosser H. Taylor, *Slaveholding in North Carolina: An Economic View* (Chapel Hill: University of North Carolina Press, 1926); Ralph Betts Flanders, *Plantation Slavery in Georgia* (Chapel Hill: University of North Carolina Press, 1933); Charles S. Sydnor, *Slavery in Mississippi* (New York; D. Appleton-Century Company, 1933); J. Winston Coleman, *Slavery Times in Kentucky* (Chapel Hill: University of North Carolina Press); and James B. Sellers, *Slavery in Alabama* (University: University of Alabama Press, 1950).

[10] Review in *Mississippi Valley Historical Review* 5 (1918–1919): 480–2, 480 (first quote), 481 (second quote).

Negro Past, published six years later, he went further and attacked the whole concept of a peculiar African American personality as had been defined by Phillips. In 1936 Carter Woodson added to the development of this new perspective with his *The African Background Outlined,* a study that argued African Americans were developing their own culture under slavery and in the process were drawing heavily upon African folkways in their efforts.[11]

Even among some mainstream white historians criticism of Phillips started to emerge as scholars began to test his other conclusions. A major point of contention centered around his idea that slavery had not been profitable. In 1933 Lewis Gray's *History of Agriculture in the Southern States* challenged Phillips's conclusions and contended that the continued expansion of slaveholding and the refusal to divert investment capital into areas other than the production of staple crops argued for the profitability of slavery and the plantation. Robert R. Russel added weight to Gray's assessment with an article on the impact of slavery on economic progress in the South that appeared in 1938.[12]

The debate moved onto more empirical grounds in 1942 when Thomas P. Govan looked at the question in his "Was Plantation Slavery Profitable?" Much of Phillips's argument had been based upon assertion, but Sydnor had developed a systematic analysis of profits and losses on a theoretical Mississippi plantation. It was Sydnor's model that Govan attacked. He concluded that some of the sums Sydnor had charged against profits in his assessment of the income of the plantation were not warranted. As a result, Govan found that Sydnor's model plantation was very profitable with a return of 13 percent on its investment. Everyone did not accept Govan's argument, as evidenced by Robert W. Smith's 1946 article "Was Slavery Profitable in the Ante-Bellum South?"

[11] Melville J. Herskovits, "What Has African Given America?" *New Republic* 84 (September 4, 1935): 92–94; Melville J. Herskovits, *The Myth of the Negro Past* (New York and London: Harper & Brothers, 1941); and Carter G. Woodson, *The African Background Outlined, or Handbook for the Study of the Negro* (Washington, D.C.: Associated Publishers, 1936).

[12] Lewis Gray, *History of Agriculture in Southern United States to 1860,* 2 vols. (Washington, D.C.: Carnegie Institute, 1933); Robert R. Russel, "The General Effects of Slavery upon Southern Economic Progress," *Journal of Southern History* 4 (January 1938): 34–54.

Nonetheless, Govan had raised serious questions about this key element in the Phillips thesis.[13]

An equally serious question raised about Phillips's work was the representativeness of the plantations that he used as the basis for his study. In 1944 Richard Hofstadter point out that Phillips had drawn most of the cases upon which his conclusions were based from among plantations with one hundred or more slaves. This was hardly representative of the typical slaveholding in the antebellum South. While perhaps 19 percent of slaves lived on such holdings, only 1 percent of slaveholdings were that large. Hofstadter doubted that conditions on the larger holdings were the same as those on the smaller ones, although he believed that the topic needed further investigation.[14]

Phillips's views on the benign character of slavery also came under attack from several directions. African American sociologist E. Franklin Frazier's *The Negro Family in the United States* appeared in 1939 and offered serious criticism of the effect of slavery on the African American family. He agreed with Phillips that slaves had left behind the institutions of their African past, including ideas of the family. Frazier argued, however, that this showed the evil of slavery, since he attributed the absence of an African culture among the slaves to their enslavement. As to the African American family, he believed that slavery was profoundly injurious for that institution and had destroyed it as a stable platform upon which African Americans could develop a functioning community.[15]

A further assault upon the idea of the moderation of the slave regime came from works such as Frank J. Klingberg's *An Appraisal of the Negro in Colonial South Carolina* that was published in 1941. Klingberg's work was a study of the observations of missionaries from the Anglican Church's Society for the

[13] Thomas P. Govan, "Was Plantation Slavery Profitable?" *Journal of Southern History* 8 (November 1942): 513–35; Robert W. Smith, "Was Slavery Profitable in the Ante-bellum South?" *Agricultural History* 20 (January 1946): 62–64.

[14] Richard Hofstadter, "U. B. Phillips and the Plantation Legend," *Journal of Negro History* 29 (April 1944): 109–24.

[15] E. Franklin Frazier, *The Negro Family in the United States* (Chicago: University of Chicago, 1939).

Propagation of the Faith in Foreign Parts. The work detailed planter attitudes toward their slaves and also described their treatment. While his description of conditions paralleled that of Phillips to a degree, Klingberg brought a different perspective to this material. Rather than finding the treatment of the slaves moderate, he concluded that it was cruel.[16]

As Phillips faced challenges to his ideas concerning African culture and its transfer to the Americas, slave profits, and slave treatment, his ideas concerning slave personality also encountered objections. Race had been a continuing concern in many areas of American scholarship through the early twentieth century, and by the 1940s research in basic sciences and social sciences had seriously weakened theories of racial uniqueness. By the 1940s it was impossible to argue that African slaves were suited to enslavement because of their race.[17]

Within the framework of this new interpretation of African American character, a variety of slave behaviors took on new meaning. Both Raymond A. and Alice H. Bauer's "Day to Day Resistance to Slavery" from 1942 and Herbert Aptheker's *American Negro Slave Revolts* in 1943 portrayed the slaves as imbued with a human spirit that could not be satisfied with enslavement. Aptheker in particular concluded that for the slave day-to-day life involved a constant struggle to be free. Both studies found the slaves to be anything but submissive. Instead, slaves resisted oppression, striking out at their masters in whatever way that they could. Their tools ranged from work slowdowns, designed to deprive the master of the fruits of their labor, to open rebellions, such as that of Nat Turner. Rather than obedience and resignation, discontent and rebellion constantly characterized slave life.[18]

[16] Frank J. Klingberg, *An Appraisal of the Negro in Colonial South Carolina: A Study in Americanization* (Washington, D.C.: The Associated Publishers, 1941).

[17] See in particular Gunnar Myrdal, *An American Dilemma: The Negro Problem and Modern Democracy* (New York and London: Harper & Brothers, 1944); Otto Klineberg, ed., *Characteristics of the American Negro* (New York and London: Harper & Brothers, 1944).

[18] Raymond A. and Alice H. Bauer, "Day to Day Resistance to Slavery," *Journal of Negro History* 27 (October 1942): 388–419; Herbert Aptheker, *American Negro Slave Revolts* (New York: Columbia University Press, 1943); see also Harvey Wish, "American Slave Insurrections before 1861," *Journal of Negro History* 28 (1937): 299–320.

John Hope Franklin summed up the direction the work of scholars such as Frazier, Klingberg, the Bauers, and Aptheker was taking historical scholarship and many of his conclusions in *From Slavery to Freedom* which appeared in 1947. In this general study of the history of African Americans, Franklin brought the insights of the historical revisionists to his examination of slavery, introducing materials on African civilization and on slave perspectives of slavery. This discussion of slavery not as the masters thought it should be but rather through the eyes of the slaves offered a new perspective that required a total reassessment of slavery.[19]

By the 1950s Phillips's work remained central to most mainstream history, but enough studies challenging his methodology and his central assumptions regarding race had appeared that it was obvious that the generalizations he had made were inadequate. When James B. Sellers's 1950 study *Slavery in Alabama* appeared and approached the topic using the same questions asked by Phillips, it was not well received. Weymouth T. Jordan's review of the book in the *Journal of Southern History* noted the absence of an effort to see slavery through the eyes of the slaves. "As in other studies," he noted negatively, "the Alabama slave's own concepts and reactions to his condition are presented only through a discussion of some of his protests, such as crimes committed and efforts to run away." That a change in how historians viewed Phillips was made even clearer in Kenneth Stampp's 1952 article in the *Journal of Southern History* in which Stampp concluded: "We are still waiting for the first scientific and completely exhaustive study of the institution which is based upon no assumptions whose validity cannot be thoroughly proved."[20]

When Orville Taylor began working in the 1950s on his study of slavery in Arkansas as his dissertation at Duke University, scholarship in the field was on the verge of revolutionary change. The result of his research placed him at the edge of the revolution,

---

[19] John Hope Franklin, *From Slavery to Freedom* (New York: Alfred A. Knopf, 1947).
[20] Weymouth T. Jordan review in *Journal of Southern History* 16 (November 1950): 539 (first quote); Kenneth M. Stampp, "The Historian and Southern Negro Slavery," *Journal of American History* 57 (April 1952): 613 (second quote).

approaching his topic in a very traditional manner but bringing a host of new insights and differing personal attitudes to the study. The traditional approach was to be expected. Taylor worked with Charles S. Sydnor and the methodology, even to the topics examined, showed Sydnor's influence.

Like his mentor Sydnor, Taylor devoted much of his book to a detailed portrait of slavery in Arkansas as an institution defined by the law or conceived of by whites. His discussion of the demographic aspects of slavery and its legal framework under the French and Spanish, the territorial government, and then the state remain unsurpassed in the material provided on these topics. He developed significant information on the internal slave trade, the character of slave sales and pricing, plus the extent of the practice of slave hiring. His discussion of the character of work engaged in by slaves was exhaustive, and he provided a detailed description of such matters as slave housing, food, clothing, and health. He devoted whole chapters to white efforts to promote religion among the slaves and the character of the slave family promoted by whites. He carefully described the existence of free blacks in Arkansas.

In offering an analysis of the topic, Taylor came closest to the interpretations of Phillips in his discussion of the way slaves worked and how the masters treated them. He believed fear of damaging slave property stood as a factor that limited the degree of punishment masters and overseers imposed upon their slaves. He thought that incentives were used to secure labor more commonly than whippings, although he recognized that at times whites treated their slaves with enormous cruelty. He attributed such action to overseers or to instances when in the heat of anger an individual forgot the value of their property. Still, he concluded that "while whipping was common, it is doubtful that it was usually as brutal as often alleged."[21]

On the other hand, Taylor's work was not a simple replication of the Phillips analysis. His bibliography indicated his awareness

---

[21] Orville W. Taylor, *Negro Slavery in Arkansas* (Durham, N.C.: Duke University Press, 1958), 204 (first quote), 105, 106.

of the pioneering works of Gray and Sellers on the profitability of slavery. He also had read Apetheker's study of slave revolts, and he was familiar with the ideas of Carter Woodson. As the list of his secondary sources would suggest, *Slavery in Arkansas* was a work that was aware of changing views. Taylor's introduction also suggested another difference: his acceptance of new white attitudes towards blacks. His purpose in writing the book, this native Arkansan stated, was his hope that it would somehow help produce some understanding of "racial problems in Arkansas and the South today."[22]

As a result of his different perspective, Taylor broke with Phillips and his mentor in major aspects of the study. His assessment of the growth and expansion of slavery in the antebellum years led him to conclude that slavery in Arkansas was, throughout its existence, a "vital and growing institution."[23] Ultimately, he devoted an entire chapter to the topic and applied his own quantitative assessment to the question of slave profitability. He cautiously concluded, however, that while the local evidence supported the contentions of Gray and Govan, it was "not necessary to disagree wholly with Phillips, Sydnor, and like thinkers," who had admitted that slavery could be profitable in favorable circumstances.[24]

Another theme introduced but not well developed was his observation that slavery was an institution of pervasive importance throughout white society in Arkansas and that planters had not monopolized the slaves or wealth of the state. Demonstrating that as many as 17.5 percent of whites either owned slaves or were in families that owned slaves, plus showing that slave smallholdings were spread throughout the state, he concluded that slavery was important in every section and across class lines.[25] The initial observation was of particular significance for it challenged traditional views that Arkansas divided on the question of slavery

[22] Ibid., vii.
[23] Ibid., 48.
[24] Ibid., 121.
[25] Ibid., 56, 58.

along regional lines because of the absence of slavery in the mountainous regions of the state.

As to the character of the institution, Taylor did not agree that it was the benign institution portrayed by Phillips. Looking at the slave trade in the state, he recognized that many slaveowners wanted to preserve slave families, but he noticed that in practice that often did not take place. Noting an advertisement for the purchase of two girls, aged ten to fourteen, Taylor concluded that they "hardly could have been obtained without separating them from their mothers!" He recognized that masters attended to their slaves' health, but saw it primarily as an expression of "mercenary concern." He saw the religious efforts of the masters as intended largely to promote obedience among their slaves. He also hypothesized a considerable degree of sexual relations between slaves and masters and reasoned it to be a matter of exploitation, with powerful men making advances on powerless women.[26]

On slave marriages and the slave family, Taylor's investigation of conditions in Arkansas brought him to conclusions very similar to those reached by E. Franklin Frazier in his work. Taylor found that the lack of legal marriages and the "varying standards and requirements concerning the marital relationships of their slaves" held by different owners contributed to "sexual promiscuity" in the quarters, and he believed this stood in the way of the development of more stable marital relations.[27]

Taylor further broke with previous studies as he tried to inject slave views of slavery into his story. As has been true of all historians who have tried to find the voices of slaves, he was limited by existing evidence. The typescripts of the WPA slave narratives, which subsequently became a major source providing this perspective, were not at the time generally available. However, Taylor did use material from that collection that had been published by B. A. Botkin in *Lay My Burden Down*. He also mined the autobiography of Scott Bond, a former slave in Arkansas, for insights into the institution.

[26] Ibid., 67 (first quote), 151 (second quote), 201.
[27] Ibid., 195 (first quote).]

Taylor's work was an important case study that modified much of the traditional history of slavery. Despite Taylor's accomplishments, however, the assault upon that view was just beginning and almost every aspect of the field changed rapidly after *Negro Slavery in Arkansas* appeared. Any future student of slavery in Arkansas will have to consider Taylor's work but must also be aware of the drastic changes that have taken place in the field since Taylor and following the publication of two books that marked the beginning of a virtual revolution in slavery studies, those of Kenneth M. Stampp and Stanley Elkins.

The first, Stampp's *The Peculiar Institution,* appeared in 1956, while Taylor was teaching in Africa. Many of its revisionist conclusions were similar to those formed by Taylor in his research. Stampp attempted to bring the slave's perspective to his study of slavery, although his critics believed he had imposed the standards of white scholars in the mid–twentieth century. In fact, like Taylor, Stampp had difficulties finding the sources that would allow the slaves to speak for themselves. His differing perspectives, however, allowed him to turn traditional interpretations on their head. Stampp saw slavery as a brutal system underpinned by greed that produced profits by exploiting slave laborers. He brushed aside Phillips's view of the masters as paternalistic. The power of the masters and their willingness to use ruthless means to control their labor kept the system going, certainly not any contentment with their situation on the part of the slaves. "They [the slaves] longed for freedom and resisted bondage as much as any people could have done in their circumstances," he wrote. In the end, however, after Stampp it would be impossible to study slavery without considering the slaves. Stampp ended his book with a telling quote from a former slaves: "Tisn't he who has stood and looked on, that can tell you what slavery is,—'tis he who has endured."[28]

[28] Kenneth M. Stampp, *The Peculiar Institution: Slavery in the Ante-Bellum South* (New York: Alfred A. Knopf, 1956), 140 (first quote), 430 (second quote); Stampp's book was not received well by all scholars. In his review of the book for the *Journal of Southern History,* Chase C. Mooney, working on his study of slavery in Tennessee at this time, charged that Stampp had introduced no new information to the study of slavery but simply applied twentieth-century values to create his reinterpretation. See review of Chase C. Mooney in *Journal of Southern History* 23 (February 1957): 125–28.

Stampp demanded slavery be viewed from the slave's perspective, but equally important in setting the agenda for future studies was Stanley Elkins's *Slavery,* published in 1959. Elkins agreed with Stampp's view concerning the evils of slavery and went on to argue that North American slavery was a brutal and closed system comparable to Nazi concentration camps during World War II. He suggested that these conditions denied African American slaves significant role models within their own community upon which they could build personalities. Instead, their character was formed in reaction to the demands of their masters. The result was the creation of the Sambo character. In fact, Elkins concluded that such a personality was most likely to appear among the gang workers on large plantations, and he recognized that many slaves lived in more complex environments. His interpretation generated a strong and hostile response, but his ideas challenged scholars to discover the extent to which African cultural models survived in North America and the cultural forces at work within slave communities.[29]

Was slavery the paternalistic institution portrayed by Phillips or the exploitive system seen by Stampp? How did the slaves perceive their lives? What were the characteristics of their lives and what forces contributed to them? Even though scholars have explored a variety of topics associated with slavery, almost every study of slavery since Stampp and Elkins has attempted to answer these questions. The result of these works has been a revolution in our understanding of slavery.[30]

One of these areas was a continued exploration of the economic aspects of the institution where questions of its paternalistic versus exploitive character hinged. Much of this work was done by economic historians and economists who applied statistical analysis to the slave economy. In 1958 Alfred H. Conrad and John R. Meyer were the first to enter the discussion with an

---

[29] Stanley Elkins, *Slavery: A Problem in American Intellectual and Institutional Life* (Chicago: University of Chicago Press, 1959).

[30] The discussion of slave historiography that follows does not pretend to be exhaustive. I have chosen to omit the literature comparing North American slavery with slavery elsewhere in the world, the development of slavery, the evolution of slave law, and urban slavery because these topics do not appear as relevant to the Arkansas case as other topics introduced.

article that used extensive statistical evidence to support their contention that for the individual planter slavery usually was profitable and that the rate of return they received on their investment was as good as was received elsewhere in the nation at this time. Even more conclusive was Robert W. Fogel and Stanley L. Engerman's *Time on the Cross* that appeared in 1974. Fogel and Engerman not only argued that slave investment produced profits but went further to claim that the slave system was profitable to the South. Their work set off something of a firestorm of reaction, however, when they went on to conclude that the institution was relatively benign, with conditions for slaves comparable to those of contemporary manufacturing workers in the North.[31]

The work of Fogel and Engerman appears to have settled the question of the profitability of slavery for individual planters, but the issue of slavery's impact on the southern economy remains unresolved and a topic that has generated an extensive literature hostile to Fogel and Engerman's conclusion. While many scholars have used the same methodology as Fogel and Engerman to suggest that slavery restricted economic development, one of the major contributors to that discussion, Eugene D. Genovese, has argued that actual profits or losses are irrelevant to the question. Genovese contended that reliance on slave labor gave the South's elites a precapitalist outlook that made them resist economic change that might have threatened their social position and consequently kept the South from developing in alternative ways.[32]

An area of research that has produced an even greater amount of scholarship has been the investigation of the character of the slave community and the influences at work within it. John Blassingame's *The Slave Community* published in 1972 was both a summing up of already existing insights into the slave world through the eyes of the slaves and a response to Elkins. If the state

[31] Alfred H. Conrad and John R. Meyer, "The Economics of Slavery in the Ante Bellum South," *Journal of Political Economy* 66 (April 1958): 95–130; Robert W. Fogel and Stanley L. Engerman, *Time on the Cross: The Economics of American Negro Slavery*, 2 vols. (Boston: Little Brown and Co., 1974).

[32] Eugene D. Genovese, *The Political Economy of Slavery* (New York: Pantheon Books, 1965); see also his *The World the Slaveholders Made* (New York: Pantheon Books, 1969) and *Roll, Jordan, Roll* (New York: Pantheon Books, 1974).

studies that followed Phillips can be considered footnotes to his work, it may be said that much of the literature since Blassingame has been an elaboration on his conclusions.

Blassingame responded directly to Elkins, arguing that Sambo was not the dominant slave personality nor was slavery a closed system. Instead, he saw slavery as a complex institution within which slaves possessed a variety of resources that allowed them to maintain their self-esteem. Blassingame pointed particularly to life in the quarters as providing slaves with African traditions, African American religious ideas, stable family life, and African American role models that were more important in shaping personality than the contributions of the masters. The result was slaves who were hostilely submissive, who simulated deference, who in the end preserved their manhood. Blassingame's basic ideas were reinforced by other general studies that appeared at about the same time.[33]

While Genovese believed actual profitability was irrelevant to the question, much of this literature has focused on statistical measurements in an effort to determine slavery's impact on the South. Most of this research has suggested that slavery placed serious limits on the region's economic development. See in particular Gavin Wright, *The Political Economy of the Cotton South: Households, Markets, and Wealth in the Nineteenth Century* (New York: W. W. Norton and Co., 1978). Other works in the same category include Alfred H. Conrad, et al., "Slavery as an Obstacle to Economic Growth in the United States: A Panel Discussion," *Journal of Economic History* 27 (December 1967): 518–60; Marvin Fishbaum and Julius Rubin, "Slavery and the Economic Development of the American South," *Explorations in Entrepreneurial History,* 2nd ser., 6 (1968): 116–27; Julius Rubin, "The Limits of Agricultural Progress in the Nineteenth-Century South," *Agricultural History* 49 (1975): 362–73; and Norris W. Pryer, "Why Did Industrialization Lag in the Old South?" *Georgia Historical Quarterly* 55 (1971): 378–89.

That there remains no agreement on this issue may be seen in Fred Bateman and Thomas Weiss, *A Deplorable Scarcity: The Failure of Industrialization in the Slave Economy* (Chapel Hill: University of North Carolina Press, 1981). In this study the authors agree that the development of southern manufacturing lagged behind that of the northeast (although not the northwest), but blamed this on limitations on markets created by the South's inadequate transportation system.

[33] John Blassingame, *The Slave Community* (New York: Oxford University Press, 1972).

For other studies offering similar views, see George P. Rawick's first volume to the published slave narratives, *From Sundown to Sunup: The Making of the Black Community. The American Slave: A Composite Autobiography,* vol. 1 (Westport, Conn.: Greenwood Publishing Co., 1972); Eugene D. Genovese's *Roll, Jordan, Roll* and *The World the Slaves Made*; Thomas L. Webber, *Deep Like the Rivers: Education in the Slave Quarter Community, 1831–1865* (New York: W. W. Norton and Co., 1978); and Paul D. Escott, *Slavery Remembered: A Record of Twentieth-Century Slave Narratives* (Chapel Hill: University of North Carolina Press, 1979).

Most scholars since have agreed with Blassingame's basic idea concerning the viability of the slave community as a force in establishing independent personalities among the slaves and have focused on identifying the character of that community. One aspect of that research has been an effort to pinpoint the degree to which African traditions survived among American slaves, with scholars seeing factors as time, size of the slave population, and isolation from whites as playing roles in the extent to which Africanisms endured. Nonetheless, all agree that African traditions remained present in the slave community and played a role in the emergence of African American culture. African religious beliefs and practices, concepts concerning life, folk knowledge, music, dance, and even language all contributed to the creation of a creole culture that was African and American.[34]

Another major area of investigation has been the slave family where researchers have produced a picture of the slave family that

---

[34] Much of this literature emerged out of the pathbreaking work of Melville Herskovits, and a considerable amount of it was concerned with African influences on religion. See in particular Leonard E. Barrett, *Soul-Force: African Heritage in Afro-American Religion* (Garden City, N.Y.: Anchor Press, 1974) and Albert J. Raboteau, *Slave Religion: The "Invisible Institution" in the Antebellum South* (New York: Oxford University Press, 1978); Sterling Stuckey, *Slave Culture: Nationalist Theory and the Foundations of Black America* (New York: Oxford University Press, 1987); and Mechal Sobel, *The World They Made Together: Black and White Values in Eighteenth-Century Virginia* (Princeton: Princeton University Press, 1987).

For a look at the survival of African musical styles see Dena J. Epstein, *Sinful Tunes and Spirituals: Black Folk Music to the Civil War* (Urbana: University of Illinois Press, 1977).

Lawrence W. Levine, *Black Culture and Black Consciousness: Afro-American Folk Thought from Slavery to Freedom* (New York: Oxford University Press, 1977) explores the influences of African cosmology and folk knowledge on African American life.

Among the most recent explorations of African survivals is Joseph E. Holloway, ed., *Africanisms in American Culture* (Bloomington and Indianapolis: Indiana University Press, 1990); William D. Piersen, *From Africa to America: African American History from the Colonial Era to the Early Republic, 1526–1790* (New York: Twayne Publishers, an Imprint of Simon & Schuster Macmillan, 1996); and Michael A. Gomez, *Exchanging Our Country Marks: The Transformation of African Identities in the Colonial and Antebellum South* (Chapel Hill and London: University of North Carolina Press, 1998).

For local studies that emphasize the importance of African heritage see Peter H. Wood, *Black Majority, Negroes in Colonial South Carolina from 1670 Through the Stono Rebellion* (New York: W. W. Norton, 1974) and Gwyndolyn Midlo Hall, *Africans in Colonial Louisiana: The Development of Afro-Creole Culture in the Eighteenth Century* (Baton Rouge: Louisiana State University Press, 1992).

differed markedly from that of Frazier. In his 1976 study *The Black Family in Slavery and Freedom, 1750–1925*, Herbert G. Gutman advanced a new interpretation that saw the slave family as a stable unit, despite the restrictions placed upon it by the masters. Gutman concluded that most slaves lived in and valued the traditional nuclear family, but also recognized that slavery encouraged as a matter of survival the development of an extended kinship network that ultimately encompassed an entire plantation, with all adults ultimately taking some responsibility for the rearing of children. For Gutman the family became the repository of black culture in North America, especially as the importation of new slaves from Africa declined, and the means through which slave children achieved an identity and acquired a sense of self-worth. Subsequent scholarship largely has reinforced Gutman, although recent works have emphasized the varieties of family life generated by different circumstances, such as the size of a slave holding, location in a border state, or rural or urban residence.[35]

A spin-off of family studies and of the growing historical interest in gender has been the development of a rich literature on slave women. Much of this work has emphasized the critical role women played in the development of the slave community and in the acculturation of black children. Deborah Gray White's *Arn'n't I a Woman? Female Slaves in the Plantation South* from 1985 was among the first serious scholarly studies of the subject, and she showed how the tendency to organize plantation labor along gender lines allowed women to establish contacts among themselves and create networks of relationships that made it possible for them

---

[35] Herbert G. Gutman, *The Black Family in Slavery and Freedom, 1750–1925* (New York: Pantheon Books, 1976); Larry E. Hudson Jr., *To Have and to Hold: Slave Work and Family Life in Antebellum South Carolina* (Athens and London: The University of Georgia Press, 1997).

For studies suggesting variations in the nature of the slave family see Orville Vernon Burton, *In My Father's House Are Many Mansions: Family and Community in Edgefield, South Carolina* (Chapel Hill and London: University of North Carolina Press, 1985); Ann Patton Malone, *Sweet Chariot: Slave Family and Household Structure in Nineteenth-Century Louisiana* (Chapel Hill and London: University of North Carolina Press, 1992); and Brenda E. Stevenson, *Life in Black & White: Family and Community in the Slave South* (New York and Oxford: Oxford University Press, 1996).

to play a major role in the creation of the African American community.[36]

In addition to family life and gender issues, the religious culture of slaves has also attracted considerable scholarly attention. Luther P. Jackson pioneered this work with his 1931 article, "Religious Development of the Negro in Virginia from 1760 to 1860," but the field exploded in the 1970s as scholars began their search for the roots of African American and slave culture. Scholars such as Lawrence Levine, Eugene Genovese, Olli Alho, Albert Raboteau, and Mechal Sobel produced works that concluded that the slaves were able to create a religion that served their own purposes within that established by their masters. This religion synthesized the ideas of their African past, Christian theology, and current needs into what Raboteau called an "invisible church." This church provided a framework of support for slaves within which they could assert their individual worth as equal creatures of God.[37]

Emphasis upon family and religion as the source of African American culture produced something of a reaction in the 1990s

[36] Deborah Gray White, *Arn'n't I a Woman? Female Slaves in the Plantation South* (New York: W. W. Norton & Co., 1985); Jacqueline Jones, *Labor of Love, Labor of Sorrow: Black Women, Work and the Family from Slavery to the Present* (New York: Basic Books, Inc., 1985); Elizabeth Fox-Genovese, *Within the Plantation Household: Black and White Women of the Old South* (Chapel Hill: University of North Carolina Press, 1988); Patricia Morton, ed., *Discovering the Women in Slavery: Emancipating Perspectives on the American Past* (Athens, Ga. and London: University of Georgia Press, 1996); and David Barry Gaspar and Darlene Clark Hine, eds., *More than Chattel: Black Women and Slavery in the Americas* (Bloomington and Indianapolis: Indiana University Press, 1996).

[37] Luther P. Jackson, "Religious Development of the Negro in Virginia from 1760 to 1860," *Journal of Negro History* 16 (1931): 168–239; Genovese, *Roll, Jordan, Roll;* Lawrence W. Levine, *Black Culture and Black Consciousness: Afro-American Folk Thought from Slavery to Freedom* (New York: Oxford University Press, 1977); Olli Alho, *The Religion of the Slaves: A Study of the Religious Tradition and Behavior of Plantation Slaves in the United States, 1830–1865* (Helsinki, Finland: Suomalainen Tiedeakatemia, Academia Scientiarum Fennica, 1976); Raboteau, *Slave Religion* and Mechal Sobel, *Trabelin' On: The Slave Journey into an Afro-Baptist Faith* (Westport, Conn.: Greenwood Press, 1979).

See also Sylvia R. Frey, "'The Year of Jubilee Is Come'; Black Christianity in the Plantation South in Post-Revolution America," in *Religion in a Revolutionary Age,* Ronald Hoffman and Peter J. Albert, eds., (Charlottesville: University Press of Virginia, 1994). See also the relevant essays in John B. Boles, ed., *Masters and Slaves in the House of the Lord: Race and Religion in the American South, 1740–1870* (Lexington: University Press of Kentucky, 1988).

among scholars exploring slave labor. This work has suggested that labor also played a role in giving slaves the autonomy within which they could work out their own lives. Numerous ways have been found in which the slaves secured this autonomy in their work. The development of internal economies involving the growing of foods for consumption, fishing and hunting, and the construction of household objects all worked to give some slaves the resources to improve their lives. Studies of slaves in industrial and urban labor situations have also emphasized the degree of autonomy allowed slaves in such situations.[38]

A further aspect of the development of the modern analysis of the roots of black culture has been the focus on resistance as an element of that culture. While African tradition, family, religion, and even labor provided ways in which the slaves took control over their own lives, in a system where the master possessed overwhelming power, individual or community resistance was the only way for slaves to protect themselves. Studies of slave resistance turned the racial stereotyping of earlier generations on its head, discovering in many of the traits believed to prove black inferiority resistance to enslavement. Breaking tools, mistreating animals, destroying crops, slowing down work, theft, and running away were all seen by whites as evidence of black inadequacies. The new

---

[38] For discussions of these internal economies see the essays in Ira Berlin and Phillip Morgan, eds. *The Slaves' Economy: Independent Production by Slaves in the Americas* (Portland, Ore., and London: Frank Cass & Co., Ltd., 1991); and Ira Berlin and Philip Morgan, eds., *Cultivation and Culture: Labor and the Shaping of Slave Life in the Americas,* Carter G. Woodson Institute Series in Black Studies (Charlottesville and London: University Press of Virginia, 1993); see also Roderick A. McDonald, *The Economy and Material Culture of Slaves* (Baton Rouge: Louisiana State University Press, 1993).

Concerning slaves in industrial or urban work see Robert S. Starobin, *Industrial Slavery in the Old South* (New York: Oxford University Press, 1970); Charles B. Dew, "Disciplining Slave Ironworkers in the Antebellum South: Coercion, Conciliation and Accommodation," *American Historical Review* 74 (April 1974): 393–418; and *Bond of Iron: Master and Slave at Buffalo Forge* (New York and London: W. W. Norton & Company, 1994); and Ronald L. Lewis, *Coal, Iron, and Slaves: Industrial Slavery in Maryland and Virginia, 1715–1865* (Westport, Conn.: Greenwood Press, 1979).

William L. Van Deburg, *The Slave Drivers: Black Agricultural Labor Supervisors in the Antebellum South* (Westport, Conn. and London: Greenwood Press, 1979) offers a unique perspective on the slave driver, contending that they used their position to protect slaves.

scholarship saw such behavior as part of an emerging culture that allowed slaves to maintain a degree of control over their lives.[39]

By the 1990s it may be said that historians had built a new consensus concerning slavery. Numerous state and local studies added to the evidence supporting this new view, and Ira Berlin's recent *Many Thousands Gone* has offered a superb summary of the field at its current stage. Slavery has come to be seen as a profitable endeavor for planters, although discussion continues as to its overall effect on the South. Likewise, the character of the masters remains somewhat in question. As to the slaves, however, the consensus view is that their world was not the sole product of their white masters but rather the result of an interactive process in which slaves successfully struggled to create a world of their own that gave them an identity that transcended that of the masters. The new scholarship has not created a monolithic view of slavery, however, for one of the major trends has been to see the institution as differing over time and in location.[40]

By the 1990s at least one scholar had concluded that histori-

[39] Gerald W. Mullin, *Flight and Rebellion: Slave Resistance in Eighteenth-Century Virginia* (New York: Oxford University Press, 1975); Leslie Howard Owens, *This Species of Property: Slave Life and Culture in the Old South* (New York: Oxford University Press, 1976); Sylvia R. Frey, *Water from the Rock: Black Resistance in a Revolutionary Age* (Princeton: Princeton University Press, 1991); and her "Between Slavery and Freedom: Virginia Blacks in the American Revolution," *Journal of Southern History* 49 (August 1983): 375–98. The most recent contribution to this literature has been John Hope Franklin and Loren Schweninger, *Runaway Slaves: Rebels on the Plantation* (New York and Oxford: Oxford University Press, 1999).
    Studies of larger slave uprisings may be seen in Eugene D. Genovese, *From Rebellion to Revolution: Afro-American Slave Revolts in the Making of the Modern World* (Baton Rouge: Louisiana State University Press, 1979) and Douglas R. Egerton, *Gabriel's Rebellion: The Virginia Slave Conspiracies of 1800 and 1802* (Chapel Hill: University of North Carolina Press, 1993).
[40] Ira Berlin, *Many Thousands Gone: The First Two Centuries of Slavery in North America* (Cambridge: The Belknap Press of Harvard University Press, 1988); Betty Wood, *Slavery in Colonial Georgia, 1730–1775* (Athens: University of Georgia Press, 1984) and *Women's Work, Men's Work: the Informal Slave Economies of Lowcountry Georgia* (Athens, Ga. and London: University of Georgia Press, 1995); Charles Joyner, *Down by the Riverside: A South Carolina Slave Community* (Urbana: University of Illinois Press, 1984); Allan Kulikoff, *Tobacco and Slaves: The Development of Southern Cultures in the Chesapeake, 1680–1800* (Chapel Hill: University of North Carolina Press, 1986); Lois Green Carr, Philip D. Morgan, and Jean B. Russo, eds., *Colonial Chesapeake Society* (Chapel Hill: University of North Carolina Press, 1988);

ans had gone too far in their emphasis upon the degree to which slaves were able to establish autonomy within the slave system. Scholarship intended to disprove Phillips seemed to suggest a benignity to slavery. William Dusinberre's 1996 volume, *Them Dark Days: Slavery in the American Rice Swamps* may mark a major shift in the direction of slave scholarship. In his examination of slavery in the lowcountry of Georgia and the Carolinas, Dusinberre concluded that scholars have overdrawn the degree to which slaves were able to create autonomous families and communities within the slave system, although recognizing that his conclusions were based on slavery as practiced on rice plantations. He recognized the constant struggle of slaves to achieve a degree of autonomy, but concluded that the system imposed on slaves proved too formidable for the slave to achieve much in this way. Whether or not Dusinberre's work represents a stepping back from the dominating historiographical trend that have existed since the 1950s, however, remains to be seen.[41]

By the year 2000 the trends that began with Stampp and Elkins have barely touched the study of slavery in Arkansas. Recent general histories have included chapters that reevaluated slavery within Stampp's interpretive framework. A few articles appearing in a recent volume of the *Arkansas Historical Quarterly* have attempted tentative probes into the topics that are a part of the new scholarship. Little original research has been done offering insights into the variety of new topics concerning slavery that have developed since Taylor's study was published. As a result, *Negro Slavery in Arkansas* remains the only major work on the peculiar institution in Arkansas. The detailed information that it offers and its exploration of primary source materials makes it still

---

Randolph B. Campbell, *An Empire for Slavery: The Peculiar Institution in Texas, 1821–1865* (Baton Rouge and London: Louisiana State University Press, 1989); Marvin L. Michael Kay and Lorin Lee Cary, *Slavery in North Carolina, 1748–1775* (Chapel Hill: University of North Carolina Press, 1995); and Lorena S. Walsh, *From Calabar to Carter's Grove: A History of a Virginia Slave Community* (Charlottesville: University Press of Virginia, 1997).

[41] William Dusinberre, *Them Dark Days: Slavery in the American Rice Swamps* (New York and Oxford: Oxford University Press, 1996).

a valuable resource for understanding slavery in the state. It is the essential starting point for anyone interested in studying the institution in the future.[42]

[42] For recent general studies incorporate the Stampp interpretation into their assessment of slavery, see S. Charles Bolton, *Arkansas 1800–1860: Remote and Restless* (Fayetteville: University of Arkansas Press, 1998) (A revised version of his chapter on slavery was published as "Slavery and the Defining of Arkansas," in *Arkansas Historical Quarterly* 68 (spring 1999): 1–23) and *Territorial Ambition: Land and Society in Arkansas 1800–1840* (Fayetteville: University of Arkansas Press, 1993); Michael B. Dougan, *Arkansas Odyssey: The Saga of Arkansas from Prehistoric Times to Present* (Little Rock: Rose Publishing Company, 1993); and Carl H. Moneyhon, *The Impact of the Civil War and Reconstruction on Arkansas, Persistence in the Midst of Ruin* (Baton Rouge: Louisiana State University Press, 1994).

For examples of new efforts at basic research on slavery see Gary Battershell, "The Socioeconomic Role of Slavery in the Arkansas Upcountry," *Arkansas Historical Quarteely* 58 (spring 1999): 45–60; and Carl H. Moneyon, "The Slave Family in Arkansas," *Arkansas Historical Quarterly* 58 (spring 1999): 24–44.

Negro Slavery in Arkansas

I

Red, White, and Black

THE RED MAN was there first, but the white man came early to
Arkansas. And the black man, the third of that trio of races
which made Arkansas, came not long after. Arkansas Post, the
first white settlement within the limits of the present state of
Arkansas—as well as in the entire lower Mississippi River Valley
—was founded near the mouth of the Arkansas River by the
French explorer Henri de Tonti in 1686.[1] The first settlement
was not occupied continuously, but in 1720 German colonists sent
by John Law, the famous Scottish financier, made another near
the same spot, bringing with them the first Negro slaves in Arkansas. Law's grant of land on the lower Arkansas River had been
given to him by the king of France.[2]

Law's colony was not, however, the first attempt to develop
Louisiana, of which Arkansas was a part, into an economically
profitable area. In 1699 the French adventurer d'Iberville found-

[1] De Tonti wrote: "When we were at Arkansas, ten of the Frenchmen
who accompanied me asked for a settlement on the River Arkansas, on a
seignory that M. de la Salle had given me on our first voyage. I granted
the request to some of them. They remained there to build a house surrounded
by stakes." Henri de Tonti, "Memoir Sent in 1693, on the Discovery of the
Mississippi and the Neighboring Nations, from the Year 1678 to the Time of
his Death, and by the Sieur de Tonty to the Year 1691," B. F. French, compiler,
Historical Collections of Louisiana (7 vols.; New York, 1846-1875), 1, 68.
A similar account is in Henri de Tonti, *An Account of Monsieur de la Salle's
Last Expedition and Discoveries in North America* (London, 1698), pp.
129-130.

[2] J. Hanno Deiler, *The Settlement of the German Coast of Louisiana and
the Creoles of German Descent* (Philadelphia, 1909), p. 10. Deiler was the
most thorough student of the early history of the Germans in Louisiana.
Although his study is chiefly concerned with the "German Coast" on the
Mississippi River above New Orleans, it also gives considerable information
about the Arkansas settlement, since there was a close relationship between
the two.

ed a settlement on the site of the present town of Ocean Springs, Mississippi, and in 1702 another, called Fort Louis de la Louisiane, was made on the Mobile River. A flood in 1707 overflowed the fort and the small village which had grown up around it, and the whole establishment was then moved to the site of the modern city of Mobile, Alabama.[3] None of these settlements, nor others which developed in the same area, proved profitable. The people had expected to find gold, silver, precious stones, and pearls, as the Spaniards had in Mexico and other parts of Central and South America, and they were not willing to devote their efforts to agriculture. Instead, they hunted fruitlessly for easily gotten riches, traded a little with the Canadian hunters who came down the Mississippi with boatloads of furs, and hoped that a lucrative trade with the Spaniards in Mexico would develop.[4] Nothing came of these hopes, and with the exception of a few pearls of poor quality from the Pearl River—hence the name—no riches were found.[5]

By 1712 the government of France had come to realize that new steps must be taken if the colony of Louisiana were to survive. The handful of settlers—no more than 340—had at times been reduced to living on acorns, and in 1710 most of them had been forced to live with the Indians to keep from starving.[6] Aware of the deplorable conditions, King Louis XIV, on September 14, 1712, granted all of Louisiana to the Marquis du Chatel, more commonly known as M. Anthony Crozat.[7] The grant was prompted by the high regard which Louis held for Crozat, and by the hope that Louisiana could at last be made profitable by good management. In the patent Louis wrote:

Crozat's zeal and the singular knowledge he has acquired in maritime commerce, encouraged us to hope for as good success as he has hitherto had in the divers and sundry enterprises he has gone upon, and which have procured to our kingdom great quantities of gold and

[3] Deiler, *German Coast*, p. 10.
[4] *Ibid.*, p. 9.
[5] *Ibid.*, p. 9 n.
[6] Charles Gayarré, *History of Louisiana* (4 vols.; 3rd ed.; New Orleans, 1885), I, 101-102.
[7] *A Letter to a Member of the P--------t of G----t B-----n, Occasion'd by the Privilege Granted by the French King to Mr. Cozart* (London, 1713), pp. 3444.

silver in such conjunctions as have rendered them very acceptable to us.[8]

Crozat was a prominent merchant and financier, and Secretary of the Household, Crown, and Revenue. His powers in Louisiana were practically unlimited. For a period of fifteen years he was to have a monopoly of all trade between France and Louisiana and within the colony. He was permitted to open mines of any type, with the king to receive one-fifth of the yield. He was given a monopoly of the fur trade with the Indians. The grant also made provision for the agricultural development of Louisiana, permitting importation of slaves from Africa.[9] Had Crozat taken full advantage of this right, the first Negro slaves might have entered Arkansas several years earlier than they did.

Despite an auspicious beginning, Crozat's grand scheme for the development of Louisiana soon came to naught. It proved impossible to protect the chartered privileges from the Canadians on the north, the Spaniards on the southwest, and the English and unlicensed French traders throughout the grant. The old lure of gold proved stronger than the attractions of agriculture. There was jealousy and dissension among the leaders and settlers. Finally, admitting his inability to operate the colony successfully, Crozat in 1717 was permitted to relinquish the grant.[10]

The Crozat undertaking was a failure. Nevertheless, lessons were learned as a result, and thus some good came of it. For one thing, plans were made to move the capital of the colony from Mobile Bay to the banks of the Mississippi, a more favorable location for control of the Mississippi Valley. More important, there had come a gradual realization that the real future of the colony lay in agriculture and not in foolish searching after mineral wealth.[11] Finally, there had been a growing sense of the necessity of a plentiful labor supply in the form of Negro slaves. Despite the permission to import slaves granted to Crozat, by 1716 there

[8] *Ibid.*, p. 35.
[9] *Ibid.*, pp. 37-43.
[10] Deiler, *German Coast*, p. 10.
[11] Maro O. Rolfe, "State of Arkansas," Weston A. Goodspeed, ed., *The Province and the States, a History of the Province of Louisiana under France and Spain, and of the Territories and States of the United States Formed Therefrom* (8 vols.; Madison, Wisconsin, 1904), I, 147.

were only a few Negroes in the colony, all of them in the vicinity of Mobile.[12]

Immediately after Crozat relinquished his concession in Louisiana, Louis XIV granted (on August 23, 1717) a trade monopoly in Louisiana to the Western Company, an ambitious stock enterprise under the presidency of John Law.[13] In many respects the charter of the Western Company resembled Crozat's, but there was an important difference in that more emphasis was placed upon agriculture. The charter spoke of "undertaking the different species of husbandry and plantations that may be established there,"[14] and stipulated that the company must "in the course of her charter . . . carry over to the lands granted to her, no less than six thousand white persons and three thousand negroes."[15] The company failed to bring this many people, but the Negroes imported were the first slaves to enter Arkansas.

The Western Company was empowered to sell or give away land in Louisiana,[16] and Law secured two of the largest and best concessions for himself, one on the Mississippi near New Orleans, and the other, somewhat larger, on the lower Arkansas near the "Post of Arkansas," found by De Tonti a number of years before.[17]

The complete story of John Law's colony on the Arkansas and of Negro slavery as it existed there lies buried in the obscurity of centuries. The total life of the colony was short, and Law himself ceased to have any connection with it before the first colonists and their slaves arrived in Arkansas. Therefore it is well to dispose of Law at the outset. His fantastic plan for bringing the government of France out of its financial straits through a system of credit and almost unlimited issues of paper money collapsed in December, 1720, and Law, completely bank-

---

[12] Gayarré, *History of Louisiana*, I, 161.

[13] *A Full and Impartial Account of the Company of Mississippi, otherwise called the French East-India-Company, Projected and Settled by Mr. Law* (London, 1720), p. 3. This is by no means a "full" account, for it contains little information of the Law colony itself. The translation of the charter granted Law which was consulted is in Benard de la Harpe, "Historical Journal of the Establishment of the French in Louisiana," French, *Historical Collections of Louisiana*, III, 49-59.

[14] *Ibid.*, III, 49.   [15] *Ibid.*, III, 58.

[16] *Ibid.*, III, 51.

[17] *Ibid.*, III, 21, 85; Deiler, *German Coast*, pp. 10-11.

rupt and disgraced, fled to the Belgian frontier.[18]   When news of
this turn of events reached Louisiana, where advance agents and
a number of colonists had already been sent, there was indecision
as to the disposition of the concessions, for Law himself had
been the guiding spirit of the whole enterprise.[19]   Without Law,
it soon failed.

Law had begun his plans for the Arkansas settlement soon
after the Western Company was chartered in 1717.   He knew
from reports of former governors and concessionaires in Louisiana that the French people had proved themselves poorly adapted
to agriculture; therefore he decided to secure Germans and Alsa-
tians to settle his grants.   A great recruitment campaign was
launched throughout Germany, with particular success in the Palatinate.   Many Germans—perhaps as many as nine or ten thousand[20]—left their homes for Louisiana, but only a small portion
of these ever reached Louisiana, and even fewer got to Arkansas.
Some died of epidemics in the ports; others on the voyage.   Deiler,
the modern historian, estimated that about two thousand Germans
actually reached Arkansas.[21]

The Germans secured the slaves to be used on the Arkansas
concession from among the several shiploads which arrived at Old
Biloxi from Guinea during the years 1720 and 1721.[22]   As with
the Germans, the number of slaves finally reaching Arkansas is
unknown.   The slaves and their new German masters traveled
from Old Biloxi to the Arkansas by boat on the inland route—
Lake Borgne, Lake Pontchartrain, Lake Maurepas, Amite River,
Bayou Manchac, and up the Mississippi River.[23]   Exactly where
they landed and began to develop the land is unknown, since there

[18] La Harpe, "Historical Journal," p. 88 n.; Adolphe Thiers, *The Mississippi Bubble: A Memoir of John Law* (New York, 1859), p. 187.
[19] La Harpe, "Historical Journal," p. 89.
[20] Father Charlevoix, a Jesuit priest who traveled in Arkansas a few years later, wrote that "nine thousand Germans were to be sent, which were raised in the Palatinate." Father Charlevoix, *A Voyage to North America: Undertaken by Command of the Present King of France. Containing the Geographical Description and Natural History of Canada and Louisiana* (2 vols.; Dublin, 1766), II, 184.   Deiler estimated the number at ten thousand. Deiler, *German Coast*, p. 14.
[21] Deiler, *German Coast*, pp. 15-17, 21, 27-30.   Deiler drew much of his information on numbers from La Harpe, "Historical Journal," pp. 75-80.
[22] La Harpe, "Historical Journal," pp. 75-95.
[23] Deiler, *German Coast*, p. 21.

are no physical vestiges of the colony remaining and contemporary descriptions and landmarks are difficult to utilize. The Frenchman Dumont, who had first hand knowledge of the settlement, wrote: "The people sent by Law came and settled about a league from the Arcansas Post, in the depths of the woods, where they found a beautiful plain surrounded by fertile valleys, and a little stream of fine, clear, wholesome water. . . ."[24] La Harpe said the settlement was "situated north-northwest from the Sotouis or Arkansas villages, and on the right of the river, ascending about two leagues and a half by river and one and a half by land. This establishment is about a quarter of a league inland, and you cross a bayou to get to it."[25]

The Law concession was large—by some accounts containing as much as 2500 square miles—but little of it was ever occupied.[26] The Arkansas colonists encountered hardships from the very beginning. The land was fertile, but it would take time to produce a crop, even after the land had been cleared and crude shelters had been constructed against the coming winter.[27] To add to the difficulty no supplies were received from the Western Company, which was in a completely disorganized state after the fall of Law. The colonists were forced, therefore, to seek help from Indians in the neighborhood. During the winter of 1720-1721 many of them suffered from smallpox.[28]

With the coming of spring in 1721 prospects for success of the Arkansas colony brightened. The main body of immigrants

[24] Dumont de Montigny, *Mémoires Historiques sur la Louisiane* . . . (2 vols.; Paris, 1753), II, 68. A translation of this work appears in French, *Historical Collections of Louisiana*, V, 1-233.

[25] La Harpe, "Historical Journal," p. 107. Local tradition has it that the stream mentioned by both Dumont and La Harpe is Moore's Bayou—although the water is not now "fine and clear"—and that the settlement was nine miles south of the present town of Gillette, just east of the road leading south to Pendleton Ferry across the Arkansas River. Interview with Judge J. H. Henderson, De Witt, Arkansas, June 1, 1951.

[26] Letter from Father du Poisson, Missionary to the Akensas, to Father Patouillet, Reuben Gold Thwaites, ed., *The Jesuit Relations and Allied Documents; Travels and Explorations of the Jesuit Missionaries in New France, 1610-1791* (73 vols.; Cleveland, 1896-1901), LXVII, 259; Antoine Simon Le Page Dupratz, *The History of Louisiana, or of the Western Parts of Virginia and Carolina, Containing a Description of the Countries That Lie on Both Sides of the River Mississippi* . . . (2 vols.; London, 1763), I, 53. Also see map opposite p. 79 of Deiler, *German Coast.*

[27] Deiler, *German Coast,* p. 36.

[28] *Ibid.,* p. 37.

was due to arrive that year, and ahead lay a long growing season in which to store up food for winter. But the summer had hardly begun when the full account of the fall of Law reached the Germans. For a time there was some hope that the Western Company would continue with the projected plans of Law, but the hope never materialized because Law's manager, Levens, refused to transfer the grant to the company or even to manage it for the company. Consequently the settlers had no one to whom they could turn for aid until the first major crop was harvested. All these problems led to a growing feeling among the colonists that, deserted in the wilds of Arkansas, they must eventually abandon the concession.[29]

The new and larger group of Germans reached the shores of Louisiana in the spring of 1721 as planned, but, since Law himself had failed, the Western Company realized that it would be impractical to send them to Arkansas, "as Law could not support the people . . . until they could make their first crop to support themselves."[30] Instead, the company decided to establish a new and more readily accessible settlement for the newly arrived Germans on a forty-mile-long strip of land along both banks of the Mississippi River, beginning twenty-five miles upriver from New Orleans, where a small number of Germans employed by Law had been settled already. The new colonists were installed there under the leadership of a Swedish-German nobleman, Karl Freidrich d'Arensbourg, and the area has been known since that time as the German Coast.[31]

Meanwhile, most of the Germans and slaves on the Arkansas had deserted en masse and sailed down the Mississippi to New Orleans. When the Jesuit priest Charlevoix passed the Law concession in December, 1721, the grandly conceived project had declined to such an extent that he wrote: "Over against the Kappa Village we see the sad ruins of Mr. Law's Grant, of which the company remain the proprietors."[32] In March, 1722, Benard de la Harpe, who had been sent by the Western Company to inspect

---

[29] *Ibid.*   [30] *Ibid.*, p. 53.
[31] La Harpe, "Historical Journal," p. 85 n.; Deiler, *German Coast,* p. 54. While traveling in the region in 1952, the author saw "Darenburg's Grocery," perhaps operated by a descendant of the original D'Arensbourg.
[32] Charlevoix, *Voyage to North America*, II, 184.

the Arkansas concession and instal a new director, Dudemaine Dufresne, in place of Levens, found only forty-seven Germans and their slaves.[33] The rapid decline of the Arkansas settlement is also confirmed by an official census of Louisiana taken in 1721 by M. Diron, Inspector General of the French troops in Louisiana. Unfortunately the census itself did not enumerate in detail the inhabitants of Arkansas, but in fifteen appended pages of "Remarks and Observations on Louisiana," an unknown contemporary writer noted that only eighty colonists remained in Arkansas at the time.[34] When La Harpe again visited the concession in April, 1723, after a voyage up the Arkansas River, he found it entirely deserted.[35]

The colonists from Arkansas who arrived at New Orleans in 1721 and 1722 must have considerably outnumbered the 169 residents of the town. Embittered by their experiences, they demanded return passage to Europe. But Governor Bienville, wanting to keep such desirable settlers, offered them tracts on the German Coast, which in most cases were accepted.[36]

So ended one of the most ambitious ventures in early American history, a venture which, if successful, might have altered completely the course of Arkansas history. The population of Arkansas probably would have increased rapidly, and Negro slavery might have become extensive a full century earlier than it actually did.

Little is known of the work or management of the Negro slaves on the Law concession during the short time it existed. Even legal control of slavery was not standardized, since the Black Code, which regulated slavery in Louisiana for nearly a hundred years, was not formulated until 1724, by which time all except a few stragglers had left Arkansas. The little information available suggests, however, that the great gulf between master and slave had not yet developed, and that the slave was regarded as something of a lesser member of the family. The historian Dumont indicated no difference in living quarters of masters and

[33] La Harpe, "Historical Journal," p. 107.
[34] Deiler, *German Coast*, p. 74.
[35] La Harpe, "Historical Journal," p. 108.
[36] Deiler, *German Coast*, p. 38.

slaves, a natural arrangement under primitive conditions.[37]   An extensive official census of Louisiana compiled in 1724 casts some light, at least by implication, upon the life of the Arkansas slaves. The census gives detailed information concerning a number of Germans and their Negro slaves living on the German Coast, including some who had formerly lived on the Arkansas.   It is apparent from the census that, although living conditions were still relatively harsh and crude, the slaves—usually no more than one or two to a family—were well treated and well fed, and were considered valuable members of the family group.[38]   Doubtless the same relationships had prevailed in the Law colony.

Abandonment of the Law concession did not mark complete termination of settlement on the lower Arkansas River, for a few of the settlers chose to remain, with their slaves, in the vicinity of Arkansas Post.   The post had been occupied only intermittently since its establishment by De Tonti in 1686, but it became a permanent French military establishment in 1722, when La Harpe, at the time of his first visit to the Law colony, installed Lieutenant de la Boulaye as commandant.[39]   There continued to be some agriculture—mostly wheat-growing—carried on in the area, but Arkansas Post served principally as an outpost for trade with the Indians living on or near the Arkansas River and as a way-station between the French settlements in New Orleans and vicinity and those up the Mississippi in Illinois and Missouri.   Several attempts were made to move the post to a location nearer the Mississippi River which would be more convenient to travelers, but each time disastrous floods forced the French to return to the site continuously occupied since that time—the first high ground, about thirty miles from the mouth of the Arkansas.[40]

The . . . settlers of the post were hunters and trappers.   Married to Indian women, these white men took up Indian manners and customs; dressed like them; lived like them.   From hunting came their livelihood.   Excursions were made up and down the White and

[37] Dumont, *Mémoires Historiques sur la Louisiane*, II, 68.
[38] For pertinent items in the census, see Deiler, *German Coast*, pp. 77-96. One appended comment was that the settlers "feed their negroes very well on account of the great quantities of vegetables they raise."
[39] La Harpe, "Historical Journal," pp. 99-107.
[40] *Arkansas Gazette*, Nov. 20, 1819.

Arkansas Rivers, and when sufficient furs, hides, buffalo robes, and bear oils were gathered, these were sent to New Orleans.[41]

Population of the Arkansas Post area remained small, showing no great increase until nearly the end of the eighteenth century, when small settlements were beginning to appear in other parts of Arkansas. As one writer has said, "probably the shock of the bursting of John Law's Mississippi Bubble was too much" for Arkansas.[42] An official census taken in 1744 showed only 12 white male inhabitants and 10 Negroes of both sexes in the Arkansas district.[43] By 1769, seven years after France ceded Arkansas to Spain, the population had increased to 88, with the official census of 1771 (based on figures assembled in 1769) enumerating 32 white males, 30 white females, 9 Negro males, and 7 Negro females.[44] In 1785 there were 196 people of both races in Arkansas, with no indication of the number of slaves,[45] but the next three years saw a drop to 119.[46] After that time, with the coming of settlers from the former English colonies after the American Revolution, the population again began to increase and to become more widely distributed over Arkansas.[47] Especially was this true after the United States acquired Arkansas as a part of the Louisiana Purchase in 1803.

Although there were relatively few slaves in Arkansas during the eighteenth century, they occupied a distinct place in the little, struggling frontier settlements. Some engaged in that age-old task of slaves—farming. Others were personal servants, and still

[41] U. S. Congress, Senate, *Arkansas 1836-1936: A Study of its Growth and Characteristics in Observance of its Centennial Year, 1936,* Senate Document No. 191, 74th Congress, 2nd Session (Washington, 1936), p. 7.

[42] *Ibid.*

[43] Census of Louisiana, 1744, printed in Gayarré, *History of Louisiana,* II, 28.

[44] Census of Louisiana, Sept. 2, 1771, Lawrence Kinnaird, ed., *Spain in the Mississippi Valley, Annual Report of the American Historical Association, 1945* (4 vols.; Washington, 1949), II, 196.

[45] Census of Louisiana, 1785, printed in Gayarré, *History of Louisiana,* III, 170.

[46] Census of Louisiana, 1788, printed in Gayarré, *History of Louisiana,* III, 215.

[47] A few sympathizers with the English settled in Arkansas even before the Revolution was over. Russell W. Benedict, grandson of one of the earliest settlers, wrote of one group: ". . . when Bunker Hill fell . . . and when all hopes of British success vanished, the **Massengills, Wyleys,** and **Flanagins,** Torys as they were, fled for safety to the western wilderness. . . ." Ted R. Worley, ed., "Story of an Early Settlement in Central Arkansas," *Arkansas Historical Quarterly,* X (Summer, 1951), 129.

others served their masters as boatmen on the long trading voyages among the Indian tribes up and down the rivers. There is no sustained record of slavery in Arkansas during the period, but the few documents which have been preserved give some insight into its nature. There is, for example, the record of the activities of Luis and Sezar, slaves of Don Bentura Orueta, Spanish merchant and trader of Arkansas Post.[48] In the spring of 1787 two Indian tribes were brought to the brink of open warfare by illegal sale of liquor to them by the slaves. Several years before, a former commandant of the post had encountered similar difficulty, and when the current commandant, Don Joseph Vallière, had arrived, he had issued orders for all merchants and other inhabitants to refrain from trading liquor to the Indians, "not only to prevent any disturbance that might result among them, but also for the tranquillity and quiet of the town."[49] But the trader Orueta ignored the order. Upon hearing of the approach of a party of Abenaqui Indians from farther up the river, he sent the slaves Luis and Sezar out with a pirogue-load of liquor to trade with them before they reached the post. The Abenaquis traded pelts for liquor, became drunk, and attempted to attack a party of Arkansas Indians, their traditional enemies, who were encamped at the post. Vallière checked the incipient clash by placing the Arkansas warriors inside the stockade, and then proceeded to investigate the affair fully. When confronted with facts obtained from the Abenaquis, Luis and Sezar at first denied guilt, but Vallière obtained a confession by placing them in stocks and threatening punishment of a hundred lashes unless they told the truth. The slaves then admitted the illegal sales, but attempted to justify their acts by saying that they were only slaves who did as their master ordered. Vallière then placed Orueta under house arrest and turned the case over to the governor of Louisiana for further action.

There were also skilled artisans among the slaves at Arkansas Post, as is shown by an incident concerning the small vessel *La Flèche*, which stopped there on February 2, 1793, for repairs. By that date the post had grown considerably, but was still only a

[48] Kinnaird, *Spain in the Mississippi Valley*, III, 203-208.
[49] *Ibid.*, III, 204.

village, with a white-oak stockade, thirty shingled houses ranging along the streets below the fort, and a dozen more houses on larger plots of farm land nearby.[50]   The master of the *La Flèche* recorded in his log:

I went ashore to ask the commandant if he had some blacksmiths. He replied that he had an old Negro. I requested that he send for him immediately in order that he might take the measurements of the iron bindings of my rudder to make new ones and to mend the old one also.   The Negro came and took the measurements.[51]

Some slaves were used in the frequent campaigns against the Indians in Arkansas and neighboring regions, especially during the earlier French period.   The Chickasaw Indians, living in what is now western Tennessee, were extremely troublesome for a time. In the spring of 1739 Governor Bienville of Louisiana organized a large expedition to move against them, and a fort, to serve as a rendezvous for troops from Canada, New Orleans, and the Arkansas settlements, was constructed at a point in Arkansas near the juncture of the St. Francis River with the Mississippi.   The army which gathered there and later moved opposite the present city of Memphis preparatory to attack upon the Indians consisted of twelve hundred white troops and twice that many friendly Indian and Negro troops.   Battle against the Chickasaws proved unnecessary at the time, for a peace was arranged.[52]

Legal regulation of slavery in Louisiana (and thus in Arkansas) during the French and Spanish periods was through the *Code Noir,* or Black Code, adopted by the French in 1724.[53]   The Black Code is a comprehensive and detailed instrument of fifty-three sections covering almost every aspect of slavery.   Some of its provisions were later carried directly or indirectly into Arkansas territorial and state laws; consequently an examination of the code seems doubly in order.

Much of the Black Code was devoted to regulations concerning

[50] Log of His Majesty's Galiot *La Flèche,* Jan. 5 to March 5, 1793, Kinnaird, *Spain in the Mississippi Valley,* IV, 111.
[51] *Ibid.*
[52] Dumont, *Mémoires Historiques sur la Louisiane,* II, 232-239.
[53] The translation employed here is in French, *Historical Collections of Louisiana,* III, 89-95.   In most instances citations to specific sections will not be made.

care and welfare of the slaves. Particular concern was shown for their religious lives. Masters were required to give religious instruction, and only the Roman Catholic religion was permitted. Even overseers of the slaves were required to be Catholic. Strict Sabbath and religious holiday observance was decreed, with slaves barred from working. And when a Christian slave died he, like a deceased Christian white man, must be buried in consecrated ground.

Several sections of the code specified in detail how slaves should be clothed and fed, and ample provision was made for them to make complaints against masters who did not properly feed, clothe, or otherwise care for them. The master was allowed considerable leeway in punishing a wayward slave, but severe penalty for the master was prescribed in case the slave were killed or mutilated in administration of punishment. After the productive life of a slave was over, the master was still required to care for him just as he had previously done. Consideration for normal family relationships among slaves was shown. Regular religious marriage ceremonies were required, and husbands and wives belonging to the same master could not be sold separately. Slave children under the age of fourteen could not be sold away from their parents. Although marriage between slaves was considered wholly valid, there was rigid prohibition of marriage, either regular or irregular, between slaves and whites and between slaves and free Negroes.

In contrast with the humanitarian attitudes noted above, many of the provisions of the Black Code were severe, and some even cruel. Special attention was given to acts of violence against free individuals by slaves. Section XXVIII decreed: "With regard to outrages or acts of violence committed by slaves against free persons, it is our will that they be punished with severity, and even with death, should the case require it." A slave was also subject to corporal punishment for theft. Whipping was the standard punishment for minor crimes or infraction of disciplinary rules, with branding with the "flower de luce" a not unusual accompaniment. Perhaps the cruelest punishment was reserved for the runaway slave. For a first offense—if he remained absent for as long as a month—the slave was to have his ears cut off and be branded on one shoulder. After a second offense, he was to be hamstrung and branded on the other shoulder. Punishment for the third offense was the ultimate—death.

Running through the Black Code is the philosophy that the slave was not a free agent, and that his master was largely responsible for his acts. Section XXIII, for example, says: "Masters shall be responsible for what their slaves have done by their command." The master was required to make amends for any theft committed, or any damage done, by his slave. A slave could never be a party to a civil suit, but it was possible for the master to act for him in civil cases and also to demand criminal action for any wrong done his slave. Slaves could, of course, be tried in criminal courts, but they could not serve as witnesses except in rare instances. In no case could a slave serve as witness either for or against his master.

Numerous restrictions were placed upon the activities of slaves. They could not carry "offensive weapons or heavy sticks," except when sent out to hunt game by their masters and carrying a written statement to that effect. Assembling of slaves without the supervision of white persons was forbidden, with capital punishment being the penalty in some cases. Slaves could not sell produce or other articles of any sort without written permission from their masters, nor could they own any sort of property. In the event a slave acquired property, title automatically passed to the master.

The Black Code made liberal provision for freeing of slaves. A freed slave still had certain responsibilities toward his former master and family, Section LIII directing: "We command all manumitted slaves to show the profoundest respect to their former masters, to their widows and children, and any injury or insult offered by said manumitted slaves to their former master, their widows or children, shall be punished with more severity than if it had been offered by any other person." The code made it clear that freed slaves nevertheless were to enjoy "the same rights, privileges, and immunities which are enjoyed by freeborn persons." These liberal attitudes and provisions determined that Louisiana would, in statehood days, have a large free Negro population relatively unhampered by restrictive legal regulations. It will be seen later, however, that these attitudes and provisions were not carried over into the territory and state of Arkansas, where there would be few free Negroes, and these closely restricted by the laws.

II

Forecast of the Missouri Compromise

WHEN ARKANSAS passed into the possession of the United States as a part of the Louisiana Purchase in 1803, the existence of slavery within its borders remained undisturbed.[1] Later, repeated attempts would be made to abolish slavery or to prohibit indefinite perpetuation of it in Arkansas, but all would be unsuccessful until the final abolition of slavery on a national scale.

Arkansas progressed rapidly through a series of governmental changes during its first sixteen years under the control of the United States. In 1804 Congress created the Territory of Orleans out of the region around New Orleans, and the remainder of Louisiana became the District of Louisiana. In 1812 the Territory of Orleans was enlarged and became the state of Louisiana, but in the meantime the District of Louisiana, of which Arkansas was a part, had been reorganized repeatedly. It had been attached for a time to Indiana Territory, but in 1805 Louisiana became a separate territory with its own government. In 1812 the name was changed to Missouri Territory; in 1819 Arkansas Territory was created from the southern portion of Missouri Territory.[2]

The governmental changes during this period had only superficial effect upon the people of Arkansas and upon slavery within its bounds. Whether the seat of government was in New Orleans

---

[1] Article III of the treaty by which Louisiana was transferred from France to the United States reads in part: "The inhabitants of the ceded territory . . . shall be maintained and protected in the free enjoyment of their liberty, property, and the religion which they profess." U. S. Congress, Senate, *American State Papers; Documents Legislative and Executive, of the Congress of the United States* (38 vols.; Washington, 1832-1861), *Foreign Relations*, II, 507.

[2] *The Statutes at Large of the United States of America,* (68 vols.; Boston and Washington, 1855-   ) II, 283-289, 331-332, 743-747.

or Indiana or St. Louis, population continued to increase at a steady, if not spectacular, rate. Prior to 1803 most of the population had been concentrated in the vicinity of Arkansas Post, but settlers from other parts of the United States now began to move in greater numbers into other areas. The United States census of 1810, compiled while Arkansas was still a part of the District of Louisiana, provides the first official figures compiled by the United States government on the slave population of Arkansas. In the "Settlements of Hope Field and St. Francis" there were 188 people, classified as follows: 90 free white males, 69 free white females, and 29 Negro slaves.[3] The "Settlements of Hope Field and St. Francis," in eastern Arkansas along the Mississippi and lower St. Francis rivers, had sprung up in the last years of Spanish occupation. Hopefield, opposite present-day Memphis, Tennessee, was the only concentration of population in the area. The Arkansas Post section, referred to in the census as "Settlements on the Arkansas," still led in both slave and total population with 463 free white males, 302 free white females, 2 "free persons, except Indians not taxed" (evidently free Negroes), and 107 slaves, for a total of 874 people.[4]

Life in the Arkansas Post area was described in detail in 1805 by John B. Treat, United States factor at the post, in a letter to Henry Dearborn, Secretary of War:

The population here is between sixty and seventy Families . . . all of whom either reside in the Village, or within a circuit of between three and four Miles; there are also scatter'd up the River, seven or eight Families . . . divided amongst those in this Neighbourhood, are sixty Blacks, seldom more than three in a family, and with one, or two exceptions, the whole of them are slaves.—

The pursuits of these People are either Farming, Trading or Hunting . . . but I must admit that agriculture here is yet in its Infancy; the Lands although not so fertile as are those water'd by the Ohio, and its tributary streams; Yet are sufficiently so for industrious cultivation; the past Harvest, has produc'd from fifteen to eighteen Bushels of Wheat, per Acre; weighing sixty-two English

[3] United States Bureau of the Census, *Census of 1810* (Washington, 1811), p. 84.
[4] *Ibid.* See p. 16 above for legal provisions concerning free Negroes in Arkansas prior to the Louisiana Purchase. A later chapter will treat the free Negro in territorial and statehood days.

pounds; and I am told that has been the average for a number of years past, and occasionally has not only been more abundant, but sixty five and six pounds per bushel; which I think will be admitted a good crop in any part of the Union. . . .[5]

In addition to the people living along the Arkansas, Mississippi, and St. Francis rivers in 1810, there were also some in northeastern Arkansas in what are now Randolph, Lawrence, and Independence counties. In 1810 that area was a part of the District of New Madrid, which had a total population of 2,103, including 287 slaves and 5 free Negroes.[6] Since the District of New Madrid included territory later divided between Arkansas and Missouri, it is not possible to ascertain from the census exactly how many slaves there were in the Arkansas portion. Lawrence County, as the Arkansas section was later named, developed rapidly, and during the greater part of the first quarter-century of American control was the most thickly settled part of Arkansas. There had been a few Frenchmen and Spaniards there before 1800,[7] but the new settlers, coming down the military road which led from St. Genevieve, Missouri, to the Red River in Arkansas, were largely Americans from the older states—Tennessee, Kentucky, Virginia, North Carolina, Georgia, and others.[8] Bringing their slaves with them, they settled in the wilderness along the Black, White, Strawberry, Spring, and Current rivers and numerous tributary streams and attempted to re-create the agricultural life of the older sections.[9] Most of the individual slaveholdings were quite small, and despite the early lead which Lawrence County took in both white and slave populations, it failed to develop into one of the leading slave counties in statehood days.

On March 2, 1819, President James Monroe signed the bill,

[5] John B. Treat to the Secretary of War, Nov. 15, 1805, Clarence E. Carter, ed., *The Territorial Papers of the United States* (20 vols.; Washington, 1934), XIII, *The Territory of Louisiana-Missouri, 1803-1806,* 278-279.
[6] *Census of 1810,* p. 84.
[7] Walter E. McLeod, *Centennial Memorial History of Lawrence County* (Russellville, Arkansas, 1936), p. 10; Lawrence Dalton, *History of Randolph County* (Little Rock, 1946), pp. 9-10.
[8] McLeod, *History of Lawrence County,* p. 11.
[9] *Ibid.,* p. 20.

effective July 4, 1819, creating Arkansas Territory.[10] The eastern, northern, and southern boundaries of the new territory were much the same as those of the state of Arkansas today, but on the west Arkansas included almost all of present-day Oklahoma, the western boundary of the United States having been fixed by the Florida Treaty with Spain on February 22, 1819, only eight days before Monroe signed the act creating Arkansas Territory.[11] Arkansas was reduced to its present area by treaties with the Choctaw Indians in 1825 and the Cherokees in 1828.[12]

In the debates and voting in Congress preceding passage of the bill creating Arkansas Territory, the continuing existence of the institution of slavery in Arkansas was severely tested. Slavery survived, although at one point by the extremely narrow margin of two votes. When the bill authorizing creation of the territory was introduced in the House of Representatives on February 18, 1819, Representative John W. Taylor of New York offered an amendment of two sections which would have prohibited the further introduction of slaves into Arkansas and provided for the final emancipation of all slaves already there within twenty-five years.[13] The Taylor amendment was a duplicate of the more famous Tallmadge amendment to the bill for admission of Missouri as a state, which had been presented in the House only five days previously and which had set off a series of debates on slavery occupying several days prior to the introduction of the Arkansas bill.[14] The questions of whether Missouri should be admitted as a slave state and whether Arkansas should be created a slave territory were so closely interrelated in chronology, personalities, and arguments that they are almost inseparable. Missouri was not permitted to enter the union as a slave state until more than a year later (and then only by compromise), but the decision in favor of slavery in Arkansas at this time proved to be an accurate

---

[10] The act creating the territory may be found in *United States Statutes at Large,* III, 493-496.

[11] *American State Papers, Foreign Relations,* V, 127-132.

[12] United States Congress, Senate, *Indian Affairs, Laws and Treaties,* Senate Document No. 452, 57th Congress, 1st Session (5 vols.; Washington, 1903-1941), II, 149-151, 493-496.

[13] U. S. Congress, *Annals of the Congress of the United States, 1789-1824* (42 vols.; Washington, 1834-1856), 15th Congress, 2nd Session, II, 1222.

[14] *Ibid.,* pp. 1170-1217.

forecast of the geographical demarcation line—36° 30′, the northern boundary of Arkansas—drawn between slave and nonslave
areas by the Missouri Compromise of 1820. This prediction
seems to have been largely ignored by recent students of the
period,[15] but not by contemporary observers. One wrote concerning passage of the Arkansas bill:

> It would almost seem as if an understanding prevailed, that a line
> of demarcation should take place in the west, so that a certain por-
> tion of the new states should be assigned for the non-slave-holding
> states of the Atlantic—while the more southern new states and terri-
> tories, were to be left for the accomodation [*sic*] of emigrants from
> the old slave-holding states.[16]

The burden of the argument in favor of Arkansas as a slave
territory was borne by Henry Clay of Kentucky, Speaker of the
House, and Felix Walker of North Carolina, while the antislave
position was voiced chiefly by Representative Taylor, who had
introduced the restrictive amendment. Arguments on both sides
were much the same (and made largely by the same people) as the
earlier and later arguments concerning Missouri. The antislave
proponents voiced the hope that farmers from the nonslaveholding
states could emigrate to Arkansas and participate in cultivation of
the Southern crops of cotton and tobacco without having to compete with slave labor, as would be the case if they went to the
Southeast. They asserted that Congress had the constitutional
power to prohibit or restrict slavery in a territory. They charged
that the South had degraded labor and predicted that if the area
west of the Mississippi were opened to slavery, enforcement of
laws against the African slave trade would prove impossible, for
the need for additional slaves would stimulate smuggling. Finally, they predicted that in the long run the trans-Mississippi region
with slavery would suffer economically by comparison with the
nonslaveholding North.[17]

The proslavery faction in the House attempted to refute the

---

[15] A notable exception is Glover Moore, author of the thorough and comprehensive *The Missouri Controversy* (Lexington, Kentucky, 1953). Professor
Moore pays due attention to the Arkansas controversy, and notes the significance
of its outcome in relation to the Missouri Compromise.
[16] New York *Daily Advertiser*, Feb. 24, 1819, quoted in Moore, *Missouri
Controversy*, p. 60.
[17] *Annals of Congress*, 15th Congress, 2nd Session, II, 1222-1239.

arguments of Taylor and the other opponents and offered some of their own. They admitted that the condition of slaves was inferior but claimed that their lot would be improved if they were spread over a wider area. (This was the "diffusion" theory). Since a great deal of labor was needed to open up the area, Southerners would practically be banned unless they could take their slaves, they asserted, thus in effect giving the region to Northerners. Henry Clay accused the antislave faction of suffering from "negrophobia," and wondered what Southerners had done to warrant proscription. To the hope that nonslaveholding farmers could emigrate to Arkansas without fear of having to compete with slaves, Felix Walker replied that Arkansas was so far south that only slaves could cultivate the land anyway. None of the Southern congressmen defended the institution of slavery itself, although they did assert that it was a matter in which the Northerners should not meddle.[18]

There was one important difference between the Arkansas and Missouri questions: in the case of Arkansas the controversy was over creation of a slave territory, while for Missouri it was over admission of a slave state. Most Southern congressmen seemed to acknowledge the constitutional power of Congress to prohibit slavery in a territory, although not in a state. Some, however, even denied the power of Congress over slavery in a territory. Felix Walker, for example, maintained that in the organization of a territorial government only the people of the area "have the right, and are the proper judges of that policy best adapted to their genius and interest, and it ought to be exclusively left to them."[19] Thus he saw no fundamental difference between restricting slavery in a territory and restricting it in a state.

The House voted on each section of the Taylor amendment separately; the first was defeated by a vote of seventy-one to seventy, and the second was passed by a vote of seventy-five to seventy-three. Thus continued importation of slaves into Arkansas was to be permitted, but gradual emancipation was to be provided for. Not satisfied with this turn of events, proslavery forces moved that the bill be referred to a special committee in-

[18] *Ibid.*   [19] *Ibid.*, p. 1227.

structed to strike out the second section. Vote on this motion was eighty-eight to eighty-eight, with Speaker of the House Henry Clay breaking the tie with an affirmative vote. The committee to which the bill was referred recommended striking out the section providing for emancipation of the Arkansas slaves, and the House accepted the recommendation by the narrow margin of eighty-nine to eighty-seven on February 19. Shortly thereafter the bill creating Arkansas Territory was passed with no restrictions on slavery.[20]

The bill had less difficulty in the Senate, where North and South were more evenly balanced than in the House, which had a substantial majority of members from nonslave states. Senator James Burrill of Rhode Island attempted to amend the bill to prohibit further importation of slaves into Arkansas, but the Senate rejected the amendment by a vote of nineteen to fourteen, passed the bill, and sent it to President Monroe for signature.[21]

Votes in the House and Senate on the Arkansas bill reveal clearly that the proslave triumph was achieved only by help from non-Southern sections; in both houses the margin of victory was provided by votes of men from the Old Northwest states of Ohio, Indiana, and Illinois, where many Southern people had settled. In the eighty-nine-to-eighty-seven House vote which eliminated the emancipation provision, the shifted votes of Representatives John McLean of Illinois and William Henry Harrison (later president of the United States), Philemon Beecher, and John W. Campbell of Ohio were responsible for the victory. These four votes comprised half of the congressional strength of the Old Northwest at that time. Otherwise, practically every Southerner voted for elimination of the provision and almost all Northeasterners against it; only one Southerner and fourteen Northeasterners crossed sectional lines, and most of the latter had voted with the South from the beginning of the issue. The nineteen-to-fourteen Senate vote on Senator Burrill's amendment prohibiting further importation of slaves into Arkansas was even more markedly sectional: every Southern senator voted against the amendment, and every Northeastern senator for it. The amendment was

[20] *Ibid.*, pp. 1271-1282.   [21] *Ibid.*, p. 1274.

rejected only as a result of the vote of four senators from the Old Northwest, Jeremiah Morrow of Ohio, Waller Taylor of Indiana, and Jesse B. Thomas and Ninian Edwards of Illinois, all men of Southern birth or leanings.[22]

It is readily apparent from the voting in Congress on the issue of slavery in Arkansas Territory that while the South-Northeast rivalry was fully crystallized by this time, the Old Northwest, or at least a majority of its senators and congressmen, was still sympathetic with the South and slavery.

The United States census of 1820, taken the year after the territory was created, reveals 1,617 slaves in Arkansas in a total population of 14,273. Thus approximately one-ninth of the entire population was slave. Each succeeding census would show great growth in the number of slaves, as well as increase in their proportion to the total population. It is evident from the census that most of the people living in Arkansas in 1820 were not slaveholders or members of slaveholding families, since there was an average of little more than one slave to each two families. The majority of the population was engaged in farming (3,613 heads of families as compared to 79 in commerce and 179 in manufacturing), but most of the farms were of the small, pioneer sort cultivated by members of the family.[23]

Arkansas had seven counties in 1820.[24] Lawrence County led in both slave and total population, with 490 slaves in the 5,602 total. Trailing closely in number of slaves but lagging far behind in total population was Hempstead County, with 481 slaves in the 2,248 aggregate. Next was Arkansas County, having 178 slaves in a total of 1,260, followed by Pulaski, with 171 in 1,923; Phillips, with 145 in 1,201; Miller, with 82 in 999; and Clark, with 70 slaves in a total population of 1,040.[25]

[22] *Ibid.*, pp. 1273-1274.
[23] U. S. Bureau of the Census, *Census of 1820* (Washington, 1821), p. 41.
[24] Arkansas County, formed Dec. 31, 1813, by the legislature of Missouri Territory, was the first county in Arkansas, including about two-thirds of the area of the present state of Arkansas. Lawrence County was created in 1815. These two, along with Hempstead, Clark, and Pulaski, created in 1818, comprised Arkansas at the time it became a territory. Miller and Phillips Counties were formed in 1820, shortly before the census was taken. Dallas T. Herndon, ed., *The Arkansas Handbook,* 1949-1950 (Little Rock, 1950), p. 144.
[25] *Census of 1820*, p. 41.

The ten years from 1820 to 1830 saw a marked gain in the number of slaves in Arkansas, as well as in the ratio of slaves to the total population. The census of 1830 shows 4,576 slaves, almost a threefold increase over 1820. During the same period the total population increased to 30,388, a little more than twice that of 1820.[26] While in 1820 slaves had composed one-ninth of the total, in 1830 they represented more than one-seventh. During the decade sixteen new counties were created,[27] including several formed from land acquired from Indians to the west, and new settlers had pushed through the forests and up and down the rivers into every section of the territory. In 1830 Lawrence County still led in total population—2,806—but had dropped to sixth in number of slaves, with only 325. This was also an overall loss in number of slaves, but the decline may be accounted for by the creation of new counties out of parts of Lawrence County rather than by actual departure of the slaves. The leading slave county in 1830 was Hempstead in the southwest, which was second in total population; it had 522 slaves in a total of 2,512 people. In order, the other most important slaveholding counties were Pulaski, in the center of the territory, with 439; Arkansas, in the southeast, with 369; Crawford, on the western border, with 352; and Lafayette, in the southwest, with 340. All counties had some slaves, the smallest number—17—being found in Jackson, on the White River, created less than a year before the census of 1830 was made.[28]

The major streams of emigration in the 1820-1835 period were into the northern and western sections of Arkansas, and as a consequence the eastern and southern counties, which in later years would comprise the most important cotton-producing section with the heaviest slave population, lagged considerably behind in development. For example, Phillips and Chicot counties along the Mississippi River, Jefferson on the lower Arkansas River, and Union on the Louisiana border ranked far down the list in both total and slave population in 1830, whereas in 1860 they led

[26] U. S. Bureau of the Census, *Census of 1830* (Washington, 1832), p. 155.
[27] Chicot, Conway, Crawford, Crittenden, Hot Spring, Independence, Izard, Jackson, Jefferson, Lafayette, Monroe, Pope, St. Francis, Sevier, Union, and Washington.
[28] *Census of 1830,* p. 155.

the state in slave population in the order listed.[29] An imaginary line bisecting Arkansas from northeast to southwest marks the approximate division between the highlands and the lowlands, the former lying north and west of the line. In 1830 approximately 68 per cent of the total population and 61 per cent of the slaves lived in the twelve counties which could be classified generally as in the highlands.[30] The highland counties continued to lead in total population until the end of the slavery period, and not until about 1840 did the lowland area exceed the highlands in number of slaves. It should be pointed out, however, that many of the highland counties of Arkansas had some of the characteristics of the lowlands; of the twelve highland counties existing in 1830, all except Washington lay along important navigable rivers, the Black and the White of northeastern and north central Arkansas, the Arkansas in the central and western sections, and the Ouachita and the Red in the southwestern part of the territory. Later, as new counties were created from the mountain sections of the twelve counties, there was an increased number of true highland counties, usually with very few slaves.

The trend toward more rapid settlement of the northern and western counties, despite their remoteness from previously settled areas, began almost as soon as Arkansas became a territory. Official recognition of the trend came in 1821, when the territorial capital was moved from Arkansas Post, where it had been located originally, to Little Rock, in the center of the state at the point where the highlands begin.[31] Access to good land was much easier in the uplands, since the lowlands were subject to floods for a great part of the year. Disease was more prevalent along the Mississippi, lower Arkansas, and lower White rivers than on the upper reaches of the White and the Arkansas. And, very important to anyone who wished to travel away from the rivers, virtually all important roads followed the uplands. In later statehood days, as the lure of the rich cotton lands in the south and east be-

[29] U. S. Bureau of the Census, *Census of 1860 (Population)* (Washington, 1864), p. 18.
[30] *Census of 1830,* p. 155.
[31] For a detailed account of circumstances surrounding selection of Little Rock as the new seat of government, see Dallas T. Herndon, *Why Little Rock Was Born* (Little Rock, 1933).

came stronger, new settlers populated them rapidly and attempted
to overcome their disadvantages. But during most of the territorial period, northern and western Arkansas continued to be the
mecca for most of the thousands of settlers coming into the region.

The editor of the *Arkansas Gazette* wrote in 1830 concerning
emigration to northwestern Arkansas:

> At no period since the organization of the Territorial government,
> has the tide of emigration to Arkansas, been so strong, as during the
> past autumn, and it appears to increase, as the winter advances.
> Nearly 200 emigrants came up during the past week, in the steam-
> boats Industry and Waverley, and we understand several boats are on
> the river, filled with movers. Several of them have stopped in this
> place and vicinity, others are destined for different points on the river,
> but the mass of the movers are bound for Washington and Crawford
> Counties, and the country acquired from the Cherokees, by the late
> Treaty. The former County, and the late Cherokee country, have in-
> creased astonishingly in population the last twelve months, and the
> influx of settlers from Alabama, Tennessee, Mississippi, and other
> states east of the Mississippi River, and from Missouri, on the north,
> appears to be daily increasing. The country appears to have acquired
> much fame abroad, and, from information derived from intelligent
> persons who possess opportunities of judging, we are inclined to
> think the many advantages which it combines, have not been over-
> rated. For fertility of soil, salubrity of climate, and fine, healthy
> situations, it is said not to be exceeded by any country. Some of
> the settlements are already quite dense, and present appearances
> justify the belief that it will, in a very short period, become the most
> populous section of our territory.[32]

Settlement of other parts of the territory was not completely
neglected, however. The editor of the *Gazette* hastened to comment:

> While the tide of emigration is setting so fast toward the newly-
> acquired country to the west, it is gratifying to be able to state, that
> almost every other section of our Territory is receiving a steady acces-
> sion to its strength . . . . The counties bordering on the Mississippi
> are rapidly settling, as are also those on White River and its tribu-
> taries; and the southern countries are receiving their share from the
> emigrants daily passing through our town, and crossing the Arkansas

[32] *Arkansas Gazette,* Feb. 2, 1830. Similar reports are in the *Arkansas
Gazette* of Oct. 20 and Nov. 10, 1830, and Oct. 31, 1832.

Highlands and Lowlands: Relief Map of the State of Arkansas
*Shaded relief image courtesy of the Center for Advanced Spatial Technologies,
University of Arkansas*

at other points, as well as from great numbers who ascend Red River.[33]

Many of the new settlers brought with them their "wooly-heads," as one editor bluntly termed slaves,[34] and slavery in Arkansas continued to expand.

Various aspects of slavery as it existed in Arkansas during both territorial and statehood days will be examined in detail later, but some attention should be given here to legal control of the institution during the thirty-three years between 1803, when Arkansas was acquired by the United States from France, and 1836, when it became a state. Most of the laws regulating slavery in Arkansas Territory were inherited from the governments of Louisiana Territory and Missouri Territory. On October 1, 1804, the legislature of Louisiana Territory, which included Arkansas, passed a comprehensive set of laws concerning slavery, using the Black Code of 1724 as a basis. After Missouri became a separate territory (with Arkansas a component part), a few additional laws were enacted, and during the existence of Arkansas Territory a very few others went into effect. Not until the last year of territorial status—1835—was there a systematic compilation of the laws of Arkansas. In that year John Steele and James McCampbell of Little Rock, under direction of Governor John Pope, edited and published the first digest of Arkansas laws, which included all slave laws enacted since 1803 by the various governments to which Arkansas had been subject.[35]

Some of the harsher provisions of the Black Code were eliminated in the 1804 slave laws passed by the Louisiana legislature. No longer could a slave be branded or have his ears cut off. Whipping remained the principal mode of punishment. For example, a slave who "lifted his hand" against any free person might be given punishment not exceeding thirty lashes by a justice of the peace. All reference to any particular religion was omitted. The same general restrictions were placed on activities of slaves as in French and Spanish days: they could not carry

[33] *Arkansas Gazette*, Feb. 2, 1832.
[34] *Arkansas Gazette*, Nov. 10, 1830.
[35] J. Steele and J. M'Campbell, eds., *Laws of Arkansas Territory* (Little Rock, 1835).

guns except on frontier plantations, and only then by license of a
justice of the peace. Assembling of slaves—with some exceptions,
such as in church or on the home plantation—was prohibited.
Slaves could not prepare, exhibit, or administer any sort of medicine, nor could they buy or sell any commodity. A pass when off
the home plantation was required. Slaves could testify in court
only in cases where other slaves were involved.[36]

The growing importance of the slave as a piece of property
was emphasized by numerous laws dealing with him in that
status. Slaves were declared to be personal estate and were to be
taxed as such. They could be willed, deeded, or presented as
gifts by the owners, and could be emancipated by will or other
written instrument. In order to protect the interests of creditors,
however, the law provided that an emancipated slave was still
subject to seizure to satisfy a debt contracted by the owner prior
to emancipation. An emancipated Negro who failed to pay his
taxes could also be seized and hired out long enough to earn the
required amount of money.[37]

The local justice of the peace occupied a key position in the
legal control of slavery, since higher judicial officials were few and
likely to be far away, and also because the majority of infractions
of the law by slaves were minor ones which would never reach the
higher courts under any circumstances. The justice was given
authority to mete out punishment (usually whipping) for most
of the offenses previously listed—illegal assemblies, selling goods,
traveling without a pass, and so forth. As already indicated, the
justice also had power to license a slave to carry a gun. The law
gave in detail the procedure to be followed in taking and punishing runaway slaves, and in this the justice had an important function. He was required not only to issue warrants for the arrest
of known fugitives, but also to go out, in company with the sheriff
if necessary, in search for them.[38]

Few lasting additions to the slave code of 1804 were made in
the remaining years during which Arkansas was a part of Louisiana. One law, passed on November 4, 1808, provided that any
slave who refused to obey the lawful commands of his master

[36] *Ibid.*, pp. 437-438, 521-524, 528.
[37] *Ibid.*, pp. 526-527.   [38] *Ibid.*, pp. 521-523.

should be committed to jail until he should "humble himself to the . . . master's satisfaction," and, further, that a slave who assaulted his master might be punished with a maximum of ten lashes upon conviction by two or more justices of the peace.[39] Another, passed at the same time, imposed the mandatory penalty of death upon a slave convicted of murder or arson. A third law provided means for a slave to sue for freedom on grounds that he was being held illegally in slavery.[40]

Most of the laws concerning slavery passed during the seven years (1812-1819) Arkansas was a part of Missouri Territory dealt with the descent of slaves upon death of the owner.[41] Others re-emphasized the responsibility of the master for the acts of his slave: when a slave was convicted of any offense which carried restitution of money or property as part of the penalty, the master was required to make the restitution, and in all cases the master was to be responsible for any depredation or trespass committed by his slave.[42] A tax not exceeding one dollar was levied upon each slave.[43] Finally, slaves were forbidden to work on Sunday, penalty for violation naturally falling upon the masters rather than the slaves.[44]

After Arkansas became a territory in 1819, several important laws pertaining to slavery were added to the code. Prior to this time enforcement of laws regulating the activities of slaves had been left largely to authorities such as the sheriff and the justice of the peace, but in 1825 the slave patrol, an important device in the system of slave control, was introduced into Arkansas for the first time. The patrol, composed of a varying number of citizens, was charged with inspecting slave quarters, searching out places of unlawful assembly, and otherwise enforcing the law.[45] New and more comprehensive laws concerning runaway slaves were passed,[46] an indication that runaways had become a greater problem by territorial days. As the population of Arkansas increased, the justice of the peace began to lose some jurisdiction over the

---

[39] *Ibid.,* p. 191. An interesting commentary on the nature of slavery at the time was that this law also applied to a disobedient child.
[40] *Ibid.,* pp. 197-268.　　　　　[41] *Ibid.,* pp. 210, 212-214, 225.
[42] *Ibid.,* pp. 197-198, 549-550.　　[43] *Ibid.,* p. 461.
[44] *Ibid.,* p. 553.　　　　　　　　[45] *Ibid.,* pp. 530-532.
[46] *Ibid.,* pp. 528-530.

more important cases involving slaves. For example, after 1827 the law provided that "negro slaves should not be subject to any execution or other process issued from a justice of the peace," and that only circuit or superior courts could handle such matters.[47] The lawless white element present on the frontier made necessary in 1829 passage of a very severe law against "Negro-stealing." Under its provisions there was only one permissible penalty for the offense—death. That a slave was considered as little more than a very valuable animal is attested to by the fact that theft of a horse, mare, gelding, mule, or ass carried precisely the same punishment.[48]

By 1835 slavery in Arkansas, although not universally prevalent, had become firmly established as a part of the life and economy of the territory. The population was approaching the size when statehood would be possible, and a majority of the leaders were determined that Arkansas should enter the Union as a slave state. The struggle to achieve that end would not be easy, but, as in 1819, it would be successful.

[47] *Ibid.,* p. 350.   [48] *Ibid.,* p. 175.

III

"...wolf by the ears...."

AT LEAST as early as 1831 some citizens of Arkansas began to hope that the territory could become a state as soon as it had satisfied the population requirements for entrance into the union.[1] Since the population had more than doubled—from 14,273 to 30,388—between 1820 and 1830,[2] it was clear that the time was not far in the future. Memories of the struggle over the slavery issue which accompanied creation of Arkansas Territory in 1819 were still fresh in the minds of many of the people, and it was evident that when Arkansas did apply for statehood, there would be attempts to block her admission unless she abandoned or limited slavery; this despite the Missouri Compromise of 1820, which clearly placed Arkansas in the slaveholding section of the country geographically.[3] Since only a minority of Arkansans were slaveholders, some opposition within the state was also to be expected.

The first important public expressions on the possibility of statehood came in 1831 during the campaign between Benjamin Desha and Ambrose Sevier for election as delegate of the territory to Congress. Desha, in a statement to the electorate in the *Arkansas Advocate*, promised that if elected he would, as soon as Arkansas has attained the necessary population, promote its entrance into the union.[4] Sevier, on the other hand, was more cautious. While admitting the possibility of statehood soon, he added:

[1] The requisite population at that time was 47,700. *United States Statutes at Large*, V, 50.
[2] *Census of 1820*, p. 41; *Census of 1830*, p. 43.
[3] *United States Statutes at Large*, III, 548.
[4] *Arkansas Advocate*, May 11, 1831.

It would be, in our present situation, a grave consideration whether we should accept state government or not. . . .Taxed highly and deeply in debt, I believe we should be pursuing our best interests by remaining as we are. [But] when we are out of debt, and when we have the population and the means to support a state government, I am anxious as the most impatient to see this territory become a state.[5]

Sevier won the election, and although he had advocated deliberation in the matter of seeking statehood, once in Congress his attitude changed and he became the most ardent supporter of that objective. On December 17, 1833, he introduced the following resolution in the House of Representatives:

Resolved, That the Committee on the Territories be instructed to inquire into the expediency of permitting the people of the Territory of Arkansas to form a constitution and state government, and for the admission of such State into the Union, on an equal footing with the original States.[6]

On January 29, 1834, Senator John Tipton of Indiana introduced in the Senate a similar measure, which was referred to a select committee already considering a bill for the admission of Michigan.[7]

In a letter to his constituents through the *Arkansas Gazette,* Sevier explained that the slavery question was his chief motivation:

Michigan is now applying for admission, and I have every reason to believe that her application will be granted. Michigan, of course, will be a free state, and should she go into the Union as such, the happy balance of political power now existing in the senate will be destroyed, unless a slave state should go in with her. . . . At this time, also, we should be able to come in without trammels upon the subject of slavery. . . .[8]

To people who might believe that the whole matter of geographical limitations of slaveholding and nonslaveholding regions had been settled permanently by the Missouri Compromise, Sevier

[5] *Ibid.,* April 11, 1831.
[6] U. S. Congress, *The Congressional Globe* (46 vols.; Washington, 1834-1873), 23rd Congress, 1st Session, p. 36.
[7] *Ibid.,* p. 133.
[8] *Arkansas Gazette,* March 30, 1834.

pointed out: "It is true that a compromise was made, but . . . no congress has a right to bind a succeeding congress on the subject of slavery, . . . and the same body who made the compromise might rescind or disregard it."[9]

Neither Sevier's nor Tipton's measures succeeded in getting approval during the 1833-1834 session of Congress; in fact, neither ever got to the floor for a decisive vote. It appeared as if most members of both houses of Congress wanted to defer as long as possible final action on the admission of new states, since the controversial issue of slavery must inevitably be injected. Sevier attempted to force a decision on his Arkansas resolution on April 10, 1834, by introducing a resolution providing that the House would "on the 4th Tuesday of this month, proceed to consider such bills in the order in which they stand on the calendar, as relate exclusively to Territorial concerns." But the House postponed any action,[10] and ignored the matter for the remainder of the session.

Although Tipton's Senate bill to authorize Arkansas to form a constitution received a little more consideration than Sevier's resolution, it likewise was not permitted to come to a floor vote. The bill was taken up on May 12, but immediately Senator Thomas Ewing of Ohio moved to table it, and the Senate agreed by a vote of twenty-two to nineteen. No Southern solidarity is discernible in this vote; only eight senators from slave states voted against tabling the bill, while nine voted for tabling.[11] Near the end of the session, on June 26, Senator Tipton again tried to secure a vote on the bill, saying that "his only object was that the people of the Territory might be authorized to have the census taken, preparatory to their final admission." The first vote to take up the bill proved favorable by seventeen to sixteen, and while the bill was being read a motion by Senator Daniel Webster of Massachusetts to table it was defeated by a single vote, sixteen to fifteen. Before the reading of the bill had been completed, however, another motion to table it, this time by Senator Peleg

[9] *Ibid.*
[10] *Congressional Globe,* 23rd Congress, 1st Session, p. 303.
[11] *Ibid.,* p. 379.

Sprague of Maine, was approved by a vote of seventeen to four-teen.[12]

Sevier renewed his efforts to get favorable House action on authorization of an Arkansas constitution when Congress reconvened in December, 1834, but with no greater success than before. The House agreed to set aside February 9, 1835, for considering bills relating to the territories, including the Arkansas bill; when that day came, the only action taken was to turn the bills over to a "Committee of the Whole on the State of the Union."[13] On February 14 the Committee on Territories attempted to get the territorial bills before the House, but a decision was delayed until the next Monday. That day, largely occupied with heated discussions on the proposed abolition of slavery in the District of Columbia, passed with no action on the Arkansas bill.[14]

Despite an appeal by Sevier a few days later for the House to "take up . . . several bills, which had some days previous passed through committee, relating to the Territories, and which were of great importance to those concerned," the House took no action, and adjourned for the session on March 3.[15] The Senate did not consider Tipton's bill concerning the admission of Arkansas at all during the session.[16]

After these setbacks, Sevier decided to abandon attempts to get an enabling act passed in Congress, and suggested that the people of Arkansas should—following the lead of Michigan, rebuffed in the same manner—go ahead and form a constitution and present it to Congress with an application for statehood at the next session. There was, he said, "a battle to fight with fanaticism upon the subject of slavery . . . . Our rights are secured to us by the third article of the treaty of April 30, 1803. They are secured to us by the constitution itself. Our ancestors tired of colonial vassalage, and so have we."[17]

Meanwhile, public interest in the statehood question was at a high level in Arkansas, with proponents in the majority. Many public meetings were held during the spring and summer of 1835

---

[12] *Ibid.*, p. 473.
[13] *Congressional Globe*, 23rd Congress, 2nd Session, pp. 177-178, 223.
[14] *Ibid.*, pp. 244, 251-255.   [15] *Ibid.*, pp. 266, 332.
[16] *Ibid., passim.*
[17] *Arkansas Gazette*, June 9, 1835.

to consider what action should be taken: in Jackson County, April 26-28; Pulaski County, June 13; Pope County, June 27; Arkansas County, July 4; Independence County, July 6; St. Francis County, July 7 and July 11; Crittenden County, July 14; Lawrence County, July 20; and Washington County, August 10.[18] Resolutions were passed at most of the meetings; the Jackson County resolution was typical. It requested Governor William S. Fulton to call a special session of the legislature to provide for a constitutional convention and emphasized the importance of maintaining the balance of power between the slaveholding and the nonslaveholding states, in view of "the disposition of many of our northern and eastern brethren to interfere with and disturb us in the possession of our slaves."[19] The Jackson County resolution also clearly expressed what appears to have been the dominant attitude in Arkansas toward the institution of slavery, an attitude prompted by what one writer called having "the wolf by the ears" and hesitating before turning him loose:[20]

This is a species of property which, perhaps, it might have been well for the national quiet, harmony, and union of the United States had it never been known among them.

But our slaves are now here. They have been entailed upon us by our ancestors. Our knowledge has been coeval with the possession and use of them; and whether they be to us a blessing or a curse, they have grown upon our hands, and involved our means and support to such an extent that now to rid ourselves of them, either by emancipation or colonization abroad, without encumbering ourselves with a still greater evil and incurring an insupportable loss, would be a thing impossible; at least, a task which we are not willing, and which no human power can reasonably coerce upon us, to bear.[21]

Two other very immediate and practical reasons for the maintenance of slavery in Arkansas were advanced by Albert Pike,

[18] *Ibid.*, May 8-Aug. 15, 1835.   [19] *Ibid.*, May 8, 1835.
[20] Jesse Turner, "The Constitution of 1836," *Publications of the Arkansas Historical Association* (4 vols.; Fayetteville and Conway, 1906-1917), III, 122.
[21] *Arkansas Gazette*, May 8, 1835. An insufficient number of individual expressions of opinion concerning attitudes toward slavery were encountered to permit an absolutely certain evaluation of the prevailing feelings in Arkansas at this time. It is the opinion of the author, however, based upon thorough examination of the sources of the period, that few people in Arkansas vigorously defended slavery—most of them merely accepted it as a part of the pattern of life. The impression is also received that few people condemned slavery itself, even though they might object, on political or economic grounds, to its spread or continuation.

editor of the *Arkansas Advocate* and later an important political and military figure. He pointed out that if Arkansas were to become a free state "surrounded, as she would be, by Missouri, Tennessee, Mississippi, Louisiana, Texas and the Indian tribes— all of them slave countries—our state would become the land of refuge for runaways and vagabonds, and besides this, our revenue is to be raised from, and our rich lands settled by, the slaveholders."[22]

The feeling of some of the opponents of statehood that the institution of slavery in Arkansas, although not especially desirable, was in no danger and that statehood would be economically unsound, was expressed by an unknown correspondent of the Little Rock *Times* who signed his series of letters "Arkansas":

Conceive . . . the justice of the apprehensions of the slaveholders for the safety of their property, and how is the case affected by it? Of the whole white population, for one who has twenty slaves, we will find you twenty who have no slaves. The one, then, will be the sufferer by the abolition of slavery in the Territory, and to enable him to loll in ease and affluence and to save his own delicate hands from the rude contact of the vulgar plow, the twenty who earn their honest living by the sweat of the brow are called upon with the voice of authority assumed by wealth to receive the yoke. They must consent to a tenfold increase of tax for the support of a state government, because my lord is threatened with danger of desertion from his cotton field if we remain as we are.

To this the nonslaveholders who compose, as will appear by the new census, an overwhelming majority of the population of the territory, cannot submit. They are willing to forego the advantages to *themselves* of the abolition of slavery . . . but a greater sacrifice cannot, in justice, be expected. . . .[23]

Territorial Governor William S. Fulton opposed framing a constitution prior to passage of an enabling act in Congress, although he favored statehood as soon as possible after proper authorization. He believed that such action would be unlawful and therefore void.[24] Fulton clung to this position, even securing an opinion from the attorney general of the United States to

[22] *Arkansas Advocate*, June 10, 1835.
[23] *Times*, June 13, 1835.
[24] *Arkansas Gazette*, Aug. 4, 1835; *Times*, Aug. 8, 1835.

support it; nevertheless, the territorial legislature later overrode him and enacted a law to provide for a constitutional convention.[25] While this procedure was certainly irregular, there was no real spirit of defiance of the federal government, nor did officials in Washington long interpret it as such. Sevier, the congressional delegate, stated the Arkansas position:

. . . that we contemplated no [rebellion]; that treason against the federal government never entered into the mind of a single individual in Arkansas. That we intended to form a constitution, . . . and, until it should be accepted by congress, that we expected to remain . . . in allegiance . . . to territorial authorities. This seemed satisfactory to everybody.[26]

While the controversy raged over the propriety of an unauthorized constitutional convention, elections to what would be the last territorial legislature in Arkansas were taking place. At the same time the voters expressed their approval or disapproval of calling a convention in a sort of "straw vote" suggested by the *Arkansas Gazette* on May 26, 1835. Results showed that a large majority of those voting favored the convention.[27] A territorial census taken during the same period revealed that Arkansas had a population of 51,800, sufficient for statehood.[28]

Almost the first item of business of the legislature, which convened on October 5, 1835, was referral of the matter of seeking statehood to a joint committee. The committee promptly introduced a bill providing for election of members to a constitutional convention. Some members of the committee did not agree, however, asserting that the action was "unnecessary, impolitic, and illegal." The committee majority report was adopted, nevertheless, by a vote of twenty-nine to two.[29]

When the bill itself came up for action, there arose a serious controversy, involving slavery, over the basis of representation in the proposed convention. Members of the joint committee from

---

[25] *Times,* Oct. 19, 26, Nov. 29, 1835.
[26] *Arkansas Advocate,* Jan. 1, 1836.
[27] *Arkansas Gazette,* May 26, 1835; *Times,* Aug. 22, 29, 1835; David Y. Thomas, ed., *Arkansas and Its People, a History, 1541-1930* (4 vols.; New York, 1930), I, 87.
[28] *Arkansas Gazette,* Aug. 25, 1835.
[29] *Times,* Oct. 19, 1835.

the northern and western part of the territory insisted that representation should be distributed equally among the free white male inhabitants.[30]   This group was led principally by David Walker of Washington County.   On the other hand, the southern and eastern faction, whose chief spokesman was James H. Walker of Hempstead County, favored some arrangement in which the slave population would also be used in determining distribution of members of the constitutional convention.   Without its slaves, they argued, Arkansas would not have a population large enough to seek admittance to the union, and therefore the slaves should be counted for representation—if not all of them, certainly three-fifths, as in computing representation in the national congress.[31]

After several days of heated discussion, the legislature passed a compromise bill fixing the number of representatives to the convention at fifty-two, twenty-six from the northwest and the same number from the southeast, "thus leaving the two grand divisions equally balanced, and the people free to determine at the polls whether they [would] have slave representation, or a representation of freemen."[32]   The compromise was more favorable to the southeastern group, for not only was the freeman population of that section less than that of the northwest, but the total population was also smaller.[33]   The controversy over the basis of representation was not prompted solely by opposition to slavery by the northwestern leaders, for some of them, including Walker, held slaves themselves.[34]   Much more important was their fear that the southeast might gain political advantage if slaves were used in determining the basis of representation.[35]   As will be seen, however, the temporary political advantage gained by the southeast was not fully maintained when the constitution was drawn up. Governor Fulton refused to sign the bill passed by the legislature, but it became law nonetheless after he retained it without action for three days.[36]

[30] *Arkansas Advocate,* Oct. 30, 1835.
[31] *Ibid.*   [32] *Times,* Nov. 2, 1835.
[33] See p. 27 above.
[34] *Arkansas Gazette,* Dec. 15, 1835; Tax Assessment Lists, Crawford County and Washington County, 1835.
[35] For a full expression of the northwestern feeling, see the long statement of David Walker in the *Times,* Nov. 30, 1835.
[36] *Times,* Nov. 9, 1835.

The Arkansas constitutional convention met on Monday, January 4, 1836, at the "Baptist meeting house" in Little Rock, and three days later moved to the Presbyterian church, which offered better facilities. It concluded its work a little less than four weeks later with official adoption of the constitution on January 30.[37] The document was never submitted to the people of the state for approval, since that action had not been called for in the legislative act authorizing the convention.

Only the actions of the convention pertaining to slavery will be considered here. There was general harmony in enactment of sections of the constitution dealing directly with slavery, but it was inevitable that the basis of representation in the General Assembly should cause disagreement, since essentially the same matter had so recently been dealt with in the territorial legislature authorizing the convention. The advantage fluctuated rapidly between the northwest and the southeast during the week beginning January 19 in which the basis of representation was the chief question before the convention. The legislative committee at first recommended that representation be drawn from districts comprised of equal numbers of inhabitants, whether white or black, an obvious concession to the southeast with its greater proportion of slaves.[38] But upon motion of John Ringgold of Independence County this provision was stricken out and replaced by another providing for districts to be composed of equal numbers of free white male inhabitants.[39] Further motions and substitute motions and amendments and substitute amendments were offered by both sides, during discussion of which arguments practically identical with those in the last territorial legislature were heard. Again a select committee for the purpose of working out some sort of compromise had to be resorted to.[40]

The report of the select committee, adopted by the convention a few days later by a vote of twenty-eight to twenty-two, had some of the elements of a compromise, but the advantage lay with the northwest. The principal of representation based on the free white male population was adopted for both Senate and House of Rep-

[37] *Journal of the Constitution Convention of 1836* (Little Rock, 1836), pp. 3, 5, 119.
[38] *Ibid.*, p. 70.   [39] *Ibid.*, p. 72.   [40] *Ibid.*, pp. 80-81.

resentatives. There were to be sixteen senatorial districts, with
the ratio of representation to be one senator for each fifteen hundred free white males, and fifty-four representatives apportioned
among the thirty-four counties, one representative to each five
hundred free white males, with a further provision that each
county then organized should always have at least one representative.[41] Although having failed to secure adoption of their
basic principle, southeastern members could derive some con-
solation from the fact that since there were fewer free white males
in the southeastern half of the state, senatorial districts there
would be larger geographically and each senator would represent
more people (even though some of them were slaves). They also
recognized that several of their counties had less than five hundred
free white males, thus giving to the southeast, at least until the
population grew, a larger number of representatives in proportion to the total free white male population. Collectively, the
southeastern group emerged at a disadvantage, since there would
be fewer senators and representatives from that section, but individually, southeastern senators and representatives could wield
proportionately greater power in the General Assembly than their
northwestern colleagues.[42]

That two representative bodies—the territorial legislature and
the constitutional convention—should have taken different stands
within three months on the question of the weight of the slave
population in determination of bases of representation was indicative of the almost even division of opinion in Arkansas in the matter. Furthermore, the willingness of both sides to compromise
demonstrated that admission into the union was far more important than how petty internal differences over slavery were to be
settled.

With the exception of that involving the basis of representation, only three sections of the constitution dealt directly with
slavery. Article IV, Section 23, gave the General Assembly
"power to pass all laws that are necessary to prohibit the introduction into this State, of any slave or slaves, who may have commit-

---

[41] *Ibid.,* p. 89.
[42] Albert Pike, a close contemporary observer, commented that the method
of apportionment was "a compromise between the friends of district representation and those opposed to it." Turner, "Constitution of 1836," p. 116.

ted any high crime, in any other State or Territory."[43] Section 25 of the same article provided:

The General Assembly shall have the power to prohibit the introduction of any slave or slaves, for the purpose of speculation, or as an article of trade or merchandise: To oblige the owner of any slave or slaves to treat them with humanity: And in the prosecution of slaves for any crime, they shall not be deprived of an impartial jury; and any slave who shall be convicted of a capital offense, shall suffer the same degree of punishment as would be inflicted on a free white person, and no other; and courts of justice, before whom slaves shall be tried, shall assign them counsel for their defense.[44]

Article VII, Section 1, would prove to be very controversial when the constitution was presented to Congress for approval:

The General Assembly shall have no power to pass laws for the emancipation of slaves, without the consent of the owners. They shall have no power to prevent emigrants to this State from bringing with them such persons as are deemed slaves by the laws of any one of the United States. They shall have power to pass laws to permit owners to emancipate them, saving the right of creditors, and preventing them from becoming a public charge. They shall have power to prevent slaves from being brought to this state as merchandise, and also to oblige the owners of slaves to treat them with humanity.[45]

Several other sections or clauses pertaining to slavery were considered by the convention but were stricken out prior to passage. Among them were requirements that an emancipated slave be removed from the state shortly after emancipation, that a freed slave be re-enslaved if he returned to the state, and that a person who inflicted injury or death on a slave should suffer the same degree of punishment as if the offense had been committed on a free white person, except in case of insurrection of the slave.[46]

[43] Constitution of the State of Arkansas, printed in William McK. Ball and Sam C. Roane, compilers, *Revised Statutes of the State of Arkansas, Adopted at the October Session of the General Assembly of Said State, A. D. 1837* . . . (Boston, 1838), p. 24. The constitution is also printed in Francis N. Thorpe, ed., *The Federal and State Constitutions, Colonial Charters, and other Organic Laws of the States, Territories and Colonies now or heretofore forming the United States of America*, House Document No. 357, 59th Congress, 2nd Session (7 vols.; Washington, 1909), I, 268-286.

[44] *Revised Statutes, 1838*, p. 24. Laws implementing the first two parts of this section were never passed.

[45] *Ibid.*, p. 37.

[46] *Journal of the Constitutional Convention*, pp. 39, 43.

On March 10, 1836, President Andrew Jackson forwarded to Congress the Arkansas constitution, which he had received officially a few days before.   Further action was immediately referred to a select committee.[47]   Ambrose Sevier, still territorial delegate to Congress, predicted the ensuing struggle over approval of the constitution in a letter to the *Arkansas Gazette:* "Don't be astonished if we have another Missouri discussion upon the subject of slavery."[48]

While Sevier's estimate proved to be somewhat exaggerated, there was considerable opposition in Congress to the constitution, directed in both Senate and House principally at Article VII, Section 1, which deprived the Arkansas General Assembly of the power to pass laws emancipating slaves without the consent of their owners.   In the Senate on April 4 Senator Benjamin Swift of Vermont expressed the common opinion of the antislavery forces when he asserted that he could not vote for the admission of Arkansas because the section provided for the maintenance of slavery in perpetuity.[49]   In the House of Representatives opposition to admission of Arkansas was led by John Quincy Adams of Massachusetts, former President of the United States, and William Slade of Vermont.   On June 9 Adams proposed an amendment to the bill for admission which declared that "nothing in this act shall be construed as an assent by Congress to the article in the constitution . . . in relation to slavery and the emancipation of slaves."[50]   Slade also proposed an amendment, providing that Arkansas should not enter the union until it should

expunge from its present constitution so much thereof as prohibits the General Assembly from passing laws for the emancipation of slaves without the consent of their owners; and should also provide . . . that no negro or mulatto born in, or brought into, said state, after its admission into the Union, shall be held . . . as property or in any way be subjected to slavery.

After a great deal of discussion before the House, whose members were—after twenty-five hours' continuous session—"sleepy, tired,

[47] *Congressional Globe,* 24th Congress, 1st Session, p. 240.
[48] *Arkansas Gazette,* April 5, 1836.
[49] *Congressional Globe,* 24th Congress, 1st Session, p. 315.
[50] *Ibid.,* p. 542.

and drunk," both amendments were soundly defeated.[51]   Four days later, on June 13, the House approved the bill admitting Arkansas by a vote of 143 to 50, shortly after the bill admitting Michigan as a free state was passed.[52]   Action for that day was concluded with the famous remark of Representative Henry W. Connor of North Carolina, that "as the House had been delivered of twins, after the operation they might adjourn."[53]

Meanwhile, the Senate, where opposition was lighter, had already passed bills for admission of Arkansas and Michigan, the Arkansas bill by the decisive vote of thirty-one to six.[54]   Although the vote shows that there was relatively little opposition, Senator James Buchanan (later President of the United States), to whom the bill had been entrusted, helped smooth the way for its passage by pointing out that

. . . on the subject of slavery this constitution was more liberal than the constitution of any of the slaveholding States that had been admitted into the Union.   It preserved the very words of the other constitutions in regard to slavery; but there were other provisions in it in favor of the slaves, and among them a provision which secured to them the right of trial by jury, thus putting them, in that particular, on an equal footing with whites.[55]

Senator Buchanan's analysis of the slavery provisions of the Arkansas constitution was somewhat exaggerated, for all of them evidently were taken directly from the constitutions of one or another of the slave states.   The greatest resemblance in language is to the Alabama constitution of 1819; the only additional provision found in the Arkansas constitution is that "any slave who shall be convicted of a capital offense, shall suffer the same degree of punishment as would be inflicted on a free white person, and no other."   The Missouri constitution of 1820 is perhaps the most similar in meaning to the Arkansas constitution, even containing the exact provision concerning the degree of punishment of a slave quoted above.   Other constitutions which contain some of the same provisions on slavery as that of Arkansas include the Mississippi constitution of 1832, the Kentucky constitution of

[51] *Ibid.*, p. 543.   [52] *Ibid.*, p. 551.
[53] *Ibid.*   [54] *Ibid.*, p. 316.
[55] *Ibid.*, pp. 315-316.   Buchanan referred to Article IV, Section 25.

1799, and the Georgia constitution of 1798. Apparently the various constitutions borrowed heavily from those drawn up previously.

Several constitutions in effect at the time the Arkansas constitution was written contained no direct reference to slavery: Virginia (1830), Louisiana (1812), South Carolina (1790), North Carolina (1776), and Maryland (1776). These states relied upon statute laws for regulation of slavery. Senator Buchanan's implication that only the Arkansas constitution guaranteed the right of trial by jury to slaves was not correct. The Missouri constitution contained almost exactly the same statement as that of Arkansas: "In prosecution for crimes, slaves shall not be deprived of an impartial trial by jury. . . ." The constitutions of Alabama and Kentucky did not directly guarantee right of trial by jury, but provided that "the general assembly shall have no power to deprive them of the privilege of an impartial trial by petit jury" in case of major crimes. While only the Arkansas, Missouri, Kentucky, and Alabama constitutions mentioned trial of slaves by jury, all of the other slave states made statutory provision for jury trials, at least in major cases.[56] It may be concluded, then, that although the slavery provisions in the Arkansas constitution were not more liberal than those of all of the other constitutions, they were more liberal than most, and no less liberal than any.

On June 15, 1836, President Jackson signed the bills admitting the far-from-identical twins, Arkansas and Michigan, into the United States.[57] Thus Arkansas entered its brief period of less than thirty years as a slaveholding state.

[56] Constitutions of the states named in Thorpe, *Federal and State Constitutions, passim;* Thomas R. R. Cobb, *An Inquiry into the Law of Negro Slavery* . . . (Philadelphia, 1858), pp. 268-269.
[57] *United States Statutes at Large,* V, 49-52.

Addition and Multiplication

NEGRO SLAVERY was a vital and growing institution during its existence in Arkansas. In numbers, slaves continued to increase; until the Civil War dealt it a death blow, slavery constantly thrust itself into new areas of the state and increased at a rapid rate in the already heavily slave area. Although only six counties in Arkansas (Arkansas, Chicot, Desha, and Phillips in the eastern part of the state, Union in the southern, and Lafayette in the southwestern) had more slaves than whites in 1860,[1] there is little doubt that had slavery endured, within a short span of years Arkansas would have resembled in racial composition the state of Mississippi, where by 1850 there was an excess of slaves over whites in all the counties adjacent to the Mississippi, in most of the second tier of counties, and in others scattered over the state.[2] It is true that nearly half of Arkansas was not adaptable to slave-operated, mass-production agriculture, but the eastern lowlands had the same extremely fertile, level land found in the more highly developed Mississippi delta country. Only the time required to clear and place the Arkansas lands in cultivation accounted for the lag between the development of Arkansas and that of Mississippi as slave states, and that lag was rapidly being made up.

Perhaps the most convincing proof of the vigorous and expanding nature of slavery in Arkansas is the fact that from 1820 to 1850 the percentage of increase in number of slaves was far

[1] *Census of 1860 (Population),* p. 18.
[2] For a graphic representation of density and distribution of the slave population of Mississippi in 1850, see the frontispiece of Charles S. Sydnor, *Slavery in Mississippi* (New York, 1933).

greater than that in any other state, and that from 1850 to 1860 it was second only to that in Texas. From 1820 to 1830 the percentage of increase was 182; from 1830 to 1840, 335; from 1840 to 1850, 136; and from 1850 to 1860, 135. The second-place states in rate of increase each decade did not even closely approach Arkansas: in 1830 Missouri showed a gain of 145 per cent in a decade; in 1840 Mississippi had experienced a ten-year increase of 197 per cent; and in 1850 Mississippi again ranked second, with an 1840-1850 increase of 58 per cent. The 1850-1860 rate of increase in Texas, which exceeded that of Arkansas, was 213 per cent.[3]

In actual numbers of slaves Arkansas ranked throughout the slavery period much lower than it did in percentages of increase, but by 1860 its relative rank among slaveholding states was beginning to rise more rapidly. In 1820 there were 1,617 slaves in Arkansas, a smaller number than in any other Southern state, and even less than in two of the Middle Atlantic states, New Jersey and New York, which still had 7,557 and 10,088 respectively. The next decade saw an increase of slaves in Arkansas to 4,576, and a climb to thirteenth rank among slave states. In that year—1830 —Arkansas exceeded only one of the slave states, Delaware. The census of 1840 reported 19,935 slaves, again placing the state thirteenth, and again exceeding only Delaware. In 1850 Arkansas still held thirteenth place, but had surpassed Florida in number of slaves, with 47,100 as compared to 39,310. By 1860 there were 111,115 slaves in Arkansas, giving the state twelfth rank and a lead over Maryland and Florida as well as Delaware. In every census year the state of Virginia held first place in number of slaves by a considerable margin.[4]

It has been seen that the slave population of Arkansas increased very rapidly; another indication of the vigorous nature of the institution in the state was that the slave population increased at a considerably faster rate than did the white. This was in large measure due to continuous importation of slaves from the older states, for obviously the slaves could not reproduce themselves so rapidly. Beginning with the 1820-1830 period, the comparative

[3] *Census of 1860 (Population)*, pp. 598-604.
[4] *Ibid.*, pp. 594-95, 600-604.

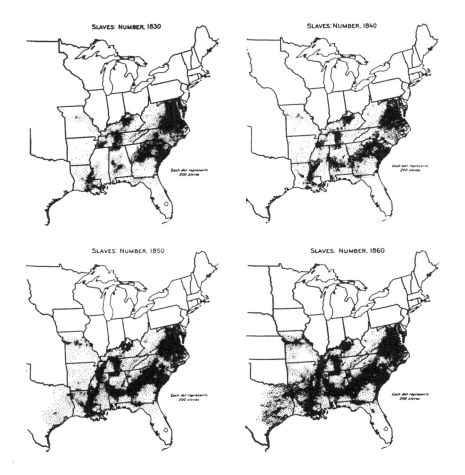

Growth and spread of slavery in Arkansas and other slave states

(From Lewis C. Gray, History of Agriculture in the Southern United States to 1860, *Washington, 1933, II, 654-655. By permission of the Carnegie Institution of Washington.)*

percentage rates of increases during successive decades were as follows: 1820-1830, slave 182, white 104; 1830-1840, slave 335, white 200; 1840-1850, slave 136, white 110; 1850-1860, slave 135, white 99. The over-all percentage of increase in slave population from 1820 to 1860 was 6,771, as compared to a white increase of 2,476 per cent.[5] Consequently slaves composed an ever-increasing proportion of the total population of Arkansas. Whereas only 11 per cent of the people were slaves in 1820 and 15 per cent in 1830, 20 per cent were slaves in 1840, 22 per cent in 1850, and 25 per cent in 1860.[6] The total population of Arkansas in each of the census years was as follows: 1820, 14,255; 1830, 30,388; 1840, 97,574; 1850, 209,897; and 1860, 435,450.[7]

As during the territorial period, slaves in the state of Arkansas continued to be distributed throughout all of the counties. Some counties always had few, however, and the greatest concentrations of slaves were found in the lowland counties, or those lying south and east of the imaginary line bisecting the state from northeast to southwest. During territorial days there had been more slaves in the highlands of the north and west,[8] but shortly after Arkansas became a state in 1836, the lowland counties gained a lead which continued to increase until the end of slavery. At the time of the first census after Arkansas entered the Union (1840), 52 per cent of the slaves, or 10,066 of the 19,935, were found in the fifteen counties which could be classified as lowland, while the remainder lived in the twenty-four highland counties. At the same time the greater proportion of the total population was still (as it would continue to be) in the uplands, with 55,942 people living there as compared to only 31,942 in the lowlands.[9] By 1850 the proportion of slaves living in the twenty-one lowland counties had increased greatly, to about 70 per cent, or 32,845 of the total of 47,100 slaves in the state. By this year Arkansas had fifty-one counties. The highlands, containing 122,855 people of the state total of 209,897, continued to be the most thickly populated, irrespective of race.[10]

[5] *Ibid.*, pp. 599, 602-604.
[6] *Ibid.*, p. 599; U. S. Bureau of the Census, *Census of 1850* (Washington, 1853), p. 548.
[7] *Census of 1860 (Population)*, pp. 599, 602-604.
[8] See p. 27 above.   [9] *Census of 1850*, p. 535.   [10] *Ibid.*

The preponderance of slaves in the southern and eastern counties was even more marked by 1860. In that year 80,698 slaves, or about 74 per cent of the 111,115 in the entire state, were located in the twenty-four lowland counties, the remainder being distributed throughout the thirty-one counties of the north and west. The lowlands, although still lagging in total population, showed a much greater increase in the 1850-1860 decade than did the rest of the state, and in 1860 were rapidly approaching the highlands in population density. The census of that year showed 203,357 people of all races in the southeastern half of the state, and 232,093 in the northwestern.[11]

Thus it is evident that by 1860 the emigration pattern of the 1820's and 1830's had reversed itself. No longer were Washington and Crawford and other northwestern counties, with their healthful upland valleys, the principal attraction for farmers coming into Arkansas. The highland counties continued to increase in population, but the attraction of the southern cotton lands, in spite of the numerous disadvantages for pleasant living, grew stronger and stronger. And as the cotton lands filled up, the slave population increased.

These items from Little Rock newspapers, typical of many appearing in the press of the state during the forties and fifties, illustrate the change in patterns of emigration:

There is a large demand for corn in our market. The crowd of emigrants is so large that it is sold along the Memphis and Washington[12] road at from fifty cents to one dollar per bushel. Small lots brought into our market are readily sold for 50 cents.

Emigrants for South Arkansas and Texas are crowding through our city thicker and faster than ever. The rush is tremendous. The two ferries are constantly engaged in crossing the movers.[13]

[11] *Census of 1860 (Population)*, p. 18.
[12] Washington, in southwestern Arkansas, was the seat of Hempstead County at that time. Although never very populous, it was one of the most important Arkansas towns, center of a well-developed plantation area and a point of departure for travelers to Texas. From 1863 to 1865, while Little Rock and a major portion of Arkansas were occupied by Federal troops, Washington was the Confederate capital of the state. A good, if somewhat uneven, history of Washington is Charlean Moss Williams, *The Old Town Speaks* (Houston, 1951).
[13] *Arkansas State Democrat*, Nov. 2, 1849.

We are pleased to find that the tide of emigration to Arkansas has recommenced this fall, with renewed vigor. The ferry, at this place, has been crowded, for several days, with movers, going South, some to Texas, but principally to settle the fertile lands in the Red River country. Among those who have passed through town, since Sunday morning, we presume there were not less than 300 negroes. We also understand that the road leading from Memphis to this place, is literally lined with movers—all destined for the southern part of the state. They are generally from Tennessee and Alabama, and a large number from North Carolina.[14]

The lead in slave population among individual counties in Arkansas in successive decades shifted in the same manner as did the over-all concentration of Negroes—from northwest to southeast. Of the ten counties with the largest numbers of slaves in 1840, only five (Chicot, Lafayette, Jefferson, Union, and Phillips) were located in the southern and eastern sections of the state, while four (Hempstead, Pulaski, Sevier, and Clark) occupied positions along the highland-lowland line, and one (Washington) was a true upland county. By 1850 a distinct change had occurred. No northwestern counties and only two of the borderline counties (Hempstead and Sevier) were among the leading ten in slave population; the remaining eight were all southeastern counties. The next ten years saw a continuation of the trend, and in 1860 only one county among those with the greatest slave populations (Hempstead) was not of the true lowland group.[15]

The real significance of the size of the slave population in a given county is not apparent without some consideration of the total population of the county. The following table compiled from the federal censuses shows both slave and total population in each of the ten leading slave counties for the years 1850 and 1860. It may be seen that in both years Chicot County far exceeded any other in proportion of slaves to total population. Its population was 78 per cent slave in 1850, and 81 per cent slave in 1860. With its flat fertile fields along the Mississippi and preponderance of large plantations and slaveholders, Chicot was more nearly

---

[14] *Arkansas Gazette*, Oct. 27, 1845.
[15] *Census of 1840*, p. 41; *Census of 1850*, p. 535; *Census of 1860 (Population)*, p. 18.

representative of the idealized Southern plantation country than any other Arkansas county.

LEADING SLAVE COUNTIES IN ARKANSAS, 1850 AND 1860

	1850			1860	
COUNTY	POPULATION		COUNTY	POPULATION	
	Slave	*Total*		*Slave*	*Total*
Union	4,767	10,298	Phillips	8,941	14,876
Chicot	3,984	5,115	Chicot	7,512	9,234
Lafayette	3,320	5,220	Jefferson	7,146	14,971
Ouachita	3,304	9,591	Union	6,331	12,288
Jefferson	2,621	5,834	Hempstead	5,398	13,989
Phillips	2,591	6,935	Arkansas	4,921	8,844
Dallas	2,542	6,877	Ouachita	4,478	12,936
Hempstead	2,460	7,672	Lafayette	4,311	8,464
Arkansas	1,538	3,245	Desha	3,784	6,459
Sevier	1,372	3,240	Ashley	3,761	8,590

Although the lowland counties of Arkansas continued to increase their lead in total slave population, it must not be assumed that the counties of the hill and mountain region were at the same time actually losing slaves. In the decade between 1850 and 1860 the only counties which did were Newton, with a decline from 47 to 24 slaves while the total county population increased from 1,758 to 3,393, and Crawford, where the number of slaves dropped from 933 to 858, with the total county population also declining from 7,950 to 7,860.[16] All other northwestern counties showed varying gains in slaves, but in almost every instance the white population increased much more than the slave.[17] For example, Washington County, second most populous in the state in 1850, experienced an increase of from 1,199 to 1,432 slaves and from 8,757 to 13,133 whites; Benton County gained in slave

[16] *Census of 1850*, p. 535; *Census of 1860 (Population)*, p. 18. The decline of slavery in Newton County, in the rugged mountains of northern Arkansas, was of negligible importance in the over-all status of the institution in the state. It was the beginning of a trend, however, which within a few years established Newton County as one of the few in Arkansas with no Negro residents. Crawford County's loss in population, both white and Negro, is largely accounted for by the creation on January 6, 1851, of Sebastian County, partially from territory taken from Crawford County. Herndon, *The Arkansas Handbook, 1949-1950*, p. 144.

[17] A notable exception was White County, where the number of slaves increased almost fivefold, from 308 to 1432, while the white population gain was only threefold, from 2309 to 6884. *Census of 1850*, p. 535; *Census of 1860 (Population)*, p. 18. This rapid gain in slaves can be attributed, however, to the existence of good agricultural land along White River within the county.

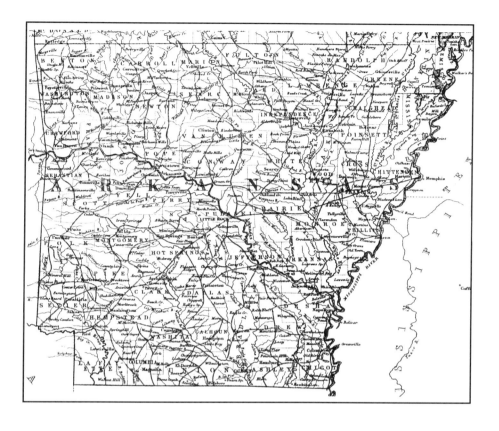

Arkansas near the end of the slavery period, 1860
Map #1323 Courtesy of Arkansas History Commission

population from 201 to 384 and in white population from 3,508 to 8,921; and in Marion County slaves increased in number from 126 to 261, with whites showing a gain of from 2,308 to 6,192.[18] The northwestern section of Arkansas was becoming more and more predominantly white in racial composition.

Negro slavery in Arkansas was primarily a rural institution, just as the state itself was primarily rural. As late as 1860 there were only a half dozen centers of population which might be considered cities: Little Rock with 3,727 people, Camden with 2,219, Fort Smith with 1,530, Pine Bluff with 1,396, Van Buren with 969, Fayetteville with 967, and Arkadelphia with 817.[19] Even these "cities"—in spite of proud claims such as that of Robert F. Kellam of Camden, who wrote that "Camden is destined to become one of the leading cities of the South very soon"[20]—were in reality little more than frontier villages. They had few buildings of brick and stone,[21] and the streets were so muddy in winter they were virtually impassable and so dusty in summer that the residents suffered real discomfort.[22] Other than the larger centers, only twelve places in the state were listed in the federal census as towns, and the populations of these ranged as low as 76 in Mt. Ida.[23]

Of the towns, Camden had the largest number of slaves in 1860—875—although not the largest in proportion to the total population. Little Rock had 846 slaves, Pine Bluff 340, Fayetteville 294, Van Buren 213, and Arkadelphia 217. One of the smaller towns, Spring Hill in Hempstead County, had by far the highest proportion of slaves to total population, 372 of 401.[24]

Most of the slaves in the cities and towns were house servants, artisans, or laborers, but the substantial number of slaves occasionally listed in the census as the property of a single person indi-

[18] *Census of 1850,* p. 535; *Census of 1860 (Population),* p. 18.
[19] *Census of 1860 (Population),* p. 19.
[20] Diary of Robert F. Kellam, March 27, 1859.
[21] Perhaps the best proof of the temporary nature of most of the pre-Civil War buildings in Arkansas is that few have survived down to the present.
[22] Diary of Robert F. Kellam, Jan. 14, 1859, Aug. 20, 1860.
[23] *Census of 1860 (Population),* p. 19.
[24] *Ibid.* The published census lists no slaves in Fort Smith, although it is known there were a number. Helena is not listed among the towns and cities in the published census, but according to the manuscript census schedules, it contained 526 slaves, a number exceeded only by Camden and Little Rock. MS Census Schedule, Slave Population, Town of Helena, 1860.

cates that some planters quartered their slaves in town at the family home and sent them out to work on the nearby plantation each day.   Such would seem to be true in the case of Jasper Parchal of Helena, who owned 49 slaves living within the town. Most of the other holdings in Helena were quite small, averaging a little less than 6 slaves per owner; the 93 slaveholders of the town owned a total of 526 slaves.[25]   Other towns usually had one or more fairly large slaveholders also,[26] with the remainder of the slaves held singly or in small family groups.   For example, in 1860 there were 33 slaves in Little Rock belonging to Peter Hanger, but with 846 slaves in the city owned by 144 men, the average number per owner was approximately the same as in Helena—slightly less than six.   Many men well known in early Arkansas history were among the slaveholding group in Little Rock, and most of them held only small numbers (living within the city, at least).   William E. Woodruff, founder of the *Arkansas Gazette* and its publisher for many years, was somewhat above the average with his fourteen slaves.   Another printer and publisher, R. S. Yerkes, owned three slaves, as did Justice Elbert H. English of the Arkansas Supreme Court.   John Pope, famous jurist, and Albert Pike, lawyer, poet, Mason, and later general, each held four slaves.[27]

In the city of Pine Bluff, a great majority of the slaves were held singly, being employed as cooks, house servants, carriage drivers, or the like.   The average holding was only a little more than two slaves per owner, much smaller than in the other towns. The 340 slaves were in the possession of 123 owners.   In Fayetteville, slaveholders owned, on the average, more slaves than those in any other of the larger Arkansas towns—375 slaves to 47 owners, or 8 each.   One man, Isaac Taylor, owned 32.[28]   The high average is somewhat surprising, since Fayetteville was in the northwestern section of the state.   In the towns of the state as a

[25] MS Census Schedule, Slave Population, Town of Helena, 1860.

[26] Many residents of the towns owned large numbers of slaves living in the rural areas, but these were usually listed separately, especially if they were in a different township.

[27] MS Census Schedule, Slave Population, City of Little Rock, 1860.

[28] MS Census Schedules, Slave Population, City of Pine Bluff and Town of Fayetteville, 1860.

whole, the average number of slaves per owner was a fraction more than four.

The 3,799 slaves listed in the census of 1860 as living in the towns and cities of Arkansas comprised only a little more than one-thirtieth of the total slave population of 111,115 in that year.[29] Thus the town slave was relatively unimportant numerically in Arkansas. Since, however, only one twenty-fifth of the total population (15,503 of 435,450) lived in the towns and cities, town slaves were only slightly less numerous, proportionately, than the whole urban class.[30]

Considering the state of Arkansas as a whole, the average slaveholder owned more slaves than did the average slaveholder in the towns. According to the census of 1860, there were 11,481 slaveholders and 111,115 slaves in the state,[31] an average of 9.6 slaves to each individual owner. Actually, neither the number of slaveholders as given in the census nor the size of the average holding is strictly correct, for since the census was compiled by counties, no recognition of multiple county holdings was made. Consequently, a man who held slaves in two or more counties was counted in the census two or more times, and the total number of slaveholders is thus too large. Also because of the county method of compilation, the true average holding was something more than 9.6, since the census did not record total holding of individuals. But since relatively few men had multiple holdings, neither of the figures given is seriously in error.

Among the fifteen states which had significant numbers of slaves in 1860, Arkansas ranked about midway in the average size of slaveholdings, which ranged from fifteen in South Carolina downward to 4.6 in Missouri. The states of the lower south —Florida, Georgia, South Carolina, Alabama, Mississippi, and Louisiana—exceeded Arkansas in the size of slaveholdings, while the border states and others of the upper south—Virginia, North Carolina, Maryland, Tennessee, Missouri, and Kentucky—had smaller average holdings. Also in the latter group was Texas, which, although an increasingly important slave state, was some-

[29] *Census of 1860 (Population)*, p. 19.
[30] *Ibid.*
[31] U. S. Bureau of the Census, *Census of 1860 (Agriculture)* (Washington, 1864), p. 224.

what in the status of Arkansas in that the institution of slavery was still growing very vigorously. Size of the average holding in Arkansas was only a fraction less than the average of all the slave states, which was slightly more than ten.[32]

In understanding the impact which Negro slavery had upon the white people of the state of Arkansas, the size of the average holding is by no means the only factor which should be considered. Equally important is the proportion of slaveholders in the white population. In 1860 there were 11,481 slaveowners in the white population of 324,143, or approximately 3.5 per cent. At first glance it would thus seem that only about one of every twenty-eight white people had contact with slaves in the status of master. Slaveowners, however, were usually heads of families, so considerably more than one person in twenty-eight was, if not the legal owner of slaves, at least a member of a slave-owning family. A conservative figure for the size of the average Arkansas family in 1860 would be five; on that basis, 17.5 per cent, or a little more than one person in six, either owned slaves in his own name or was a member of a family which owned slaves. An even clearer impression of the total significance of slavery in the state in 1860 may be gained by adding the percentage of slaves in the population—25—to the 17.5 per cent. Thus it may be seen that 42.5 per cent of the population of Arkansas was directly involved in the institution of slavery.[33]

The figures given immediately above are not indicative of the importance of Negro slavery in the southern and eastern counties of Arkansas, however, for there the average white man owned a great many more slaves than the state-wide average, and at the same time a much larger percentage of the white population owned slaves. In 1860 the average number of slaves to each owner in the six counties in which slaves outnumbered whites was as follows:

[32] Compiled from figures given in *ibid.*, p. 247. Care must be exercised in the use of statistics given in the printed census. For example, the number of slaveowners in Arkansas in 1860 is given as 1149 on p. 247 and 11,481 on p. 224. The last figure is evidently correct; the first apparently lacks one digit. Use of the incorrect figure has at times given the erroneous impression that slaveholding was relatively unimportant in Arkansas. See, for example, James G. Randall, *The Civil War and Reconstruction* (New York, 1937), p. 61. Correct figures have been used where the tables are in error.

[33] *Census of 1860 (Population)*, p. 593; *Census of 1860 (Agriculture)*, p. 247; Sydnor, *Slavery in Mississippi*, p. 193.

Chicot, 33.3; Arkansas, 18.9; Desha, 18.5; Phillips, 16.2; Lafayette, 15.9; and Union, 10.4. In contrast to this, the average number of slaves per owner in six northwestern counties selected at random was much lower: Washington, 4.9; Benton, 3.5; Van Buren, 3.8; Izard, 5.8; Scott, 4.3; and Pope, 4.6.[34] It may be seen from these figures that while a typical holding in the northwestern section of the state was no more than a small family of slaves, one in the southeast consisted of from two to six families. In contrast to the statewide average of only 3.5 per cent of the white population as slaveholders, percentages of owners to total white population in the counties where slaves were preponderant were as follows: Chicot, 13; Union, 10.2; Phillips, 9.2; Desha, 7.6; Arkansas, 6.4; and Lafayette, 6.3. Again assuming five persons in the average white family, more than 43 per cent of the white people in these counties were members of slaveholding families—Chicot County, with 65 per cent, leading the others.[35]

By far the majority of the large individual slaveholdings were along the Mississippi River and in the southern part of Arkansas. Of the seven holdings in the state of two hundred or more slaves in 1860, three were in counties on the Mississippi (Chicot and Mississippi), three in Arkansas County, only a few miles inland, and the seventh in Hempstead County, on Red River in the southwestern section. The only holding of more than five hundred slaves, that of Elisha Worthington, was in Chicot County. There were sixty-six owners of a hundred or more slaves in Arkansas in 1860, and all but eleven of these lived in the lower counties. In slaveholdings of diminishing size the trend was also for most to be concentrated in the south and east. There was one notable exception, however; in Chicot County few of the individual holdings were of less than ten slaves, a natural condition in a county where large scale production of cotton was dominant.[36]

Examination of the table below, adapted from the *Census of 1860 (Agriculture)*, will show that in the state as a whole, the greatest single category of owners held only one slave each, and that more than 50 per cent of the owners owned four or less each.

[34] *Census of 1860 (Agriculture)*, p. 224.
[35] *Census of 1860 (Population)*, p. 18; *Census of 1860 (Agriculture)*, p. 224.
[36] *Ibid.*

These widely distributed small holdings, along with the large ones of the plantation areas, served to maintain a consciousness of slavery in every section of Arkansas.

SLAVES AND SLAVEHOLDERS IN ARKANSAS, 1860

Number of Slaves	Number of Owners	Number of Slaves	Number of Owners
1	2,339	15 & under 20	641
2	1,503	20 & under 30	586
3	1,070	30 & under 40	275
4	894	40 & under 50	157
5	730	50 & under 70	161
6	569	70 & under 100	118
7	463	100 & under 200	59
8	404	200 & under 300	6
9	369	300 & under 500	0
10 & under 15	1,136	500 & under 1,000	1

Total number of slaves 111,115
Total number of owners 11,481

V

"Likely Negroes for Sale and for Hire"

NEGRO SLAVES in Arkansas, like other pieces of property, were frequently transferred from one owner to another. Some were given to friends or relatives, either during the lifetime of the owner or by will, but the most common method of transfer was by sale. And since, as we have seen, the number of slaves in the state increased very rapidly—far more rapidly than could be accounted for by the natural increase—a great many more were bought than were sold and sent outside the state. From 1850 to 1860—to select a period for which records and statistics are more plentiful than for any other—the number of slaveowners in Arkansas increased from 5,999 to 11,481, while the number of slaves increased from 47,100 to 111,115.[1] These figures show that the average number of slaves held by a single owner increased during the decade from 7.8 to 9.6, or approximately 23 per cent. Thus the average owner increased his individual holdings substantially during the decade, in most instances by purchase. Most significant, however, was the proportionately greater increase in the slaveholdings of large size. In 1850 Arkansas had no slaveowners with more than 300 slaves, only 2 with more than 200, 21 with more than 100, and 130 with more than 50 slaves each. By 1860 one man owned more than 500 slaves, 66 more than 100, and 345 more than 50 each. Whereas only one owner in 46 had owned 50 or more slaves in 1850, one in 33 had that many in his possession in 1860.[2] And naturally the number of slaves in the larger holdings was proportionately even greater. Of course the great

[1] *Census of 1860 (Agriculture)*, pp. 224, 248.
[2] *Ibid.*

increase in slaves within the state in the decade cannot be attributed solely to purchases in Arkansas, for as farmers and planters came in from the older states, they brought their slaves with them, and slaves were often inherited. Rare indeed, however, was the slaveowner who did not add to his holdings by purchase as the years passed.

A few examples will serve to illustrate the rapidity with which certain slaveowners increased the size of their holdings. In 1855 Gideon J. Pillow, who owned 3,825 acres of land near Helena in Phillips County, had 120 slaves valued (for tax purposes, which was usually considerably below the current market value) at $72,000, or an average of $600 each.[3] Four years later, in 1859, Pillow owned 6,788 acres of land and 160 slaves assessed at $120,000, an average of $750 each.[4] Even if 10 per cent of the increase in number of slaves could be accounted for by reproduction (a liberal estimate), Pillow's outlay for slaves in the four years was not less than $18,900, certainly a considerable sum for a man whose entire estate, including land, slaves, horses, mules, cattle, and buildings, was assessed at only $110,400 in 1855.[5] A much more marked increase in number of slaves was achieved by John A. Jordan of Arkansas County, who in 1850 owned 64 slaves worth, for tax purposes, an average of $400 each.[6] By 1860 Jordan had 273 slaves valued at $700 each.[7] If Jordan's slaves reproduced themselves by 25 per cent during the decade, and if $600 may be accepted as an average price for slaves in that period, Jordan expended at least $109,200 for new slaves, an amount nearly three times as large as the entire assessed valuation of his estate in 1850 ($38,348).[8] Numerous such examples could be cited.

Although thousands of slaves were purchased by citizens of

[3] Tax Assessment List, Phillips County, 1855.
[4] Tax Assessment List, Phillips County, 1859.
[5] Tax Assessment List, Phillips County, 1855.
[6] Tax Assessment List, Arkansas County, 1850.
[7] Tax Assessment List, Arkansas County, 1860.
[8] Tax Assessment List, Arkansas County, 1850. Frederick Bancroft, the authority on Southern slave trading, estimated rates of increase of slaves by reproduction at 24.2 per cent in the 1830's, 26.6 per cent in the 1840's, and 23.4 per cent in the 1850's. Frederick Bancroft, *Slave-Trading in the Old South* (Baltimore, 1931), pp. 383-384. The round figure 25 per cent was used in these computations.

Arkansas, the organized slave trade within the state was of very small proportions as compared to that of most of the other slave states. Arkansas had few slave auction businesses, plentiful in other states.[9] There were no permanent slave markets to which licensed traders brought slaves from Virginia and Kentucky and other states which had a surplus, as they did to Memphis and New Orleans and Natchez and Montgomery and other well-known slave-trading centers of the South.[10] Only occasionally did announcements of Arkansas slave dealers appear in Arkansas newspapers, and then only in connection with the sale of other commodities. The following advertisement is typical of the few which did appear:

A CARD

The undersigned has taken the well-known store recently occupied by S. H. Tucker, Esq., for the purpose of conducting and transacting an Auction and Commission business. . . . He is now fully prepared to receive consignments of any description whatever. Sales will be effected at any and all times, at the "Auction Mart", upon Slaves, Real Estate, Merchandise, Household Furniture, &c., &c. Returns made immediately after sales with promptness. Liberal advances will be made upon consignments, when required. The Auction Mart will have regular sales on Monday, Wednesday, and Saturday's, and on Tuesday, Thursday, and Saturday evenings.

F. R. Taylor[11]

March 25, 1836

Since there was no official discouragement of an organized slave trade in Arkansas,[12] other reasons to explain its small scope

[9] In all the materials consulted in preparation of this study there were very few references to professional slave trading in Arkansas, and no evidence that a well-organized, widespread trade existed at all within the state. The standard work on slave trading in the South refers several times to the great demand for slaves in Arkansas and the heavy sale of slaves to Arkansas buyers, but cites no instance of a slave trader carrying on an organized business within the state. Bancroft, *Slave-Trading*, pp. 250, 272, 319, 383, 387, 399, 401.

[10] For descriptions of operation of the slave trade in these centers, see Bancroft, *Slave-Trading, passim*; Sydnor, *Slavery in Mississippi*, pp. 131-180; and James B. Sellers, *Slavery in Alabama* (University, Alabama, 1950), pp. 141-194.

[11] *Arkansas Gazette*, April 1, 1836.

[12] It will be recalled that the Arkansas constitution of 1836 authorized the General Assembly to "prohibit the introduction of any slave or slaves, for the purpose of speculation, or as an article of trade or merchandise. . . ." No such prohibitions were enacted, however. Most Southern states at one time

must be sought. Arkansas was at the far edge of the frontier, and by 1860 had not developed any major centers of population, to which professional slave traders naturally gravitated. There were ready markets in areas less remote than Arkansas for as many slaves as were brought to them, and possibly the slave traders felt that the additional time, expense, and effort necessary to transport slaves into Arkansas were unwarranted, especially when they knew that because of the great demand for slaves in Arkansas the planters would go outside of the state in search of them. Finally, no important market of any sort developed in Arkansas; with planters largely dependent upon New Orleans and Memphis for supplies of all sorts and for marketing of crops, it is understandable that they also sought slaves in those cities. All this should not be interpreted as minimization of the importance of slave trading in Arkansas—dealings on a local scale will be discussed later—but merely to emphasize that organized, large-scale traffic in imported slaves within the state was almost non-existent.

New Orleans was the most important out-of-state market for Arkansas planters and thus one in which there was a great deal of buying and selling of slaves. Steamboats plied regularly between New Orleans and the plantations and towns on the major Arkansas streams—the Arkansas, the White, the Ouachita, and the Red—as well as, when the depth of water permitted, smaller streams such as the Black, Little Missouri, Little Red, Petit Jean, Cache, and St. Francis rivers, and the numerous creeks and bayous of the southeastern section.[13] Arkansas planters wanting to buy additional slaves or to sell surplus ones frequently did so through the many commission merchants or factors in New Orleans. Frederick Bancroft wrote of this aspect of the trade:

---

or another had laws prohibiting the importation of slaves as articles of merchandise, but in all cases they were eventually repealed. Bancroft, *Slave-Trading*, p. 272.

[13] General accounts of river transportation in Arkansas may be found in Mattie Brown, "A History of River Transportation in Arkansas from 1819-1880" (Unpublished M. A. thesis, Department of History, University of Arkansas, 1933) and Herbert and Edward Quick, *Mississippi Steamboatin': A History of Steamboating on the Mississippi and its Tributaries* (New York, 1926).

"Orders from commission merchants respectfully solicited", said Thomas Foster's (a slave dealer) advertisement. That refers to a phase of slave-trading then little noticed by the public and now almost forgotten. The agent that disposed of a planter's crop and bought for him supplies not easily obtained near home was called his commission merchant or factor. The accounts were expected to be settled annually. The sugar planters were within easy reach of New Orleans and usually went there at least once a year for business and pleasure. It was quite different with the cotton planters in northern and western Louisiana, Arkansas, and Mississippi. If they sent their produce and orders to New Orleans, their commission merchant or factor also bought or sold slaves for them according to whether they had a surplus or a marked deficit with him. And he dealt with a regular trader, a commission merchant or an auctioneer.[14]

James Sheppard, who owned and operated Waterford Plantation at New Gascony, on the Arkansas River near Pine Bluff, dealt in the New Orleans market in the manner described by Bancroft. During the years from 1851, when he acquired Waterford and moved the nucleus of his slave working force from Copiah County, Mississippi, until his planting operations were disrupted by the Civil War, Sheppard regularly sold cotton, bought plantation supplies, and bought and sold slaves in New Orleans through a number of different commission merchants. On July 10, 1858, the firm of Bradley, Wilson and Co. of New Orleans wrote Sheppard: "Refering to our letter of the 27th ult we now . . . advise of the sale of the Girl Mary at Eleven Hundred Dollars. Herewith we hand you amount of sale, $1072.50."[15] Early the next spring, Sheppard sold a Negro man in the New Orleans market through H. N. Templeman. Templeman reported on the sale:

I do not believe I could of sold your man Austin for nine hundred dollars without a full guarantee I have given the guarantee and sold him at auction got $1260. and after paying all expenses he will net you eleven hundred and forty dollars 1140$—that is the net amount I sold him for a 12 months bill the loss on the bill commission and all expenses my charge included. . . .[16]

[14] Bancroft, *Slave-Trading*, p. 319.
[15] Bradley, Wilson & Co. to James Sheppard, July 10, 1858, Sheppard Papers. The $27.50 commission charged represented 2.5 per cent of the sale, standard for such transactions. Bancroft, *Slave-Trading*, p. 318.
[16] H. N. Templeman to James Sheppard, March 11, 1859, Sheppard Papers.

Other New Orleans commission merchants with whom Sheppard had dealings included Byrne, Vance & Co., Bartley, Johns and Co., and Moses Greenwood and Co.[17]

Sheppard also bought slaves in Memphis, which, according to Bancroft, "of the cities in the central South, . . . had by far the largest slave-trade" and "was the most convenient place for the planters of Arkansas . . . to obtain their slaves."[18] On at least one occasion, Sheppard purchased slaves from the famous Nathan Bedford Forrest, the leading dealer in the busy Memphis slave market in the late 1850's and later one of the ablest of the Southern cavalry generals during the Civil War. On May 29, 1859, Forrest placed Dick and Edmund, two Negro boys whom Sheppard had purchased in person two days earlier, on board the steamboat *Jennie Whipple,* bound for Pine Bluff and points above. Late the next day, after a voyage down the Mississippi and up the Arkansas, Captain James A. Gray delivered the slaves to Sheppard's overseer in Pine Bluff, who paid these charges incurred in delivery: two days' board at the Forrest slave jail at forty cents each per day, board and room for two days aboard the boat, a total of $3.00, and passage from Memphis to Pine Bluff, $14.00.[19]

Both New Orleans and Memphis slave dealers used advertisements in various Arkansas newspapers to announce the availability of their wares to buyers in the state. In March, 1858, Walter L. Campbell of 71 and 73 Baronne St., New Orleans, was advertising:

VIRGINIA AND MARYLAND NEGROES

FOR SALE

REMOVAL FROM ESPLANADE STREET

Walter L. Campbell has purchased Nos. 71 and 73 Baronne street, where he will be found early in the fall with a large lot of Maryland and Virginia

[17] There are numerous letters, receipts, etc. from these firms in the Sheppard Papers.
[18] Bancroft, *Slave-Trading*, pp. 250, 264.
[19] N. B. Forrest to James Sheppard, May 29, 1859, and receipt for payment of passage of "Boys Dick and Edmund," May 30, 1859, Sheppard Papers. Transportation of individual, unattended slaves was not uncommon. Occasionally, however, the slaves used the unusual degree of freedom as an opportunity to run away. *Arkansas Gazette,* Sept. 8, 1821, June 21, 1836, April 14, 1857.

Negroes for sale. He is preparing ample and
healthy quarters for the increased business he
intends conducting for the coming season.[20]

Representative of the Memphis advertisers was the firm of M.
& Wm. Little, who announced in 1856: "We . . . have just
received a lot of likely young Negroes from Middle Tenn. And
will keep a good supply throughout the season . . . and will receive
and sell on commission. Also accomodate trancient [*sic*] traders
with good rooms for fifty negroes."[21]

Although the majority of slaves purchased from professional
slave dealers came from the nearer markets such as New Orleans
and Memphis, some prospective buyers went as far afield as Virginia and Georgia in search of Negroes to their liking. Among
those who did so was Jared Martin of Little Rock, never a large
slaveholder, but a man who bought regularly over a period of
more than thirty years, and whose records of purchases of slaves
have been well preserved. While in Richmond, Virginia, in
June, 1856, Martin bought Peter for $1100 and George for $1000
from Dickinson, Hill & Co., Sally from Carroll and Peterson for
$995, and a slave family consisting of Henry, his wife Jane, and
three small children, Joe, Sarah, and Austin, for $3300.[22] Five
days later while on the return journey to Arkansas, Martin purchased an eleven-year-old boy, Tom, from A. Howell in Marietta,
Georgia, for $815.[23] Martin also bought slaves in St. Louis, a
market approaching Memphis and New Orleans in importance.[24]
On April 2, 1852, he purchased three slaves, Anthony, William,
and John, for a total of $2150 from B. M. Lynch, listed in
Green's Directory for 1851 as a "negro trader," with headquarters
at 104 Locust Street.[25] The three slaves ranged in age from
sixteen to thirty,[26] the age group considered most desirable; a
few years later, a single "prime field hand" would often sell for
twice as much as each of these.

[20] *Ouachita Herald,* March 4, 1858.
[21] *True Democrat,* April 15, 1856.
[22] Bills of sale, Martin Papers.
[23] Bill of sale, A. Howell to J. C. Martin, June 9, 1856, Martin Papers.
[24] "St. Louis . . . was one of the five or six cities that sent the most Negroes
to the insatiable 'Southern market.'" Bancroft, *Slave-Trading,* p. 139.
[25] *Ibid.,* p. 138.
[26] Bill of sale, B. M. Lynch to J. C. Martin, April 2, 1852, Martin Papers.

Out-of-state buying and selling such as has been described took
place frequently, but probably the majority of all slave sales involving Arkansas owners and slaves was carried out within the state
between individuals who were not professional slave dealers.
Slaves were sold for a wide variety of reasons. Sometimes it
was necessary to sell the slaves of a deceased slaveowner in order
to pay claims against his estate. Shortly after Charles Whitson
of Franklin County died in 1846, the administrator of his estate,
Alfred Coffee, appeared in the probate court and presented an
affidavit stating that "the personal estate in the hand of said
administrators is not sufficient to pay the debts exhibited against
said estate." Judge Thomas Aldridge then authorized Coffee to
sell two slaves, William and Lucinda. The sale was to be held at
the courthouse in Ozark on the fourth Monday in February.
and Coffee was required to give sufficient notice of the sale by
advertising in the Van Buren *Intelligencer* for two weeks previous
to the date.[27]

The slaves of a deceased man might also be sold in order to
make a fair distribution of the estate among the heirs.[28] Sometimes the owner of a family of slaves decreed in his will that they
be sold as a group to prevent possible separation of the slave
family after his death. William R. Thorn, who died in Pulaski
County in October, 1850, was especially solicitous of the welfare of his slaves after his death. He appointed E. H. English
his executor, instructing him to sell one slave family "in a group
for the best price that can be had so that they may remain together
as a family," and to sell the slave woman Mariah and her infant
child to a friend for the ridiculously low price of $100, the obvious
purpose being to secure her a good home and keep mother and
child together rather than to derive income.[29]

Certainly many slave families were separated by sales, but
many instances are recorded in which sales were made only as a
family unit, or were prompted by no other reasons than to keep

[27] Franklin County Probate Record, 1840-1849, p. 215. Records of similar
cases are in Union County Probate Record "A," 1845-1855, p. 57, Desha
County Probate Court Record, 1852-1857, p. 151, and in the probate court
records of practically every other Arkansas county which existed before the
Civil War.
[28] Franklin County Probate Court Record, 1852-1859, p. 47.
[29] Pulaski County Will Book "B," p. 10.

a family together or to reunite one previously separated. A slave family had no legal status, and practically all records identify a slave child only by its mother, but many owners considered the feelings of their slaves and did what they could to preserve the family relationship.[30] A few examples will serve to illustrate this. B. Smith and Chester Ashley of Little Rock offered a mulatto woman named Charlotte, aged forty, and her son Lewis, aged eighteen, for sale in 1829 "to some respectable person, who will treat them humanely, and not separate them."[31] Sometimes a series of sales was necessary to accomplish the end of reuniting a slave family. Early in 1860 Robert F. Kellam, Camden merchant, sold his Negro woman Sarah, aged twenty-two, and her two children, aged three and five, to Lucius Greening for $2500. Two months later a Mr. Fuller of Camden sold his slave Sheridan to Greening also, which, in Kellam's words, "gett our former Servant Sarah with her husband."[32] That mixed motives sometimes entered into sale or purchase of slaves is shown by an advertisement appearing in the *Arkansas Gazette* in 1835: an unnamed person was seeking to buy a "family of Negroes," thus respecting the existence of the slave family, and yet at the same time was willing to take as an alternative "several young *Negro Girls,* from 10 to 14 years of age,"[33] who hardly could have been obtained without separating them from their mothers!

In times of economic depression and financial distress the sale of slaves in Arkansas increased, sometimes because of foreclosures on estates, and in other instances simply because the owner found it necessary to raise money. The Panic of 1837 seems to have caused fewer forced sales of slaves than that of 1857, chiefly because of the relatively slight economic development of Arkansas at the earlier date. But Arkansas underwent severe "hard times" after 1857, as did the entire United States. The price of slaves remained high, but money was difficult to obtain. The editor of a Little Rock newspaper complained that "at New

[30] Arkansas had no legal restrictions against separating families, or even mothers and small children. Any effort to keep families together was thus prompted by humanitarianism, or sometimes practical motives, since separating families often created disciplinary problems, such as running away.

[31] *Arkansas Gazette,* April 15, 1829.

[32] Diary of Robert F. Kellam, Jan. 4, March 28, 1860.

[33] *Arkansas Gazette,* Oct. 20, 1835.

Orleans a quarter of a dollar is not considered worthy of notice," but that nevertheless "Negroes are selling from $1,300 to $2,000 and lands from $20 to $50 per acre."[34]   At about the same time John Brown, lawyer, insurance agent, and slave owner of Camden, commented that "everything that we live on is at higher rates than usual and money hard to get."[35]   In such a period a man known to be in the market for slaves and to have a ready supply of cash was likely to be offered many slaves.   Within a few months in 1857 Jared Martin of Little Rock received several letters from prospective sellers.   Excerpts from two of them follow:

> I have four likely Negroes a woman and 3 children I wish to sell . . . if you have not all the money a few hundred dollars will not split us let me hear from you early on the subject . . . I am bound to raise $1500 and if you would come soon I know we could trade.[36]

> I want you to write me amediately or by next Fridays mail wheather you intends to bye my negro boy or not I have come to the conclusion to take nine hundred dollars for him he is thirteen years old . . . the only reason for my selling him is that I am in debt and want to pay out. . . .[37]

Others who needed money during economic depression advertised in the newspapers, as did John Collins of Little Rock, who offered nine slaves for sale in December, 1858, "all sound and likely, and sold for no fault, but for the reason, that the subscriber wants money."[38]

Some slaves were sold to satisfy provisions of Arkansas law. A statute passed in 1837 provided that when a slave was committed to the county jail as a runaway, the sheriff was required to publish notice of the detention in the papers of the state for a year.[39]   At the expiration of that time, if the owner still had not

[34] *Arkansas State Gazette and Democrat,* March 22, 1857.
[35] Diary of John Brown, March 27, 1857.
[36] W. B. Isbell to Jared Martin, Aug. 18, 1857, Martin Papers.
[37] S. R. Gray to Jared Martin, March 18, 1857, Martin Papers.
[38] *Arkansas True Democrat,* Nov. 24, 1858.
[39] A typical advertisement of this sort, published in the *Arkansas State Democrat* on Dec. 14, 1849, and for several months thereafter:

Negro Boy in Jail

Was committed to the custody of the jailor of Pulaski county, on the 3rd inst., as a runaway slave, a Negro Boy, who says his name is *Henry,* and

appeared, the slave was auctioned by the sheriff, and the proceeds of the sale, after deduction of expenses of apprehending, advertising, maintaining, and selling, were to be paid into the county treasury. Sale of a runaway slave in this manner did not necessarily mean total loss to the owner, however, for if he could prove ownership of the slave within three years, he was entitled to draw from the county treasury the proceeds of the sale.[40] Scarcity of records of such sales indicates that few slaves were held the full period before being claimed by the owners.

Legal requirements also dictated the sale of a slave when an owner was unable to satisfy a judgment levied against him in the civil courts. For example, Antoine Barraque, a famous early citizen of Pine Bluff for whom one of the principal streets of the city was named, was forced to sell his slave woman Chaney, aged twenty-eight, to Richardson C. Anderson in 1842 to satisfy a civil judgment. Since the sale price of $550 was more than the amount of the judgment, Barraque received the balance—$100—in cash.[41]

An unusual slave sale was that of a man named Bobb, aged twenty, by Lorenzo N. Clarke of Jefferson County to John J. Hammett for $450 on August 27, 1844. Bobb had run away from Clarke and been captured by Hammett;[42] perhaps both men felt that sale of the runaway was simpler than transferring him back to the home plantation.

One of the simplest and most effective ways of arranging for the sale or purchase of slaves was through advertising in the newspapers of the state. Practically all newspapers regularly carried advertisements such as these:

---

says he belongs to William Perry, of Jefferson county. Said boy is supposed to be about 19 years of age, is about 5 feet 5 inches high, dark copper color, weighs about 145 to 150 pounds, and has some scars on the inside of both arms between the wrist and elbow.

The owner of the above boy, is requested to come forward, prove his property, pay charges, and take him away, or he will be dealt with according to the law.

Ben F. Danley, Sheriff
and Jailor, Pulaski county, Ark.

[40] *Revised Statutes, 1838,* pp. 713-714.
[41] Jefferson County Chattel Mortgage Record, 1841-1868, p. 16. Despite its title, this volume contains records of many slave sales.
[42] *Ibid.,* p. 46.

MULATTO WOMAN FOR SALE

She is a likely and genteel servant, about 20 years of age, no children, and is a good cook, washer, ironer, pretty good sempstress, and is well acquainted with all kinds house-work. Inquire at the *Gazette and Democrat* office.[43]

FOR SALE

A likely *Negro Man,* about 25 years of age, tall, strong, and athletic, an excellent chopper, teamster, and farmer, and handy at almost any kind of servant's work. Inquire at the *Democrat Office.*[44]

CASH FOR NEGROES

Several young Negroes are wanted, for which cash will be paid. Inquire at the *Gazette* Office.[45]

Personal, informal negotiations between prospective buyer and seller, or through intermediaries, were also used to arrange sale of slaves. The activities of Jared Martin, already mentioned as a regular buyer of slaves, afford many good examples of this, as well as of general procedures of buying and selling slaves. Martin carried on a wide correspondence with relatives in Missouri, Tennessee, and other parts of Arkansas in which the purchase of slaves was regularly mentioned. Apparently he and his relatives had standing agreements that he should be notified when slaves were available, and when necessary he made long overland trips to purchase even a single slave. Jared's brother John, still living on the family homestead at Jackson, Missouri, from which Jared had migrated to Arkansas in the 1820's,[46] was often of assistance in the search for slaves. In 1831 he wrote Jared:

On the 19th of next month there is several negroes to be sold in Jackson among which there is a very fine girl about 11 years old I have been thinking this Girl might suit you verry well provided she can be had on Reasonable terms the Terms of the Sale is twelve months Credit I think it likely She will hardly go Over two hundred and fifty dollars or very little over, perhaps not quite that much if

[43] *Arkansas Gazette and Democrat,* Sept. 27, 1850.
[44] *Ibid.,* March 8, 1850.
[45] *Arkansas Gazette,* Oct. 20, 1835.
[46] Interview with Miss Blanche Martin, Little Rock, Arkansas, July 23, 1951.

you wish it and can let me know by that time I can purchase her for you if the price is low enough which I think may probably be the case.[47]

Jared bought the young slave girl,[48] but the next year he again enlisted the aid of his brother, this time seeking brood mares as well as slaves. John wrote: "I am waiting anxiously your arrival in this country I feel myself bound to give you every assistance in my power in making your selection for a Servant and brood mares Valuable Negro girls of the age you speak of comes high in this country. . . ."[49] It was no mere coincidence that Jared was searching for brood mares and young Negro girls at the same time; he, like all slaveowners, was fully aware of the profits to be realized when the girls began to bear children. Martin's bills of sale show a number of purchases of young girls, and his correspondence indicates a continuing interest in acquisition of them.

A nephew of Jared's, John F. Martin of Ripley County, Missouri, wrote of the availability of slaves in 1843:

You wanted to by Negroes if you do you can get them in this parte of the worlde thar is to bee some I expecte solde shortly after the first of January at Greene ville . . . a good family of Negroes to be sold for to be devided betwene hares of an estate . . . I shall want to hear frome you or Uncle Allen soone and write what you woold give for sutch Negroes as I have spoke of I think that one of you had better come one about the time those negroes ar solde if you will I will Write to you when tha are to be sole.[50]

By 1853 John Martin had moved from Jackson, Missouri, to Independence County, Arkansas, but was still helping Jared locate slaves for purchase. He wrote:

Conserning the negroes you wish to by I have heard of one that I have reason to believe can be had for 900 dollars if he will suit you he is 19 or 20 years old rather Small Sized keen and active . . . I have heard of another that is about 17 years old verry large of his age his owner offered him for 700 dollars but when Offered his price

[47] John Martin to Jared Martin, Aug. 24, 1831, Martin Papers.
[48] Bill of Sale, Richard Owen to Jared C. Martin, Sept. 21, 1831, Martin Papers.
[49] John Martin to Jared Martin, Oct. 10, 1832, Martin Papers.
[50] John F. Martin to Jared C. Martin, Nov. 23, 1843, Martin Papers.

backed Out the individual that told me what I have here stated said he didn't think the man would take a thousand or Sell a tall. I am to hear more about the matter next week. . . ."[51]

Not all of Jared Martin's relatives were as helpful as these. When he inquired about the possibility of buying slaves at Memphis in 1837, another nephew, W. M. Dunn, replied that "negroes . . . are the scarcest article that could be enquired for in the country there is more demand for negroes here now than I ever knew 100 men would not supply the wants of Shelby County Father and myself wants ten from 16 to 22 years of age we expect to have to go some distance. . . ."[52] The consistency with which Jared Martin sought slaves inside and outside of Arkansas for a generation and the trouble he was willing to go to in securing them show clearly that the supply of slaves never equaled the demand in Arkansas.

Many slaves were sold at the annual sale days held in the major towns at the first of January. Few firsthand descriptions of these events have survived, but doubtless they were much like public auctions of stock and farm equipment still held in some small Arkansas towns. Robert F. Kellam of Camden wrote in his diary on one sale day: "A busy Day city full of People Several sales of property at enormous prices. Negroes fellows 17 to 1800$ women 1400$ children 6 to 800$"[53] Another Camden resident, John Brown, also mentioned the sales days in his diary. On the same day mentioned by Kellam he commented on the activity in El Dorado, a neighboring town where he was visiting a daughter: "We spent the day as usual except that I went to town with Mr. C. and witnessed the excitement of the sales, hirings, and arrangements of the New Year."[54]

The usual legal instrument by which ownership of a slave was transferred was a bill of sale. Some bills of sale were very simple documents giving only the barest details of the transaction: names of buyer and seller, name of the slave, the amount paid, and the date. More often, however, they were more detailed,

[51] John Martin to Jared Martin, April 28, 1853, Martin Papers.
[52] W. M. Dunn to Jared Martin, Sept. 18, 1837, Martin Papers.
[53] Diary of Robert F. Kellam, Jan. 2, 1860.
[54] Diary of John Brown, Jan. 2, 1860.

describing the physical condition of the slave, listing the guarantees given by the seller, and giving the slave's age in addition to the other information. Purchasers naturally were interested in the physical condition of slaves and usually insisted that they be in good health. The slave John, purchased by John F. Hanks of Helena from John F. Talbot in 1847, was described as "sound in mind and body,"[55] a phrase commonly used. The five-year-old slave girl Eliza, sold by Simon Vanarsdale to Louis Fletcher of Lawrence County in 1819, was declared to be "free from any latent disease whatever."[56] Should a slave fail to live up to the guarantee of soundness given by the seller, the buyer was almost certain to demand that the slave be taken back and the money refunded, or at least that some adjustment be made in the purchase price. In 1852 Samuel Carson purchased the slave boy Phillip from Jared C. Martin through the intermediary services of William H. Sutton. Immediately after transfer of ownership, Phillip became ill, first with chills and fever, then with pains in the side and chest. Carson called in a Dr. Rosell, who pronounced the slave "unsound." Phillip remained "on foot, but not able to work," and Carson called upon Sutton to help him to "get clear of" the slave.[57]

Another guarantee usually found in bills of sale was that the slave being sold was a "slave for life."[58] One reason for this guarantee was that some wills stipulated that certain slaves be freed upon death of the owner or at a specified time later. For example, Eli Crow of Yell County willed: "I hereby do emancipate my slaves and discharge them . . . from all slavery . . . after my death,"[59] and Allen T. Wilkins of Lafayette County provided that his "negro woman, Sarah Jane, and her child, John, be emancipated . . . as soon as John . . . shall arrive at the age of twenty-

[55] Bill of sale, John H. Talbot to John F. Hanks, Aug. 20, 1847, Hanks Papers.
[56] Bill of sale, Simon Vanarsdale to Louis Fletcher, Aug. 18, 1819, in possession of Miss Mary P. Fletcher, Little Rock, Arkansas.
[57] Samuel Carson to William H. Sutton, Dec. 6, 1852, Martin Papers. This letter was readdressed by Sutton to Jared Martin.
[58] Bill of sale, John H. Talbot to John F. Hanks, Aug. 20, 1847, Hanks Papers; bills of sale, Andrew Caldwell to Jared C. Martin, Nov. 30, 1841, S. H. Tucker to J. C. Martin, Oct. 12, 1857, John F. Kellam and Benjamin C. Woodruff to J. Martin, June 14, 1848, Martin Papers; Chicot County Deed Record "A," p. 1.
[59] *Bob, alias Robert Crow* v. *Powers,* 19 Ark. 424.

one years."[60] Another reason was for protection against fraudulent sale of free Negroes. A case which illustrates the need for
such a guarantee concerns the Negro boy Bill. A mulatto, Bill
was secured in Indian Territory in August, 1854, by William
Houser of Van Buren, and the next month was turned over to
Samuel Strayhorn of Dardanelle with instructions that he be
sold "for any price whatever." Shortly thereafter Bill sued for
his freedom in Crawford County Circuit Court, which gave a
judgment of liberation in August, 1856. But for some reason
Bill was not notified of his right to liberation, and in November,
1856, he was sold for $1000 to Josiah M. Giles, who received a
bill of sale containing the usual "slave for life" guarantee. Within a few months Giles discovered the misrepresentation and
brought suit against Strayhorn as agent for Houser, alleging that
Strayhorn had made false and fraudulent representations concerning Bill. Eventually, after it had been disclosed that Strayhorn
was aware that Bill was a free Negro, the Arkansas Supreme
Court upheld Giles in his contention, ruling:

> The sale of a free negro to Giles, with warranty that he was a
> slave, was a fraud on the part of Houser, in whose name, and by
> whose authority the sale was made; and it must be assumed, upon
> the finding of the court below, . . . that Strayhorn participated in
> the fraud.[61]

Guarantees of the title to the slave, protection against transfer
of a slave not the legitimate property of the seller, were also found
in bills of sale. In selling the slave Syrus to John A. Stone of
Hempstead County in 1849, James M. Nolen promised to "warrant and defend the title against all claim or claims whatsoever."[62]
Ira G. Halleman, when selling the eighteen-year-old boy Disum
to Stone in 1860, warranted "the title to said slave to be good to
the said Stone his heirs and assigns against the lawful claims of
any person furthermore I consider this title binding on myself my
executors and administrators against any person or persons law-

---

[60] *Abraham* v. *Wilkins,* 17 Ark. 292.
[61] *Strayhorn* v. *Giles,* 22 Ark. 519.
[62] Bill of sale, James M. Nolen to John A. Stone, Dec. 28, 1849, Stephenson
Papers.

fully claiming the same."[63]   Certainly no more thorough guarantee of title could have been given.

One of the guarantees found less frequently in bills of sale was
that the slave was "free of vice," as thirteen-year-old Maria was
described when sold by William C. Gaveston to N. H. Fish in
Jefferson County in 1847.[64]   This may have meant that the slave
was not sexually promiscuous, or merely that she was of generally
good character.

In some instances slaves were transferred from one person to
another through a mortgage, which usually amounted to a sort of
conditional sale.   In 1840 Sam C. Roane (co-compiler of the 1838
digest of Arkansas laws) loaned Richard C. Byrd $7,500, payable
in six months, and in return received nine slaves from him.   A
"deed of mortgage" was drawn up stipulating that when Byrd had
repaid to Roane the amount of the note the slaves would again
belong to him, but that "if such payment shall not be made as
aforesaid then this deed shall be and remain in full force. . . ."
Four of the slaves were small children, so their total valuation
must have been considerably less than the amount of the note;
this suggests that they were merely being used as security.[65]
Jared Martin of Little Rock was once approached by Charles
Rapley, who wanted to go into the grocery and provision business in partnership with S. H. Tucker, about a loan to be secured
by a "Mortgage either upon Negroes or Lands."[66]   Another sort
of mortgage or conditional deed used was that given by Conway
Oldham of Desha County to James Hibbard in 1840.   Oldham
delivered the slave Allen to Hibbard in lieu of payment of a debt
of $185.31, and it was agreed that if Oldham later paid the debt,
the slave would be returned to him.[67]

The general trend of slave prices in Arkansas throughout the
slavery period was upward, although during the 1840's they fell
below previous levels, only to recover in the 1850's and move
even higher.   The major controlling factors in this general price

[63] Bill of sale, Ira G. Halleman to John A. Stone, March 17, 1860, Stephenson Papers.
[64] Jefferson County Chattel Mortgage Record, 1841-1868, p. 83.
[65] *Ibid.,* p. 1.
[66] Charles Rapley to Jared C. Martin, Jan. 19, 1854, Martin Papers.
[67] Desha County Deed Record "A," 1839-1843, p. 202.

rise were the continuing scarcity of slaves and the constant demand
for them. Prices or valuations of a great many slaves will be
considered here for the purpose of showing by decades the upward
price trend.[68] Factors which contributed to differences in slave
prices at a given time, such as age, health, sex, and special skills,
will be considered in detail later. The earliest specific valuation of
a slave encountered is in a letter written in 1815 to the Missouri
Fur Company of St. Louis by John C. Luttig, a fur trader at
Polk Bayou (now Batesville). Luttig had bought a sixteen-year-
old girl "raised to house Work and Cooking" for $300, noting
that she was a great bargain and that he would not have been able
to buy her so cheaply except for the scarcity of money in the
region.[69] By the 1820's slaves were worth somewhat more: eight
slaves of varying ages belonging to the estate of G. W. Ferebee,
recently deceased, were sold at public auction on July 5, 1823,
for an average of $380 each. But four of the slaves were evident-
ly small children or very old men or women, since prices paid for
them were small; the four highest-priced slaves sold for an average of $510 each.[70] Samuel Gibson of Arkansas County received
about the same average price for nine slaves which he sold on
October 7, 1823, to various buyers. Ranging in age from eight to

[68] Information concerning the value or selling price of slaves was found
in a wide variety of sources: bills of sale, inventories of estates, deed records,
will records, tax assessment lists, probate court records, county records of
other types, diaries, plantation records, newspapers, and personal letters and
papers of all types. These sources were of varying usefulness in attempting
to make a valid analysis of slave prices and price trends. For example, inventories of estates are merely estimates of the appraisers, tax assessment lists
tend to show slaves at somewhat less than market value, and many records give
no information on ages or special qualifications of the slaves, which had direct
bearing upon value. The most useful documents were the bills of sale, although
even they are often far from detailed. In each instance individual judgment
was used to determine whether to include prices in the computations. The
county tax assessment lists contain by far the largest quantity of slave valuations, but these were not used at all, since the proportion of true value at
which the slaves were assessed varied greatly between counties. It is recognized that valuations and selling prices do not always have the same degree of
validity, but an inadequate number of actual sales prices made it necessary to
include appraisal valuations. "Value" and "price" are used here synonymously.
Because of their number, not all sources from which prices were derived can
be cited, although many of them are referred to in other connections.
[69] John C. Luttig to Christian Wilt, April 16, 1815, Arkansas Manuscripts
Collection, University of Arkansas.
[70] Phillips County Circuit Court Record 1, 1821-1831, p. 23. Like many early
county records, this volume contains various documents—wills, deeds, estate
records and others—as well as court records.

forty, they brought an average of $388 each.[71] The average value
of all slaves sold or appraised—for which records were examined
—during the 1820's was $380.

Although the average value of slaves of all ages is significant
in showing the trend of values, it must be borne in mind that the
most productive and sought after slaves were worth much more
than the average. Ulrich B. Phillips worked out the following
formula showing the relationship of prices of different categories
of slaves to each other. While Arkansas prices might not have
conformed to it in every respect, it is useful as a general guide:

. . . artizans often brought twice as much as field hands of similar
ages, prime women generally brought three-fourths or four-fifths as
much as prime men; boys and girls entering their teens, and men and
women entering their fifties, brought about half of prime prices for
their sexes; and infants were generally appraised at about a tenth or
an eighth of prime. The average price for slaves of all ages and both
sexes, furthermore, was generally about one-half of the price for male
prime field hands.[72]

During the 1830's slave prices rose sharply, with single slaves
being valued at more than a thousand dollars for the first time.
In 1830 Eli J. Lewis of Little Rock received only $500 for Dick,
aged seventeen or eighteen,[73] but in 1837 John H. McLeod of
Phillips County paid $1200 for William, twenty-two.[74] Values
of other slaves sold or appraised during this decade varied considerably, from $30.00 for Adam to $1000 each for Addison, Jeff,
Tom, Dennis, and John.[75] On the basis of available records,
the average value of all slaves sold or appraised during the 1830's
was $485, an increase of $105 and 28 per cent over the 1820's.

Slave values fell to slightly lower levels in the 1840's than in
the 1830's, but the drop, in the wake of the Panic of 1837, was
much less severe in Arkansas than in most of the rest of the
South, where it amounted to 25 per cent or more.[76] The smaller

[71] Chicot County Deed Record "A," 1823-1835, pp. 1-2.
[72] Ulrich B. Phillips, *American Negro Slavery* (New York, 1918), p. 370.
[73] Bill of sale, Eli J. Lewis to Peter C. Parker, Aug. 10, 1830, Hanks Papers.
[74] Bill of sale, Nathaniel Bolton to John H. McLeod, July 24, 1837, Hanks
Papers.
[75] Appraisal of the Estate of John Davis, Jan. 19, 1836, Stephenson Papers.
[76] For a graphic depiction of the trends of slave prices in several major
Southern market areas, see the chart opposite p. 370 of Phillips, *American*

decline in Arkansas may be accounted for by the greater demand
for slaves there than in most other areas. Significant, too, is
that in Arkansas, an almost wholly slave-importing state, prices
were always among the highest in the South. Referring to the
group of states, including Arkansas, which imported slaves most
heavily, Frederic Bancroft wrote: ". . . as a rule, slaves were
dearer and opportunities to use them profitably on cheaper fertile
land were greater in Florida and Alabama than in Georgia, still
greater in Mississippi and Louisiana, and, in some respects, greatest in Arkansas and Texas. . . ."[77] Sales or appraisal prices for
the 1840's which were examined reveal an average slave value of
$455, $30 and 6 per cent less than in the previous decade.

The rate of increase in average value of slaves again moved
upward during the 1850's. The $627 average valuation of all
slaves for which records during the decade were available was an
increase over the 1840's of $172, or 38 per cent. This figure
does not give a true indication of the more sharply rising prices
at the very end of the decade and in the early 1860's, however.
The Camden merchant Robert F. Kellam noted this trend when
he wrote early in 1860 of the "enormous prices" slaves were
bringing.[78] The best single available source for comparison and
analysis of slave values in Arkansas, and also one which shows
the high 1860 prices, is a detailed appraisal of the 211 slaves on
Bellevue and Yellow Bayou Plantations in Chicot County, owned
by the estate of Junius W. Craig, which was made on July 14,
1860.[79] Although the slaves were not actually sold for the ap-

---

Negro Slavery. Arkansas prices most nearly conformed to New Orleans prices,
although they were sometimes higher. Note that prices were much higher
in the lower and Western South than in the upper and Eastern South, a
natural reflection of the buying and selling character of the regions.

[77] Bancroft, *Slave-Trading,* p. 399.

[78] Diary of Robert F. Kellam, Jan. 2, 1860.

[79] Appraisement of the Personal Property of the Estate of Junius W. Craig,
as made on the 14th day of July, A. D., 1860, Exhibit C-No. 3, of Bill of
Complaints in case of Joshua M. Craig and John A. Craig vs. Emma J. Wright
and others, in Circuit Court, County of Chicot, State of Arkansas, April Term,
A. D. 1861. Junius Craig made a will on July 17, 1858, at Louisville, Kentucky,
bequeathing half of his estate to his fiancée, Emma J. Wright, the other half
to be used in improvement of his plantation during her lifetime and after her
death in establishing a college at Helena. Junius died shortly thereafter, and
his brothers brought suit in an attempt to break the will and secure the property
for themselves. Chicot County Will Book "D," p. 37. Slave prices in Arkansas
seem more significant if compared to prices for other items during the same
period. The average value of all farm land in Arkansas in 1860 was $10.00

praisal prices, there is no doubt of the accuracy of the valuations, since the appraisal was made by three disinterested men in compliance with a court order in a highly controversial court suit. The appraisal gives name, age, and value of each slave, and in some instances information about physical condition and special skills. The slaves ranged in age from six-weeks-old John Chicot through Judge Isaac Shelby, twenty-two, and Big Sarah, forty-five, to sixty-one-year-old Dinah, and were divided fairly evenly between males and females of all ages. The group, then, may be considered a representative cross-section of all Arkansas plantation slaves at that time. Since Bellevue and Yellow Bayou were impersonal commercial enterprises, they perhaps had proportionately fewer nonproductive slaves than the state as a whole, which would tend to make the average price a bit high; this probably would have been offset, however, by the proportionately small number of skilled artisans and house servants, which were often worth more than field hands. Average value of the Craig slaves was $881, which was $254 and 40 per cent more than the average value of all slaves for which records of the 1850's were examined.

The Craig appraisal illustrates many of the factors governing the value of slaves. Skilled artisans usually were the most valuable slaves, with the exception of "fancy girls" in houses of prostitution, and there is no evidence that slaves were used in such establishments in Arkansas;[80] the most valuable Craig slave was Elias, a twenty-five-year-old blacksmith, worth $2800. Next in value, at $2000, was Cyrus, aged twenty-seven, doubtless the "driver," or field foreman. Nineteen male slaves from seventeen to thirty-six years of age were next in the scale of values, each appraised at $1500, closely followed by eleven men aged sixteen to thirty-nine, worth $1400 each. With the exception of three,

---

per acre, a substantial home could be built in a city for $900, and cows were worth about $8.00 each. *Census of 1860 (Agriculture)*, p. 6; Diary of John Brown, Nov. 17, 1858. Thus an average slave was worth approximately as much as an eighty-acre farm, a city house, or a herd of a hundred cattle. It is the author's conservative opinion that on the basis of the purchasing power of the 1958 dollar, an average Arkansas slave in 1860 was worth at least $5,000, with those worth twice that not uncommon.

[80] For accounts of sales of slave girls for purposes of prostitution and concubinage, see Winston Coleman, *Slavery Times in Kentucky* (Chapel Hill, 1940), pp. 121, 137, 159, and Bancroft, *Slave-Trading*, pp. 328-333.

Lewis and Jackson, both thirty-six, and Wesley, thirty-nine, these thirty male slaves were the prime field hands, in the most vigorous and productive age range—from the late teens to the late twenties. Lewis, Jackson, and Wesley probably were either artisans or house-servants, for most slaves in the middle and late thirties were worth somewhat less than they. For example, four of the remaining thirty-six-year-old men on the plantations, Russell, King George, Verdeman, and Will Graves, were each valued at $1200, and the fifth, Big Jim, at only $700. The slave nearest in age to Wesley, thirty-eight-year-old Colbert, was worth $1200.

Forty-two of the male slaves were appraised at from $1000 to $1200 each. These, along with the prime field hands, comprised the bulk of the male plantation working force. They ranged in age from eleven-year-old Henry Clay to forty-six-year-old Ned, with few, however, past forty.

Among the women, the most valuable single slave was Hannah, aged twenty-seven and mother of two children, appraised at $1400. She must have possessed some special skill to justify the valuation, for all of the nine women in the next most valuable group, worth $1200 each, were younger than she, ranging from nineteen through twenty-six years of age. The capacity to bear children had definite effect upon the value of slave women: most of the women in this group were mothers of small children, with one, twenty-two-year-old Mary Bob, having several from seven years of age downwards. One woman, Little Sarah, seventeen, was valued at $1100, and eighteen were worth $1000 each. These varied in age from twelve-year-old Kizzy to thirty-five-year-old Big Charlotte, but with two exceptions—Maria and Lucy, both twenty-three—they were in the age groups twelve through seventeen and twenty-nine through thirty-five, just below and just above the group most productive of both labor and children.

With the exception of the very small children and the older slaves whose productiveness had largely passed, the remaining Craig slaves were valued at from $500 to $900. This value-category included slaves of both sexes and all ages from six to fifty-six. A large number were children between six and twelve, with boys usually attaining higher values at younger ages than girls; the others were men and women from the teens to the fifties.

A slave child, if healthy, was worth at least $100 at birth, and by five or six $500 or more.   Six-year-old Amanda, for example, was already valued at $700, and four-year-old Warner at $500. The decline in value of slaves considered old by standards of that day was as precipitate as increase in value of the children was rapid.   Of the eleven Craig slaves aged fifty or more, only one, fifty-one-year-old John, was worth more than six-year-old Amanda; two, Will Cowden and Martin, were worth the same amount; seven were appraised at $400 to $600 each; and Dinah, matriarch of the Craig plantations and doubtless considered an ancient crone at sixty-one, was worth only $300—slightly more than half the value of four-year-old Juliet Ann.

Eight of the slaves were described in the appraisal as suffering from some physical handicap or disease and consequently had reduced values or none at all.   The close correlation of health and value will be discussed in a later chapter.

On the basis of the Craig appraisal, these conclusions as to the values of slaves appear valid: at most ages beyond infancy male slaves were a little more valuable than females.   For both sexes values rose rapidly from birth, reaching a peak in the early or middle twenties, and declining thereafter, much more rapidly after about age forty.   By age eight, most slave children were worth more than most adult slaves past fifty.   Finally, some slaves, because of special skills or abilities, were valued at considerably more than others of the same age group.

There is much evidence, in addition to that derived from the Craig inventory, of characteristics or abilities which helped to determine the values of slaves.   The three slaves which John Collins of Little Rock offered for sale in 1858 doubtless justified the "valuable" description given them: Jim, twenty-six, was a "numberone cook," Henry, twenty, was a "valuable family Servant and Pastry Cook," and Charlotte, at thirty already the mother of six children,[81] fitted into the category of "special woman," who bore children regularly and long.   The "Likely Negro Woman," an

[81] *Arkansas True Democrat,* Nov. 24, 1858.

"excellent spinner, outservant, and good plain cook"[82] and the mulatto woman, "likely and genteel servant, . . . good cook, washer, ironer, pretty good sempstress . . . well-acquainted with all kinds housework,"[83] who were offered for sale in Little Rock certainly commanded higher prices than women of similar ages without those skills.   One especially desirable young slave man was described as "healthy vary stoute willing and quicke he is black & a good looking boy."[84]   Blackness was a desirable characteristic in slaves, for a light-colored slave, especially if he were almost white, might be inclined to run away more readily than a black one, since detection and capture would be more difficult.   Many light-skinned slaves in Arkansas did run away, and some attempted to pass themselves for free white men.[85]   Temperament had direct bearing on value; a slave known to be recalcitrant or quarrelsome was normally worth less than an easily manageable one.[86]

Hiring out of slaves was a common practice in Arkansas. Probably the majority of hired slaves were those belonging to estates and hired out either temporarily pending division among the heirs, or for longer periods if there were minor heirs or a widow dependent upon proceeds of their labor for a living.   Details of the hiring-out process were handled by administrators of the estates, who filed annual reports with the probate courts.   Examples of such hirings follow.   When Robert M. Desha died in Helena in 1823, Frances A. Desha and George W. Ferebee, administrators, sold the household furniture and personal effects of the deceased man at public auction and hired out the slaves belonging to the estate for the remainder of the calendar year.[87]

[82] *Arkansas Gazette,* Oct. 6, 1830.
[83] *Gazette and Democrat,* Sept. 27, 1850.
[84] John F. Martin to Jared C. Martin, Nov. 23, 1843, Martin Papers.
[85] *Batesville News,* July 11, 1839; *Washington Telegraph,* Aug. 12, 1846; *Arkansas Gazette,* April 19, 1836, June 28, 1836.   One of James Sheppard's New Orleans factors wrote concerning a slave woman placed with them for sale: "There is but little probability of finding a purchaser for this girl shortly at a fair price. . . . A great objection to this girl is her color, but few persons are disposed to buy a servant that is so white. . . ." Bradley, Wilson & Co. to James Sheppard, May 1, 1857, Sheppard Papers.
[86] Diary of John Brown, April 23, 1857; Robert W. Miller to James Sheppard, June 16, 1859, Sheppard Papers.
[87] *Arkansas Gazette,* Oct. 27, 1823.

James Colter, who died in Pulaski County in 1841, leaving two minor children, willed that his slaves were to be hired out until they had brought enough money—if proceeds of the sale of his corn, fodder, and stock were not sufficient—to pay his debts. The slaves were to remain hired out until the children became of age or married, and then they and the "proceeds of their hire" were to be divided equally between the children.[88] Alfred Coffee of Franklin County served as administrator of the estate of Charles Whitson for several years, paying proceeds from hire of the slaves to Whitson's widow.[89]

Some slave owners, especially if they became involved in activities other than farming, preferred to hire out their slaves as a regular source of income rather than to sell them or hire an overseer. In 1854 John Brown, who for a number of years had been operating his plantation near Princeton, Dallas County, with from twenty to twenty-five slaves, moved to Camden to engage in the insurance business and the practice of law. He left his plantation and slaves under the direction of an overseer for a time, but when the crop year was over he sold the plantation and a few of the slaves, moved the remainder to Camden, and from that time until the abolition of slavery hired them out, some by the day or week and others on yearly contracts. Brown continued to own land in various parts of Arkansas, but his own slaves were not used on any of his land.[90]

Slaves were often hired out for limited periods to fill a demand for special skills or equipment or simply because the hirer needed them for only a limited time. After John Brown moved to Camden he kept his most valuable slave, Thom, hired out regularly on a short-term basis as a teamster or skilled laborer, also furnishing wagon and team when necessary. In September of 1854 Thom was working for a dollar a day for a Judge Strain of Camden,[91] and later the same month, along with the slave Willis, he began working on a railroad right-of-way near the town.[92] In the early spring Thom plowed gardens in Camden,[93] and sometimes he,

[88] Pulaski County Will Book "A," p. 102.
[89] Franklin County Administrators' Record, 1840-1866, pp. 34, 40, 44.
[90] Diary of John Brown, 1854-1861, *passim.*
[91] *Ibid.,* Sept. 24, 1854.   [92] *Ibid.,* Sept. 26, 1854, Jan. 20, 1855.
[93] *Ibid.,* Feb. 7, 1855.

along with other Brown slaves, spent longer periods working on farms in the vicinity.[94]	Thom worked during May, 1855, in the woods making laths, which Brown had contracted to deliver for two dollars a thousand,[95] and at other times he cut, hauled, and sold firewood,[96] helped at housemoving,[97] and built fences.[98] Before Brown gave up the Princeton plantation he occasionally hired out slaves to pick cotton for neighbors.[99]	Some doctors and lawyers hired slaves on a regular part-time basis to care for their offices. For example, James H. Caruthers, a lawyer, paid three dollars per month for the services of Dick in "cutting wood, making fires, and attending office."[100]

Slaves were not always hired out by preference, but sometimes because a satisfactory sale could not be arranged.	A twenty-eight-year-old blacksmith, "stout, likely, and trusty, and a first-rate workman, having served a regular apprenticeship in the blacksmith's trade," was offered for sale in Little Rock in 1838, but the owner was also willing to hire him out.[101]

The practice of hiring slaves was useful to the hirer as well as to the owner.	As has been pointed out, people who had no labor supply of their own often needed slaves for special tasks or short periods.	Practically all public works projects or other large-scale, short-term enterprises used hired slaves.	Many were used during the 1850's by the United States government in clearing the "Raft," a huge obstruction to navigation stretching for miles up and down Red River in southwestern Arkansas.	The following advertisement appeared in the *Washington Telegraph,* published nearby:

NEGROES WANTED

WANTED, for the ensuing four months or longer, at the option of the owner, THIRTY GOOD, ABLE BODIED NEGRO LABORERS, to work on the *improvement of Red River,* at and in the vicinity of the RAFT. Wages, Thirty Dollars per month, with good and wholesome food.

[94] *Ibid.,* Feb. 24, 1855.	[95] *Ibid.,* May 25, 1855.
[96] *Ibid.,* Jan. 11, Feb. 8, 1856.	[97] *Ibid.,* Sept. 25, 1856.
[98] *Ibid.,* March 14, 1859.
[99] *Ibid.,* Nov. 14, Dec. 5, 1853.
[100] Statement, James B. Borden to James H. Caruthers, Feb. 23, 1852, Stephenson Papers.
[101] *Arkansas Gazette,* May 30, 1838.

For further particulars, apply at the office of the Washington Telegraph, or to

CHAS. A. FULLER

U. S. Ag't and Eng'r[102]

Hired slaves were also used in road-clearing and building. Allen and Jared Martin of Little Rock, whose own slaves were busy on their farms, planned to use from twelve to twenty-five hired slaves in opening up a road from Little Rock to Columbia, on the Mississippi River in southeastern Arkansas, in 1835.[103] Street work in the towns occupied some hired slaves,[104] and a few were employed in the little railroad building which went on in Arkansas before the Civil War.[105]

Hired slaves were sought as domestic servants, especially by business or professional people in the towns who preferred not to make the large investment necessary in buying a servant. Newspapers frequently carried advertisements for house servants. In 1835 an unnamed advertiser in Little Rock wanted *"to Hire By the Year,* On or about the 10th of November next, A Negro Woman, to cook, & c., for a family of two persons."[106] Mrs. Burnett, who operated a boarding house in Little Rock, sought "A NEGRO BOY, from 14 to 18 years old, who is acquainted with housework,"[107] and Dan R. Mills, operator of a ferry across the Arkansas River in Little Rock, needed a "Negro Woman, who is acquainted with cooking and washing, and who is steady and trusty."[108] Advertisements offering domestic servants for hire were rarer, an indication that the demand was greater than the supply. Sometimes Robert F. Kellam, the prosperous Camden merchant, had no slaves of his own, but hired a cook from someone in the vicinity.[109] Many of John Brown's female slaves were hired out as domestic servants, for they usually were sent out individually, and sometimes to doctors.[110]

[102] *Washington Telegraph,* July 23, 1856.
[103] *Times,* July 11, 1835; Allen Martin to Jared Martin, June 21, 1835, Martin Papers.
[104] Diary of John Brown, Sept. 12, 1857.
[105] Diary of John Brown, Sept. 26, 1854, Jan. 20, 1855.
[106] *Times,* Oct. 26, 1836.   [107] *Gazette and Democrat,* March 22, 1850.
[108] *Arkansas Gazette,* Nov. 10, 1835.
[109] Diary of Robert F. Kellam, Jan. 8, Feb. 1, 3, 1860.
[110] Diary of John Brown, Dec. 20, 1854, Jan. 6, 1855, Sept. 18, 1856, Jan. 4, 1858, Feb. 14, 1859.

Procedures by which slaves were hired out varied from the simple verbal agreements employed by John Brown in placing his slaves by the day or week to detailed contracts when the hiring was on an annual or longer basis. Unlike bills of sale, which served almost wholly to protect the buyer, hiring contracts or agreements were designed largely to protect the interests of the owner of the slave. For example, when James Estill hired seven slaves from an estate in Chicot County for a period of five years, he agreed to pay all doctor's bills, feed and clothe the slaves "in the same manner and way that he does his own," not to remove them from the county, to "make due diligence in recovering them the same as if they were his own" in case they ran away, and to return them at the expiration of the term of service.[111] These were all fairly standard conditions; in addition, most agreements required bond or security of the hirer, and some specified "good comfortable wearing apparel and bedding"[112] and "wholesome diet."[113] Of course the agreements also stipulated the amount to be paid and the length of the contract. If on an annual basis, most contracts began with the first of the calendar year.

Guarantees such as those listed above had sound basis, for a person who hired a slave was not likely to be as careful of his welfare as the owner, since he had no large investment involved. John Brown of Camden was especially careful in placing his slaves. During one hiring period he commented: "I am hiring out the negroes at private hiring at a slight advance on last year. I don't aim at getting the highest prices for hire, as I want them at good places—not abused."[114] At another time: "I have hired out all my negroes at about the same rates as heretofore but I never have had the highest prices, as I have regarded the place I put them more important than the price of the hire."[115] While most agreements stated that the hirer was to pay all medical bills, Brown insisted that in case of serious illness of a slave he was to be notified, and that he would then "take the expense of the physician and control of the case";[116] once he brought an ill hired slave back home so

---

[111] Chicot County Deed Record "A," p. 77.
[112] *Arkansas Banner,* May 21, 1845.
[113] *Gazette and Democrat,* Dec. 20, 1850.
[114] Diary of John Brown, Dec. 31, 1858.
[115] *Ibid.,* Jan. 24, 1861.   [116] *Ibid.,* Jan. 4, 1858.

that he could look after her.[117] Brown did not hesitate to revoke a contract if a slave were treated badly, as when he "took Cy home from Dr. Lamars on account of the treatment of the overseer and permitted by the doctor. . . ."[118]

The "private hiring" of which John Brown wrote, meaning informal personal negotiation, was a method widely used. Many slaves, however, were placed at public hirings, held annually in the larger towns on the first day of January along with the public sale of slaves, or at other times of the year when necessary. Regardless of when held, public hirings normally took place "at the Courthouse Door" or some other well-frequented location, but sometimes at the farm or home of the owner. Actual spoken bids for the hire of the slaves were taken, just as in public slave sales; in fact, public hirings were often referred to as "Public Auctions."[119] It was this impersonal procedure to which John Brown objected, since he preferred to select personally the places for his slaves.

Amounts for which slaves were hired varied widely, dependent to greater or lesser degree upon the same factors as those determining the sale prices of slaves. Skilled slaves brought more than unskilled, and men usually more than women. Age had less effect upon the hire value of a slave than upon the sale value, for the hirer was concerned primarily with the slave's ability to perform the task at hand and not with his long-term value. Hiring prices tended to follow the fluctuations of sale prices, but inadequate data prevent determination of the precise degree of correlation of the two. James Estill paid an average of only $60.00 per year for the slaves, mostly men, he hired in 1830,[120] but in 1852 J. W. Irwin of Jefferson County, guardian of the heirs of Thomas Holcombe, received $135 for Ben, $92.00 for Edmond, $72.00 for Sarah, and $21.00 for Celia, a small girl.[121] John Titsworth of Franklin County paid $120 each for the hire

[117] *Ibid.,* Sept. 26, 1857.
[118] *Ibid.,* Jan. 24, 1861.
[119] *Arkansas Gazette,* April 8, 1823, Dec. 15, 1835; *Arkansas Banner,* May 21, 1845; *Arkansas Intelligencer,* Dec. 29, 1849; *Gazette and Democrat,* Dec. 20, 1850.
[120] Chicot County Deed Record "A," p. 77.
[121] Jefferson County Record of Settlements "A," p. 8.

of the slaves Jim and Henry in 1855, and the same amount in 1856.[122]

The records of John Brown indicate that hiring rates increased steadily, if not spectacularly, during the late 1850's and early 1860's. And of course Brown did not insist on top prices for his slaves. Brown's slave woman Ann brought $90.00 per year in 1855 and $110 in 1858; Willis, one of Brown's more valuable slaves, hired for $190 in 1856 and $200 in 1858; and even the hire of Edmund and Polly, an elderly couple who were usually hired together, increased from $100 in 1856 to $110 in 1858.[123] For the last years of the decade and the early 1860's Brown merely indicated that he was getting a "slight advance" or "about the same rates as heretofore." On hiring day in 1860 Brown made an entry in his diary which gives some insight into the relationship of hiring price to slave value: "Judging from these a high degree of prosperity would seem to prevail in the country, negroes selling from $1500 to $1800 and hiring from $200 to $250 for the year."[124] On the basis of these figures, slaves were hired for about one-seventh of their sale value per year, a figure in line with those compiled for other states.[125] Naturally this ratio would not hold true for young slaves, whose hire would be lower in proportion to sale value, nor for low-priced but still productive older slaves, whose yearly hire would be proportionately more.

Since, as has been pointed out, sale prices of slaves in Arkansas were consistently among the highest in the South, it is not surprising that yearly hiring prices were also higher than in most of the states. The following tabulation of average hiring prices of slaves in the various states in 1860 was made by the federal Bureau of Agriculture:

	Men	*Women*	*Youth*[126]
Virginia	$105	$ 46	$39
North Carolina	110	49	50
South Carolina	103	55	43

[122] Franklin County Probate Court Record, 1852-1859, p. 241.
[123] Diary of John Brown, Dec. 20, 1854, Jan. 2, 1856, Jan. 4, 1858.
[124] *Ibid.*, Dec. 31, 1858, Jan. 2, 1860, Jan. 24, 1861.
[125] Sydnor, *Slavery in Mississippi,* p. 175; Bancroft, *Slave-Trading,* pp. 156-157.
[126] *Report of Commissioner of Agriculture, 1866,* p. 416, cited in Matthew B. Hammond, *The Cotton Industry* (Ithaca, New York, 1897), p. 90.

Georgia	124	75	57
Florida	139	80	65
Alabama	138	89	66
Mississippi	166	100	71
Louisiana	171	120	72
Texas	166	109	80
Arkansas	170	108	80
Tennessee	121	63	60

Only in Louisiana did both slave men and women hire for more than in Arkansas, and this was probably due to the heavy seasonal demand for labor in the sugar mills. In all three categories, Arkansas hiring prices ranked at or near the top.

Daily, weekly, and monthly rates for hire of slaves were proportionately greater than annual rates, but an owner faced with the choice of short-term or annual hiring had more to consider than the higher possible over-all earning from short-term hiring. There was more limited demand for slaves for short periods than for entire years, and in addition the owner had the constant trouble of keeping the slave employed and of engaging in numerous small financial transactions. An additional disadvantage was that the owner normally fed, housed, and clothed the slave who worked at short jobs, while these obligations rested upon the hirer when the slave was hired for a year. Few slaves, therefore, were hired out regularly for short periods. The highly skilled slave, such as John Brown's Thom, was the most likely to prove financially remunerative to his owner over a long period of time, for he was consistently in demand and brought a higher rate. While Brown's other men were hiring for a dollar a day, Thom brought $1.25; on a monthly basis, Thom's rate was often $25.00 while the maximum for the others was about $20.00. The hirer sometimes boarded the slaves when they were working by the month.[127] The maximum monthly rate encountered was the $30.00 offered by the United States government for work on the Red River Raft. Many slaves of lesser abilities earned much less than the more-or-less standard dollar a day for reasonably capable men. The daily rate for Brown's elderly Edmund was only fifty cents. Women sometimes brought even less. Eveline, a young girl, was hired for

[127] Diary of John Brown, 1854-1861, *passim.*

$4.00 a month in 1855, but by 1860 was bringing $10.00. Young Louisa's hire ranged from $10.00 a month to three months for $25.00.[128] During this same period Henry Pernot, a Van Buren doctor, was paying from $4.00 to $6.00 per month for the hire of various young boys.[129]

A law passed at the first session of the General Assembly of the state of Arkansas, and effective continuously thereafter, prohibited slaves from hiring their own time, a practice common in some states. A fine of from twenty to a hundred dollars was to be levied upon the master who permitted his slave to hire his own time.[130] It is impossible to say how frequently the law was violated, but it might be inferred that John Brown had been permitting his slaves to hire their own time from his statement about Willis: "He pays his dollar per day."[131] No instances of trial or conviction under this law were found, however.

Slave-hiring appears to have been generally profitable and satisfactory for both owner and hirer. The owner was freed of management and maintenance of his slaves in most instances, and, under ideal conditions, might expect the slave to earn the equivalent of his value in six or eight years, after which the profit would be even greater. The slave would eventually become unproductive and wholly dependent on his master for a livelihood, but every slave owner had to be prepared for that obligation anyway. The hirer of a slave, without investing more than a few hundred dollars at most, had at his disposal a labor supply—if only for a limited period—which would have required a much larger outlay had he purchased the slave. Another advantage was that productiveness in relation to outlay was fairly predictable, since hiring rate and the slave's capabilities were closely correlated and could be adjusted periodically if necessary. Over a long period of time, hiring a slave rather than buying him might prove uneconomic, but the frequency with which hired slaves were shifted from one hirer to another indicates that few people contemplated long-term

---

[128] Diary of John Brown, July 11, Nov. 7, 1854, June 2, 1855, Jan. 4, 1858, Jan. 14, 1859, Nov. 15, 1860.
[129] Account Book of Henry Pernot, M. D., 1852-1856, flyleaf and p. 146.
[130] *Revised Statutes, 1838,* pp. 731-732.
[131] Diary of John Brown, June 20, 1859.

hiring—they merely wanted a labor supply for a particular purpose at the time. As to the slave, who of course was not consulted in the matter, he probably preferred a settled life among familiar surroundings on his own master's farm to the transient existence of a hireling under a temporary master who expected full and visible return for every dollar expended.

VI

"All hands at the new ground ...."

ARKANSAS CITIZENS sought to buy and to hire Negro slaves for one reason—because of the work they could do. And work they did in Arkansas: on the large plantations along the Mississippi and the other rivers of the state, on the hundreds of small farms scattered throughout every county, in the towns, on the rivers, in the forests—everywhere.

By far the majority of Arkansas slaves lived and worked in the rural areas of the state, little more than one in thirty, as we have seen, being found in the towns even at the height of development of slavery in 1860.[1] Of the approximately 107,000 slaves living in the rural areas in that year,[2] about 51,000 were on what may be considered plantations as distinguished from farms. A reasonable criterion for distinguishing between plantations and farms in Arkansas is that, in general, plantations were those agricultural enterprises with twenty-five or more slaves on which overseers were employed.[3] Of course there were exceptions to this rule, but in most cases it seems valid.

[1] See p. 55 above.
[2] *Census of 1860 (Agriculture)*, p. 224; *Census of 1860 (Population)*, p. 19.
[3] Sydnor, the authority on slavery in Mississippi, drew the line between farms and plantations at thirty slaves, basing his decision upon the fact that the number of slaveholdings of at least that size in the state in 1860 coincided closely with both the number of persons listed in the census as planters and the number listed as overseers, the assumption being that a farm became a plantation when it was necessary to employ an overseer. Sydnor, *Slavery in Mississippi*, p. 67. Other authorities have drawn the line of distinction at lower and higher points; Sellers, for example, although not distinguishing clearly between farmer and planter, said that "a large planter was one who owned fifty slaves or more." Sellers, *Slavery in Alabama*, p. 40. With characteristic thoroughness, Lewis C. Gray in his general history of Southern agriculture separated planters into two groups: those with from ten to fifty slaves, and those with fifty or more, although he did not employ the criterion

Virtually all of the larger plantations were located in the southern and eastern counties of the state, especially in the last decade of slavery in Arkansas. The one usual exception to the southeastern group was Hempstead County in the southwest, which, because of its location along Red River, resembled the southeastern counties more than it did the others of its own geographical section.[4]

Production of cotton was the primary concern of the owners of the large plantations, and thus the activity in which the great majority of plantation slaves were engaged. Arkansas was the sixth-ranking state in the production of cotton in 1860, with 367,-393 bales.[5] Since Arkansas ranked only twelfth in number of slaves, it is evident that cotton production was somewhat more important in the state than in the average Southern state. Much of that increasing importance had come in the previous ten years; in 1850 only 65,344 bales had been grown,[6] at a time when the slave population of the state was 47,100. Cotton production multiplied almost six times in ten years, while during the same period the slave population was only a little more than doubling. This marked increase was caused by the very rapid rate at which the fertile and highly productive lowlands were being brought into cultivation, and also by the fact that the greatest growth in size of

---

of use of an overseer in distinguishing a plantation. Lewis C. Gray, *History of Agriculture in the Southern United States to 1860* (2 vols.; Washington, 1933), I, 483. In Arkansas there obviously was not the same relationship between the census categories of "planter" and "overseer" as in Mississippi, for in 1860 there were only 438 planters, but 1071 overseers. Nor was there close correlation between the number of slaveholdings of thirty or more and the number of overseers; there were 777 slaveholdings of that size as compared to the 1071 overseers. The number of slaveholdings of twenty or more was 1363; since the number of overseers coincides almost exactly with the midway point (1070) between 1363 and 777, twenty-five slaves seems a reasonable distinguishing point. *Census of 1860 (Population)*, p. 21; *Census of 1860 (Agriculture)*, p. 224.

[4] Of the sixty-nine plantations in 1860 in the largest census category—a thousand acres or more—nineteen were in Chicot County, eight in Union, seven in Hempstead, five in Jefferson, and four each in Phillips and Desha. With four exceptions—one each in Independence, Pulaski, Johnson, and Sebastian counties—all of the plantations of a thousand acres or more were in the southern and eastern sections of the state. The tendency for larger holdings of land to be concentrated in the southeast was also true of progressively smaller farms. Chicot County, for example, had only six farms of twenty acres or less, while Carroll, a typical northwestern county, had 237 in that category. *Census of 1860 (Agriculture)*, p. 193.

[5] *Census of 1860 (Agriculture)*, p. 185.

[6] *Ibid.*, p. xciv.

individual slaveholdings was shown on the larger plantations, which were devoted more exclusively to cotton and produced it more efficiently than smaller units. In virtually all instances, counties which led in cotton production also ranked high in the number of large plantations.

Before the Arkansas lands could be planted to cotton, clearing of the dense virgin timber and undergrowth was necessary, and in this strenuous activity slaves played an important part. Few indeed were the planters who did not continually bring more and more land into cultivation. As late as 1860 only a small percentage of the total acreage in farms within the state was considered "improved": 1,983,313 acres as compared to 7,590,393 acres unimproved.[7] The same general proportion of cleared to uncleared land may be noted in information available about individual plantations. For example, Council Bend Plantation, near Helena, had only a hundred of 747 acres cleared in 1848,[8] and of the 1,040 acres on Jenifer Farm, also near Helena, only 200 acres were in cultivation in 1850. In season, the thirty-nine slaves at Jenifer labored at cultivation of cotton and operation of the plantation gin, but during the winter months they cleared additional acres and "deadened" others for future clearing.[9]

A vivid and informative account of the process of hewing cotton fields from the virgin Arkansas woodlands was written by Henry M. Stanley, later famous as an African explorer, who visited the Saline County plantation of a Major Ingham in 1860. The Ingham domain was large, but still "mostly a pine forest, in the midst of which some few score black men had cleared a large space for planting." The numerous Ingham slaves were principally employed in clearing more of the pine forest for future planting of cotton, although there were several house slaves, who "curtsied and bobbed joyfully" to their master when he returned from New Orleans with Stanley as his guest.[10]

Divided into work gangs, the slaves attacked the forest wall with vigor early each morning. On the edge of the clearing one gang felled trees with axes. Another gang chopped the timber

[7] *Ibid.,* p. 6.
[8] *Southern Shield,* Dec. 16, 1848.   [9] *Ibid.,* Jan. 5, 1850.
[10] *The Autobiography of Sir Henry Morton Stanley* (New York, 1909), pp. 146-147.

into logs small enough to be moved, and still another rolled the logs to the blazing fire in the center of the clearing. Members of each gang chanted and sang lustily at their work and vied with other gangs in contests of speed and stamina. "They appeared to enjoy it," commented Stanley, "and the atmosphere, laden with the scent of burning resin, the roaring fires, the dance of the lively flames, the excitement of the gangs while holding on, with grim resolve and honor bound, to the bearing spikes, had a real fascination for me."[11]

Clearing of the land was by no means the end of the struggle to control natural growth. Even after the forests had been cleared and the resulting "new ground" had been planted to cotton, constant additional work by the field slaves was necessary. Periodically fields had to be "scrubbed."[12] Sprouts had to be cut.[13] Stumps had to be burned.[14] Years elapsed before the frontier cotton field was smooth and unbroken.

Ulrich B. Phillips pointed out that the culture of cotton extended throughout the year, and that "at the Christmas holiday when the old harvest was nearly or quite completed, well managed plantations had their preliminaries for the new crop already in progress."[15] That statement applies well to cotton production in Arkansas, whether on the large plantations or the small farms, for methods of culture were much the same on both in that day before the widespread use of machinery. The principal difference was in the number of slaves employed on each, or, in some instances, that a larger amount of the work on the small farms was done by free white labor than by slaves.

The year-round nature of cotton growing is illustrated thoroughly by entries in the diary of John Brown, the Dallas County cotton grower whose classification lay on the boundary between farmer and planter. The number of slaves he owned varied between twenty and twenty-five, and in some years he employed an overseer, while at other times he supervised the slaves himself.

---

[11] *Ibid.,* p. 148.
[12] Diary of John Brown, July 27, 1852.
[13] *Ibid.,* Jan. 29, 1853, Jan. 16, 1854.
[14] *Ibid.,* Nov. 6, 1852, Jan. 19, 1853.
[15] Phillips, *American Negro Slavery,* p. 207.

His diary entries provide excellent insight into the problems and duties involved in producing the "white gold" of the South.[16]

On January 25, 1853, Brown wrote, "All hands at the new ground . . . rolling logs." And a few days later, "I have Steven [a slave] grubbing but he does little of it. My present clearing is the first which I have grubbed at this place." Bad weather during the first of February kept the slaves out of the fields and required Brown to use them at other necessary tasks around the farm, but by the middle of the month one plow was at work in the new ground, while most of the other men worked at getting the cotton gin in operating order. Of this process, Brown wrote: "As usual, we have patched up the screws so that we can make some bales by putting a band around the part that was cracked by the negroes putting oxen to it in my absence. Gin starts again." The cotton being ginned was the last of the previous season's production.

The whole slave labor force resumed work in the new ground toward the end of February. The men plowed, and the women pulled up the old cotton stalks. In April and May the cotton crop was planted, earlier in the upland fields than in the "bottoms," since the lower areas required longer to dry out sufficiently after the winter rains.

June was a month of especially great activity in the cotton fields. Brown and his slaves worked long and vigorously to keep the cotton clear of grass and weeds in order that it might grow well and rapidly. The press of work became so great that it was necessary for Brown's oldest son, William, to drop out of school temporarily "for the assistance of him and his horse in the present pinch." There were usually nine "hoes" and three "ploughs" in the fields;[17] the remainder of the twenty-two slaves were either house servants or children too small to work in the fields. So important was close attention to the cotton crop at this time that Brown only occasionally had his slaves work in the other crops, and then only when the cotton was in good condition.

[16] Diary of John Brown, *passim*. Individual citations will not be made here to entries in the diary.
[17] Brown, like other Southerners of his era, customarily referred to his slaves in terms of their tasks in the fields, as one "plough," two "hoes," etc.

June 8: Spent morning in cleaning out the patches and gardens with the hoes, 2 ploughs dirting the cotton. At noon commenced the upland cotton the second time having got over the bottom yesterday. Three ploughs dirting cotton and 8 hoes.
June 16: Finished the upland cotton second time over. It looks like doing something now, but is too small for the season. We finished dirting all the cotton and have two ploughs preparing and hands planting late corn in the valley, say 6 acres. I am planting two rows corn and 1 of peas. Land exceedingly rough—so I have for my crop for the season 65 acres of cotton and 44 of corn, altogether 110 acres.[18]

Shortly after the middle of July the cotton crop was "laid by" until mature enough for picking. In celebration of the occasion Brown gave the slaves a half-day holiday before starting them on the variety of tasks which had accumulated around the plantation while they were busy with the cotton.

Cotton picking started on a small scale on August 30, and full-time on September 10. From that day until almost the end of the year, cotton picking was the primary activity of Brown's slaves. In early October the cotton gin was placed in operation to bale the cotton which had been accumulating at the rate of about twelve hundred pounds each picking day, enough to make one ginned bale. The gin produced, according to Brown, "a beautiful article." By the middle of November all of Brown's own cotton was picked, and throughout the rest of the month and most of December the slaves picked regularly for neighbors, with Brown receiving fifty cents per hundred pounds for their labor.

The profitable year prompted Brown on December 5 to employ an overseer for the next season. Relieved from what he called the "particular oversight" of the slaves, Brown had more leisure time, but cotton picking for the neighbors and operation of the gin went

[18] Contemporary statements from other states concerning the amounts of cotton and corn one slave should be able to cultivate bear out Brown's evident belief that the five and one-half acres of cotton and four acres of corn cultivated by each of his slaves was below standard. Some years earlier it was reported from Georgia that the average was six acres of cotton and eight acres of corn. *The American Farmer,* II, 359, cited in Phillips, *American Negro Slavery,* p. 207. R. Abbey of Yazoo County, Mississippi, believed that a slave should be able to cultivate six acres of cotton, and another Mississippi planter estimated that each hand cultivated ten acres of cotton and six of corn. *De Bow's Review,* II, 134; X, 66. Another estimate was eight and one-half acres of cotton and four and one-half acres of corn. Sydnor, *Slavery in Mississippi,* p. 14 n. The sources above were also cited by Sydnor.

right on, with a few days interlude for the "holy days." But early in January the slaves were back in the fields again, almost exactly duplicating the work of a year before: "The negroes are grubbing and cleaning up the new ground . . . and breaking cotton stalks." So went the regular routine of a year's cotton cultivation on a small plantation in southern Arkansas, a routine duplicated thousands of times on other farms and plantations throughout the state.

While Arkansas plantation slaves spent more time in cotton cultivation than in any other single activity, they performed many other tasks regularly, including work in the numerous other crops produced. Among crops grown in important quantities in Arkansas, according to the census of 1860, were wheat, rye, Indian corn, oats, rice, tobacco, peas and beans, garden products, Irish potatoes, sweet potatoes, and orchard products. In addition, there was considerable production of wool, butter, cheese, sorghum molasses, beeswax, and honey, and finally, a livestock industry in which horses, mules, milk cows, beef cattle, sheep, and hogs were grown.[19] With the exception of corn, potatoes, livestock, butter, peas, and beans, production of these items was proportionately less in most of the heavy slave-holding counties, but since there was rather wide distribution of production throughout the state, it is evident that slaves did work at producing and growing them. In some cases, leading slave-holding counties were also among the leaders in the state in production of crops other than cotton. For example, Union County, fourth in number of slaves, ranked first in orchard products, second in rye, peas, beans, and sweet potatoes, and fifth in wool. Hempstead, fifth-ranking slave county, ranked first in production of swine, and fourth in peas, beans, and corn. The leading slave county, Phillips, was third in production of corn and second in orchard products, while Chicot County, with the second largest number of slaves in the state, ranked first in rice production. Jefferson, third in number of slaves, was second in amount of rice grown.[20] These statistics

[19] *Census of 1860 (Agriculture),* pp. 6-9.
[20] *Ibid.* Non-slave-operated farms in these counties doubtless raised proportionately more food crops than the slave-operated plantations, but not enough more to minimize the importance of slaves in their production.

imply, then, that the time-hallowed belief that slaves on cotton plantations raised very little of their own food—or little of anything else except cotton—is by no means valid in relation to Arkansas on the eve of the Civil War.

Most of the available records of slave agricultural activities in Arkansas contain frequent references to cultivation of the crops mentioned above. Each of the succession of overseers employed by James Sheppard of Waterford Plantation during the years from 1851 to the Civil War reported to him regularly on the progress of the crops while he was absent on visits to his family home in Virginia. In July, 1852, J. R. McNeely, the current overseer, wrote that "it is very warm & dry here now I am pulling fodder this week and it will take me all next week to finish."[21] The next spring D. T. Weeks, McNeely's successor, expressed his concern for the corn crop: "The corn crop is quite likely to the age of it exception of the wet bottoms it seems like corn does not like to come up nor grow either on nor around them William says it was so last year and I see the best corn in them when I came here."[22] In August of 1854 the "foder was all saved."[23] "The corn was suffering some for want of rain" in the summer of 1855.[24] The report of the overseer I. M. Key in August, 1860, was fuller than most:

the corn crop on this place is only a moderate one Corn is very high and will continue so for the crop in this country will be a short one we have millet in abundance I have 20 large stacks the weather has been so dry and I was late getting the millet off of the ground I declined planting the peas have used the upper millet patch for a turnip patch . . . I must say something about my sweet potato crop I think they are very fine indeede. . . .[25]

On John Brown's Princeton plantation, somewhat smaller and more diversified than Waterford, the slaves customarily used time that could be spared from cultivation of the cotton for working

[21] J. R. McNeely to James Sheppard, July 29, 1852, Sheppard Papers. Fodder, used in winter feeding of horses, mules, and cattle, consisted of green corn leaves bound into small bundles with a single blade of corn.
[22] D. T. Weeks to James Sheppard, May 4, 1853, Sheppard Papers.
[23] D. T. Weeks to James Sheppard, Aug. 10, 1854, Sheppard Papers.
[24] D. T. Weeks to James Sheppard, July 15, 1855, Sheppard Papers.
[25] I. M. Key to James Sheppard, Aug. 12, 1860, Sheppard Papers.

in the food crops. Early corn was planted before the cotton,[26] and late corn after,[27] therefore full attention could be devoted to the cotton at the time necessary. Oats were planted at least as early as cotton, and sometimes earlier.[28] After the cotton was laid by in July, the slaves did more work in the corn, including plowing, "cutting grass and bushes in the late new ground corn in the bottoms," and the inevitable fodder-pulling.[29] The early corn matured before the end of August, and the pleasure of using "new corn meal" elicited a special notation in John Brown's diary.[30] During the spring and summer, Brown's family and slaves cultivated a turnip patch which furnished food for themselves as well as for the cattle.[31] Another turnip crop, which would be used during the fall and winter, was sown in September before the fall rains came.[32] Later in the fall, after most of the cotton was picked, Brown put "all hands at the sweet potatoes except Tabby and the chaps picking and got in the cellar and filled it completely."[33]

The variety of tasks which slaves performed on Arkansas plantations in addition to actual cultivation of crops was almost endless. On the larger plantations, such as Junius W. Craig's Yellow Bayou and Bellevue in Chicot County, with a combined total of 211 slaves, well-organized division of labor was standard. Certain slaves were assigned more or less permanently to particular duties, as blacksmithing, working in the cotton gin, tending stock, driving the wagons, or making and repairing harness for the work animals.[34] On smaller establishments, however, as for example John Brown's Princeton plantation, tasks were apportioned among the slave force as circumstances dictated, a given slave becoming a field hand, a cotton ginner, or a fence-repairer at different times.[35]

On the basis of various types of records, male plantation slaves in Arkansas are known to have worked as carpenters, teamsters, "ostlers" [hostlers], blacksmiths, well-diggers, shoe and harness

[26] Diary of John Brown, March 25, 1853.
[27] *Ibid.*, June 16, 1853.   [28] *Ibid.*, March 25, 1853.
[29] *Ibid.*, Aug. 5, 1852, July 11, Aug. 8, 16, 1853.
[30] *Ibid.*, Aug. 29, 1853.   [31] *Ibid.*, July 13, 1852.
[32] *Ibid.*, Sept. 10, 1853.   [33] *Ibid.*, Nov. 1, 1853.
[34] Appraisal of Craig Estate.
[35] Diary of John Brown, July 17, 1852, Jan. 19, 29, 1853.

makers, chair-makers, musicians, ginners, sawyers, rail-splitters, shingle-makers, gardeners, and basket-makers.[36] Doubtless they did many other types of work of which there is no surviving record.

Many women slaves worked in the fields along with the men, hoeing the cotton, corn, and other crops, picking cotton, burning fallen timber, "grubbing" bushes, breaking and pulling cotton stalks, hoeing the gardens, or sometimes even plowing.[37] Other women, or in many cases the same, spun cotton on hand spinning wheels and wove the thread into coarse cloth,[38] washed and ironed clothing,[39] and helped tend the stock.[40]

An especially select group were the house servants, numerous on the large estates of the lowlands and less so on the smaller farms and plantations, but widely used throughout the state in households of all sizes. As pointed out earlier, well-trained house servants, both male and female, were in great demand and often sold for more than ordinary field hands.[41] House servants worked as cooks, pastry cooks, washers and ironers, "out servants," spinners, weavers, table waiters, wet nurses, nursemaids, personal maids, houseboys, bodyservants to the men of the family, butlers, or seamstresses.[42] Most of the house work was done by hand, but little more than ten years after Elias Howe invented the sewing machine in 1846, the Arkansas plantation owner could

[36] Diary of John Brown, *passim;* D. T. Weeks to James Sheppard, Sept. 20, 1854, Sheppard Papers; *Gazette and Democrat,* Jan. 15, 1850; *Batesville News,* Oct., 17, 1839; *Arkansas State Democrat,* June 1, 1849; *True Democrat,* Oct. 18, 1854; J. H. Henderson, "The Negro in Arkansas County" (unpublished MS in possession of the author, De Witt, Arkansas), p. 7; Willie Empie to James Sheppard, July 16, 1859, Sheppard Papers.

[37] Diary of John Brown, *passim;* letters of various overseers to James Sheppard, Sheppard Papers; Samuel H. Chester, *Pioneer Days in Arkansas* (Richmond, 1927), p. 42.

[38] Diary of John Brown, Feb. 7, 1853; Henderson, "The Negro in Arkansas County," p. 6.

[39] *Gazette and Democrat,* March 8, 1850; *Batesville News,* Oct. 17, 1839; Diary of John Brown, Oct. 29, 1852.

[40] Diary of John Brown, Aug. 5, 1852.

[41] See pp. 81-82 and 85 above.

[42] W. B. Isbell to Allen or Jared Martin, Aug. 18, 1855, Martin Papers; Diary of John Brown, *passim; Batesville News,* Oct. 17, 1839; Henderson, "The Negro in Arkansas County," p. 6; Thomas J. Sherrard, *The Sherrard Family of Steubenville, Together with Letters, Records, and Genealogies of Related Families* (Philadelphia, 1890), p. 288; Mrs. George H. Stinson, "Mrs. Mary Washington Graham" (unpublished MS in possession of John Stinson, Sr., Camden, Arkansas); *Gazette and Democrat,* March 8, 1850.

increase the productivity of his plantation seamstresses by heed-
ing advertisements such as this one which appeared in a Little
Rock newspaper:

Singer & Co's Sewing Machine

It is well adapted to plantations for the purpose of
making negro clothing, as it can do the work of 11 or
12 seamstresses.[43]

While most house servants were women, some were men.   The
Chester family of Columbia County, like many other Arkansas
families, had a houseboy who could perform any necessary domestic task well.[44]   In describing a dinner served at Little Bay Plantation, near Camden, in 1850, Virginia Stinson wrote: "O my!
such a dinner and how we enjoyed it.   Men and maid servants
flitted here and there."[45]   Lycurgus Johnson of Lakeport, Chicot
County, who owned and operated a plantation of two thousand
acres with 150 slaves in the days immediately before the Civil
War, had seven or eight house servants, one a male dining-room
servant for whom he had paid $1700.[46]

At the heart of the labor system of the Arkansas plantation was
the overseer.   As previously noted, in 1860 there were 1,071
persons in the state whose occupation was listed as overseer.[47]
Overseers were somewhat more numerous than teachers and a
little less so than blacksmiths;[48] it is evident, then, that they had
considerable impact upon the labor system of the state, even though
the majority were found in the area of large plantations.

The duties and responsibilities of an overseer varied considerably from plantation to plantation, dependent upon the size of the
plantation, the number of slaves, and especially the degree to
which the owner participated personally in the management of
plantation affairs.   On a small plantation, such as John Brown's
at Princeton, the overseer might be little more than a foreman of

[43] *True Democrat,* Oct. 27, 1857.
[44] Chester, *Pioneer Days in Arkansas,* p. 45.
[45] Stinson, "Mrs. Mary Washington Graham."
[46] Sherrard, *Sherrard Family,* p. 288.
[47] See p. 92 n.
[48] *Census of 1860 (Population),* 21.

the slaves, with the owner making the major decisions concerning the types and acreage of crops, buying the supplies and marketing the crops, and even handling some of the details of management of the slaves.[49]   On a larger plantation, as for example James Sheppard's Waterford, with sixty or more slaves, the owner was necessarily less concerned with the details of plantation and slave management, which consequently fell to a greater extent upon the overseer.   Practically every year Sheppard was absent for several months at a time on visits to Virginia; during his absences the overseers were fully responsible for everything—housing, feeding, and clothing the slaves, punishing them if the need arose, doctoring their ills, supervising the planting, cultivating, harvesting, and marketing the crops.[50]   Under such circumstances the overseer did not merely oversee the work of the slaves, but was the plantation manager in every sense.   Sheppard was not a true absentee owner, since he spent a major part of each year at Waterford, but there were numerous owners who resided permanently away from their plantations, visiting them only occasionally.[51]   In such instances the responsibility of the overseer was greatest.   But whether a plantation owner was resident or absentee, a good overseer was not expected merely to perform routine work, but always to strive for a profit for the owner.   Many did not succeed, as is evidenced by the generally high rate of turnover of overseers;[52] others, however, remained profitably in the employ of the same planters for years, then rose to the status of planters or businessmen themselves.[53]

Whether or not all overseers lived up to the responsibilities

[49] Diary of John Brown, 1853-1854, *passim.*
[50] Letters of various overseers to James Sheppard, 1852-1860, Sheppard Papers. Many of these letters are cited in other connections.
[51] Scattered throughout the manuscript census schedules, but especially in those of the heavy slaveholding counties, are notations that information was given the census-taker by the overseer rather than by the owner of the slaves. Both census and county tax records indicate multiple plantation holdings, with the owner sometimes living on none of them.
[52] Richard Finn of Hempstead County, for example, had four or five in the same year. 9 Ark. 674.
[53] One such instance was related by Mrs. Hannah J. Knight. Her husband came to Little Rock to serve as overseer of thirty slaves on the Byrd plantation, most of which now lies in the wholesale district in the eastern part of the city. After several years he quit to become co-editor of the *Arkansas Gazette* with William E. Woodruff. Mrs. Hannah D. Knight, "Hospitality of Early Days," *Arkansas Pioneers,* I (Sept., 1912), 12.

placed upon them, they were continually conscious of the necessity of pleasing the plantation owner. Several of the letters written to James Sheppard of Waterford Plantation by his overseers contain reassurances that they had his best interests at heart and that they were striving to do the best job possible. D. T. Weeks wrote in 1854:

> . . . I am & have been using every precaution to keep health and prevent sickness among the slaves ever since you went away for it is no little pleasure for me to take a person's property and manage it in his absence and make and save as I can and be able when he returns to find all he left with me well. but on the other hand if misfortune & accident hapens so that I lose some Mules or negroes I do not expect Any man regrets it any more than I do. . . .[54]

I. M. Key, a later overseer, wrote, after giving a detailed report of progress of the crops, health and discipline of the slaves, and related matters, ". . . make yourself easy about the plantation. I will certainly do anything in my power to enhance your interest."[55]

Certainly the position of the overseer was a difficult one. If he were too lenient in disciplining the slaves and in exacting work from them, he stood in danger of incurring the displeasure of his employer by failing to produce a satisfactory crop. A good example of this is afforded by the experience of Smirl, the overseer hired by John Brown of Princeton at the end of his profitable crop year of 1853. A few months after hiring Smirl, Brown and his family and some of the slaves moved into the nearby river town of Camden, leaving Smirl in complete charge of the plantation and the remaining slaves. By July of 1854, potentially as good a crop year as the previous one, it was obvious that Smirl was a failure at his job. Brown wrote:

> Went through Princeton to my farm. Found all well and the crop almost lost. I feel it very severely. It will make it very difficult to get along, a sad misfortune at present but the thing is done and what can't be cured must be endured. My negroes do badly and I ought to have employed a strict overseer who would have pushed them up. They have not worked.[56]

[54] D. T. Weeks to James Sheppard, Sept. 10, 1854, Sheppard Papers.
[55] I. M. Key to James Sheppard, Aug. 12, 1860, Sheppard Papers.
[56] Diary of John Brown, July 20, 1854.

By January, 1855, the extent of the year's failure was fully apparent. The plantation had produced only six or seven hundred bushels of corn and seven or eight bales of cotton, a small fraction of the abundant yield of the previous year, and Brown placed the blame largely upon the "want of skill and energy" of the overseer Smirl. He went on to philosophize somewhat ruefully: "I however have to bear with it and blame it on what I have often done before, by employing the wrong sort of overseer, to favor my negroes, but all experience shows that a very decided and commanding man must be had to make anything on a plantation without the presence of the owner." Needless to say, Smirl was not rehired. In fact, Brown was so disgruntled with the financial loss of the year that he sold the plantation, moved the slaves into Camden, and thenceforth hired them out as day-laborers or on yearly contracts.[57]

If the overseer, taking the other extreme from that followed by Smirl, drove the slaves too hard or punished them too severely for infractions of plantation discipline, he stood equally in danger of censure or discharge for undue damage to valuable property,[58] and at the same time risked the loss of part of his slave force through temporary disability, with resulting loss in crop production. Doubtless the average overseer felt caught between the "upper and nether millstones," and there is little wonder that the turnover among them was so great.

Many of the Arkansas overseers were quite young, further indication that the occupation could not hold men permanently. Harvey Gulley of Missouri Township, Ouachita County, was an overseer in 1850 when he was only nineteen. James Gunter, born in Tennessee, at twenty-one was overseer of the slaves of I. B. Lea in Liberty Township, Ouachita County.[59] Other overseers were referred to as young, as for example in the following account in a letter from D. T. Weeks to James Sheppard: "Mr. Nichols had A negro drowned in the Ark River lately on the river place The young overseer there went to chastice him & he refused to

[57] *Ibid.,* Jan. 1, 6, Feb. 7, June 1, 1855.
[58] For an account of an overseer being discharged for harsh treatment of a slave, see the case of *Brunson* v. *Martin,* 17 Ark. 270.
[59] Schedule of Free Inhabitants, Ouachita County, Arkansas, 1850, pp. 137, 148.

submit he called 3 more negroes & he run into the river an got drowned. . . ."[60] Transient in nature as the occupation might be, overseeing did offer to young, landless, moneyless men moving west an opportunity above that of the common farm laborer, with prospect of saving money and becoming planters themselves.

Since the days of the abolition movement preceding the Civil War, the Southern plantation overseer has been considered in the popular mind as the ultimate in cruelty and lack of moral principle, just as from the same period there have been transmitted the idealized portraits of the kindly old Negro mammy and the faithful old male retainer. Certainly these were not typical of all Negro slaves; neither were all overseers immoral brutes. There are numerous known instances of cruelties by Arkansas overseers, it is true, but it is in the nature of man to remember and record the extreme in human conduct rather than the mean. The very nature of the position of the overseer—that it was he who must directly enforce the edicts of the ruling class—insured that he would rarely be remembered in a favorable light by the slaves themselves.

Henry M. Stanley, in reminiscing about his experiences on the Ingham plantation in Saline County, recorded an extremely caustic criticism of an Arkansas overseer. Stanley was a native of Great Britain, a country which had long led the fight against the slave system throughout the world, and so it was natural that he had preconceived unfavorable opinions of almost everything connected with slavery. Nevertheless, Stanley's description of the unnamed overseer gives insight into the characteristics and actions of a man who represented one extreme in his occupation. Of his first encounter with the overseer Stanley wrote:

. . . I began to feel the influence of the charm [of the Ingham home], and was ready to view my stay in the western woods with interest and content. But there was one person in the family that caused a doubt in my mind, and that was the overseer. He joined us after supper, and, almost immediately, I conceived a dislike for him. His vulgarity and coarseness revived recollections of levee men. His garb was offensive; the pantaloons stuffed into his boots, the big hat, the slouch of his carriage, his rough accents and the manner of his

[60] D. T. Weeks to James Sheppard, Sept. 20, 1854, Sheppard Papers.

half-patronising familiarity. I set him down at once as one of those men who haunt liquor-saloons, and are proud to claim acquaintance with the bartenders.[61]

Before many days passed Stanley had opportunity to observe the overseer in the performance of his duties, and the first impressions were not dispelled, but rather were intensified, the overseer by now seeming to be "a compound of a Legree and Nelson, with an admixture of mannerism peculiarly his own." Stanley, because he enjoyed the work, was helping the slaves clear the pine forests, and whenever the overseer came by his gang, he noted that "the men became subdued, and stopped their innocent chaff and play." The overseer always kept the slaves aware of his presence by repeatedly cracking a "blacksnake" whip. Within a few days the brewing quarrel between Stanley and the overseer came to a head.

One day . . . he was in a worse humor than usual. His face was longer, and malice gleamed in his eyes. . . . He cried out his commands with a more imperious note. A young fellow named Jim was the first victim of his ire, and, as he was carrying a heavy log with myself and the others, he could not answer him so politely as he expected. He flicked at his naked shoulders with his whip, and the lash, flying unexpectedly near me, caused us both to drop our spikes. Unassisted by us, the weight of the log was too great for the others, and it fell to the ground crushing the foot of one of them. Meantime, furious at the indignity, I had engaged him in a wordy contest; hot words, even threats, were exchanged, and had it not been for the cries of the wounded man who was held fast by the log, we should probably have fought. The end of it was, I retired from the field, burning with indignation, and disgusted with his abominable brutality.[62]

Stanley reported the matter immediately to Major Ingham, who heard him without great concern, attempting to explain— and this was the general philosophy of slaveowners—that if there were to be effective control of the slaves the overseer must be left in full charge. The upshot of the conversation with Ingham was that Stanley packed and left for the Arkansas River, unwilling to continue living where such attitudes prevailed.[63]

[61] Stanley, *Autobiography,* p. 147.   [62] *Ibid.,* pp. 148-149.
[63] *Ibid.,* pp. 149-150.

While at times overseers did treat slaves with a degree of severity beyond all reason, at other times some of them displayed remarkable patience. Following is an account of the difficulties between one of James Sheppard's overseers and an especially recalcitrant slave girl.

Nora is still on hand, the most impudent and disobedient piece I ever saw. She wont mind me at all, unless I watch her & she knows I wont whip her because she is sick and weak. The hands had a beef on their holiday. I ordered Nora positively not to touch any of it in the quarters & perhaps Id send her some from the house so soon as my back was turned she sent Wiley or William for a piece of liver which he sent her & she downed it all. Consequently all day Saturday, Sunday & Monday she had a high fever. . . . I ordered her to take quinine but she said she wouldn't take it. . . . I went down there found her standing in the middle of the floor mad as a hornet—she wouldn't take the medicine, & i gave her 15 or 20 cuts with my little cowhide & not wanting to whip her called in Aggy and Patsy & told her I'd gap her if it took the whole plantation she took it then & afterwards . . . but swore she'd run away—that she had done swore so when you whipped her before. . . . I don't know what to do with her cant whip her as she has had her courses on her 8 times since you left and they have made her weak & I cant whip her. She's the most insufferable liar & quarrels with everybody. She's too delicate to stand this climate and your best plan is to sell her, she can never suit your family—will never give you anything but trouble for running away she is not a proper woman to have among the children.[64]

Sometimes differences between overseers and slaves erupted into serious trouble and violence—even murder. There are recorded instances of slaves killing overseers, as well as of overseers killing slaves. On August 11, 1859, a slave belonging to J. W. Carpenter, a planter near Helena, killed Robert Bickers, the plantation overseer, by crushing his skull with an axe. The slave hid in the hayloft of a barn on the plantation until he was forced by hunger to emerge, when he was seen by other slaves and captured. With no pretense of a trial, the slave was hanged on August 17 near the spot where he committed the murder, and the body was permitted to remain hanging for a day as a warning to other slaves of the community.[65] An overseer who killed a slave was James

[64] Robert W. Miller to James Sheppard, June 16, 1859, Sheppard Papers.
[65] *Des Arc Weekly Citizen*, Aug. 24, 1859.

Martin, the employee of Robert A. Brunson of Hempstead County. Martin killed the slave Nathan with a shotgun in 1853 after Nathan had said "shoot and be damned" and had advanced threateningly. Brunson discharged Martin, believing that the shooting had been unnecessary. Immediately Martin brought suit to recover his contract wages for the year. Testimony and result of the trial give further indication of the great degree of authority which overseers, by law and by custom, held. Brunson, the slave's owner, contested Martin's suit for recovery of wages with this statement:

> . . . you, without necessity, and contrary to and against your duty, as my overseer, and manager upon my farm, did wrongfully kill and destroy my property, then under your care and control, as my overseer and manager, . . . to wit: a Negro slave named Nathan, of great value, to wit: of the value of fifteen hundred dollars, and that I shall cut-off and keep back, the entire sum claimed by you in the suit aforesaid, for the damage by me sustained in this behalf, and take judgement against you for the balance to which I am entitled on account of same.[66]

In the trial evidence was introduced showing that Martin had been drinking the afternoon of the shooting, that he had said he "had a rough and saucy set of negroes on the farm, and that he would make the negroes obey him, or he would kill them," and that the slave Nathan was unarmed. Nevertheless, the jury held that Martin had shown no negligence in management of the slaves which would justify Brunson in withholding his wages or collecting damages. This was later upheld by the Arkansas Supreme Court.[67] The very existence of the institution of slavery was based upon force or threat of force, and court decisions such as this helped to maintain the authority of the whites over the slaves.

Overseers customarily were hired for a year at a time, most often in the winter after one crop had been harvested and before work on the new crop had gotten fully underway. Usually the employment agreement was a formal contract signed by both the overseer and the employer. If the work of the overseer proved

[66] *Brunson v. Martin,* 17 Ark. 270.
[67] *Ibid.,* 270-278.

satisfactory, the contract might be renewed annually. A typical contract, one of a number preserved in the James Sheppard Papers, follows:

This article of agreement made and entered into this day between James Sheppard and Robert W. Miller, Witnesseth, that I the said Sheppard have employed the Said Miller to oversee my plantation for the balance of the present year and for well and truely performing the said services as overseer the said Sheppard is to pay five hundred dollars and to furnish five hundred pounds of pork and to also furnish said Millers family with Meal and feed his horse. Said Miller is to furnish his own cook. It is also agreed between the parties that if either should become dissatisfied that this contract shall be dissolved at any time during the year by giving notice in person a week before hand. In case this contract should be broken and the parties separate the said Sheppard is to pay and furnish the said articles in proportion to the time that this bargain may continue. Said Sheppard is also to furnish a cow. Said Millers woman is to cultivate the garden. Signed this the 7th day of February 1859.

JAMES SHEPPARD
ROBERT W. MILLER[68]

The five hundred dollar yearly salary Miller received was slightly lower than those paid to other Sheppard overseers during the period, but it was nevertheless a substantial sum of money in that day of generally low prices for everything except slaves.[69] Miller's predecessor, D. T. Weeks, had begun in 1853 at $600 per year, and his pay had gradually increased to $700 by 1858, the year he left Sheppard's employ.[70] In 1860, the year following Miller's one-year tenure, there were two overseers in rapid succession, the first, William F. Black, receiving pay at the rate of $800 a year,[71] and the second, I. M. Key, at $850 a year.[72] Evidently the pay of all Sheppard's overseers was above average, for

[68] Contract between James Sheppard and Robert W. Miller, Feb. 7, 1859, Sheppard Papers.
[69] For example, the three slaves owned by the author's great-great-grandfather, George L. Green of Hillsboro, Union County, were valued at $2,000, while the remainder of his property, consisting of a 320-acre farm, a horse, and ten cows, was valued at only $1,400. Tax Assessment List, Union County, 1853.
[70] Contracts between James Sheppard and D. T. Weeks, 1853-1858, Sheppard Papers.
[71] Contract between James Sheppard and William F. Black, April 9, 1860, Sheppard Papers.
[72] Contract between James Sheppard and I. M. Key, July 2, 1860, Sheppard Papers.

reliable witnesses in a court suit concerning payment of an overseer's salary testified in 1854 that the usual price for overseeing a
plantation was "from $300 to $400 per annum, none of them going higher than the latter sum."[73] The number of slaves to be
supervised had some bearing upon the amount of the salary. In
1845, when the general price level was somewhat lower than ten
or fifteen years later, J. W. White, overseer for two large plantations at Spanish Moss Bend, Chicot County, wrote a friend that
"I don't think I will live with Faulkner next year he is one of the
best men I ever saw but has not the force that will justify him in
paying big wages I had rather live with him than any man I ever
lived with if he could give as big wages as I can get on other
places," and at the same time reported: "I have flatering induce-
ments held out to me and have been told that one of our neighbour
planters intends for me to oversee for him next season if a
thousand dollars will take he has a large force. . . ."[74] It is not
known whether White secured the job or not, but in any event
the $1000 salary figure is the largest encountered in Arkansas.

As noted earlier, the number of slaves living in the towns of
Arkansas in 1860 was only 3,799, and many of these worked on
farms on the outskirts. A majority of the remainder performed
the same types of work as the house servants and artisans on the
rural farms and plantations. Some, however, worked in the small
industrial enterprises of the period, in spite of the general opposition among the nonslaveholding white population to the use of
slaves in skilled jobs. At times this opposition was expressed in
an open and organized manner. In the fall of 1858 several protest
meetings of white mechanics and artisans were held in Little
Rock, with C. O. Haller, a German immigrant, and A. J. Ward,
owner of a blacksmith and carriage shop, in charge. The group
passed resolutions protesting the use of slaves and free Negroes
as mechanics, the practice of teaching negroes the mechanic
trades, and—this had only indirect bearing upon slavery—the
use of convict labor in the skilled mechanic trades. They also
pledged themselves to urge passage of laws which would remedy

[73] *McDaniel as ad* v. *Parks,* 19 Ark. 673.
[74] J. W. White to Jared C. Martin, Aug. 20, 1845, Martin Papers.

the existing situation.[75]   No such laws applying to slaves were ever passed, however, and slaves continued to work in the blacksmith shops, carriage shops, tanyards, sawmills, lumber yards, and other small industries of the towns.[76]

The town houses of wealthy Arkansas slaveowners were staffed with a variety of house servants.   Notable among such establishments was the mansion of Chester Ashley, which with its grounds occupied the entire block now bounded by Scott, Cumberland, Markham, and Second Streets in downtown Little Rock. The house itself was a large two-story brick structure with great columns supporting a long portico.   Behind it were formal gardens, hothouses, slave quarters, stables, and other outbuildings. A number of slave gardeners, stableboys, and carriage drivers were required to staff the place, and the frequent and lavish entertainments given by Ashley called for cooks, maids, and other house servants.   Seven of Ashley's male slaves also played brass and stringed instruments, giving frequent concerts on the lawn in front of the house, as well as playing for the less frequent slave entertainments during the various holidays.[77]

Slaves worked in the hotels, boarding houses, and taverns of the towns.   As previously noted, a Mrs. Burnett, who operated a boarding house in Little Rock, was attempting in 1850 to hire a Negro boy from 14 to 18 years old who was "acquainted with housework."[78]   Joseph Anthony, operator of the Anthony House, most famous of the early Little Rock hotels, owned five slaves in 1853, and it is reasonable to suppose that they worked in the hotel.[79]   Among tavern operators who used slave labor were a man named Harris in Camden and another named Powell in Van Buren.[80]

Town slaves are also known to have worked as draymen, garden-plowmen, house painters, house movers, and street laborers.[81]

[75] *Arkansas State Gazette and Democrat,* Sept. 25, Oct. 9, 16, 1858.
[76] *Arkansas Gazette,* May 30, 1838; *Mooney* v. *Brinkley,* 17 Ark. 345.
[77] Mrs. Fanny Ashley Johnson, "The Ashley Mansion and the Ashley Band —the Johnson Residence," *Arkansas Pioneers,* I (Sept., 1912), 10-11. Mrs. Johnson was a descendant of Chester Ashley.
[78] *Gazette and Democrat,* March 22, 1850.
[79] Tax Assessment List, Pulaski County, 1853.
[80] Diary of John Brown, Jan. 4, 1858; *Powell* v. *State,* 21 Ark. 509.
[81] Diary of John Brown, 1852-1860, *passim;* Diary of Robert F. Kellam, Oct. 10, 1860.

Much of the street repair work in the incorporated towns was done by slaves in compliance with ordinances such as that passed by the town council of Little Rock in 1835, which required all owners of one or more slaves to furnish for a specified period "one hand in addition to the services now required of such slave-owner." A fine of one dollar was set for failure to comply.[82]

In general, land transportation was still in an almost primitive state in Arkansas up to the end of the slavery period, but some progress was being made, and slaves were used in building public roads and bridges and even in constructing the few miles of rail-road which were completed before the Civil War. Away from the environs of the larger towns, most of the roads were little more than cleared rights-of-way through the forests, with crude bridges crossing the smaller streams and ferries across the larger. Probably the best-developed road in the state was the Military Road, which entered north of Pocahontas in northeastern Arkansas, progressed southwest down the highland line through Little Rock, and crossed into Texas at the Red River not far from the town of Washington. Other fairly well-developed roads ran from Little Rock to DeVall's Bluff on White River, from Little Rock to Van Buren and Fayetteville in northwest Arkansas, and from Little Rock to the Mississippi River in the southeastern corner of the state. Of course there were also many shorter local and connecting roads.

Correspondence between Allen and Jared Martin while they were in process of negotiating the contract for clearing the road between Little Rock and the Mississippi River at Columbia in 1835 gives considerable information concerning the use of slaves in road building. Allen wrote Jared:

I enclose bids for the part of the road from Fourche to Pine Bluffs—from Bayou Bartholomew coming up to Abels Creek, and from Abels Creek to Bayou Bartholomew below the Bluffs. the prices are such as will afford us good proffit and nothing more—from Fourche to Bluffs is much the hardest to clear on account of the brush—but I have put the lower section at the same price on account of it being to far from home—the middle section will be verry light

[82] *Arkansas Gazette,* June 23, 1835.

clearing—from information that I have gathered upon which I can rely. on the middle and largest part of the lower section twelve hands can cut a mile a day—it will take twenty or twenty five hands to cut (on an average) a mile a day on the uper section. if I enter into this business, I wish to get enough to pay me well for the labor. I mean enough of work—for we will have to go to as much expense in the outfit for 40 miles of road (or verry nearly) as for 90.[83]

A much more universal use of slaves was in the maintenance of local roads. The detailed statute on roads and highways passed by the Arkansas legislature on February 14, 1838, provided that

All free male inhabitants, between the ages of sixteen and forty five years, except such persons as are exempted from performing militia duty, and all male slaves of the same age, shall be subject to work on any public road within their respective townships, when assigned by the justice of the peace appointed for that purpose by the county court, if they shall have resided in the township previous to being warned to work on the same.[84]

The law outlined in detail the penalties which could be levied against slaveowners who neglected or refused to send their slaves to work on the roads when directed to do so. The fine was two dollars for each day of absence from road duty, the amount to be recovered "by action of debt" in a justice of the peace court. The maximum amount of time any person, free or slave, could be required to work on the public roads was "twelve days in one year, or four days at any one time or in any one month." Road workers were required to furnish their own hand tools.[85] This law, which was based on the old territorial statute, remained in effect without change throughout the slavery period.

Most slaveowners sent their slaves to work on the roads when required to do so by the local road overseer; no instances of deliberate refusal to comply with the law were encountered in county records. Occasionally, however, slaveowners became involved in legal proceedings with county officials over the time and place of road work by slaves. James Sheppard of Waterford Plantation engaged in a year-long controversy with Jefferson County officials in 1858 and 1859. Early in 1858 Sheppard was called upon by

[83] Allen Martin to Jared C. Martin, June 21, 1835, Martin Papers.
[84] *Revised Statutes, 1838*, pp. 703-704.
[85] *Ibid.*, pp. 704-710.

road overseer Thomas Watkins to send his slaves to work on the "Waters Road District No. 1 beginning near Mrs. Rones Bridge and ending at the Bogy Township line." Sheppard refused to send his slaves, asserting that under the law he was not required to furnish workers for this road, which was some distance from his plantation. The road overseer then brought proceedings against Sheppard. Sheppard's overseer, D. T. Weeks, with the assistance of a Pine Bluff lawyer, a General James, secured suspension of the proceedings by a decree from the county court, which assigned Sheppard's slaves to work on "Road District No. 2 down River leading from Vaugine Township line to Bogy Township line." Sheppard was given until April 15, 1858, to complete the work.[86]

The press of work during the planting season was upon Waterford Plantation at this period of the year, and Weeks did not send the slaves to work on the road. The matter dragged on, with J. W. Vaughan, the road overseer, giving Sheppard several extensions of time in which to accomplish the work. Finally, Vaughan filed suit in early 1859, at the same time indicating that he was willing to give Sheppard one more chance.[87] On February 14, 1859, Vaughan sent this notice to Sheppard:

Mr. James Sheppard or Overseer or Agent.
You are hereby notified to attend with all your force subject to work roads (consisting of 17 in number) . . . the object is to work out the five days due said Road by law. . . . You will please send some 5 or 6 shovels or spades if you have them the ballance axes if you have no shovels or spades send all axes Mr. Weeks will also attend at same time to make out his five days. . . .[88]

Faced with the loss of use of his slave force for a double length of time—for both the current and previous year—Sheppard decided to pay his 1858 road work obligations in cash, and was given until May 11 to discharge his 1859 obligations.[89] Thus the controversy was ended, at least for the moment. The affair

[86] D. T. Weeks to James Sheppard, March 20, 1858, Sheppard Papers.
[87] J. W. Vaughan to James Sheppard, Feb. 12, 1859, Sheppard Papers.
[88] J. W. Vaughan to James Sheppard or Overseer or Agent, Feb. 14, 1859, Sheppard Papers.
[89] Receipt, J. W. Vaughan to James Sheppard, March 31, 1849, Sheppard Papers.

illustrates the difficulties which a planter often had in fitting the closely scheduled work of his slaves into a public works program.

Use of slave labor in railroad construction in Arkansas was very limited, since the state had so few miles of railroad before the Civil War. Among the few slaves known to have worked in railroad construction were John Brown's. Brown hired them out for $21.25 each for one month to a Mr. Lear, who held the contract for building a railroad right-of-way near Camden.[90]

Slaves were used extensively in water transportation, easily the most important means of transportation in Arkansas before the Civil War.[91] Long before Arkansas became a state, slaves served as oarsmen for the numerous traders plying the rivers and smaller streams of the region. Jacob Barkman of Blakeleytown (later Arkadelphia) opened regular commercial shipping service between New Orleans and the upper Ouachita River prior to 1820, using pirogues manned by six slaves. Barkman transported skins, furs, tallow, and bear grease down the river, and returned with coffee, sugar, powder, lead, flints, cotton and woolen goods, buttons, pins, and needles. The round trip required six months.[92]

After steamboats began to replace more primitive craft, slaves were used in a wide variety of tasks. According to one close student of river transportation in Arkansas and surrounding states, they soon "made up more than half of the crews of the steamboats." They "cooked and served the meals, made the bunks, stoked the fires, and rolled the freight up and down the gangplanks."[93] Some slaves even rose to become steamboat engineers. Reuben, the tall, two-hundred-pound slave of Emzy Wilson of Palarm, near Little Rock, worked for several years as an engineer on boats on the Mississippi and Cumberland rivers.[94]

Steamboats brought employment for slaves ashore also. Practically all of the boats used wood for fuel, which necessitated wood-yards along the banks of the rivers at frequent intervals. Slaves chopped and stacked the wood and carried it aboard the boats

[90] Diary of John Brown, Oct. 26, 1854.
[91] Brown, "River Transportation in Arkansas," pp. 35-36.
[92] *Southern Standard*, June 21, 1895; Laura Scott Butler, "History of Clark County," *Publications of the Arkansas Historical Association* (4 vols., Fayetteville and Conway, 1906-1917), I, 375-376.
[93] Quick, *Mississippi Steamboatin'*, p. 236.
[94] *Arkansas Gazette*, Feb. 9, 1836.

when they put into shore.[95]   Occasionally slaves aided in salvaging steamboats which had sunk in the rivers.   On May 16, 1837, Noah H. Badgett, with the assistance of his slaves, salvaged the contents of the wrecked and abandoned steamer *Compromise,* about fifteen miles below Little Rock.   Badgett claimed salvage in the amount of $1074.75.[96]   Slaves were also instrumental in salvaging the contents of the steamer *America,* which sank in the Mississippi River bordering Mississippi County in 1827 while carrying a cargo of shot, bar lead, and more than three thousand pigs of lead.   Slaves living near the Arkansas bank of the river witnessed the sinking and remembered the location.   Within two years, because of a change in the current of the river, the wreck became covered by a tow head and island which within twenty years produced trees thirty or forty feet high.   In the early 1850's the current of the river shifted again, and the tow head and island were washed away.   During the early spring of 1855 the wreck of the *America* was located, chiefly through the assistance of the same slaves who had seen the sinking nearly thirty years before, and a professional salvaging company recovered almost $5000 worth of lead.[97]   Since there were many steamboat wrecks and sinkings on the Arkansas rivers, other slaves must also have participated in salvaging operations.

[95] *Memphis Daily Eagle,* April 26, 1850.
[96] *Arkansas Gazette,* July 4, 1837.
[97] *Eads et al.* v. *Brazelton,* 22 Ark. 499.

VII

The Balance Sheet

THE SYSTEM [of slavery] was unprofitable for [Arkansas] as a whole," declared David Yancey Thomas, a leading recent Arkansas historian, in 1930.[1] This statement expresses one view of the profitableness of slavery, in the entire South as well as in Arkansas, which has been widely held. Many authorities, on the other hand, have asserted that slavery was profitable.

Most famous of the historians who believed that slavery was either unprofitable, or profitable only under ideal conditions, was Ulrich B. Phillips, who wrote that "by the close of the 'fifties it is fairly certain that no slaveholders but those few whose plantations lay in the most advantageous parts of the cotton and sugar districts and whose managerial ability was exceptionally great were earning anything beyond what would cover their maintenance and carrying charges." A historian who usually wrote more descriptively than analytically, Phillips offered little direct or detailed evidence to support his conclusion. He apparently based his opinion largely upon a belief that the price of slaves was too high in comparison with the amount they produced, but he also believed that the profit on a slave was only that amount realized beyond what would be a fair rate of return in the form of interest on the capital invested in the slave.[2] The latter point will be discussed later.

Writing on slavery in Alabama, Charles S. Davis asserted that "profits in cotton planting have been largely over-estimated," and, echoing Phillips almost precisely, "one might justly conclude that

[1] Thomas, *Arkansas and its People,* I, 114.
[2] Phillips, *American Negro Slavery,* pp. 391-392.

since slave prices were so high, the Alabama planter could receive only a small return on his investment, and that only by efficient management in the cultivation of good lands."[3]   Ralph Betts Flanders, the historian of plantation slavery in Georgia, was another follower of Phillips, but with less extreme views.   Flanders singled out a number of instances of what he considered low profits in the use of slavery and described slave labor as "expensive and inefficient," but believed that "with proper management of slave labor and the application of scientific methods to the planting industry, large profits could be made."[4]

Charles S. Sydnor also minimized the profitableness of slave labor, producing a formidable body of evidence to support his conclusions.   He set up a hypothetical but typical Mississippi cotton plantation of the 1850's with six hundred acres of land and fifty slaves, valued altogether at $36,000.   The income in a typical year was $6,320, and the expenses of operation $5,440.   Interest and depreciation on the value of the land and slaves accounted for $4,140 of the expenses, while the remaining $1,300 was expended for plantation supplies and the hire of an overseer.   Thus Sydnor's hypothetical planter made a profit of $880, or a little less than 2.5 per cent on his invested capital.   And, wrote Sydnor, "if anything, the above statement is too optimistic."[5]

Several historians, most of them writing since those mentioned above, have either concluded independently that slavery was profitable, or have challenged directly the conclusions of Phillips, Sydnor, and the others.   The most thorough, and probably the most convincing, was Thomas P. Govan, who attacked the views of both Phillips and Sydnor, but devoted most of his attention to Sydnor, who presented more challengeable evidence than Phillips.   One of Govan's major objections to Sydnor's method of computing profit concerned the treatment of the large items of interest on land and slaves as expenses of operation of the plantation.   Instead of the interest being a cost of doing business, Govan said, "according to many economists and the generally accepted definition of

[3] Charles S. Davis, *The Cotton Kingdom in Alabama* (Montgomery, 1939), pp. 180-189.
[4] Ralph Betts Flanders, *Plantation Slavery in Georgia* (Chapel Hill, 1933), pp. 217-231.
[5] Sydnor, *Slavery in Mississippi*, pp. 196-197.

accountants and businessmen, profit is a combination of this interest on investment and wages for management."[6] In other words, the amount of profit on Sydnor's plantation was dependent upon the definition of profit. Sydnor recognized this to some extent, for he wrote that the planter "was, of course, free to spend the interest on his investment in negroes and land, and this was the item that caused the profits on Mississippi plantations to appear high."[7] Sydnor was thus actually admitting that slavery was profitable, even though a major part of that profit was return on investment in capital.

Govan also objected to charging substantial sums for depreciation of slaves and land as expenses of doing business. He pointed out the commonly accepted fact that slaves more than reproduced themselves, asserted that improvements to the land more than compensated for any loss in fertility, and noted the continuous increase in prices of land and slaves up to the Civil War. Finally, Govan objected to Sydnor's capitalization of the land and slaves at the current market value, saying that in most instances the initial investment in land and slaves was less than current value, since the land and some of the slaves had been purchased when prices were lower, and many of the slaves had been reared on the plantation.

After eliminating the items of interest and depreciation which he believed had been unjustly charged as expenses of Sydnor's plantation, Govan refigured the profit and concluded that it would have been $5,020, or an entirely satisfactory return of approximately 13 per cent on the invested capital. He believed, however, that the figure was somewhat too high, since Sydnor had not made adequate deductions for such actual plantation expenses as corn, pork, freight, factors' commissions, and so forth.[8]

Writing several years later, Robert W. Smith agreed substantially with Govan. Smith added only the obvious point that it was legitimate to charge interest as an expense of operation

[6] Thomas P. Govan, "Was Plantation Slavery Profitable?," *Journal of Southern History,* VIII (Nov., 1942), 521.
[7] Sydnor, *Slavery in Mississippi,* p. 197.
[8] Govan, "Was Plantation Slavery Profitable?," pp. 520-525.

when the planter had borrowed money to purchase the plantation or slaves and was still in process of repaying the loan.[9]

A final writer to be mentioned here who believed that slavery
was profitable was Lewis C. Gray, author of the comprehensive
history of Southern agriculture. The writer of the introduction
to Gray's work said, "He appears to have been the first to explain the paradox of the unprofitableness of the system so generally
alleged by antislavery critics and even by historians and the ability of the plantation system to displace the small farm economy
under certain favorable conditions." Gray believed that slave
labor was efficient, and that "far from being a decrepit institution, the economic motives for the continuance of slavery from
the standpoint of the employer were never so strong as in the
years just preceding the Civil War."[10]

Some of these writers, as well as others, have singled out as
another indication of the profitableness of slavery the great rise in
general agricultural wealth in the South, demonstrated by increases in number of farms, cash value of farms, number of slaves,
and number of slaveholders.[11]

Insofar as Arkansas was concerned, the author agrees, in
general, with those writers who have contended that slavery was
profitable, and yet in so doing it is not necessary to disagree wholly
with Phillips, Sydnor, and like thinkers. They all admitted that
slavery was profitable under favorable conditions, and Sydnor,
who marshaled the most evidence in support of his views, nevertheless basically admitted that even under typical conditions it was
profitable. The author agrees with Govan that interest should not
be considered an item of expense of the planter, for that interest
was spendable profit, no matter what it was called. No evidence
on this point appears necessary; Sydnor's hypothetical Mississippi
plantation could also be considered typical of Arkansas, and the
choice between considering interest as expense or as a profit—

[9] Robert W. Smith, "Was Slavery Profitable in the Ante-Bellum South?," *Agricultural History*, XX (Jan., 1946), 62-64.
[10] Gray, *History of Agriculture in the Southern United States*, I, viii, 470-471, 476.
[11] A recent authority who pointed this out is Clement Eaton in *A History of the Old South* (New York, 1949), p. 278.

and the plantation thus operating at little or at substantial profit —is purely an intellectual one.

The author also agrees with Govan that it was unfair to charge depreciation on the slaves as an expense of operation. Certainly in Arkansas, as will be pointed out in greater detail later in this study, slaves more than reproduced themselves. As to whether it would be fair to charge depreciation of the land as an expense in Arkansas there is little evidence, for most of Arkansas had not been settled long enough to suffer from the soil erosion and depletion so common in the older states. In general support of Govan's contention, however, is the fact that despite the widespread soil depletion land values throughout the South increased steadily.[12]

Govan's objection to capitalization of the slaves and land at current market value is less valid in relation to Arkansas than to most of the other Southern states, for in Arkansas, a new state, planters did buy a large proportion of their land and slaves at the relatively high prices of the 1850's.

With the contention of Lewis C. Gray that slavery was far from a "decrepit institution" the author wholly agrees, and enough evidence has already been presented concerning the vitality of Arkansas slavery to make further proof unnecessary.

Since all authorities agree that slavery was profitable under favorable conditions, it is hardly necessary to demonstrate that such was the case in southern and eastern Arkansas, for certainly most of that region was in what Phillips called the "most advantageous parts of the cotton . . . districts." The experiences of one southeastern Arkansas planter will be related, though, to show that cotton-planting with slave labor could be not only moderately profitable, but phenomenally so. That planter was

[12] This table, adapted from Gray, *History of Agriculture in the Southern United States*, II, 643, shows average value per acre of farm land and buildings in some of the Southern states:

	1850	1860		1850	1860
Alabama	$ 5.30	$ 9.20	North Carolina	$ 3.23	$ 6.03
Arkansas	5.88	9.57	South Carolina	5.08	8.62
Georgia	4.20	5.89	Tennessee	5.15	13.13
Louisiana	15.20	22.04	Texas	1.44	3.48
Mississippi	5.22	12.04	Virginia	8.27	11.95

James Sheppard of Jefferson County, to whom frequent reference has been made previously.

In order to trace Sheppard's planting career in Arkansas clearly, it is necessary to go back some years prior to his moving to Arkansas.[13] Sheppard was the son of Joseph M. Sheppard, a Virginia doctor who practiced in Richmond and vicinity, but who as time went on devoted most of his attention to farming and speculating in railroad stocks and bonds. In the early 1830's Dr. Sheppard purchased White Sulphur Springs, a large cotton plantation in Copiah County in southwestern Mississippi, which he operated through an overseer for several years. James Sheppard had been born in 1816; after completing his studies at the College of William and Mary in 1836, he worked with his father in business and farming in Virginia until the fall of 1839, when he went to Mississippi to assume management of the Copiah County plantation. He had no financial share in the enterprise until 1847, meanwhile merely working for his father for all expenses and a salary of $800 per year.

James Sheppard maintained close social connections with Virginia, usually spending several months there during the summer and fall "fever season," and on September 30, 1847, he was married to Kate Empie, daughter of Dr. Adam Empie, a former president of the college of William and Mary. The day before the wedding Dr. Sheppard sold the Mississippi plantation to James and his younger brother John William. The valuation placed on the plantation was $36,070, divided as follows: a hundred slaves at $300 each (Dr. Sheppard wrote "times depressed"); twenty mules, $800; three wagons, $195; thirty ploughs, $75.00; and the 1,204 acres of land, $5,000. Dr. Sheppard gave James and John William $3,035 of the valuation each as legacies, and they executed bonds of $15,000 each at 6 per cent interest for the remainder.

[13] Information concerning James Sheppard was drawn largely from the James Sheppard Papers. Although the papers are extensive enough to provide a general knowledge of his planting career, they are not complete and detailed enough to make possible a full financial analysis for a single year, as has been done for plantations in other states. Nor is there sufficient information about any other Arkansas plantation to make this possible. Hundreds of papers were consulted in assembling the information, therefore individual citations will not be made.

James returned to Mississippi with his bride that fall and resumed management of the plantation under an agreement with his brother by which he received all living and personal expenses and a small salary, with all profits to be applied on payment of the bonds. Mrs. Sheppard found the Mississippi climate distasteful and returned to Virginia in the summer of 1848 to live with James's family, remaining there thenceforth except for occasional winters in Mississippi (and later Arkansas). James continued to journey regularly between the upper and lower South. In the fall of 1850 John William joined James in Mississippi, but he became ill and died there on June 14, 1851.

On the first of the year prior to the death of John William, the balance due Dr. Sheppard on each of the bonds was $7,616.69, showing that about $5,000 plus interest per year had been applied to the debt. By will of John William, a life interest in his half of the plantation went to Dr. Sheppard and his wife, and upon their deaths to James. On September 5, 1851, James paid his father the entire amount due on his bond, thus becoming clear owner of one-half of the plantation and slaves. Where he got the more than $7,000 is not clear from his records, but he must have been maintaining a surplus of cash or of credits with his New Orleans factors, for there is no evidence of other income, except perhaps a small amount from railroad stocks. In any event, starting with only slightly more than $3,000 in capital in the form of the legacy from his father, in four years of cotton-planting James Sheppard had become half-owner of a large plantation and eighty-two slaves (reduced to that number from the one hundred of four years before).

Prior to John William's death, plans had been made to purchase another and more fertile plantation in Jefferson County, Arkansas, and to move the slaves there. In the late fall of 1851 James Sheppard bought Waterford Plantation, 1,017 acres on an island in the Arkansas River a few miles from Pine Bluff, from L. R. Marshall of Natchez, Mississippi. Shortly thereafter he moved the slaves from Mississippi and began cultivation of the land. The amount paid for Waterford is not ascertainable from Sheppard's records, but since no slaves went with the land, $20,000 probably would be a liberal estimate. It was contemplated at first that Waterford would be operated as a joint enterprise of James Sheppard and his father, but in the summer of 1852 James took complete ownership and control of the plantation by repaying his father half of the amount of the down payment and agreeing to give him half of the proceeds of the 1852 crop. Dr. Sheppard retained ownership of half of the slaves, with James paying him hire at the rate of $550 per year, probably about a fifth of their actual hire value. The two continued to own the Mississippi plantation; it was rented during some years and lay idle during others. In the late 1850's Sheppard received offers ranging from $6,000 to $12,000 for it, but retained possession.

The precise annual profits from Waterford, which was largely devoted to cotton-growing, cannot be determined from the records, but they were substantial, for by January, 1859, James Sheppard had paid off the mortgage and saved a large amount of cash. He also had purchased quantities of stocks and bonds, and, freed of the mortgage, he bought more. In a single transaction in 1859 he bought $11,019.66 worth of bonds of the Virginia and Tennessee, O. & A., and R. & Y. R. railroads, and on the first of the next year he collected $1,002.79 in interest and dividends on these and on other stocks and bonds of the Central, Richmond, and Petersburg Railroad, the Midlothian Coal Mining Company, and the Albemarle Insurance Company.

By this time the number of slaves at Waterford had been reduced to sixty-four; it may be gathered from the records that Sheppard sold those in excess of the needs of the plantation deliberately. Although he lost some by death, he probably sold as many as the net decline of about twenty, for there would have been a substantial increase by reproduction in the decade. These slaves added to the general income. Despite the decline in number of slaves, the total valuation of Waterford increased greatly during the decade. As late as 1856 the valuation for tax purposes was $38,040, but in 1860 it was $65,560. Much of this increase was due to increased valuation of the slaves, assessed in 1860 at $700 each as compared to about $400 each in 1856. But even the $700 valuation was conservative for 1860, as was pointed out earlier in the discussion of slave values at that time. The value of the land, to which 160 acres had been added by 1860, increased from ten to sixteen dollars per acre from 1856 to 1860.

On January 25, 1860, James Sheppard expanded his planting operations greatly by purchasing nearby Blenheim Plantation from James B. and Mary Payne and Elizabeth H. Robinson for $116,-140. He paid $30,000 in cash and agreed to pay the remainder in five annual instalments of $17,228. Blenheim was exceptionally fertile and in a high state of cultivation, with its 620 acres valued at $60.00 each, more than six times the average value of all Arkansas farm land. The forty-six slaves were valued at $1,250 each. Also included in the purchase were all corn, horses, mules, hogs, cattle, oxen, fodder, farming equipment, tools, gin-stands, household and kitchen furniture, wagons, and meat on the plantation. The deed transferring the property gives no information concerning the buildings on Blenheim.

Thus on the eve of the Civil War James Sheppard had, conservatively, a net worth of $90,299.66, which included the value of Waterford Plantation and half of its slaves, half the value of the Mississippi plantation (at $10.00 per acre), the down payment on Blenheim Plantation, and the value of the stocks and bonds of which there is definite record. This was by no means the full extent of his worth a short time later, however; before the Civil War disrupted his planting he paid two of the $17,288 instalments on Blemhein,[14] and in 1863 the Union Army stripped Waterford and Blenheim of large quantities of cotton, hay, potatoes, mules, hogs, sheep, and wagons, for which his heirs later filed a claim for $73,697 with the Southern Claims Commission.[15] Even if half of the latter amount is discounted, Sheppard's net worth by 1863 was at least $161,723.66.

This, then, is the record of how one Arkansas cotton planter prospered greatly with the use of slave labor. Sheppard increased his 1847 capital of $3,000 more than fifty-fold until it became

[14] *Sheppard v. Thomas*, 26 Ark. 617.
[15] United States Congress, House of Representatives, *Ninth General Report of the Commissioners of Claims,* House Miscellaneous Document No. 10, 46th Congress, 2nd Session (Washington, 1879), p. 33; *Consolidated Index of Claims Reported by the Commissioners of Claims to the House of Representatives from 1871 to 1880* (Washington, 1892), p. 212.

$161,723 fifteen years later, during the same period living well, maintaining his wife and family separately most of the time, and making many expensive trips to Virginia. There is no doubt that the initial use of his father's capital and the use of his father's slaves at a low rate of hire aided him in his economic progress, but the value of these concessions was negligible in comparison with the total capital appreciation. It is also evident that part of the capital appreciation was due to a rising price level, but the fact remains that James Sheppard owned practically nothing in 1847, but was a wealthy man by any standard in 1863.[16]

Approximately 9 per cent of the slaveowners in Arkansas in 1860 (1,070 of 11,481) were in the planter class of which Sheppard was a member.[17] Their slaveholdings ranged in size from

[16] Sheppard's later career, although anticlimatic and of no real relevance here, is interesting and no doubt much like that of others of the time. As noted above, most of his movable property was confiscated by the Union Army in 1863, and his slaves probably were freed simultaneously. At about the same time Sheppard fled to Texas and attempted unsuccessfully to carry on planting operations on a small scale there. In 1864 he returned to Jefferson County, took the oath of allegiance to the United States provided for in President Lincoln's Amnesty Proclamation of Dec. 8, 1863, and again tried to farm, but with little success due to a lack of labor. He attempted to fill this need in 1866 by hiring sixty-one "coloured freedmen" in Otsego County, New York, and taking them to Waterford and Blenheim. The hiring arrangements bore remarkable resemblance to practices followed in hiring slaves before the war, with the obvious exception that the pay went to the Negroes. The laborers received pay ranging from six to fifteen dollars per month, housing, firewood, medical care, one peck of meal and four pounds of meat per week, and "such vegetables as could be raised on the place." There are no records of the success of the plantations with free labor, but it must not have been great, for in 1866 and 1867 Sheppard attempted unsuccessfully to sell them at prices considerably less than their prewar value. Since he had been unable to continue the payments on Blenheim, Sheppard became involved in litigation over the unpaid balance. In September, 1865, his unpaid notes were assigned by the previous owners of Blenheim to Samuel B. Thomas, who promptly sued Sheppard for the amount, $66,791.54, in Jefferson County Circuit Court. Thomas received a judgment against Sheppard for the full amount, but upon appeal to the Arkansas Supreme Court, the judgment was set aside in 1871 and Sheppard thus received clear possession of Blenheim. Sheppard's attorneys pointed out that he had already paid more than the value of the land, and asserted that he should not be held responsible for the value of the slaves, since they had proved not to be "slaves for life," as guaranteed in the purchase agreement. The Supreme Court did not reverse the lower court decision on those grounds, however, but because the deed given by the sellers to Sheppard did not provide for assignment of the notes to anyone else.

But before the favorable Supreme Court decision was rendered, James Sheppard had died (1870), leaving his family three large plantations of greatly reduced value and a large claim against the United States government, which in 1879 was disallowed. Sheppard Papers, 1863-1877, *passim; Sheppard* v. *Thomas,* 26 Ark. 617; U. S. Cong., H. of R., *Ninth General Report of the Commissioners of Claims,* p. 33.

[17] See p. 92 n. above.

twenty-five to more than five hundred, so Sheppard with his hundred-odd slaves ranked only as an "upper middle-class" planter. Since slavery was so profitable for him, it is highly probable that it was also profitable for the majority of his class, most of whom operated under much the same conditions as he.

But what of the thousands of slaveowners in Arkansas who did not operate on so grand a scale as the planters? First, let us consider the 5,806 owners who held no more than four slaves each in 1860. This group, comprising approximately 51 per cent of all owners, held a total of 12,131 slaves, only 11 per cent of those in the state. It is the author's belief that most of these owners were not greatly concerned with whether or not their slaves produced a measurable net profit each year; in fact, most of their slaves worked at tasks from which, by their very nature, no profit was expected. These slaves were the cooks, maids, houseboys, gardeners, stableboys, nurses, and extra hands on small farms, or filled numerous other positions which contributed to the comfort or pleasure of their masters. But even if the small owners were concerned with the profitableness of slave labor, the fact that their number increased from 3,334 in 1850 to 5,806 in 1860 is certainly an indication that they did not consider the ownership of slaves economically burdensome.[18]

Forty per cent of the slaveowners in Arkansas in 1860 (about 4,600) lay in the category between the small owners just referred to and the planters. This middle group, most of whom were farmers, owned 43 per cent of the slaves, about 48,000.[19] They did not have the planters' advantages of large-scale production, and yet they were doubtless more concerned with the profitableness of slavery than were the small owners. Was slavery also profitable for them? One of the strongest indications that it was lies in the great rise in agricultural wealth in Arkansas during the pre-Civil War period. Of course this also applies to the small owners and the planters. The table below, compiled from the federal censuses, demonstrates the increase in wealth:

[18] *Census of 1860 (Agriculture)*, pp. 224, 248.
[19] *Ibid.*, p. 224.

	1850	1860
Number of farms	17,758	39,004
Acreage in farms	2,598,214	9,573,706
Average acreage per farm	146	245
Cash value of farms	$15,265,245	$91,649,773
Average value of farms	$893	$2,349
Number of slaveholders	5,999	11,481
Number of slaves	47,100	111,115
Average number of slaves per owner	7.8	9.6[20]

It may be seen that in every respect the agricultural wealth of Arkansas increased during the decade: the number of farms more than doubled, the average size of farms increased more than 60 per cent, the cash value of farms multiplied more than fivefold, and the average value of farms increased more than two and one-half times. The number of slaveholders more than doubled, as did the number of slaves, and with the gain in slaves greater percentage-wise than the gain in owners, the number of slaves per owner increased substantially. It is recognized that some of the census figures apply to both slaveowners and nonslaveowners, but it is hardly likely that the slaveowning farmers and planters were affected by the general increase in wealth to a lesser degree than the nonslaveowning. In fact, the evidence points to the conclusion that the slaveowners showed a greater gain in wealth than the nonslaveowners. An examination by counties of the increase in cash value of farms between 1850 and 1860 shows that in the six counties with more slaves than whites (Chicot, Union, Phillips, Desha, Arkansas, and Lafayette), the combined cash value of farms multiplied more than sixfold, from $4,426,961 to $26,654,644. A similar examination of figures for six northwestern counties with small numbers of slaves (Washington, Benton, Van Buren, Izard, Scott, and Pope) reveals only a fourfold increase, from $1,549,908 to $6,232,245. The six predominantly slave counties accounted collectively for almost 30 per cent of the farm valuation of the state in 1860, and one of them—Phillips— for almost 10 per cent of the state total.

But not only the counties with the highest concentrations of slaves showed greater gains in farm wealth than the counties with small holdings; six counties which might be considered typical.

[20] *Census of 1850*, p. 554; *Census of 1860 (Agriculture)*, pp. 6, 222.

since their population was approximately one-fourth slave, the same as the state as a whole (Clark, Jackson, St. Francis, Bradley, and Poinsett), showed a collective gain in farm values from $1,616,563 in 1850 to $12,174,863 in 1860, an increase of more than seven times as compared to the fourfold gain in the counties with small numbers of slaves.[21]   Although these figures do not prove positively that slavery in Arkansas was profitable in its ultimate stage of development, they do, as Thomas Govan wrote, "indicate this conclusion strongly enough to place the burden of proof upon those who deny that planters were making profits."[22]

One final indication of the profitableness of slavery in Arkansas was that prices of slaves in the state were consistently among the highest in the South.[23]   Certainly planters and farmers would not have continued to buy slaves at high prices if they had not already made money, or if they did not have good reason to expect to make money with slave labor in the future.

[21] *Census of 1850*, p. 554; *Census of 1860 (Agriculture)*, p. 6; *Census of 1860 (Population)*, p. 18.
[22] Govan, "Was Plantation Slavery Profitable?," p. 519.
[23] See p. 78 above.

VIII

Down in the Quarters

FOOD, CLOTHING, AND HOUSING, the basic necessities of slave life, were provided entirely by the masters. Slaves worked at raising food, making clothing, and building houses, of course, but the initiative was always that of the master, for the slave had no responsibility for himself in any manner.

Unlike some states, Arkansas had no laws regulating the types and quantities of food for slaves.[1] The records indicate, however, that the food of most of the slaves was reasonably adequate by standards of the day and section, if somewhat unvaried at times. Since the ability of a slave to work well was in large measure dependent upon how well he was fed, good judgment on the part of the profit-seeking owner dictated that he provide his slaves with nourishing food in adequate quantities. The proportions of food raised on the home farms or plantations and that purchased elsewhere varied considerably by size, type, and geographical location of the farms. The farms of the northern and western sections of the state, along with the smaller farms in the cotton-raising sections of the southeast, probably were more nearly self-sufficient than the great plantations of the lowlands. Food for town slaves, unless the master also owned farms, was usually purchased locally.

The food of the slaves varied considerably with the seasons in that day of relatively primitive methods of preservation and distribution. The year-round staples were meat, cornmeal, and molasses, supplemented at times by products of the gardens, fields,

[1] Louisiana, North Carolina, Georgia, and South Carolina had laws of varying thoroughness dealing with food, clothing, and shelter of slaves. Laws of other slave states made no specific requirements. William Goodell, *The American Slave Code* . . . (New York, 1853), pp. 134-149.

and orchards of the plantation, and by "store-bought" groceries. The meat in most cases was pork, during the greater part of the year in the form of bacon, or, as it is often still called in the South, "sidemeat."[2]   During brief periods in the winter most plantations had plentiful supplies of fresh pork—especially the portions which could not be preserved—in the few days before the meat was cured to last throughout the year.   Lack of refrigeration made hog-killing necessarily a winter activity.   John Brown of Princeton customarily killed hogs in December or January, sometimes animals penned near his home, but also those allowed to run wild in the woods—perhaps the Arkansas razorbacks of wide notoriety. In January, 1853, Brown wrote in his diary: "William and myself are hunting wild hogs in the bottom.   I have a good deal of pork running wild but it is difficult to get, but the price of green pork . . . makes us industrious.   We occasionally get a hog."[3]   And on subsequent days: "At home, occasionally hog hunting."[4]   "We are getting some meat from the woods.   I give Mr. Smirl one third of all he can kill of my wild hogs."[5]

Supplies of home-produced pork often proved inadequate, forcing slaveowners to purchase additional quantities from other sources.   James S. Conway, first governor of the state of Arkansas, wrote the overseer of his Lafayette County plantation that "I can send you from here [Conway's Magnet Cove plantation, Hot Spring County], hogs to make 35,000 pounds of pork if the farm can supply the ballance," but gave instructions to buy "some pickeled pork" if necessary.[6]   The small slaveowner was likely to buy pork from merchants in a nearby town, such as Henry and Cunningham of Van Buren, who offered "mess pork" for sale in 1849.[7]   Owners of larger numbers of slaves also purchased locally at times, but more often bought pork in quantity annually through

[2] In a letter "The Hog Question" published in the *True Democrat,* Sept. 1, 1857, a planter signing himself "Redfork" emphasized that plantation slaves should be furnished an adequate supply of "old bacon or mess pork."
[3] Diary of John Brown, Jan. 15, 1853.
[4] *Ibid.,* Jan. 19, 1853.
[5] *Ibid.,* Jan. 29, 1853.
[6] James S. Conway to E. M. Low, Aug. 29, 1839, Stephenson Papers. James Sheppard's overseers often had difficulty in raising hogs.   One reported, "I lost nearly all my hogs."   I. M. Key to James Sheppard, Aug. 12, 1860. Another: "Something continues to ketch young pigs."   D. T. Weeks to James Sheppard, March 12, 1858.   Both letters in Sheppard papers.
[7] *Arkansas Intelligencer,* Oct. 20, 1849.

the New Orleans or Memphis commission houses which also handled the sale of their cotton.[8] The uncertainty of river transportation because of both low and high water stages sometimes made getting supplies from the cities difficult, or even impossible, however. Several times during the years immediately before the Civil War John Brown had this difficulty. In March of 1847 he complained that "meat and grease is so scarce that it causes us to have to buy soap" and that "everything that we live on is at higher rates than usual and many hard to get," partially because "the river [the Ouachita] is down and much difficulty about navigation."[9] During 1860 Brown was unable to get any supplies from New Orleans. He wrote, "I have been almost eaten out by my negroes this year which came hard on me, doubly so because I was disappointed in getting my supplies last spring from N. Orleans."[10]

Pork bought through commission merchants usually came packed in barrels. An inventory of the supplies at Bellevue Plantation, Chicot County, in July, 1860, showed forty-five barrels of pork valued at $18.00 a barrel. A similar inventory at Yellow Bayou Plantation nearby showed twenty-eight barrels of pork valued at $504, also $18.00 a barrel.[11] Knowing that 211 slaves lived on Bellevue and Yellow Bayou, and that seventy-three barrels of pork would have been expected to last until the next year's supplies were received seven or eight months later, it may be estimated that each slave received, on an average, about two and one-half pounds of cured pork per week.[12] Pork prices rose gradually in the years before the Civil War. In 1836 Jared Martin of

[8] See pp. 63-64 for a list of New Orleans merchants with whom James Sheppard of Waterford Plantation dealt. John Brown of Princeton and Camden did business with these New Orleans firms: Cherry, Henderson and Co., C. W. Phelps and Co., Loyd and Freirson, and Moses Greenwood and Co.
[9] Diary of John Brown, March 27, 28, 1857.
[10] *Ibid.*, Nov. 15, 1860.
[11] Appraisal of Craig Estate.
[12] These figures provide the only opportunity encountered by the author for estimating the amount of the weekly pork ration on an Arkansas plantation. The amount of the ration was arrived at by multiplying the number of barrels by two hundred (the estimated weight of each) and dividing by the number of slaves. The two and one-half pounds seems a bit low in comparison with estimates given by writers on slavery in other states—three to five pounds— but fifty-one, or about one-fourth of the Craig slaves, were below the age of ten and would not be expected to eat an average share. This also does not take into account home-raised hogs, seventy-five on the two plantations, nor the fact that house-servants usually ate food from the owner's kitchen rather than that provided for the slaves.

Little Rock quoted the price of pork in Arkansas at from four to five cents per pound;[13] John Brown wrote in 1853 that it was selling at a little more than six cents;[14] and the pork on the Craig plantations in 1860 was worth about nine cents a pound.[15]

Beef was given to slaves much less frequently than pork and then usually as a special treat which had to be eaten soon, since no method of preservation was used. One of James Sheppard's overseers wrote of giving the slaves a beef on a holiday,[16] and John Brown mentioned the practice several times in his diary.[17] Scott Bond, a former slave who in post-Civil War days achieved a considerable measure of prosperity in St. Francis County in eastern Arkansas, told of the use of a unique bit of slang concerning hogs and cattle. "Negroes used to steal something to eat sometimes, and if it was a hog, he would call it 'Joe High.' And if it was a beef, he would call it 'Ben Low.' "[18]

The wild game which abounded in Arkansas was an additional source of meat for many slaves, as well as for their masters. Of life on a small farm in southwestern Arkansas in the late 1830's, Mrs. Nancy Cooper Guinn later wrote, ". . . bears were often killed in the bottom around us. Game was plentiful, fish, ducks, geese, squirrel, rabbits, turkey, quail and bear meat, in fact, everything of the kind we enjoyed in abundance."[19] There were two slaves, Simon and Louise, on the Cooper farm. In the 1850's one plantation in eastern Arkansas had a white employee whose sole duty was hunting wild game to be used in feeding the slaves. A secondary purpose was to protect the growing crops from the depredations of the animals—deer, turkey, bear, raccoons, opossums, and other small game.

Slade['s] . . . duty . . . was to hunt all night. He slept in the day time. He could not bring in all the game he would kill, hence the hands on our place would divide themselves into squads and take time about hunting with Slade at night until he had killed a load of coons, and they would then carry them home and go

[13] Jared Martin to John Martin, Jan. 2, 1836, Martin Papers.
[14] Diary of John Brown, Jan. 15, 1853.
[15] Appraisal of Craig Estate.
[16] Robert W. Miller to James Sheppard, June 16, 1859, Sheppard Papers.
[17] Diary of John Brown, Dec. 25, June 18, 1853.
[18] Scott Bond, *Life of Scott Bond* (Little Rock, 1917), p. 199.
[19] Mrs. Nancy Cooper Guinn, "Rural Arkansas in the '20's," in *Arkansas Pioneers*, I (Sept., 1912), 12.

to sleep, leaving Slade to make the rest of the night alone. . . . Such was the abundance of wild life in those days that whole families could subsist on game if they desired.[20]

Wild game was also sold commercially in the towns, frequently at a price higher than pork. During one winter when pork for his slaves was difficult to obtain, John Brown bought about a hundred pounds of bear meat in the town of Princeton, paying eight or nine cents a pound for it at a time when the price of pork was slightly more than six cents a pound.[21]

Poultry was not raised in quantity in Arkansas for food for slaves, or at least no production is listed in the *Census of Agriculture* for 1860. Most farms and plantations did have some chickens, ducks, and turkeys, however, and it is probable that occasionally the slaves ate some of them. Among the simple duties assigned to the small slave children was that of tending the poultry, keeping the hogs out of the rail pens and the fowls in.[22] Some planters living along the rivers supplemented the meat diet of their slaves with fish. White River, then as now, was one of the better fishing streams. Reminiscing many years later of his youth in Jackson County along the river, Robert Connell wrote:

When we boys were old enough our parents allowed us to sell the big fish to anyone who came along; but most of them went to slave owners, who would want to give their niggers a special feed. One time I took a canoe load across the water, met the sons of a slave owner and some of his niggers in a boat, who bought all of my fish.[23]

Occasionally even turtles furnished Arkansas slaves with a welcome change from the standard items of diet. Scott Bond remembered that slaves on the plantation on which he lived caught a lake turtle so big that a mule was required to pull it out of the water; it weighed 148 pounds after the shell was removed.[24]

Corn meal, usually eaten in the form of cornpone or mush, was, like pork, produced in as large quantities as possible on the home plantations. According to the United States census, more than 17,000,000 bushels of corn were produced in the state during the

[20] Bond, *Life of Scott Bond*, p. 33.
[21] Diary of John Brown, Jan. 17, 1853.
[22] Bond, *Life of Scott Bond*, p. 259.
[23] Robert Connell, Sr., *Arkansas* (New York, 1947), p. 17.
[24] Bond, *Life of Scott Bond*, p. 33.

year 1860, in amounts ranging from 88,295 to 663,540 bushels per county.[25] Since a large portion of that amount was used in feeding livestock, it is impossible to estimate the degree of self-sufficiency of the state in this respect. But in speculating on the possible self-sufficiency of the important slave counties of the state, it is worthy of note that of the four principal corn-producing counties, two—Phillips and Hempstead—were also among the leading slave counties.[26] The other two major corn-producing counties, Washington and Independence, were both in the northern part of the state, and contained relatively few slaves—1,493 and 1,337 respectively.[27] Large planters operated their own water- or animal-powered grist mills, producing meal for their own use, and at times grinding corn "on shares" for small farmers of the vicinity.[28] No less than 254 men in the state reported their occupation as miller in 1860,[29] so it is evident that there was no shortage of mills. But the numerous notations of purchase of cornmeal at local stores and through commission merchants which are found in plantation records indicate that the ideal of self-sufficiency was rarely reached. Meal was purchased in large quantities by the barrel and in smaller quantities by the bushel, with the price, depending upon transportation conditions, the level of the economy, and other factors, ranging from $1.00 to $2.00 a bushel.[30]

Wheat was grown in Arkansas long before statehood days,[31] and in substantial quantities during the period in which slavery was important,[32] but it is unlikely that slaves ate wheat bread to any great extent. The high prices of wheat flour as compared to corn meal prevented the widespread use of wheat bread for slaves,[33] as well as for many of the white people of the period. The moderately prosperous or well-to-do planter kept a barrel of

[25] *Census of 1860 (Agriculture)*, p. 7.
[26] *Ibid.*   [27] *Ibid.*, p. 224.
[28] *Arkansas Intelligencer*, Oct. 7, 1848.
[29] *Census of 1860 (Population)*, p. 21.
[30] Diary of John Brown, Jan. 30, Feb. 7, 1855; statement, Jason Margett to James Sheppard, June 29, 1855, Sheppard Papers.
[31] See pp. 11, 19-20 above.
[32] Production was 199,639 bushels in 1850 and 957,601 bushels in 1860. *Census of 1850*, p. 555; *Census of 1860 (Agriculture)*, p. 7.
[33] According to the periodical New Orleans "Prices Current," many of which are in the Sheppard Papers, the price of flour in New Orleans ranged from about $6.00 to $9.00 per barrel during the 1850's. Prices were somewhat higher inland.

flour available most of the time, but "light bread" was considered a delicacy to be used on special occasions, such as the big "railroad barbecue" at Camden in the summer of 1854, for which John Brown and his wife furnished "1 doz. apple pies and corn and light bread."[34]

Molasses, last of the three "M's" of slave food, was more than merely a cheap substitute for much more expensive sugar. Poured over cornpone, it added flavor to the meal, and, in addition, provided minerals and other necessary nutritional substances. Of the latter the slave was completely unaware, as in most instances, no doubt, was his master. Arkansas produced more sorghum molasses than any other slave state of the lower South,[35] but the important slave counties produced very little of it, or of the widely used sugar-house molasses, which was usually imported into the state along with other bulk purchases of supplies.[36] Some sorghum molasses was shipped from the producing counties of the mountains, such as Washington, Benton, and Carroll, to the more important slave counties. The price of molasses was relatively low, even in 1860, when prices reached their pre-Civil War peak —$15.00 a barrel, or approximately thirty-five cents a gallon.[37]

A meal in which meat, meal, and molasses were among the main components was described by Henry M. Stanley:

> The breakfast at seven, the dinner at noon, and the supper at six, consisted of pretty much the same kind of dishes, except that there was good coffee at the first meal. . . .The rest mainly consisted of boiled, or fried, pork and beans, and corn scones. The pork had an excess of fat over lean, and was followed by a plate full of mush and molasses. . . .[38]

Although this was in the master's home the food differed little from that of the slaves.

As we have seen in an earlier chapter,[39] many food crops were

[34] Diary of John Brown, July 6, 1854.
[35] 115,604 gallons in 1860, while Mississippi produced only 1,427 gallons, Alabama 55,563 gallons, and Louisiana none. *Census of 1860 (Agriculture)*, pp. 5, 9, 69, 87.
[36] Most of the sugar-house molasses, a by-product of sugar manufacturing, came from Louisiana, which produced 13,439,772 gallons in 1860. *Census of 1860 (Agriculture)*, p. 69.
[37] Appraisal of Craig Estate.
[38] Stanley, *Autobiography*, p. 147.
[39] See pp. 98-99 above.

produced in Arkansas in quantities adequate for use as food for slaves. Some of them, such as sweet potatoes, beans, peas, and turnips, were grown so universally that they might almost be considered staples along with meat, meal, and molasses. In addition, they could also be stored successfully during the winter. Other vegetables and fruits, however, were largely eaten only when they matured in the spring, summer, and fall growing seasons, although some, such as apples and peaches, could be dried for winter use. Slaves on the smaller farms ate vegetables more often than did those living on the large, cash-crop producing establishments. Typical of the smaller slave-operated farms was that of the Chesters in South Arkansas, where the dozen slaves were "fed . . . from the same vegetable garden and the same smokehouse and storeroom that supplied the family table."[40] Slaves in Chicot and a few other southeastern counties of the state ate some rice along with other foods furnished them, but only Chicot produced rice in significant quantities—nine thousand pounds in 1860.[41]

This catalogue of foods eaten by Arkansas slaves would not be complete without brief mention of the wild fruits, berries, and nuts which the Arkansas fields and forests produced in abundance. Use of these was so taken for granted that few records of them have survived,[42] but every rural Arkansan, then as now, has eaten and enjoyed hickory nuts, black walnuts, chestnuts, chinquapins, plums, cherries, persimmons, red haws, black haws, "Maypops," possum-grapes, muscadines, scuppernongs, crabapples, dewberries, pecans, blackberries, and wild strawberries. Living close to the soil, as most of them did, there is no doubt that many an Arkansas slave enjoyed an informal dessert during workdays, picked a hatful of berries to take home in the evening, and cracked nuts around a winter fire, as rural Arkansans, black and white, do to this day.

Little is known definitely of methods of preparation and serving of the food of Arkansas slaves, but it is reasonable to

[40] Chester, *Pioneer Days in Arkansas,* p. 39. Although the process of canning food was known in the United States from early in the nineteenth century, no evidence of its use in Arkansas was found.

[41] *Census of 1860 (Agriculture),* p. 7.

[42] One which has is the reminiscence of Mrs. Nancy Guinn, "Rural Arkansas in the '20's," previously cited. Mrs. Guinn told of the wealth of wild fruits and nuts in the Red River region of southwestern Arkansas.

suppose that the practices which prevailed in the older slave states, from which most Arkansas slaveowners came, were followed. Sydnor, the authority on slavery in Mississippi, described practices there in this manner:

No general rule was followed in preparing the meals of the slaves. On small plantations or farms, one cook served for the master and the slaves. . . .This was impracticable when the slaves were numerous. The planter then had each Negro family prepare its own food, or else a common kitchen was built and one slave set apart to cook for all the rest.

A number of those who struggled with problems of plantation management found it advantageous to use a combination of the two systems just mentioned. On one estate each family was a unit in cooking and eating, but there was a common kitchen for the single slaves. On another, dinner was prepared at the quarters and brought to the field hands at noon, but families separately prepared their breakfasts and suppers.[43]

Arkansas slaves wore every imaginable type of clothing. Various sources reveal slaves wearing everything from the formal black cloth frock coat, black cassimere pants, linen bosom shirt and black hat of Henry, a mulatto who ran away from his master at Woodlawn, Ouachita County, in 1850,[44] to the "common plantation clothes" in which Lewis Ball, also a mulatto slave, took unannounced leave in 1858 from Nathan Ross's plantation in Chicot County.[45] Between those two extremes lay the various costumes of Arkansas slaves.

The best sources of information concerning the clothing of Arkansas slaves are lists of purchases by planters, advertisements of stores found in the newspapers, and notices of runaway slaves —also in the newspapers—which practically always gave detailed descriptions of the slave's clothing. The first two sources provide little specific information about the clothing of individual slaves, while the latter does not necessarily give a correct picture of typical clothing, for the slave who ran away, especially if he had planned the escape in advance, was likely to provide himself, by theft or otherwise, with unusual quantities or varieties of

[43] Sydnor, *Slavery in Mississippi*, pp. 36-37.
[44] *Gazette and Democrat*, Dec. 13, 1850.
[45] *True Democrat*, July 14, 1858.

clothing. It is reasonably certain, however, that runaways, at one time or another, wore every sort of clothing known to Arkansas slaves.

Appearing frequently on lists of purchases by planters and in the newspaper advertisements was osnaburg, a coarse cotton cloth used primarily for making slave clothing. Hundreds of yards per year were necessary to keep the slaves on a typical plantation supplied. In February of 1858 James Sheppard of Waterford Plantation bought 255 yards of osnaburg from the firm of Thomson and Dupuy in Pine Bluff for thirteen and one-half cents a yard.[46] Only three months later one of his factors in New Orleans, Byrne, Vance and Company, purchased and forwarded to him, along with other supplies, an additional quantity of 652½ yards, this at a somewhat cheaper price—ten cents per yard— since no middleman's profit was involved.[47] The total of more than nine hundred yards which Sheppard bought that spring would have provided an average of about fifteen yards for each of his sixty-one slaves, an adequate amount for making several changes of clothing each, whether shirts, pants, dresses, or the less elaborate clothing of the small children.

While osnaburg was by far the most common type of cloth used in making slave clothing, other types were available. The firm of Martin & Morton in Helena advertised kerseys and lindseys in 1850, identifying them as "Negro goods."[48] "Heavy Negro shirting" could be purchased from Ficklin and Rapley in Little Rock in 1834.[49] James Sheppard bought plaid lindsey from Thomson and Dupuy in Pine Bluff, but the small size of the purchase—only eight yards—indicates that the cloth was to be used by the overseer's family rather than for the slaves.[50] The 1860 inventory of supplies at Bellevue and Yellow Bayou plantations in Chicot County included large quantities of various kinds of cloth; 1,654 yards of jeans, 956 yards of lindsey, and 2,550

[46] Invoice of Supplies, Mr. James Sheppard, bought of Thomson and Dupuy, Pine Bluff, Arkansas, Feb. 17, 1858, Sheppard Papers.
[47] Invoice of supplies purchased by Byrne, Vance and Co. for a/c James Sheppard, May 26, 1858, Sheppard Papers.
[48] *Southern Shield*, Oct. 12, 1850.
[49] *Arkansas Gazette*, Dec. 23, 1834.
[50] Invoice of Supplies, March 24, 1858, Sheppard Papers.

yards of "Lowells."[51]   In advertisements of runaway slaves the following additional types of cloth have been noted: calico,[52] cottonade,[53] "hard times,"[54] wool,[55] velvet,[56] jeans,[57] linen,[58] cassinet,[59] domestic cotton,[60] and cassimere.[61]   Clothing made from several of these—velvet, linen, cassinet, and cassimere—probably had been handed down from masters to slaves.   The others, however, were cheap and considered suitable for making slave clothing.

In addition to the cloth purchased there was the indeterminable amount of homespuns, principally woolen and cotton, produced in the state, much of it on the farms and plantations by slave labor. Some cotton thread was produced by mills in Arkansas, but it would be impossible to determine how widely this was used for making slave clothing.   Cotton mills are known to have operated at Royston, on the Little Missouri River in southwestern Arkansas,[62] and at Pittsburg on the Arkansas River.   The Pittsburg mill, which had five hundred spindles, produced spun cotton which compared "favorably with that . . . imported."[63]   There were even more ambitious enterprises, such as the thousand-spindle mill which John B. Ogden proposed to open at Van Buren in 1848,[64] but none of them survived long.   As late as 1860, however, the census lists 86 persons as spinners and 120 as weavers within the state.[65]   While those two hundred-odd persons would hardly have constituted a thriving textile industry, no doubt they contributed in part to providing clothing for the slaves.

Most slave clothing was made at home.   The mistress of the house on a small plantation might sew the clothes herself, assisted by a house servant if there were one.   On a larger establishment,

[51] Inventory of Craig Estate.   [52] *Southern Shield,* Oct. 16, 1852.
[53] *Arkansas State Democrat,* June 1, 1849.
[54] *Ibid.,* June 25, 1850.   [55] *Arkansas Gazette,* April 12, 1836.
[56] *Ibid.,* Sept. 8, 1821.   [57] *Batesville News,* March 7, 1839.
[58] *Arkansas Gazette,* Oct. 24, 1832.   [59] *Ibid.,* June 17, 1829.
[60] *Ibid.,* May 17, 1836.
[61] *Gazette and Democrat,* May 31, 1850.
[62] "Journal of Bishop Henry C. Lay, 1862-1863," printed in *Historical Magazine of the Protestant Episcopal Church,* VIII (March, 1939), 85.
[63] *Arkansas Intelligencer,* Dec. 8, 1849.
[64] *Ibid.,* Sept. 16, 1848.
[65] *Census of 1860 (Population),* p. 21.   The census lists only occupations of the free population, so there is no indication of how many slaves worked primarily at spinning and weaving.

one or more slaves might be used as seamstresses long enough to make the year's supply of clothing. Only on the largest plantations was there sufficient work of this sort to warrant the use of full-time seamstresses the year around. For slave owners who preferred them, ready-made clothes were available, such as the "30 suits negro clothing" advertised for sale by R. C. Byrd & Co. of Little Rock.[66]

Certainly the simplest of all slave clothing to make was that of the small children, who, regardless of sex, wore a single uniform garment until they were practically old enough to work in the fields. Scott Bond described the garment as "a long sack-like slip with holes cut for arms and head."[67] Shoes were little problem either, for the children customarily wore none until they were twelve or fourteen years of age. Once Scott Bond's mother had another slave on the plantation make a pair of shoes for the small boy from a pair of old boot tops. Scott obediently wore them when sent out to get wood for the cabin fire, but their unfamiliar weight so hindered his walking that he took them off and hid them in the woodpile.[68]

Shoes for the slaves were often purchased ready-made from local dealers, such as T. A. Boone of Pine Bluff, "Wholesale and Retail Dealer in Boots, Shoe Leather, Calf Skins and Shoe Findings," who on November 6, 1857, sold James Sheppard of Waterford forty-seven pairs of brogans (heavy work shoes) for $1.55 per pair.[69] Other planters bought tanned leather from the numerous tanyards in the state and had shoes made on the plantation by specially trained slaves.[70] Other items of wearing apparel are encountered less frequently in the newspapers and lists of purchases, but hats, boots, and wool socks, all designated as "Negro goods," also were sold.[71] Not strictly speaking clothing, "Negro blankets" were sometimes listed along with clothing.[72]

In examining the lists of cloth and clothing used by slaves on

[66] *Arkansas Gazette*, Oct. 3, 1837.   [67] Bond, *Life of Scott Bond*, p. 259.
[68] *Ibid.*, p. 258.
[69] Statement, T. A. Boone to James Sheppard, Dec. 31, 1857, Sheppard Papers.
[70] Henderson, "Negro in Arkansas County," p. 6.
[71] *Southern Shield*, Oct. 12, 1850; *Arkansas Gazette*, Sept. 23, 1854; *Arkansas Intelligencer*, Sept. 16, 1848.
[72] *Southern Shield*, Oct. 12, 1850; *Memphis Daily Eagle*, April 8, 1850.

the plantations, one gets the impression that Arkansas slaves were drably and monotonously dressed in nondescript clothes made from coarse cotton cloth. But practically the opposite impression is gained from reading the descriptions of slave clothing in the newspaper advertisements of runaways. The variety of clothing was great, and at times the combinations approached the fantastic, possibly because in their haste slaves took whatever clothing was at hand—their own or their master's. Here are descriptions of only a few of the costumes worn by runaway slaves in Arkansas: John Bird, a mulatto who escaped from a flatboat on the Mississippi River in 1821, wore "an olive colored surtout of superfine cloth, half worn, and a pair of dark velvet pantaloons."[73] More appropriately dressed for flight through the forests was a slave with the unusual name of Boatswain, who wore a pair of shoes with "the soles filled with iron tacks" and a gray jeans coat, and carried a new pair of boots and "a good deal of other clothing" when he ran away from the Walnut Bend, Phillips County, plantation of Alfred Swearingen in 1839.[74]

Harry, the property of Daniel Harkleroad of Crittenden County, outfitted himself well for winter weather when he ran away in November, 1831, wearing "an old big coat of coarse bear-skin cloth, a flax linen shirt made in the form of an overshirt, with a pocket in front, and a new wool hat."[75] When Truman, aged twenty, escaped in 1850 from the N. H. Badgett plantation seven miles below Little Rock on the Arkansas River, he was clad in "a purple lindsey coat, very much worn . . . patched with new cloth of the same kind . . . and a blue cloth cap. He carried off with him a black cloth coat, and a pair of black cassimere pants, somewhat worn. The pantaloons were patched on the inside of the legs, down toward the foot."[76]

The quantity of clothing worn and taken by some escaped slaves leaves no doubt that they were trying to make a permanent getaway. For example, Nancy, who belonged to Zachariah N. Ratcliff of Jefferson County, wore or carried three calico dresses

[73] *Arkansas Gazette*, Sept. 8, 1821.
[74] *Batesville News*, March 7, 1839.
[75] *Arkansas Gazette*, Nov. 2, 1831.
[76] *Gazette and Democrat*, March 1, 1850

and one homespun wool dress when she ran away in 1851,[77] and Jacob and Charles, slaves of Samuel D. Walker, took "a variety of clothing," in addition to wearing black fur hats and, oddly enough, "coats and hunting shirts . . . of the U. S. Dragoon uniform, with eagle buttons."[78] Certainly there should have been little difficulty in identifying Jacob and Charles.

No matter how nondescriptly Arkansas slaves were dressed during the remainder of the year, when special holidays, such as the Fourth of July or Christmas, came along they dressed themselves in their "best rigging"[79] in preparation for the customary entertainments. Of an especially elaborate "negro-ball" in Fort Smith in 1854, Ida Pfeiffer, an English traveler, wrote:

> The costumes were European, of course. The gentlemen were in black, with white neck-cloths and white waist-coats; the ladies in tulle, and other pretty white dresses; and there was no lack of gold chains and jewelry, or of ribbons and flowers in the hair.[80]

Even allowing for possible exaggeration on the part of this observer, it is apparent that on occasion slaves could and did blossom forth in resplendent finery.

Arkansas was in large measure still a frontier state up until the Civil War, with most of its white inhabitants living in log cabins or other unpretentious houses; it is not surprising, then, that most of the slaves also lived in dwellings of the simplest sort. Even the homes of the wealthiest planters were usually frame houses; few brick homes of any sort were constructed in Arkansas before the Civil War.[81] A house built for Creed Taylor, a famous early settler of southeastern Arkansas, at Napoleon in

---

[77] *Ibid.,* Jan. 31, 1851.

[78] *Arkansas Gazette,* Aug. 9, 1836. Army surplus clothing was sometimes sold to the general public, and possibly the clothing of these two slaves was of this type. For example, a large quantity of army uniforms "of the old pattern" was sold at auction at Fort Gibson, Indian Territory, on Oct. 29, 1835. The advertisement of the sale asserted that "many of the above articles are suitable for laboring hands. . . ." *Times,* Oct. 26, 1835.

[79] Diary of John Brown, Dec. 25, 1853.

[80] Ida Pfeiffer, *A Lady's Second Journey Round the World . . .* (New York, 1856), p. 422.

[81] In the course of extensive travels through every important slaveholding county and many others of lesser importance in Arkansas, the author found very few pre-Civil War plantation homes still standing, and even fewer slave cabins.

1844 was typical of many homes occupied by slaveowners up to the time of the Civil War. Built by Lewis I. Boyd in exchange for a piece of land, the house was

. . . a frame building 40 ft long x 37½ ft. wide, 12 ft. story and which is furnished in a workmanlike manner as follows, it is divided into four rooms, each of which is neatly ceiled inside and the house aforesaid is weatherboarded and roofed and otherwise in every respect is finished and furnished . . . for a family residence.[82]

During the several years John Brown operated his Princeton plantation with more than twenty slaves he lived with his family in a log house.[83] His first house in Camden, where he lived after 1854, continuing to own a number of slaves, he described as an "old house" and an "old shanty." At one time he wrote of having his slaves whitewash the house inside and out, an indication that it was built of very rough materials.[84] Later Brown built what he described as "the first mansion house" he had ever lived in in Arkansas; yet that mansion was a frame house which cost slightly more than $900.[85] Henry M. Stanley remembered that the home of his host, Major Ingham of Saline County, "was of solid pine logs, roughly squared, and but slightly stained by weather, and neatly chinked without with plaster, and lined within with planed boards, new and unpainted," but he added that "it had an air of domestic comfort."[86]

Somewhat more elaborate, and probably representative of the homes of the wealthiest planters in the most highly developed sections of the state, was the house occupied by Lycurgus Johnson at Lakeport in Chicot County about fifteen miles north of the Louisiana line. The Johnson home, still standing but in very bad repair, is a large two-story frame house built of heart cypress. The twenty-two rooms are arranged in the shape of an "L," the base being the front of the house. There is a veranda across the front, and another down the side in the hollow of the "L," leading to the semidetached kitchen. While the house is spacious and must have been quite comfortable, there is little indication of the

[82] Desha County Deed Record "A," p. 489.
[83] Diary of John Brown, Aug. 25, 1853.
[84] *Ibid.*, Aug. 29, 1856.　　[85] *Ibid.*, Nov. 17, 1858.
[86] Stanley, *Autobiography*, p. 146.

luxury and showiness so typical of the great plantation homes of the Natchez region or the Mississippi River section above New Orleans, for example. The chief decorative feature of the Johnson house is a magnificent display of iron lace in the oak leaf and acorn design surrounding a first floor porch on the northeastern corner of the house. Houses such as Johnson's were far more frequent in Arkansas than elaborate Greek Revival mansions of the type common in the older South, yet even they were relatively insignificant in number in comparison with the thousands of humbler dwellings.

There are few remaining slave cabins in Arkansas, but at least two are still standing on Yellow Bayou Plantation, about five miles north of Lake Village in Chicot County.[87] Each is built of hand-hewn cypress logs about fourteen inches square and has a single room twenty feet square with a nine foot ceiling. Wooden pegs were used almost exclusively in construction of the cabins. Each formerly had a chimney at one side, whether of brick or "dirt and sticks" it is impossible to tell now. One of the cabins has a front porch or veranda and a small shed room at the back, but these may be later additions. The floors, which probably are also later replacements, are of rough-sawn boards.

Apparently the characteristics of slave cabins were so universally taken for granted that definite description was considered unnecessary in the few references to them found in sources of the period. A description of Jenifer Farm, a short distance below Helena in Phillips County, in a "for sale" advertisement in a newspaper told of "an excellent dwelling, . . . a first rate gin house and a new gin press, and all other improvements necessary to comfort and convenience," but merely referred briefly to an unspecified number of "Negro houses."[88] The description of slave quarters on the Keen and Legrand Plantation near Laconia in Desha County, which was offered for sale in 1857, was similarly indefinite, just "negro houses."[89] Martin Guest of Indian Bay, Monroe County, gave slightly more information concerning the six

---

[87] It is possible that there are more, but alterations and additions to some of the buildings in more recent years make identification practically impossible. Descriptions of the cabins and the Johnson home are based on personal observation by the author on July 4, 1953.
[88] *Southern Shield*, Jan. 5, 1850.   [89] *Arkansas Gazette*, Nov. 10, 1857.

Negro houses on the 240-acre plantation he was attempting to sell in 1836, referring to them as "comfortable."[90]

Other and usually fairly detailed and specific sources are even more silent concerning the housing of Arkansas slaves. At no time did John Brown refer directly in his diary to the living accommodations of his twenty-odd slaves, while during the same period he wrote of numerous other aspects of slave life. It is possible to infer from scattered references in Brown's diary that some of the slaves lived in the family home, but even that is speculative. The fairly extensive papers of James Sheppard's Waterford Plantation also offer no information on slave housing.

The ideal arrangement of slave cabins on a large plantation was along a well-laid-out street. There is indication, however, that the cabins were often arranged haphazardly.[91] An old resident of Clark County signing himself "Pioneer" later described the ideal arrangement:

A planter usually built a mansion of logs, boards, or brick—just as the court houses are now built—then the houses for the slaves were built of the same materials, but laid off in a street 80 feet wide, with a row of houses on each side, the mansion at one end, and the overseers house at the other end. Then a large bell was put up near the house of the foreman, a slave that superintended the farm and other slaves, and did the bidding of the overseer.[92]

Some insight into the adequacy of slave housing may be obtained by a consideration of the ratio of number of slaves to number of slave houses on various Arkansas plantations, as given in the manuscript slave schedules of the 1860 federal census. The following table lists the number of slaves and slave houses on representative plantations in various counties of the state.

COUNTY	OWNER	NUMBER OF SLAVES	NUMBER OF HOUSES
Arkansas	Lewis J. Garrott	71	12
	James L. Garee	57	8
	Sarah Clay	227	47
	Robert C. Foster	73	13

[90] *Ibid.*, Sept. 13, 1836.
[91] There is no present physical indication that the slave houses at Yellow Bayou Plantation, where there were nearly a hundred slaves, were arranged according to any system.
[92] *Southern Standard*, Oct. 14, 1896.

Carroll	A. McLamore	38	6
Columbia	Lucinda Cook	25	4
Desha	W. P. Warfield	69	18
	F. W. Bynum	49	12
Chicot	Junius W. Craig estate	215	30
	Elisha Worthington		
	Red Leaf Plantation	145	24
	Meanie Plantation	55	10
	Eminence Plantation	94*	
	Sunnyside Plantation	234	30
Desha	C. S. Abercrombie	119	22
	George W. Graddy	28	10
Lafayette	Lewis B. Fort	59	14
Union	J. R. Bryant	46	10
Phillips	Alfred and John Swiser	83	15
	John Crenshaw	94	15
	Gideon J. Pillow	139	16
	Total	1826	318

* Disregarded in computation; number of houses not given.

On the basis of these figures, the average number of slaves living in each house was 5.74, only slightly more than the statewide average for both Negroes and whites, 5.72.[93] Considerable variation in the average per house may be noted, however, ranging from 8.6 on Gideon J. Pillow's plantation to 2.8 on George W. Graddy's. Other averages at the extremes include W. P. Warfield, 3.8, and Elisha Worthington, 7.8. In general, it may be concluded that slaves lived under somewhat more crowded conditions on the larger plantations than on the smaller ones. And since slave houses usually had only one room, most of them without doubt were inadequate by modern standards.

As in most other aspects of life "down in the quarters," housing facilities of slaves were more nearly equivalent to those of their masters on small farms than on large plantations. It has previously been pointed out that more than half of the Arkansas slaves in 1860 were in individual holdings of four or less, and that about one slaveowner in five held only a single slave. Some of these lived in the same house as the master, or, as Samuel H. Chester wrote of his family's dozen slaves in Columbia County: "They were housed in the same kind of one room log cabin that

[93] *Census of 1860 (Population)*, p. xxvii.

the boys of the family and any surplus visiting friends were housed in."[94]

Slaves in the towns also frequently lived in the master's house, especially if the number of slaves belonging to a particular family was small. The custom of presenting newly married children with slaves as personal servants was widespread; such slaves often had been companions of the new master or mistress since childhood and naturally occupied a special place in the new household.[95] The extensive town establishments, such as that of Chester Ashley in Little Rock, had quarters for their slaves to the rear or side of the main house.[96]

During most of the period of slavery in Arkansas, there was no legal restriction on the place of abode for slaves living in the towns, and the matter never became the subject of state law. In Little Rock, however, a local ordinance passed in 1856 required all slaves to live on the premises of their owners:

> Be it ordained . . . that Negroes or other slaves are prohibited hereafter from living separately and to themselves detached from the immediate and direct supervision of their owners and from the homestead of their owners, or those having charge of them; and in every case of a master, owner, or agent having the immediate control of such slave or slaves, and hereafter permitting or suffering any such slave or slaves . . . to live separately or apart . . . shall pay a penalty and fine of Five Dollars for each and every day that he or she shall permit or suffer the same. . . .[97]

That such a law was passed indicates that some slaves had been permitted to arrange for their own places of residence. Although Arkansas law prohibited slaves from hiring their own time, doubtless some of those living apart from their masters had been permitted to hire themselves out in violation of the law.

[94] Chester, *Pioneer Days in Arkansas,* p. 39.
[95] Diary of John Brown, May 9, 1854; Virginia F. Hicks, "First Columbus Settlers. . . ," Centennial Edition of the *Hope Star,* June 26, 1936; Will of Samuel D. Walker, Jan. 15, 1846, in Chicot County Will Book "C," p. 56.
[96] Johnson, "The Ashley Mansion and the Ashley Band," p. 11.
[97] Little Rock City Council Record, 1852-1860, p. 153.

"... a good deal of sickness ...."

THE STATE OF HEALTH of the slaves was a matter of constant concern to Arkansas slaveowners and others directly connected with the institution of slavery. To a considerable degree this concern was occasioned by the relationship of health to value of the slaves, both as tangible personal wealth and as a means of cultivating the crops or otherwise engaging in productive activity. The direct relationship between the health of slaves and their value is nowhere more graphically illustrated than in the list of the 211 slaves at Yellow Bayou and Bellevue Plantations in Chicot County, with their appraised values, which was compiled in 1860.[1] Parenthetical remarks indicate that eight of the slaves were diseased or suffering from some sort of injury, and in each case the appraised value was considerably less than that of other slaves of the same sex and comparable age. Alfred, a fifteen-year-old boy whose eyes were "affected," was valued at only $500, while Milor, of the same age, was worth $1000. Sevella, a twenty-two-year-old woman, was "scrofulous," and thus worth only $500; other young women of about her age, such as Mary Ann, Yellow Mary, and Mary Bob, were valued at $1200 each. If Will Hall, thirty-one, had been in good health he would have been worth at least $1200, as was Harrison, thirty-three. But since Will Hall was paralyzed, the $200 valuation placed upon him probably was a very liberal one. The rupture from which Harry, aged nine, suffered reduced his value to $500 from a probable $600 or $700 otherwise. Some diseased or afflicted slaves had little or no value: Frank ("afflicted"), aged two, was worth $50.00, while Julia Ann ("worthless"),

[1] Appraisal of Craig Estate.

aged six, Kitty ("diseased"), forty-two,[2] Lee ("worthless—diseased"), aged three, and Robert ("infant—worthless"), had no valuations at all assigned to them. Normally, a healthy slave child was worth at least $100 at birth.

Another indication of the mercenary concern of owners for the health of their slaves was the frequency with which they expressed disappointment or disgust upon loss of the services of the slaves because of illness or injury. John Brown, who in general was very considerate of the welfare of his slaves, wrote in his diary in 1856, "Thom got his ankle hurt with Arrington and Vaughan house moving and is of no service to me now."[3] In June, 1859, he wrote of Steven, who, next to Thom, was his most useful and valuable slave, "Steven is better but it seems difficult to get him up to be fit for work again. He has not worked a day for three or four months."[4] A few days later: "Steven is slowly recovering from his illness, but cannot do any work and I fear will not shortly—This shortens my cash income rather inconveniently."[5] The same attitude prevailed even toward childbirth among the slaves; Brown once commented laconically, "After much suffering, a stillborn child is born, so goes my luck with negroes."[6]

The constant concern for the health of the slaves was not caused entirely by mercenary feelings, however. In many instances the relationship between the master and slave was so close that quite naturally the master felt genuine concern and regret when the slave fell ill. Practically all slaveowners—and more especially those with relatively few slaves—habitually referred to their slaves as members of the family,[7] and expressed the same feelings for ill slaves as for ill children of their own. Such was the case when Rial, a small slave child owned by Robert F. Kellam

[2] Despite her unnamed disease, Kitty was the mother of five children, aged fifteen, thirteen, eight, seven, and one and a half, worth a total of $3,450.
[3] Diary of John Brown, Sept. 25, 1856.
[4] *Ibid.,* June 20, 1859.
[5] *Ibid.,* June 29, 1859.
[6] *Ibid.,* Aug. 11, 1860.
[7] For example, John Brown: ". . . 31 in family—to wit 22 blacks and 7 children and we, the old folks—" Diary of John Brown, June 30, 1853. Also: "Cousin Lee and Family are all well except a black woman that is a little sick." William A. Martin to Elizabeth A. Martin, Dec. 22, 1855, Martin **Papers.**

of Camden, fell ill in 1859. In February Rial was dangerously ill of "disease of the Head & Brain &c."[8] In July he fell victim of chills and fever, but by the end of the month was "now mending."[9] Early in August, however, he died suddenly of croup.[10] Throughout Rial's various illnesses, Kellam and his family gave him the best medical care available, and they felt genuine sorrow when he died. In correspondence between members of a family or between overseer and owner it was as customary to report on the health of the slaves as upon that of the children or other members of the family.[11]

Apart from such considerations as the value of the slaves and the affection felt for them, the usual great interest in the health of the slaves is not surprising, for the mid-nineteenth century was a period during which the state of health of everyone, white and Negro alike, attracted more than passing interest. This feeling was engendered by the low level of health everywhere as compared to the present, and by the knowledge that eventually almost everyone would become ill with one of the many diseases prevalent in that day, with many dying of them. The general attitude toward matters of health might best be described as one of resignation, as illustrated in this excerpt of a letter from the overseer D. T. Weeks to James Sheppard:

... I have concluded to write to you one time more to let you know if you are still living that we are all still living yet and not so much sickness ... I have concluded you must be dead as I have not heard from you but one time since you left but the Delta and Dispatch has stoped coming to the Bluff as they did for the first month after you left causes me to think you are still surviving. ...[12]

In that day good health and long life were not part of the accepted state of things; rather they were merely the hoped-for exceptions.

Arkansas slaves suffered from a varied assortment of diseases. Particularly prevalent, and especially in the lowlands of the south-

[8] Diary of Robert F. Kellam, Feb. 19, 1859.
[9] *Ibid.*, July 27, 1859.
[10] *Ibid.*, Aug. 5, 1859.
[11] D. T. Weeks to James Sheppard, Aug. 7, 1858, J. R. McNeely to James Sheppard, July 30, 1852, and numerous other letters between overseers and Sheppard in Sheppard Papers; Lee C. Blakemore to Jared C. Martin, July 4, 1855, William Allen Martin to Elizabeth A. Martin, April 5, 1856, and other letters in Martin Papers.
[12] D. T. Weeks to James Sheppard, Aug. 10, 1854, Sheppard Papers.

eastern part of the state, was malaria. Variously referred to by
people of that day as ague,[13] bilious fevers,[14] congestive chills,[15]
chills and fever,[16] or simply "the fever,"[17] and rarely as malaria,
the disease was probably a greater year-in and year-out menace to
the health and life of the slaves than any other. Henry M. Stanley, a close observer of life in southeastern Arkansas along the
Arkansas River, left this description of the disease and its effects:

Few visited our store[18] who did not bear some sign of the perni-
cious disease which afflicted old and young in the bottom lands of
Arkansas. I had not been a week at the store before I was delerious
from the fever which accompanies ague, and, for the first time in my
life, was dieted on calomel and quinine. The young physician of our
neighborhood, who boarded with Mr. Altschul, communicated to me
many particulars regarding the nature of this plague. In the form
termed by him 'congestive chills', he had known many cases to termi-
nate fatally within a few hours. Blacks as well as whites were subject
to it. Nothing availed to prevent an attack. The most abstemious,
temperate, prudent habits no more prevented it than selfish indulg-
ence, or intemperance. . . .
    . . . the frequency of ague attacks had reduced me to skin and
bone (ninety-five pounds.) It was a strange disease, preceded by a
violent shaking, and a congealed feeling as though the blood was suddenly iced, during which I had to be half-smothered in blankets, and
surrounded by hot-water bottles. After a couple of hours' shivering,
a hot fit followed, accompanied by delerium, which, after the twelfth
hour, was relieved by exhausting perspiration. When, about six
hours later, I became cool and sane, my appetite was almost ravenous
from quinine and emptiness. For three or four days afterward, unless the fever was tertian,[19] I went about my duties as before, when,
suddenly, a fit of nausea would seize me, and again the violent malady
overpowered me. Such was my experience of the agues of the Arkansas swampland; and, during the few months I remained at Cypress
Bend, I suffered from them three times a month.[20]

[13] Stanley, *Autobiography*, p. 155.
[14] *Ibid.;* D. T. Weeks to James Sheppard, Aug. 10, 1854, Sheppard Papers.
[15] Stanley, *Autobiography*, p. 155.
[16] D. T. Weeks to James Sheppard, Aug. 7, Aug. 29, 1858, Sheppard Papers;
Diary of Robert F. Kellam, July 27, 1859.
[17] D. T. Weeks to James Sheppard, July 15, 1855, Sheppard Papers; Diary
of John Brown, Sept. 21, 1857.
[18] After leaving the Ingham Plantation because of his dislike of the methods
of the overseer, Stanley had gone to Cypress Bend, on the Arkansas River
a few miles southeast of Pine Bluff, to learn the merchandise business in the
store of a Mr. Altschul, a Jewish merchant.
[19] Recurring every other day.
[20] Stanley, *Autobiography*, pp. 155-156.

Some idea of the frequency and extent of malarial attacks among the slaves in that region may be gained from examination of the letters written by James Sheppard's overseers on Waterford Plantation, only a few miles up the Arkansas River from Cypress Bend, during the years 1852-1860. Virtually every letter written during the "fever season" in the summer and fall contains references to fever among the slaves, and the collection of letters is far from complete, indicating that the extent of the disease was even greater than depicted in this source. The following are excerpts from letters of various overseers:

"I have got three hands sick of fever today."[21]

"I have had sometime back 6 cases of Bilious fever . . . all of them is up and out today but four cases have come in only 3 now. . . ."[22]

"Some little chills fever Amonge the negroes that is Edmd Fleming Sam George Walker & Wm Henry Saly Marshal was all lying up yesterdy & to day also Patrick and Vilet but I hope to start the most of them out tomorrow. . . ."[23]

"There has been some sickness here since you left Mason George Sue Emily Frank and Phoebe Ann has all had the fever but are getting well. . . ."[24]

"I have great use for quinine Now Sometimes 20 cases of chills & fevers A day However but 7 at the house to day 15 the day before & 20 day before that. . . ."[25]

". . . good deal of sickness just Now among the hands in way of chills and fevers Edy Hester Saly Marshall Jim Mary Ann Patrick Edwin & several children."[26] Although it was realized that malaria was more prevalent in the swampy regions of Arkansas than in the uplands, many years were to elapse before discovery that the swamp-bred mosquito was responsible.

Cholera was even more dreaded than malaria, although less prevalent except in epidemic years. The disease struck Arkansas most forcefully in the late 1840's and the early 1850's, and, like

[21] J. R. McNeely to James Sheppard, July 29, 1852, Sheppard Papers.
[22] D. T. Weeks to James Sheppard, Aug. 10, 1854, Sheppard Papers.
[23] Weeks to Sheppard, Sept. 10, 1854, Sheppard Papers.
[24] Weeks to Sheppard, July 15, 1855, Sheppard Papers.
[25] Weeks to Sheppard, Aug. 7, 1858, Sheppard Papers.
[26] Weeks to Sheppard, Aug. 29, 1858, Sheppard Papers.

malaria, was centered in the Arkansas River valley below Little Rock. In 1849 within a period of a few weeks nine slaves on the Notrebe plantation near Arkansas Post and three on the Byrd plantation, a few miles below Pine Bluff, died of cholera.[27] The disease struck again in the same vicinity in the summer of 1852. During that period six or seven slaves belonging to Judge John Selden Roane died, as well as several on the plantation of a Mr. Ryan. Cholera sometimes attacked with great suddenness: one slave on the Roane plantation became ill in the field and died before he could be taken to the house.[28] These are only a few instances of the many deaths from cholera during the period.

Smallpox was quite common among slaves, as of course among the entire population of that day. Advertisements of runaway slaves, such as the following, often referred to the effects of the disease:

RUNAWAY IN JAIL

Was committed to the jail of Chicot County, on the 3rd of September, 1832 . . . a Negro Boy, who calls himself HARRY . . . . He had on, when committed, a checked shirt and linen pantaloons. He has some small-pox marks in his face. . . .

H. H. Smith, *Dep. Jailer.*
Chicot County, A. T.

Villemont, Sept. 13, 1832.[29]

Small slave children were especially susceptible to disease. Scarlet fever,[30] croup,[31] and cholera morbus[32] (summer complaint) all took their toll of good health and life. Worms in children were virtually universal, and treatment for them was a regular spring routine.[33] Among adult slaves there was considerable incidence of gonorrhea and syphilis.[34] No evidence was found to indicate that any stigma was attached to having a venereal disease.

[27] *Arkansas State Democrat,* June 8, 1849.
[28] J. R. Neely to James Sheppard, July 29, 1852, Sheppard Papers.
[29] *Arkansas Gazette,* Oct. 24, 1832.
[30] I. M. Key to James Sheppard, Aug. 12, 1860, Sheppard Papers.
[31] Diary of John Brown, Aug. 5, 1859.
[32] *Ibid.,* July 7, 1855.
[33] A frequently used worm medicine was vermifuge.
[34] Dr. Henry Pernot of Van Buren made several entries in his account book referring to venereal diseases: "July 11, 1855. To visit, mileage, examining of black girl for the clap, $5.00." "May 12, 1854. To examining 3 Negroes (syphillis), $3.00." Account book of Henry Pernot, pp. 78, 133.

Accounts have also been found of Arkansas slaves suffering from eye diseases,[35] whooping cough,[36] skin diseases,[37] various respiratory diseases, and measles.[38]

In addition to the diseases named above, of which actual accounts of slave cases have been found, a few others are listed in the mortality statistics of the federal census of 1850. The additional diseases, disregarding those which claimed less than ten lives, from which Arkansas slaves died during the period from June 1, 1849, to June 1, 1850, were consumption, convulsions, dropsy, and pneumonia.

The 1850 mortality statistics afford an opportunity to make some comparisons between the state of health of the slaves and the white population of Arkansas. It is realized that the information given applies only to deaths, and not to the incidence of the various diseases, and also that there is no way to determine the percentage of fatal cases in a given disease. Furthermore, these statistics are for a single year, which might not necessarily be typical. Nevertheless, if it may be assumed that fatality rates from each disease were roughly the same in each race, a comparison perhaps has some value.

The ten chief causes of death from disease among the slaves, in descending order, were cholera, various fevers (most of which probably were malarial in character), worms, pneumonia, whooping cough, croup, dropsy, consumption, scarlet fever, and convulsions.

Among the whites, the ten major causes of death, also in descending order, were the malarial fevers, pneumonia, croup, consumption, cholera, worms, scarlet fever, dropsy, dysentery, and "inflammation of the brain."

A comparison of the two lists shows that eight of the ten diseases on each appear on the other. Whooping cough and convulsions, on the slave list, are not on the white list, while inflamation of the brain, tenth on the white list, ranked eleventh among slaves, and dysentery, ninth among whites, was an unimportant cause of slave deaths.

[35] Appraisal of Craig Estate.
[36] Diary of Robert F. Kellam, Nov. 20, 1858.
[37] Appraisal of Craig Estate.
[38] Diary of John Brown, Jan. 11, April 16, 1857.

In round figures the white population of Arkansas in 1850 was three and one-half times as large as the slave. By using this figure and the number of deaths by race from the more serious diseases during the 1849-1850 year, comparisons of the impact of the various diseases on each race may be made. In the following table the first column gives the disease, the second the number of slave deaths, the third the number of white deaths, and the fourth the degree of seriousness of the disease among the slaves as compared to the whites. The degree of seriousness was arrived at by multiplying the number of slave deaths from a disease by three and one-half and dividing the product by the number of white deaths. For example, cholera caused, proportionately, six times as many deaths among slaves as among whites, but malarial fevers only eight-tenths as many deaths among slaves as among whites.

DEATHS FROM DISEASE, 1849-1850

Disease	Slave Deaths	White Deaths	Degree of Seriousness Slaves to Whites
Cholera	155	90	6
Fevers (malarial)	85	388	.8
Worms	48	83	2
Pneumonia	47	140	1.2
Whooping cough	38	17	8
Croup	31	117	1.8
Dropsy	26	53	1.7
Consumption	22	110	.7
Scarlet fever	19	79	.8
Convulsions	11	16	2.5
Dysentery	5	53	.3
Inflammation of brain	11	51	.8

It may be seen that cholera and whooping cough were much more serious among slaves than among whites, and worms, pneumonia, croup, dropsy, and convulsions more serious, but less markedly so. On the other hand, dysentery was a much greater cause of death among whites, and scarlet fever, the malarial fevers, consumption, and inflammation of the brain also greater, although not as much so. The cholera deaths are attributable to the epidemic of 1849 and therefore have no long-term significance;[39]

[39] Some information concerning the status of medical knowledge of cholera during this period may be of interest. Discussing the change to the modern concept, a recent authority wrote: ". . . cholera had brought to mind a chain

concerning the other diseases, the generalization appears valid that slaves suffered more severely from the diseases of the respiratory organs than did the whites.

Deaths from all causes among slaves in Arkansas during the year 1849-1850 amounted to 859, 1.8 per cent of the total slave population of 47,100 in 1850, or 18 per 1,000. Deaths among white people in Arkansas that year were proportionately somewhat less, 2,157 in a population of 162,797, 1.32 per cent of the total.

Of significance equal to the percentage of deaths among the slaves and their masters was the percentage of births. During the year 1849-1850 there were 1,159 births among the slaves, 2.4 per cent of the total number, or 24 per 1,000. During the same year there were 5,841 births among the whites, 3.5 per cent of the total, or 35 per 1,000. Ten years later, during the year 1859-1860, the percentage of slave births was somewhat higher, 3.04, and the white percentage had dropped slightly to 3.36. While it may be seen that in each race there was a comfortable excess of births over deaths during the two years considered, it is equally obvious that slaves had both a higher death rate and a lower birth rate than the whites. This was generally true throughout the slaveholding states.[40]

---

of ideas having to do with decaying organic matter, effluvia, and the bodies of the sick and the dead; it had suggested poisons—miasms—arising from those processes of decay into the atmosphere and being wafted on the winds; it pictured man breathing these ubiquitous miasms, falling sick, and dying. Thinking in terms of microbes the word cholera pictures a specific family of germs descending in an unbroken line, propagating principally in the intestinal tract of man and spreading through the medium of water and food contaminated by his excretions." J. S. Chambers, *The Conquest of Cholera, America's Greatest Scourge* (New York, 1938), pp. 345-346. "Cures" for cholera were likely to be as ineffectual as the knowledge of cause was incorrect. One advocated by Dr. Samuel A. Cartwright of New Orleans in a pamphlet circulated among planters during the 1849 epidemic consisted of huge doses of pepper, calomel, gum camphor, gum Arabic, and calcined charcoal to induce sweating, cupping and bleeding, and application of mustard plasters, all in an attempt to cure the disease "by making a revulsion to the surface." Samuel A. Cartwright, *The Pathology and Treatment of Cholera* . . . (New Orleans, 1849), pp. 31, 37. The cause and mode of prevention of cholera (largely based upon good sanitary practices) were finally discovered during the 1880's by the scientists Koch and Roux and their associates. Chambers, *Conquest of Cholera*, pp. 342-350.

[40] Historians of slavery have largely ignored the fact that slave birth rates were lower than those of white people. Bancroft, for example, cited numerous instances of great fecundity of slave women, obviously implying that the reverse was true. Bancroft, *Slave-Trading*, pp. 81-86. See also Sellers, *Slavery in Alabama*, p. 147, and William D. Postell, *The Health of Slaves on Southern Plantations* (Baton Rouge, 1951), pp. 151-153. Avery O. Craven, while not

No detailed analysis of deaths in all states for the year 1859-1860 was made, but slave death rates appear to be greater in every state. Only in Tennessee among the slave states did the slaves have a higher percentage of births than the whites—3.19 to 3.17 —and the difference is so small that it proves little. The Arkansas slave birth rate ranked high among all states, being exceeded only by Tennessee, Missouri, and Texas, the latter two each having percentages of 3.09. It is not entirely clear why these states had higher slave birth rates than those of the eastern South, although one reason may be that Arkansas, Texas, and Missouri were the newest slave states, and therefore had larger proportions of slaves in the younger and more virile ages. No explanation can be offered for the high slave birth rate in Tennessee. The census of 1860, not distinguishing between slave and white, recognized the higher birth rates in the newer areas, pointing out that "the States having the highest indicated birth rates, in 1860, were Oregon, Iowa, Minnesota, Missouri, Texas, Illinois, Kansas, and Arkansas, in their order. These are chiefly pioneer, or newly-settled States."[41]

Accidents and injuries frequently incapacitated Arkansas slaves. The wise slaveowner or overseer took normal precautions to prevent accidents, knowing that the work of the farm or other slave-operated enterprise would suffer in the absence of the slave, but some accidents were inevitable.[42] There were cuts of all sorts:

---

pointing out that slave birth rates were lower, was at least aware that high birth rates by present standards were common to both races. Avery O. Craven, *The Coming of the Civil War* (New York, 1942), pp. 83-85.

[41] Data in the foregoing section were drawn from *Census of 1850*, pp. xli, 547; *Census of 1860 (Population)*, pp. xxxviii, xxxix, xli; and U. S. Bureau of the Census, *Mortality Statistics of the Seventh Census of the United States, 1850* (Washington, 1855), pp. 52-55. In some instances, because of the data provided, free Negroes have been included in the tabulations with the whites, while in others they have been excluded. Since the number of free Negroes was very small, however, the findings have not been materially affected. Some of the validity of the mortality statistics is minimized by the fact that some diseases accounting for large numbers of deaths today were unknown or incorrectly identified during slavery days. Notably absent in the statistics, for example, are cancer and heart disease.

[42] Although little information was found on the subject, it may be presumed that careful Arkansas slaveowners used precautionary measures in the prevention of disease as well as accident. Postell, in *The Health of Slaves,* pp. 90-97, has described preventive practices used in the South at large. Among them were insistence upon cleanliness of the slaves' persons, clothing, and living quarters, enforcement of regular hours for sleep and rest, provision of a pure water supply, isolation and quarantine during epidemics, and vaccina-

from hoes while chopping cotton, from scythes used in cutting hay or grain,[43] and from other sharp tools used on the farm and in the shop. Gin machinery of the period was not so well equipped with safety devices as later, and slaves who worked with it sometimes received severe injury. Edmund, a skilled and valuable slave on Waterford Plantation, received a "hard gin cut" on the back of his hand in 1854, the overseer D. T. Weeks reported to James Sheppard. He explained further: "I don't know that the leaders are injured but there is some frightful gashes to look at on the back of his hand and fingers he can work his fingers or rather open and shut his fingers causes me to have hope of the leaders." Apparently Edmund did not suffer permanent incapacitation, for a week later Weeks wrote that "all hands is well ready and waiting for work but Edmund his gin cut hand is doing well for a bad cut."[44] While such injuries could hardly be considered occupational hazards, quarrels and fights among slaves sometimes resulted in knife cuts or stabs.[45] Some slaves working at felling timber while clearing new fields or getting out logs for building purposes suffered crushed legs or feet or toes.[46] Other slaves stuck nails in their feet,[47] sprained their ankles,[48] or were injured in falls.[49] Animals and other creatures, both wild and domestic, on the Arkansas farms provided additional hazards. Slaves were bitten by dogs,[50] horses,[51] and snakes,[52] and kicked and thrown by horses and mules.[53] House slaves were almost equally subject to accidents. Only two days after Robert F. Kellam of Camden hired the slave girl Frances from Dr. Viser to serve as cook and general house servant, she scalded her feet seriously by upsetting a pot of

tion for smallpox. Postell's book is a good general study of health and medical practices among Southern slaves. It contains no information about Arkansas.
[43] *Southern Shield*, July 9, 1853; *Gazette and Democrat*, Dec. 13, 1850.
[44] D. T. Weeks to James Sheppard, Sept. 20, 27, 1854, Sheppard Papers.
[45] *Arkansas Gazette*, Feb. 1, 1832.
[46] Stanley, *Autobiography*, p. 149; D. T. Weeks to James Sheppard, Sept. 20, 1854, Sheppard Papers.
[47] D. T. Weeks to James Sheppard, Sept. 20, 1854, Sheppard Papers.
[48] Bond, *Life of Scott Bond*, p. 258.
[49] Diary of John Brown, Nov. 11, 1853.
[50] *Arkansas Gazette*, Nov. 2, 1831.
[51] *Ibid.*, Nov. 16, 1831.
[52] Bond, *Life of Scott Bond*, p. 258.
[53] *Arkansas Intelligencer*, April 14, 1845.

boiling water on them.[54]   Burns received while working around open fires were not uncommon.[55]

Physicians were available in the more populous sections of Arkansas for treatment of serious complaints, but ordinary ills and injuries of Arkansas slaves were usually treated by the slave-owner himself, or by the overseer on the larger plantations or those with absentee owners.   In some instances the wife of the planter or of the overseer looked after the "doctoring" of the slaves.   And of course there was a certain amount of self-treatment by the slaves, or administration of home medical cures by slaves to their children or other members of the slave family.

Supplies on the well-managed plantation always included a variety of medicines for use in treating the slaves.   As in the case of food, clothing, and other plantation supplies, medicines were sometimes purchased in the trading towns such as Little Rock, Pine Bluff, Camden, and Helena, or in the country general stores scattered throughout the state; large planters, however, more frequently bought medicines along with other supplies through their New Orleans or Memphis factors, paying for them when the cotton crop was sold.   James Sheppard, with a medium-sized force of slaves on Waterford Plantation, bought medical supplies both at stores in Pine Bluff and through his New Orleans factors.   During the spring of 1857 he bought the following medicines from Dr. A. W. Brewster of Pine Bluff, who operated a drugstore as well as conducting a medical practice:

Feb. 4	½ oz. sulph zinc	20
March 29	4 oz. Peru. Bark	11.00
May 3	Box Seid. powders	4/
May 16	1 lb. alum	2/
May 27	1 Bot Spts Camphor	8/
May 27	Bottle Paregoric	8/
May 27	Bot No six	8/
May 27	1 doz. Vermifuge	2.25
Nov. 9	1 oz. Borax	10[56]

A list of the medical supplies which Sheppard bought through

[54] Diary of Robert F. Kellam, Feb. 3, 1860.
[55] Thomas Pollard to James Sheppard, Jan. 24, 1854, Sheppard Papers.
[56] Statement, A. W. Brewster to James M. Sheppard, 1857, Sheppard Papers. The slash mark after some of the amounts was used during this period to indicate a "bit," or twelve and one-half cents. Thus the bottle of paregoric cost "8 bits," or a dollar.

one of his New Orleans factors, also in 1857, includes some of the same types of medicines as the list above, and additional ones as well. Listed are three bottles of turpentine, two bottles of paregoric, two bottles of sweet oil, three ounces of quinine (at $4.00 an ounce!), one bottle of vermifuge, one bottle of castor oil, and quantities of camphor, "blue mass," and carbonate of iron.[57] Sometimes the medicines which Sheppard purchased were identified only as "home medicine";[58] what this was and what diseases it was intended to treat can only be left to the imagination.

Yellow Bayou and Bellevue plantations in Chicot County also were well supplied with medicine for treatment of slave ailments. No detailed list of the medical supplies was found, but when the property of the two plantations was appraised in 1860 each had "1 lot of medicines" valued at $30.00.[59]

Quinine, or "peruvian bark," a cruder form of the same substance—called by one Arkansan "the infallible panacea"—was most commonly used by planters in treating malaria or "chills and fever" among their slaves.[60] Purging of the intestinal tract, induced by various drugs, was also considered a necessary part of the treatment. Some planters used a combination of several drugs in trying to effect a cure. In the early fall of 1857 two of John Brown's slave women fell ill. Courtney, who worked in the Brown household, became ill with "considerable fever and her eyes and face swollen" on Monday, and Brown promptly gave her "calomel in broken portions with Dovers powders." By Wednesday her condition had not improved, so Brown repeated the treatment, which "had the desired effect in a tolerable way, but still she had the same fever." Brown also noted that "her tongue became quite dark, almost black," whether from the fever or the effect of the purgatives he did not say.

On Saturday of the same week Brown received word that his slave girl Louisa, who was hired to a Mr. Works not far from

[57] Statement, Fish and Hughes to James Sheppard, Dec. 26, 1857, Sheppard Papers.

[58] On May 26, 1858, Byrne, Vance and Co. of New Orleans shipped Sheppard fourteen vials of "Home Medicine" at sixty cents per vial. The invoice is in the Sheppard Papers.

[59] Appraisal of Craig Estate.

[60] Willie Sheppard to James Sheppard, July 16, 1859, D. T. Weeks to James Sheppard, Aug. 7, 1858, Sheppard Papers.

Camden, was ill with fever. Always very careful of the health
of his slaves, Brown went to the Works farm, had Louisa moved
home to Camden in a wagon, and immediately started treatment of
the illness. He began with his specialty, calomel and Dovers
powders, in broken doses, "until they operated, with good effect,"
and seemed to be satisfied with the result. Meanwhile, there was
a recurrence of Courtney's fever, so Brown decided to broaden his
treatment. He "gave Courtney a dose of oil and turpentine which
had a fine effect, after the calomel and dovers powders cleaned her
out." Apparently the treatment helped, for Brown reported: ". . .
she is clear of fever and doing well." In continuing Louisa's
treatment, Brown relied on an even wider variety of drugs. He
used "pills [type unidentified], oil of black pepper, calomel, and
quinine," and by his own statement "prevented her fever altogether."[61]

Brown was following standard procedure in administering the
medicines to his slaves personally, for often slaves refused to take
them unless coerced. A particularly good example is that concerning James Sheppard's overseer, Robert W. Miller, and the
slave girl Nora, which has earlier been referred to in another connection. Nora so steadfastly refused to take quinine that Miller
had to threaten to whip her to make her do so.[62]

Most of the professional physicians in Arkansas treated slaves
in the normal course of practice.[63] Slaveowners in remote areas
had to rely upon their own devices for medical treatment of slaves
to a much greater degree than those living in or near the towns
unless they were prepared to pay the substantial mileage rates
which doctors of the day customarily charged for trips away from
the normal place of practice. Dr. William C. Howell, who practiced in Little Rock in the 1830's, charged a dollar per mile for
out-of-town calls in the daytime, and two dollars per mile for
night calls,[64] rates which seem well in line with those charged by
other doctors of the period. But since Negro slaves were very

[61] Diary of John Brown, Sept. 21, 23, 26, 28, 1857.
[62] Robert W. Miller to James Sheppard, July 16, 1859, Sheppard Papers.
[63] For a brief general study of early Arkansas medical practices, see Walter
Moffatt, "Medicine and Dentistry in Pioneer Arkansas," *Arkansas Historical
Quarterly,* X (Summer, 1951), 89-94.
[64] Margaret S. Ross, "Early Little Rock Doctors," *Pulaski County Historical Review,* I (June, 1953), 32.

valuable property, to be preserved at any reasonable cost, amounts expended by individual planters for professional medical care of slaves were sometimes substantial.

The fragmentary records of five physicians who practiced in three widely separated—and thus representative—Arkansas towns provide considerable information concerning professional medical care of slaves. The physicians were Henry Pernot, a Paris-born Frenchman who established a practice in Van Buren in 1852; A. Bronson, A. W. Brewster, and Thomas Young, all of whom practiced in Pine Bluff in the 1850's; and J. E. Hawkins of Stephens, Columbia County. Although the number of slaves in the areas where these doctors practiced varied greatly—from the heavy concentration around Pine Bluff to the relatively few in Van Buren and vicinity—all treated slaves with considerable frequency. These are typical entries from Pernot's account book:

M. R. Foster, June 1, 1852. To visit (black girl),
prescription, millage [mileage] (ammonia)   3.00

J. Bostick

June 6, 1853	To prescription, vial drops, black girl.	3.00
June 14, 1853	To pills, prescription, (black boy, blind of one eye.)	1.25
June 24, 1853	To vial drops prescription (black girl)	1.25
July 1, 1853	To vial drops (black girl)	".50
4	To vial drops (black girl)	".25
10	To vial drops (do)	".25
15	To vial drops (do)	".25
August 3	To bottle liniment (do)	".50
21	To vial drops (do)	".25
September 17	To vial drops (do)	".25
October 17	To vial drops (do)	".25

Josiah Foster Senior

July 11, 1855	To visit, mileage, examining of black girl for the clap	5.00

William Houser

August 12, 1854	To quinine powders (black child)	1.75
August 23	To visit pres: quinine (Black woman Margaret)	2.75[65]

Pernot's fees were more nearly comparable to those of the present day than were most other goods and services of the period,

[65] Account Book of Henry Pernot, *passim.*

but he frequently had to take his pay in commodities instead of cash. For example, Pernot's bill to Dutch Mayer, which included treatment of slaves, was $8.50 for the period from September 28, 1854, to June 10, 1855. Mayer paid it in this manner: June 10, 1855, one peck potatoes and six pounds beef, sixty-five cents; July 14, one bushel potatoes and six pounds beef, sixty-five cents; July 14, one bushel potatoes, seventy-five cents; July 24, one bushel potatoes, seventy-five cents; August 8, one bushel potatoes, seventy-five cents; August 21, two bushels potatoes, $1.50; August 21, one bushel peaches, twenty-five cents; November 6, 100 pounds flour, $3.25. This variety of food amounted to only $7.90, so Mayer paid the remaining sixty cents of the bill in cash. Calvin Phelps paid his $4.35 bill from Pernot with a thousand shingles valued at $4.00 and ten feet of timber worth thirty-five cents; John Austin paid with six loads of wood at a dollar a load.[66]

Each of the three Pine Bluff doctors treated the slaves of James Sheppard. Thomas Young treated the slaves at Waterford Plantation during the year 1851, Dr. A. Bronson served as the regular plantation doctor for the period from 1852 up until the Civil War, and Dr. A. W. Brewster, whose principal occupation may have been operation of his drugstore, occasionally was called in to consult with Dr. Bronson or to treat the Sheppard slaves alone. In 1851, when the size of Sheppard's slave force was still relatively small, Dr. Young's bill for treatment of slaves on five visits to the plantation from January to September was $29.00. The usual fee for each visit—$7.00—indicates that Young charged a fairly high mileage rate, for Sheppard lived only a few miles from the city of Pine Bluff. During the fall of 1851 Sheppard had sent some of his slaves to pick cotton for Dr. Young, for which he had charged $20.00. The net amount he owed Young on the medical bill, then, was $9.00, which he paid, as was customary for all accounts, in January of 1852.[67]

Although Dr. Bronson was the regular Waterford Plantation doctor for several years, the overseers nevertheless treated the slaves themselves on occasion. At times they did so from neces-

[66] *Ibid.*
[67] Statement, Thos. Young to James Sheppard, 1851, Sheppard Papers.

sity, as in July, 1854, when "the Asiatic Cholre was raging at a frightful rate" in the Pine Bluff region. Four of the Sheppard slaves were ill—although not with cholera—and D. T. Weeks, the overseer, sent for Dr. Bronson. The doctor sent word that he was ill with cholera himself, so, reported Weeks, "I set in to doing what I thought was the best & all is well and going about today."[68] Less than two weeks later several of the Sheppard slaves became ill again, but Weeks had the doctor come only once, and treated them himself for the remainder of their illness.[69] For 1857, the only year for which a complete record is available, Dr. Bronson's charges for medical services "rendered to negros" was $70.00.[70] During the same year Dr. Brewster also treated Sheppard's slaves several times, sending a bill for $34.00 for his services. That Sheppard sought the best medical care available when the occasion demanded is shown by Brewster's charge of $30.00 for "visit to plantation with Dr. Bronson & attending to woman during parturition—a very difficult case."[71]

Some of the charges made by Dr. J. E. Hawkins of Stephens were very low in comparison with others of the period. For example, on June 29, 1860, he charged only fifty cents for a visit, prescription, and medicine for a slave belonging to H. Bishop. This was an exception, however; his usual fees were $1.50 or $2.50 for day calls, and $3.50 for night calls, including prescription and medicine. Dr. Hawkins, as well as other doctors whose records have been examined, made the same charges for treatment of slaves as for whites; on June 28, 1860, he treated a slave of G. M. Hawkins for a fee of $1.50, and the same day visited and prescribed for the wife of D. Welch at the same rate.[72]

Full-time dentists were rare in pre-Civil War Arkansas, and physicians who treated slaves also occasionally pulled their teeth or performed other dental services. Fees for dental work were relatively low, with a dollar apparently standard for pulling a tooth.[73]

[68] D. T. Weeks to James Sheppard, July 29, 1854, Sheppard Papers.
[69] Weeks to Sheppard, Aug. 10, 1854, Sheppard Papers.
[70] Statement, A. Bronson to James Sheppard, 1857, Sheppard Papers.
[71] Statement, A. W. Brewster to James Sheppard, 1857, Sheppard Papers.
[72] Ledger of J. E. Hawkins, 1860-65, *passim.*
[73] Moffatt, "Medicine and Dentistry in Pioneer Arkansas," p. 93.

Of all aspects of medical treatment of slaves, least is definitely known of the home cures devised and administered by the slaves themselves. Knowledge of such cures was merely handed down by word of mouth from generation to generation, and since few slaves could read or write, composition of the medicines was rarely recorded in any manner. Consequently there are few surviving records of them today. Some rural Arkansans of the twentieth century, black and white alike, still rely on a variety of teas, poultices, salves, and liniments made at home from products of the fields and woods or ordinary household supplies, and there is no doubt that most of these home remedies originated at least as early as slavery days. Certainly a large percentage of all slave ailments must have been treated without benefit of scientific medical knowledge or commercial drugs.

X

Readin', 'Ritin', and Religion

On Duties to Servants

We very much regret that with the limited resources of the Convention, no satisfactory provision can be made to supply this much neglected portion of our population. But we trust and pray that the time may soon come when the Convention will be able to occupy this important field of missionary effort. In the meantime we would most affectionately and earnestly exhort Christian masters to the faithful discharge of the fearful duties growing out of this situation. Give your servants that which is just and equal, knowing that you also have a master in heaven.[1]

So read a report presented at the annual meeting of the Arkansas Baptist State Convention, meeting at Tulip, Dallas County, in 1854. This report reveals one reason many Arkansans favored religious teaching and missionary work among the slaves: genuine concern for the spiritual welfare of the slaves, who under the laws of man were merely chattels, but in the eyes of God were rational human beings who would be held responsible for their acts.

Commendable as was this attitude on the part of the master class, the following anecdote illustrates what was quite probably an equally prevalent reason for approval of religious teaching to the slaves:

Uncle Jasper . . . recalls that on the Pomprey plantation near the trading post of Benton [Saline County], Arkansas, in the old days, the preacher made one sermon do for both races. A big long shed served as meeting house. Into it the white people went to hear the

[1] *Proceedings of Arkansas Baptist Convention, 1854,* cited in J. S. Rogers, *History of Arkansas Baptists* (Conway, Arkansas, 1948), p. 474.

preacher in his powerful exhortations to right living. "Us servan's stayed outside, an' set down on de logs close by. When de preacher git all warm' up, an' had de white folks inside de shed thinkin' on de way ter glory, he stick his haid out de window now an' den ter exhort us servan's: 'You cullud people out dar—lissen at me! De way ter make good slaves, is ter obey yo' Massa an' Missis! Obey 'em constant—' Den he stick his haid back in, and preach till he had some mo' words fo' us-all."[2]

Uncle Jasper did not say what denomination the preacher represented, but that is of no consequence, since all took much the same stand: that religion lessened the difficulties, real or potential, inherent in the system of slavery. Lest by the opening quotation it be implied that Baptists had only altruistic motives in promoting religious teaching, the following excerpt from another Baptist report dealing with slaves, also presented in 1854, is given:

> Your Committee on the Colored Population ask leave to report . . . [that] all this class of persons are dependent alone upon others for devising the necessary system to communicate to them a saving knowledge of the gospel. . . .Your Committee is of the belief that if a correct system can be adopted to have the gospel regularly preached to this class of our population, that the owners would willingly, yes gladly themselves support the missionary; knowing that religion makes slaves industrious, temperate, honest and obedient![3]

Whatever the motive—to keep the slaves in peaceful subjection or to minister sincerely to the needs of their souls—all of the major denominations in Arkansas conducted religious work among slaves. In some cases slaves were members of the same churches as the whites and attended services at the same time; in others separate services were held for the slaves; in a few instances slaves had their own churches. Most of the denominations also carried on regular programs of missionary activity among the slaves in the thickly slave-populated sections of the state.

The earliest slaves in Arkansas were Catholic, of course, since their masters, French or Spanish, were also Catholic. The Black

[2] B. A. Botkin, ed., *Lay My Burden Down* (New York, 1946), p. 223. Similar reminiscences are on pp. 25 and 26.
[3] Report of Committee on the Colored Population, read at annual meeting of the Mt. Vernon Baptist Association, 1854, cited in Rogers, *Arkansas Baptists,* p. 491. The Mt. Vernon Association encompassed Phillips, St. Francis, and Monroe counties in eastern Arkansas.

Code of Louisiana, in effect prior to the Louisiana Purchase in 1803, contained, it will be recalled, several provisions concerning religion and slaves. Section II of the code made it imperative for masters to give religious instructions to slaves. Section III permitted the exercise of the Catholic creed only and prohibited every other form of worship. Section IV provided that slaves placed under the direction or supervision of any person who was not a Catholic were subject to confiscation by the government. A final religious provision of the Black Code was that Sundays and religious holidays were to be strictly observed, and that all slaves found at work on such days were subject to confiscation.[4]

With the coming of large numbers of Anglo-American, Protestant slaveowners in the years after Arkansas passed into the possession of the United States—and especially after it became a territory and a state—the Catholic faith was eclipsed by various Protestant denominations. The old French families—for example the Vaugines, the Bogys, the Notrebes, and the Barraques—who lived in the Arkansas River valley between Pine Bluff and the Mississippi River continued Catholic, however, and, presumably, so did their slaves who had grown up in the area. As additional slaves were purchased from non-Catholic owners, the percentage of Catholic slaves belonging to the old Catholic families diminished. There is no record of slaves being required to accept the Catholic religion merely because their masters were Catholic. Baptismal records of the older Catholic churches in Arkansas do contain, however, the names of slaves who were baptized in the Catholic faith.[5]

Methodists were one of the larger religious groups in Arkansas, and because of the episcopal form of organization of that body, fairly good records of their work among the slaves in Arkansas have been preserved. The chief source is the manuscript Minutes of the Arkansas Annual Conference, which have been preserved from the organization of the Conference in 1836.[6]

[4] Black Code of Louisiana, French, *Historical Collections of Louisiana*, III, 89.
[5] Baptismal Record, St. Mary's Church, New Gascony, Arkansas; Baptismal Record, St. Joseph's Church, Pine Bluff, Arkansas.
[6] The minutes are now in the archives of the Arkansas History Commission, Little Rock.

Methodist work existed for more than twenty years before the Arkansas Conference was separated from the Missouri Conference, however; the Spring River Circuit in northeastern Arkansas was established in 1815, and the Hot Springs Circuit, which covered the southern half of Arkansas, in 1816. The first Methodist church in Arkansas, named Henry's Chapel, was built in Hempstead County about 1818.[7] The first statistical report of Methodist work in Arkansas, made in 1815, showed that only four slaves in the entire area were Methodist, as compared to eighty-eight white people. Since organized work had not been started in all sections, there probably were more, however. By 1825 the number of Negro Methodists had climbed to 48, and the number of white to 664; during the next year 10 more slaves and 66 whites were brought into the church. The number of Methodists of each race continued to grow, to 22 slaves and 1,512 whites in 1831, 343 slaves and 2,306 whites in 1834, and 373 slaves and 2,326 whites in 1835, the last year Arkansas Methodists remained attached to the Missouri Conference.[8]

After 1836, with the rapid growth of population following the entrance of Arkansas into the union, the number of Methodists in the Arkansas Conference increased sharply. The proportion of slaves in the churches varied from one-seventh to one-fifth of the total number until 1854, when the Washita Conference, comprising the southern half of the state where most of the slaves were found, was created. Thereafter slaves composed only about one-tenth of the membership of the churches in the Arkansas Conference, although a much larger percentage, it may be presumed, of the churches in the Washita Conference. The following table, compiled from the conference minutes, shows the number of white, Negro, and Indian members of the churches in the Arkansas Conference for each of the years from 1836 through 1861. The component districts of the conference varied from time to time, accounting for some of the fluctuations in membership. The preponderance of Indians over Negroes during the earlier years

[7] John Hugh Reynolds, "Educational Institutions, Churches and Benevolent Societies," *Publications of the Arkansas Historical Association*, I, 155.
[8] Horace Jewell, *A History of Methodism in Arkansas* (Little Rock, 1923), pp. 56-95, *passim*.

was due to the fact that until 1844 a part of Indian Territory was included in the conference; at no time during the statehood period were there substantial numbers of Indians living in Arkansas.

MEMBERSHIP OF ARKANSAS CONFERENCE, METHODIST CHURCH, 1836-1861.

Year	White	Negro	Indian
1836	2,733	599	1,225
1837	3,054	592	960
1838	3,469	683	883
1839	4,809	809	1,216
1840	4,309	725	1,524
1841	5,066	828	1,524
1842	6,657	1,091	2,274
1843	8,770	1,804	2,840

(All districts containing Indians transferred in 1843.)

Year	White	Negro
1844	7,706	1,775
1845	7,370	1,724
1846	7,366	1,702
1847	8,007	1,731
1848	9,428	1,736
1849	10,332	1,819
1850	11,299	1,717
1851	12,756	2,430
1852	12,892	2,758
1853	15,665	2,897

(Washita Conference formed in 1854. Remaining figures apply only to northern half of state.)

Year	White	Negro
1854	9,143	833
1855	10,213	982

(After 1855, "members" and "probationers" were given.)

Year	White	Negro
1856	9,257-1,418	690-226
1857	9,052-2,289	779-221
1858	9,659-2,444	937-309
1859	11,563-2,604	1,038-416
1860	11,177-2,377	1,003-341
1861	11,447-2,463	892-170

In addition to encouraging the slaves to become members of the regular churches throughout the state, Arkansas Methodists also operated a mission program among them. The mission work was carried on through a number of "African Missions," usually located in rural areas where there were large numbers of slaves.

Most consistently mentioned in the annual reports of the Arkansas Conference was the Red River African Mission, the exact location of which was not given, but which probably was in Lafayette County in the extreme southwestern corner of the state. The mission apparently was first organized in 1840 or 1841, for it was first noted in the minutes of the Arkansas Conference in 1841, although the number of members was not given. During succeeding years, while the number of slave members increased gradually, the mission was variously referred to as "Red River Mission to Blacks," "Red River Colored Mission," and "Red River Affrican Mission." Membership of the mission was 125 from 1842 through 1844, 103 in 1845, 212 in 1848, 220 from 1849 through 1852, and 190 in 1853.[9] The same membership figures in several successive years suggest that they were only approximations. In 1853 the mission passed to the control of the Washita Conference, and no further reports were made. Several different white Methodist preachers served the Red River Mission, including A. Avery, W. B. Mason, Elijah F. McNabb, and William Mulkey.[10] Of Mulkey Dr. Andrew Hunter, famous early Arkansas Methodist, said: "Brother Mulkey served the Church for a number of years as a missionary to the colored people on the Red River plantations, the owners giving him a good support."[11]

Methodists also operated African Missions at one time or another in the following towns or communities: Helena, Princeton, Little Rock, Pine Bluff, Richland (Pine Bluff District), Mt. Vernon (Helena District), Augusta, Laconia, Bolivar (Jacksonport District), Harrisburg, and Long Lake (near Harrisburg). Since annual membership reports of all missions were not made, it is impossible to tell whether there were increases. Some had substantial memberships, however; Helena 80 in 1850, Augusta 23 members and 60 probationary members in 1857, and Little Rock 219 in 1851.[12]

More frequently than meeting in their own congregations, Methodist slaves

[9] Minutes of the Arkansas Annual Conference, 1842-1853, *passim.*
[10] *Ibid.*
[11] Jewell, *Methodism in Arkansas,* p. 210.
[12] Minutes of the Arkansas Annual Conference, 1842-1853, *passim.*

. . . received the gospel from the same Methodist preachers, and in the same churches with their masters. The galleries, or a part of the body of the house, was assigned to them. If a separate building was provided, the negro congregation was an appendage to the white, the pastor usually preaching once on Sunday for them, holding separate official meetings with their exhorters, leaders and preachers, and administering discipline and making return of members for the annual minutes.[13]

The manner in which slave members were received into Methodist congregations is illustrated by this report of a portion of the eleventh annual session of the Arkansas Annual Conference, held in 1846 at Van Buren: "The Bishop [Paine] now asked of the station preacher the success of our meeting in this house on last evening. He stated that five or six souls were converted to God, and seventeen individuals, including seven colored persons, gave their names to be admitted on trial into the church. . . ."[14]

Many Methodist preachers were themselves slaveowners;[15] some, however, were firmly abolitionist in sentiment. Most outspoken of these was Jesse Haile, whose period of service as a minister in Arkansas, from 1825 to 1829, was so turbulent that it was later referred to as the "hail storm." Haile, a fiery abolitionist "of the William Lloyd Garrison type," agitated against slavery, both in and out of the pulpit, so violently that many members of his congregations left and joined the Cumberland Presbyterian Church, whose members clung to the conservative Southern attitude toward slavery. In some instances Haile even managed to expel members who refused to emancipate their slaves at his urging. At least one young Methodist preacher, Thomas Tennant, was influenced by Haile to emancipate his own slaves, but later, when "reduced to a condition of want and suffering," regretted his action. In the interest of harmony, Haile was transferred in 1830 to the Illinois Conference, where his abolitionist fervor met with greater approval and where he served "with great acceptability to that people" for a number of years.[16]

But men with Haile's ideas were in the minority; the dominant

[13] Jewell, *Methodism in Arkansas*, p. 53.
[14] Minutes of the Arkansas Annual Conference, Nov. 30, 1846.
[15] Jewell, *Methodism in Arkansas*, p. 53.
[16] *Ibid.*, pp. 55, 73. Haile's resemblance to Garrison was merely in method; Garrison was not a preacher.

attitude of the members of the Methodist clergy in Arkansas was demonstrated some years later, on November 19, 1845, when the Tenth Session of the Arkansas Conference, at Camden, voted approval of two resolutions, one of which, in part, said: ". . . in the opinion of the Arkansas Annual Conference . . . the 'Relation of Master and Servant as it exists in the Slaveholding states of our Union' is not of itself 'necessarily sinful or a moral evil', which terms we consider synonomous."[17] The other resolution made complete the break of the Methodist Church in Arkansas with the Northern Methodists. The decisive section of the resolution read:

Resolved, that we, the members of the Arkansas Annual Conference, claiming all the rights of an annual conference of the Methodist Episcopal Church in the United States of America, do hereby declare our solemn preference for, and our determination strictly to adhere to, the Methodist Episcopal Church, *South,* in conformity to the plan of separation adopted by the General Conference of the Methodist Episcopal Church in 1844.[18]

During the period of slavery there were fewer Baptist churches in Arkansas than Methodist—281 in 1861 as compared to 505[19] —but Baptists were at least as active in their work among the slaves. The Negro's traditional affinity for Baptist beliefs is illustrated by a statement, possibly apocryphal, attributed to a Negro preacher during slavery times: "If you see a nigger who ain't a Baptist, you know some white man has been triggerin' with him!"[20] Exaggerated as this certainly was, it serves to emphasize the interest Arkansas Baptists had in the spiritual welfare of the slave population of the state.

The fact that each Baptist church in Arkansas was an independent congregation makes it impossible to secure co-ordinated statistical data on the numbers of slaves who were Baptists or who were ministered to by Baptists. There was no statewide Baptist organization until 1848, when the Arkansas Baptist State Convention was organized at Tulip, Dallas County,[21] and many Baptist churches remained outside of that organization. Evangelistic

[17] Minutes of the Arkansas Annual Conference, p. 70.
[18] *Ibid.,* p. 57.
[19] Rogers, *Arkansas Baptists,* p. 520.
[20] *Ibid.,* p. 491.
[21] *Ibid.,* p. 446.

services were a prominent part of the two-day organizational meeting of the convention, and among those converted were slaves who had accompanied their masters to the meeting. One of the organizers of the convention, the Reverend Samuel Stevenson, pastor of Mt. Bethel Baptist Church near Arkadelphia in Clark County, reported in the *American Baptist Register:*

Seldom are Christians privileged to see brighter manifestations of God's grace than were manifested in this meeting. The master and the servant, the child and parent, the self-righteous moralist and the profane sceptic bowed at the same altar of prayer and ere the meeting closed more than 40 happy hopeful converts were added to the militant kingdom of Christ. Thus the first Arkansas Conventional meeting closed, inspiring many hearts with brighter hopes.[22]

Although the exact number of slaves in Arkansas who were Baptist is unknown, some idea of their prevalence may be gained from applying figures compiled several years ago by Dr. E. P. Alldredge, statistical secretary of the Southern Baptist Convention. Dr. Alldredge wrote, "In 1860, when the War of the Confederacy broke upon the nation, there were 280,000 Baptists among the 4,000,000 Negro slaves soon to be freed—or one Baptist to every 12 Negroes of the Gospel age (10 or older.)"[23] Assuming that the percentage of Baptists among slaves in Arkansas was at least as great as in the South as a whole—and in all probability it was greater, since Arkansas had relatively few Catholics—there were at least 6,000 slaves who were Baptist in 1860.

The most extensive information concerning Baptists and slaves in Arkansas is found in the minutes of the individual churches. References to slave members are frequent, especially in the records of the churches in the predominantly slaveholding sections of the state. Minutes of associations, or organized groups of churches, are also useful. One of the oldest Baptist churches in Arkansas in continuous existence is the Point Remove Church, now located in Atkins, Pope County, but organized in 1833 at the small settlement of Point Remove, Conway County, about twelve miles north

[22] Quoted in *ibid.,* p. 448.
[23] *Southern Baptist Handbook for 1945,* cited in Rogers, *Arkansas Baptists,* p. 528.

of present-day Morrilton. There were no slaves among the charter members, but in later years several joined. The following record of a monthly conference of the church is typical of many in this and other church minutes:

1853   June
 The church met in conference Saturday Before the third Lords day in June & after worship proceded to business
1st Inviting members of our faith & order to seats with us
2nd Opend a door for the reception of members & Recd Brother
 Thomas Lemly by Experiance

JAMES BRUTON *Modr*
THOMAS HOWARD *Ch Clk*[24]

Thomas Lemly was a slave and later became a preacher. Two years later his wife, Mary, also joined Point Remove church "By Experence for Baptism." A son of the couple, Joe Lemly, was still living in Atkins in 1950.[25]

 Slaves often made up substantial portions of the membership of Baptist churches. The First Baptist Church of Pine Bluff was organized on October 6, 1853, with ten charter members, including one free Negro woman, Hannah Flanigan. A little more than a year later the membership had increased to 138, including 57 Negroes, almost all slaves. Several of the slaves belonged to Mrs. Nancy Hardwick, an especially devout member of the congregation who had great religious influence on her slaves.[26] Flat Creek Church, Ashley County, reported a membership in 1860 of 64 white people and 17 slaves. The same year the Bartholomew Baptist Association of 10 or more churches reported a total membership of 893 whites and 53 Negroes, none in separate Negro churches.[27]

 Many Baptist churches organized in Arkansas had slaves among their charter members. One of these was Muscogee Church, organized in what was then Hot Spring County (now in Polk County), in 1832. Charter members were a Reverend and

<hr>

[24] Minutes of Point Remove Baptist Church, 1833——.
[25] Statement of J. H. O'Neal, Dec. 22, 1950.
[26] Edwin Ryland and Anna Flournoy Bassett, *History of the First Baptist Church, Pine Bluff, Arkansas* (Pine Bluff, 1936), n. p.; Rogers, *Arkansas Baptists*, p. 158.
[27] E. H. Acuff, *Bartholomew Baptist Association of Arkansas, 1850-1950* (1950); Rogers, *Arkansas Baptists*, pp. 339-340, 144.

Mrs. Lewis, missionaries to the Creek Indians who at that time lived in western Arkansas; John Davis, a Creek Indian and missionary preacher; and three Negro men who were slaves of Creek Indians. Muscogee was organized primarily as an Indian mission church, but for several years more of the members were Negro slaves than Indians. During a revival campaign in 1834, thirteen slaves and six Indians joined the church.[28] Bethesda Church near present-day Alleene in Little River County had one slave among its charter members when it was organized in 1857,[29] as did Liberty Church in Union County, organized in 1832.[30]

The great majority of Baptist slaves were members of the same churches as their masters. There was little uniformity among the various individual churches in the times at which services were conducted for the slaves. In one church alone, the First Baptist of Arkadelphia, services were held at varied times, although most frequently on Sunday afternoon. On May 10, 1853, after preaching to the white members in the morning, Samuel Stevenson, the pastor, preached to the slave members in the afternoon "and opened a door for the reception of members—when Lucy and Harry Servants of S. Dickinson was recd by Experience and the ordinance of Baptism was administered the same evening."[31] Sometimes, as in July, 1860, services for the white members were held Saturday evening and for the slaves Sunday morning.

July Conference 1860. On Sabbath A. M. preaching to the colored people by Bro Horn. The door of the church was opened. Spencer a servant of Mrs. Harris Russel presented a recommendation from Mr. McDuff overseer. Spencer stated that he had lost his letter and wished to come under the watch care of the church, and he was received accordingly—[32]

Occasionally slaves attended the regular Sunday morning services and were received into the membership of the church along with white people. This was the case on September 13, 1851, when Elder Samuel Stevenson, later pastor for many years, joined the church at the same time that "three servants belonging to the

[28] Rogers, *Arkansas Baptists*, p. 127.
[29] *Ibid.*, p. 169.   [30] *Ibid.*, p. 130.
[31] Minutes of the First Baptist Church, Arkadelphia, Arkansas, 1851——.
[32] *Ibid.*

estate of W. Heard Ether Jane and David was received by letter."[33] A final variation of the arrangements for services for the slaves was that of August 5, 1860: "Sabbath evening preaching to the colored people. The door of the church was opened. Negro man George belonging to F. W. Murdock was received by Experience and Baptism."[34]

Some Baptist churches permitted the slaves to attend and participate in all of the services of the church, whatever the time they were conducted. This was particularly true in the smaller churches where services were held only one weekend a month. It was not unusual for churches to conduct services on Saturday night, Sunday morning, Sunday evening, and even Monday. New Hope Church in Clark County received slave members at each of its services during one such period of preaching in October, 1851.

Saturday before 3rd Sunday, October, 1851, received as a member a black man belong to Thos Miller. On the Lords day after servis opened the door for the reception of members Recd by Experence a Coulard man named Henry belonging to John House Recd a coulard man belonging to Wm a Striplin By the name of William by Letter. At night after servis Recd a coulard man Andrew and wife belonging to Uriah H. Parker [moderator and later pastor of the congregation] Monday after Servis opened the door . . . and recd a Black Woman by the name of Jane belonging to Br[other] McLendon on his vouching for her . . . also a Black man belonging to Prosper Lavilian by the name of Philip by Expr. . . .[35]

While joint worship services for whites and slaves were widely prevalent, some white Baptist leaders felt that the slaves could not be ministered to properly in that manner. Dr. P. S. G. Watson, one of the outstanding Baptist leaders of his day, said in 1854, "That the present plan of having the colored people attend religious worship with the whites is very defective and inefficient is evident, without argument, by the very small number of them that are professors of religion."[36] Watson's proposed solution was to have white ministers preach regularly to exclusively Negro congregations. Certainly it must have been difficult for a slave church

[33] *Ibid.*
[34] *Ibid.*
[35] Minutes of New Hope Baptist Church, Clark County, Arkansas, 1850-1860.
[36] Rogers, *Arkansas Baptists,* p. 491.

member to enjoy theoretical equality with his master in religious matters on Sunday while remaining subordinate to the master in all other matters during the week.

Despite the obstacles to fellowship between the races, there seems to have been a greater degree of informality in relationships between white and slave members in Baptist churches than in those of other denominations. A paternalistic attitude was evident on the part of white members of all denominations, of course, but in some Baptist churches, at least, the idealistic equality in the sight of God was more nearly reached. For example, slave preachers were sometimes received into the congregations, or slave members were ordained as preachers. This sort of action was made easier by the fact that each Baptist congregation, completely independent as it was, could ordain preachers without regard to any other authority, whereas ordination in churches with episcopal or other authoritarian systems of organization was much more difficult. The first minister ordained by the First Baptist Church of Pine Bluff was a slave, James Staryan, who was authorized to preach in 1854, only a year after the church was founded.[37]

An outstanding example of the slave Baptist preachers was "Uncle" Tom Clements, for many years an active member in the Mt. Zion Baptist church, still in existence in Greene County. Uncle Tom came to Arkansas before 1850 with his master, the Reverend M. E. Clements, a farmer-preacher who served as pastor of Mt. Zion church for a number of years.[38] This description of Tom's life and work was left by the Reverend R. C. Medaris, who knew him well both before and after the Civil War:

He was an outstanding soldier of the Cross. He was always present at every meeting of his church. He was always ready for every good work. He could lead in singing; he could conduct a prayer service; he could bury the dead. He could pray with more spirit and fervor than any one I ever heard, white or colored. He was true to every trust committed to him. . . .He was a good obedient slave until

[37] Ryland and Bassett, *First Baptist Church, Pine Bluff*, n. p. No records of slaves and white people partaking of the Lord's Supper, or communion, together were found. But since all other portions of services were often participated in jointly, it is quite possible that this was sometimes practiced, in Baptist churches as well as those of other denominations.
[38] R. C. Medaris, *Historical Sketch of the Mt. Zion Baptist Church, Greene County, Arkansas, also a Short Historical Sketch of Mt. Zion Baptist Association* (Jonesboro, Arkansas, 1927), p. 20; Rogers, *Arkansas Baptists*, p. 135.

he was made free, and after that remained with the Clements family until his death. . . .It is said that he officiated at the funerals of over one hundred white people in the faith.[39]

The other Protestant denominations had slave preachers, ordained or otherwise, among their membership, but knowledge of them is more scanty. In describing the religious life of slaves in the Pine Bluff area, Mrs. A. J. Marshall, widow of a pioneer Methodist preacher wrote, "It was pleasant to see the good attention to the preaching, and to hear the hearty tones with which they would sing the songs of Zion. There were some good preachers and talkers among them. Of course they 'Murdered the King's English,' but many of them seemed to understand the language of Canaan."[40]

Baptist mission work among the slaves of Arkansas was fairly extensive, if somewhat less well organized and co-ordinated than that of the Methodists. This was a normal state of affairs with Baptists, who cherished their tradition of decentralization. Sometimes mission work was promoted on a local or associational basis, as at the annual meeting of the Liberty Baptist Association, held with Salem Church, Columbia County, in 1858. Elder A. L. Hay made "a few remarks . . . upon the subject of missions, which were more particularly confined to the preaching of the gospel to the Cherokee Indians in the Nation, & to the black population [of the state]." At the conclusion of Hay's "few remarks," a collection amounting to $86.75 in cash and $20.00 "on subscription" was taken.[41] Another association which was interested in mission work among the slaves within its bounds was the Mount Vernon Association in eastern Arkansas. Slaves made up about one-fourth of the population of the three counties it covered, and the large majority of them were not being ministered to by any denomination.[42] In an attempt to remedy the condition a resolution was adopted:

[39] Medaris, *Mt. Zion Baptist Church*, pp. 7, 20.
[40] *The Autobiography of Mrs. A. J. Marshall* (Pine Bluff, Arkansas, 1897), p. 83.
[41] *Minutes of the Thirteenth Annual Session of the Liberty Baptist Association, Held with Salem Church, Columbia County, Arkansas, September 11th-14th, 1858* (Mount Lebanon, Louisiana, 1858), p. 3.
[42] Rogers, *Arkansas Baptists*, p. 491.

Resolved, That we would urge upon the Board the propriety and necessity of employing one or more suitable white ministers for labor amongst the colored population in our bounds the ensuing year and respectfully call upon owners of slaves and others to assist in sustaining such preachers. But should the Committee not succeed in procuring suitable missionaries, the churches are affectionately requested to try and afford what supply they may be able through the regular pastors.[43]

Unfortunately there is no record of the effectiveness of the resolution in securing support for the mission program. Red River Association in southwestern Arkansas probably did more successful work among the slaves than any other; during a single year in the 1850's it supported four missionaries to the slaves within its geographical area.[44]

From the very beginning the Arkansas Baptist State Convention, organized, as we have seen, in 1848, emphasized and supported missions among the slaves. At least one missionary to the slaves was employed by the Board of the Convention at the organizational meeting.[45] He, like his Methodist counterpart of the same period, was sent to work with the slaves in the Red River country. The special needs of the slaves in that section possibly stemmed from the high percentage of absentee ownership,[46] with the consequent loss of opportunity for religious training on the part of the masters. The Red River missionary produced some results during the ensuing year, but the committee supervising his work became somewhat discouraged, especially at the indifference and sometimes even antagonism on the part of some of the slave owners. The committee reported:

Your committee is to some extent distressed with the deplorable condition of many of our servants, especially in the southwestern part of our State. There are many slaves who are almost entirely deprived of hearing the gospel preached. We also know that many of them do and others doubtless would gladly hear the word of life if favorable opportunities were afforded. They often seem deeply impressed with the worth of their immortal souls. From the best information that we can obtain, in the absence of our Missionary to the

[43] *Ibid.*   [44] *Ibid.*
[45] *Ibid.*, pp. 453, 456.
[46] See MS Census Returns, Slave Schedule, Lafayette County, Arkansas, 1860.

colored population on Red River, we believe his labors have been blessed. We would therefore recommend that this field be occupied.

Your Committee would further recommend that each church appoint a committee of three or more brethren to attend the meetings that may be held with their respective churches for the benefit of this much neglected people; and also that we use our influence with masters to obtain for their servants the privilege of attending the house of God as often as practicable.[47]

The admonitions of the committee apparently bore fruit, for the report of the next year showed that B. L. Wright, Missionary to the Colored Population on Red River, had, despite the fact that "the difficulties with which he . . . had to contend might well have intimidated one less bold," baptized more than thirty "willing converts," and, furthermore, had secured the promise of additional financial aid for his work during the next year.[48] Records of Baptist mission work among the slaves for the remainder of the time up to the Civil War are fragmentary, but no doubt the Baptist Convention continued to promote the work. It is known that one missionary whose work was not primarily with slaves organized two Negro churches and ordained one Negro preacher and three deacons within a period of six months.[49]

In the Episcopal church, since all of Arkansas was a mission area until after the Civil War, work with Negro slaves was carried on as a part of the general program of missionary activity. Although many Arkansas settlers came from Virginia, North Carolina, South Carolina, and other states of the older South where the Episcopal Church was numerically important,[50] there were few Episcopal churches in the state. As late as 1850, according to the federal census, there were still only two, one in Little Rock and one in Van Buren.[51]

This was not the full extent of Episcopal work, however; three

[47] Rogers, *Arkansas Baptists,* p. 456.
[48] *Ibid.,* p. 460.
[49] *Ibid.,* p. 491.
[50] According to the 1860 census, 34,935 people, or more than 10 per cent of the white population, had been born in the three states named. There is no easy way to ascertain, of course, what percentage of these emigrants had Episcopal religious backgrounds. The small number of Episcopalians in Arkansas suggests, however, that a majority of the settlers from the South Atlantic states came from the back country, rather than from the more strongly Episcopal coastal regions.
[51] *Census of 1850,* p. 560.

years earlier, George W. Freeman, Missionary Bishop of the Southwest, reported that while Little Rock and Van Buren had the only organized parishes in the state (with the Van Buren church not especially active), there was other work on a smaller and more informal scale at Ft. Smith, Fayetteville, Cane Hill (near Fayetteville), Batesville, Helena, and Columbia (Chicot County).[52] A recent publication of the Episcopal Diocese of Arkansas indicates that the following churches now in existence were founded before the Civil War: St. John's, Camden (1850); St. Paul's, Fayetteville (1840); St. John's, Fort Smith (1847); St. John's, Helena (1853); Christ Church, Little Rock (1839); Trinity, Pine Bluff (1860); Trinity, Van Buren (1845); and Emmanuel, Lake Village (1858). These additional churches were active before the Civil War, but have either disbanded completely or have in recent years been reorganized: Grace, Jacksonport; Grace, Washington; St. Paul's, Augusta; and St. Mary's, El Dorado.[53]

Since Episcopalians were so few in number and so widely scattered, many were not members of any of the organized parishes. They had no regular services, but depended upon the occasional ministry of visiting missionaries, sometimes even the bishops themselves. During his missionary journey of 1863, Bishop Henry C. Lay visited several small places in southwestern Arkansas where there were communicants, but no churches. On April 18 he stopped at Spring Hill, an old settlement in Hempstead County, and preached five sermons within a few days, including one special sermon for the Negroes of the vicinity. He visited Washington, where there was a church, on April 23, preaching seven times, also including once to the Negroes. On April 28 Bishop Lay arrived at Royston, Pike County, where he found three communicants and preached twice, in the morning to the white people and in the evening to the slaves.[54]

By Episcopal church law, confirmation could be administered

[52] *Journal of the General Convention of the Episcopal Church, 1847,* (n.p., n.d.), p. 208.
[53] *Journal of the Eighty-first Annual Convention of the Protestant Episcopal Church in the Diocese of Arkansas, 1953* (Little Rock, 1953), pp. 7-8.
[54] "Journal of Bishop Henry C. Lay, 1862-1863," printed in *Historical Magazine of the Protestant Episcopal Church,* VIII (March, 1939), p. 85.

only by the bishop; consequently there were usually both white children and slaves to be confirmed at each of the infrequent visits of the bishops to the various churches. In the parish register of St. John's Church, Camden, under date of November 26, 1859, is recorded: "Our newly appointed missionary Bishop Henry C. Lay arrived at Camden for a visit; while here he confirmed fourteen white members and one colored, Nancy, a servant of Dr. John Seay."[55] Baptisms of slaves are also recorded. Among those baptized in Grace Church, Washington, by the Reverend Reginald H. Murphy on July 12, 1863, were seven-year-old Alexander and two-year-old Priscilla, slave children of Priscilla, cook at the rectory. Eliza G. Murphy, presumably the wife of the rector, served as sponsor of the children. Apparently slaves were baptized at the same services as white people, for several white children were baptized on the same day, both before and after the slaves.[56]

Presbyterians were the third most numerous religious denomination in Arkansas, following the Methodists and the Baptists. Beginning their work in 1828,[57] they had increased to fifty-two churches by 1850.[58] No statistics on the number of slave members of the Presbyterian churches have been found, but it may reasonably be supposed that the number was proportionately comparable to the Baptist and Methodist memberships, for slaves usually belonged to the denomination of their masters, if any. That Presbyterians were interested in the religious welfare of the slaves is evident from a resolution passed at one of the annual meetings of the Ouachita Presbytery, covering southern Arkansas. The Presbytery "recommended that all churches . . . set apart a portion of their buildings for the use of the black people, and that they cooperate with other Presbyteries in evangelistic work among the slaves. They not only regarded the right of the slave to religious privileges, but also the right to humane treatment. . . ."[59]

[55] Quoted in *St. John's Church, 1850-1950* (n.p., n.d.), p. 5.
[56] Baptismal Record, Grace Episcopal Church, Washington, Arkansas, 1860-1867.
[57] S. G. Miller, ed., *The History of Presbyterianism in Arkansas, 1828-1902* (Little Rock, n.d.), p. 11.
[58] *Census of 1850*, p. 561.
[59] Miller, *Presbyterianism in Arkansas*, p. 42.

Besides the organized denominations which have been discussed, there were a few other churches in Arkansas which may
have ministered to the slaves to some extent. The *Census of
1850* lists one "Free" church in Madison County, one "Union"
church in Madison and four in Montgomery County, and churches
of "minor sects" in the following locations: one in Madison County, ten in Scott County, and two in Yell County.[60] Since all of
these counties had very few slaves, it is not likely that many slaves
belonged to the churches.

Less is known of the informal religious training of slaves on the
plantations and in the homes of Arkansas slaveowners than of the
organized work of the churches. Only occasionally in the records
of the slavery period are there found brief allusions to the practice
which is known, from other sources, to have been widespread in
the South. When the Episcopal Bishop Lay visited the small
cotton-manufacturing village of Royston, Pike County, in 1863,
he commented, "I was gratified to find that domestic religious
teaching was begun with the factory hands—some of them being
Georgia Negroes, although ignorant of the church, knew the
Creed, by transmission from their fathers."[61] Often the wife of
the plantation owner, or "Old Missus," as she was commonly
known, served as a sort of spiritual advisor to the plantation
slaves. Such was the case in an incident related by a slave woman
applying for membership in a Baptist church in Columbia County.
In keeping with the requirements of that church, she was asked to
tell her experience of conversion to the assembled congregation.
"One day I was walkin' across de field and stumped my toe and
fell down and said 'damn it.' When I got up I felt awful bad
and went and axed Ole Missis what mus' I do. Ole Missis said,
'go pray.' I went and prayed and kep' on prayin' till at las' I
felt sho' de Lawd had forgive me."[62]

Slaveowners frequently recorded the births of the slave children
in the family Bible, as did Robert Isaac Lemon of Pine Bluff.[63]
One probably would not be in error in assuming that in devout

[60] *Census of 1850*, pp. 560, 562.
[61] "Journal of Bishop Lay," p. 85.
[62] Chester, *Pioneer Days in Arkansas*, p. 47.
[63] Bible of Robert Isaac Lemon, Pine Bluff, Arkansas, in possession of a
granddaughter, Mrs. Walter Combs, Pine Bluff.

households the slave children whose births were recorded in the family Bible were often gathered around the mistress's knee to hear the Word of God read from the very same Bible.

Often in the past the generalization has been made that Negro slaves were devoutly religious beings who bore their burdens with Christian long-suffering. Certainly there is little to bear out the validity of such a generalization insofar as the majority of Arkansas slaves was concerned. As we have seen, the number of slaves formally affiliated with the various denominations was only a small minority of the total slave population at any given time; 20,000 out of the slave population of 111,115 in 1860 probably would be a very liberal estimate. This, of course, is no positive proof of extent of religious interest, but it is an indication. It must always be remembered that the primary function of the slave was to work for his master, and only the especially religious and considerate master concerned himself with the spiritual welfare of his slaves. Left to their own devices, as most of them were, it is evident that the Negro slaves of Arkansas concerned themselves to a relatively small degree with matters of religion, at least in a formal or organized manner.

There were no laws in Arkansas forbidding the education of slaves; withholding education was merely accepted as a normal practice in the system of slavery as imported from the older states. Certainly there is no evidence that Arkansas slaveowners were any more interested in providing their slaves with even basic education than were their counterparts in states which prohibited slave education. The general Southern philosophy was that education was likely to make slaves more dissatisfied with their lot and thus more troublesome; Arkansas masters shared this belief, and, in general, withheld formal education from the slaves. Informal education was another matter, however; a master would have had to be vigilant, indeed, to prevent an intelligent slave with the desire to learn to read and write from doing so. House servants usually had access to printed matter; small slave boys and girls often accompanied their young masters and mistresses of like age so closely that inevitably they shared in some of the knowledge acquired by the white children; even field hands were not completely cut off from contact with the printed or written word.

Despite these possibilities for education, overt or secretive, there are few known instances of educated Arkansas slaves. Of course the extent of education of the slaves, especially if it were only rudimentary, is a matter about which few records of any sort would have been kept. Some information concerning the level of education of certain slaves in Arkansas may be secured from the advertisements of runaway slaves in the newspapers. Occasionally such advertisements indicated that the slave in question could read and write. For example, John A. Jordan of South Bend, Arkansas, advertised in 1854 for his "bright mulatto" slave boy William, aged 24, who could read and write, and who was expected to attempt to pass himself as a white man.[64] Fielding, a young slave who ran away from his master, J. H. Ward of Lewisburg, in 1849, could also read and write, and was expected to attempt to use his abilities to good advantage by forging a pass to aid him in his circumvention of the law.[65]

Aside from such rare cases as these, there is no positive evidence of educational accomplishments among Negro slaves in Arkansas. The job of a slave was to work, and most of the work on the farms and plantations and in the home and shops of Arkansas could be done without benefit of education.

[64] *True Democrat,* April 18, 1854.
[65] *Arkansas State Democrat,* Aug. 31, 1849.

XI

Jumping the Broomstick

IN RENDERING the decision in the case of *Gregley* v. *Jackson* in 1882, Justice James Eakin of the Arkansas Supreme Court wrote: "There were no valid marriages amongst that class [the slaves], in the slave states of America before their general emancipation near the close of the civil war, nor after that did any of the States take cognizance of marriages amongst slaves, until provisions were made by statute."[1] Written nearly twenty years after the end of the slave era, Justice Eakin's statement was a correct appraisal of the status of slave marriage in Arkansas. Arkansas had no laws which stated specifically that slave marriages did not exist in the legal sense; coming as they did from the older slave states, Arkansans merely understood generally that a slave, like any other piece of property, had no right to enter into any sort of legal contract. Frequently, however, slaves went through some sort of marriage ceremony before living together.

Information disclosed in an Arkansas Supreme Court case decided in 1950 illustrates in some detail various aspects of the marital status of slaves in Arkansas.[2] "Old Joe" Edwards was a slave of the Gant family in Union County. Before 1850 he married Susan, a slave belonging to the Wroten family, which lived six or eight miles away, in the traditional slave mariage ceremony called "jumping the broomstick." From that time on, although the requirements of the slavery system prevented them from living together constantly, Joe and Susan regarded each other as husband and wife, and during the years from 1850 to 1863 Susan

[1] *Gregley* v. *Jackson,* 38 Ark. 490.
[2] *Daniels* v. *Johnson,* 374 Ark. 216. No citations will be made to portions of the case.

gave birth to five children of whom Joe was the acknowledged father.

A few years after Joe married Susan, he became attracted to Patsy, like himself a slave of the Gant family, who lived in an adjoining slave cabin in the Gant back yard. Patsy was the "black mammy" of the Gant children, including Nancy, who was born in 1853 and lived to be more than ninety-six years old. About 1855 Joe and Patsy were married, also by "jumping the broomstick," although Joe's marriage to Susan continued to exist and to produce children. From 1856 to 1864 Patsy bore five children, all girls, whom Joe also recognized as his children. Thus Joe was "married" to two women and the father of two families of children simultaneously.[3]

Amid the confusion attendant upon the end of the Civil War and the consequent freeing of all slaves, Joe terminated his two marriages and in 1866 began to live with Aveline, also a recently freed slave. The next year the union of the two was legalized by an Arkansas statute, passed by the General Assembly on February 6, 1867, entitled "An Act to declare the rights of persons of African descent." The portion pertaining to marriage decreed:

Be it further enacted, That all negroes and mulattoes who are now cohabiting as husband and wife, and recognize each other as such, shall be deemed lawfully married from the passage of this act, and shall be subjected to all the obligations, and entitled to all the rights appertaining to the marriage relation; and in all cases where such persons now are, or have heretofore been so cohabiting, as husband and wife, and may have offspring recognized by them as their own, such offspring shall be deemed in all respects legitimate, as fully as if born in lawful wedlock.

In 1868 Joe and Aveline Edwards became the parents of J. W. (Jim), the only child born of the marriage. Both Old Joe and Aveline died by 1876, but Jim lived until 1946, leaving no descendants. During his lifetime Jim acquired property, mostly oil lands, valued variously at from $125,000 to $3,000,000, and when he died intestate, legal actions were brought by numerous

[3] This was not a unique case. In 1854 S. W. Boyer offered a $100 reward for the return of the runaway slave Henry, who had "a wife near Summerville, Tennessee, and also a wife and children in St. Louis." *True Democrat,* July 12, 1854.

relatives in attempts to secure the property. The claimants to the property were in three groups: the "Patsy line," composed of the descendants of Old Joe, father of Jim, and the Gant slave Patsy; the "Susan line," made up of the descendants of Old Joe and Susan, the Wroten slave; and the descendants of Sophronia, sister of Jim's mother Aveline.

The Union County probate judge quickly overruled the claims of the members of the Sophronia group, who had asserted that since no slave marriages had been legal, all of the children of Patsy and Susan (half-brothers and sisters of Jim) had been illegitimate, and that descent for the purpose of awarding the property should be traced from the next nearest relative, the sister of Old Joe's legal wife Aveline. The probate judge then ruled that the children of Susan and Old Joe had been legitimate and their descendants thus entitled to share the estate of Jim, but that the children of Patsy and Old Joe had been illegitimate, with their descendants deprived of a share in the estate. The judge based his decision on the fact that Old Joe's marriage to Susan had occurred first, making, in his opinion, the second, to Patsy, bigamous and the children born of it therefore illegitimate. This decision was given in spite of testimony by Mrs. Nancy Gant Britt, in whose family Patsy had been the "black mammy," that Joe and Patsy were considered properly married by standards of the slavery period:

Mrs. Britt: Everyone in the community said that when a slave man and woman were having children they were considered married. They generally lived in the same house, or near each other.

Judge: When he took up with Patsy, he called that marrying her?

Mrs. Britt: I suppose so. That is the way they did it in those days. . . .

Judge: And you say Joe and Patsy were living on the same place and were living there and had children as man and wife?

Mrs. Britt: Yes!

The descendants of Patsy appealed the decision and eventually the case reached the Arkansas Supreme Court. The court agreed that the Sophronia group had no legal claim on the estate of Jim, but ruled that the descendants of Patsy were entitled to share in the estate on an equal basis with those of Susan. The court based this decision on that part of the statute of 1867 which said ". . . in all cases where such persons . . . have heretofore been so cohabiting, as husband and wife, and may have offspring recognized by them as their own, such offspring shall be deemed in all respects legitimate, as fully as if born in lawful wedlock." In other words, since Old Joe had lived with both Susan and Patsy in the marital state, even though at the same time, and had acknowledged all children born to both slave women as his own, the children were all legitimate. It is readily apparent that the 1867 act of the legislature as interpreted by the Arkansas Supreme Court had the effect of legitimatizing children of all slave marriages in Arkansas, no matter how early they were born.

A charge leveled persistently at slaveowners through the years has been that they deliberately forced their slaves to breed and produce children as rapidly as possible in order to reap the profits. No evidence to substantiate this charge was found in Arkansas; and even if slaveowners tried to do so, they were remarkably unsuccessful, for, as we have seen, the slave birth rate was lower than the white. In all of his researches in the United States as a whole, Ulrich B. Phillips uncovered only one instance of a master forcing his slaves to cohabit regardless of their wishes, and this happened in Massachusetts in 1636.[4] A question which those accusing slaveowners of enforced breeding have neglected to attempt to answer is why it would have been necessary to compel slaves to satisfy one of the most basic of human urges.

Naturally there would have been slave children whether the slaves were married or not, but many slaveowners, especially the more religious ones, encouraged, or even insisted upon, some sort of ceremony, and after that expected a certain degree of faithfulness of the slaves to each other. One type of informal slave marriage ceremony, "jumping the broomstick," has already been mentioned; some other ceremonies were equally informal. One master near Little Rock merely wrote in the family Bible the names of his two slaves who chose to live together, admonished them to

---

[4] Phillips, *American Negro Slavery*, p. 361. For a good refutation of the myth that slaveowners systematically bred their slaves, see Craven, *Coming of the Civil War*, pp. 80-85.

refrain from "fussin' and fightin'," and thenceforth considered them married.[5] Other slave marriage ceremonies, however, were practically as formal as those of the white people. An old Negro woman who had been a slave near Dewitt in Arkansas County gave this description of slave marriages on the plantation of Colonel Jesse Chaney, who had a reputation for kindliness and consideration for his slaves:

When two of the slaves wanted to get married, they'd dress up as nice as they could and go up to the big house, and the master would marry them. They'd stand up before him, and he'd read out of a book called *The Discipline,* and say, "Thou shalt love the Lord thy God with all thy heart, all thy strength, with all thy might, and thy neighbor as thyself." Then he'd say they were man and wife and tell them to live right and be honest and kind to each other. All the slaves would be there, too, seeing the wedding.[6]

Slaveowners usually favored marriages between their own slaves, rather than between a slave of their own and one belonging to someone else, for under such an arrangement there would be less interruption of the routine of slave life and work.[7] But many slaves did marry away from home, either by choice or because of the lack of an eligible partner nearby. When marriages of this sort existed, masters permitted the slave husband to visit his wife at times (usually on weekends), or arranged to get the couple together by buying or selling one of them. Allen Martin of the Mabelvale community near Little Rock offered in 1841 to trade 237 acres of land on Crooked Creek for his slave Dick's wife and three children, who belonged to a neighbor named Thorn.[8] Previously referred to in another connection was a series of sales necessary to unite a slave couple at the home of a single owner: Robert F. Kellam of Camden sold his slave woman Sarah and her two children to Lucius Greening in January, 1860, and two months later a Mr. Sheridan sold the slave man Sheridan to Greening, which, according to Kellam, "gett our former Servant Sarah with her husband."[9]

[5] Orland K. Armstrong, *Old Massa's People* (Indianapolis, 1931), p. 165.
[6] Botkin, *Lay My Burden Down,* p. 146.
[7] Armstrong, *Old Massa's People,* p. 164; *Daniels* v. *Johnson,* 374 Ark. 216.
[8] Allen Martin to Jared C. Martin, May 15, 1841, Martin Papers.
[9] Diary of Robert F. Kellam, Jan. 4, March 28, 1860.

Since there was no legal requirement of keeping slave husbands, wives, and children together, there were many instances of separation. But the records also contain indications that many owners respected the existence of the slave family as a social, if not a legal, institution, and that they attempted to preserve it whenever possible. Advertisements of slaves for sale or hire often referred to slave families. An unnamed owner offered in the Helena *Southern Shield* to hire out "two likely negroes, man and woman; the woman is a good house girl, cook, and washer; the man is an excellent field hand," and stated that "it would be preferable to hire them together, as they are man and wife."[10] Charlotte, a mulatto woman about forty, and her son Lewis, about eighteen, were offered for sale in Little Rock in 1829 only on condition that they be treated humanely and not be separated.[11]

Slave children were always the property of the owner of the mother, which was another reason for encouragement of marriage between slaves in the same establishment. Special consideration was given to slave mothers before and after childbirth, with freedom from work "two weeks before—two weeks after" the general custom. And the owner so fortunate as to own a "special woman"—one who produced children often and over a long period of time—was even more careful of his very valuable property.[12] One such woman could soon be responsible for wealth far in excess of her own value. A major reason for the common practice of giving a slave girl to each member of the owner's family at marriage or some other time was to furnish the nucleus of a new slave working force.[13]

But all slaves did not "jump the broomstick" or enter into marriage in other ways; many merely engaged in what would be considered sexual immorality by conventional standards. The level of sexual morality of Negro slaves, however, should not be judged by the same standards which applied to white people of

[10] *Southern Shield*, May 1, 1852.
[11] *Arkansas Gazette*, April 15, 1829.
[12] Armstrong, *Old Massa's People*, pp. 165, 181.
[13] Small slave boys were also given to children of the family, but the practice of giving slave girls was more prevalent. See *Moody* v. *Walker*, 3 Ark. 147; *Hynson and Wife* v. *Terry*, 1 Ark. 38; *Carter et al* v. *Cantrell et al*, 16 Ark. 154; *Gaines as Ad.* v. *Briggs et al*, 9 Ark. 46; *Dodd* v. *McCraw*, 8 Ark. 84.

the period. Marriage, as we have seen, did not legally exist, and so to begin with the slaves were without what is probably the greatest curb to sexual promiscuity in the human social order. Certainly it would have required a high degree of social and moral consciousness for anyone, and particularly an uneducated and unsophisticated slave, to distinguish between acceptable sexual relations in an informal marriage and unacceptable relations where no such marriage existed. Especially was this true when a slave might pass successively into the ownership of men with varying standards and requirements concerning the marital relationships of their slaves. The plain fact is that probably a majority, if not all, of Arkansas slaves were sexually promiscuous by white standards at some time in their lives, partly because of the general lack of social restraint to such practices, and partly because in relation to other members of the slave class there was, legally speaking, no such thing as promiscuity. Another factor was the influence of an African background of universally polygamous marriage attaching no value to faithfulness to a single mate.

Despite widespread promiscuity, there are many instances of apparent faithfulness of slave married couples to each other. For example, "Uncle Charley" Nicholls of near Little Rock was married at an early age to Anna, his master's "house-gal," and the two lived faithfully together for many years, eventually producing, both before and after the abolition of slavery, twenty-four children, including several sets of twins.[14]

The slave social structure contained no such component as the old maid or spinster, since there was no real passage from the unmarried to the married state. Probably the nearest equivalent to this phenomenon present only in the more highly regulated societies was the slave woman who was unable to bear children for physiological reasons, and of course even this was no deterrent to cohabitation. As a rule slave girls entered into unions at a very early age, and teen-age mothers were commonplace.

It is in the cloudy realm of sexual relations between members of the white race and Negro slaves that there has been the most interest and speculation in the past. Abolitionist literature of the

[14] Armstrong, *Old Massa's People*, p. 165.

slavery period made much of white-slave relations, loudly claiming that slave women were universally made victims of the white man's lust, and intimating that this was one of the reasons for the South's persistence in maintaining slavery. Only one account from abolitionist literature referring to Arkansas need be cited here for purposes of illustration; all are very much of a type. This one was related by John Roles, who served as an overseer in the South for ten years and later published an abolitionist book.[15]

In telling of the past tribulations of his cook while in the South, Roles described her as beautiful and intelligent, but decried the advantages to be achieved by such attributes, for, he wrote, ". . . the cruel and licentious abominations of slavery had destroyed her happiness from the day that she began to bloom into womanhood, and will continue to destroy it until the grave shall hide her from the oppressor, and her beautiful but welted and scarred body shall mix and moulder with its mother earth." The slave woman was born in Virginia of—as was fitting in such fierce anti-Southern propaganda—a slave mother and a white man, who, to add further fuel to the flame, was a Methodist preacher. As a young girl she was sold to a man in Fort Smith, Arkansas, who "made her the victim of his lust when she was very young, and threatened to sell her off to a cotton plantation if she let her mistress know what he was doing." The girl was too young to realize fully the wrong of what she was doing, but such a realization would have made no difference, "for her master was a stern man, and she would not have dared to resist."

The philandering master also carried on an affair with another house slave, and when jealousy between the two arose, the second slave informed the mistress of the relations between the master and the first. At an opportune time when the master was absent from home, the mistress, with the aid of the other slave, seized Roles's heroine, stripped her, tied her hands and feet, flogged her brutally, and then ordered the other slave to continue the whipping. The next stage of the punitive and vengeful treatment consisted of application of fire in a manner which, in keeping with the ideas of that Victorian day, Roles would not even describe:

[15] John Roles, *Inside Views of Slavery on Southern Plantations* (New York, 1864), pp. 29-30.

"But I cannot give the revolting details of this cruel punishment. I have heard of jealous mistresses burning their slaves in a cruel manner, but propriety forbids me to describe the mode, for the same reasons that I cannot give the vile slang used by slave-drivers towards their female slaves." Evidently Roles was hinting broadly at injury to the sexual organs. Just before the torture was to begin, the slave girl broke free and attempted to commit suicide by cutting her throat with a butcher knife but was prevented from doing so.

A short time later the girl was sold again, this time to a merchant living on the Arkansas River. At her new home there was the same pattern of seduction, varied only by a vague promise that eventually she would be set free. But the hope never materialized, and in time she was traded off for dry goods. The new master also made glowing promises to win her sexual favors, but Roles's poor heroine never reached a status higher than that of house servant and concubine. And so went the tale.

John Roles's account doubtless contains elements of both truth and exaggeration, but it must be remembered that it, like similar literature, was written as propaganda, and naturally emphasized events which helped to prove the point of the writer. To believe that the experiences of Roles's slave girl were typical of the relationship between all female slaves and their masters in Arkansas would be like believing that *Uncle Tom's Cabin* was a completely correct picture of slavery in all its aspects.

That masters and female slaves did engage in sexual relations there is no doubt, and there is considerable evidence, even though much of it indirect, to support the assertion. The generally furtive nature of such relationships prevents, however, any reasonable estimate of their prevalence. But there is irrefutable proof in the birth to slave women of children known to have been fathered by white men. It is impossible to ascertain the frequency of such births, because for every instance in which a white man admitted paternity there certainly were many more where no such admission was made. And of the cases where white men were acknowledged fathers of slave children, probably only a small percentage were ever recorded in any form, and these

usually only when some legal question, such as a grant of freedom
or money to the slave, was involved.

It might appear that the proportion of slaves of mixed blood
would give some indication of the frequency of births of white-
fathered children, but even this can offer only insights, for when a
slave, either black or of mixed blood, cohabited with another
slave of mixed blood, obviously the children would also be of
mixed blood, but the progeny of slaves. In addition, there was
always some cohabitation between slaves and free Negroes, among
whom there was a much higher percentage of mulattoes than
among slaves, and this would tend, through the inevitable birth
of mulatto children, to increase the number of mulattoes in the
slave population, but not as a direct result of white-slave cohabitation. A final reason for the invalidity of the size of the mulatto
slave population as a key to the frequency of births of white-
fathered children to slaves is that some mulattoes eventually
moved from the status of slaves to that of free Negroes by virtue
of having white fathers. But since the number of free Negroes
in Arkansas was always small, this factor had little effect upon
the proportion of mulattoes in the total slave population.

Although it is evident, then, that the proportion of mulattoes
in the slave population can offer no direct evidence as to the number of children born of interracial cohabitation, an examination
of the available statistics is nevertheless of some interest. Prior
to 1850 the federal censuses gathered no information concerning
the color or racial composition of slaves. The following table
shows the percentage of mulattoes in the slave population of the
more important slave states for the years 1850 and 1860:

PERCENTAGE OF MULATTOES IN SLAVE POPULATION[16]

State	1850	1860
Alabama	6.73	7.89

[16] U. S. Bureau of the Census, *Compendium of the Seventh Census, 1850*
(Washington, 1854), p. 83, and *Census of 1850 (Population)*, p. xiii. The
term "mulatto" was used in no exact sense in the censuses, but merely reflected
the individual judgment of the census enumerators. A publication of the
United States Bureau of the Census contains this statement: "At the censuses
of 1850 and 1860 the terms 'black' and 'mulatto' appear not to have been
defined. In 1850 enumerators were instructed simply in enumerating colored
persons to write 'B' or 'M' in the space on the schedule, to indicate black or
mulatto, leaving the space blank in the case of whites. In 1860 no instructions
are known to have been given to the enumerators." U. S. Bureau of the

Arkansas	15.61	12.64
Florida	8.33	8.51
Georgia	6.31	7.98
Kentucky	16.40	19.19
Louisiana	8.22	9.83
Maryland	9.56	10.18
Mississippi	6.80	8.39
Missouri	17.84	19.07
North Carolina	6.19	6.94
South Carolina	3.36	5.26
Tennessee	9.29	13.63
Texas	15.27	13.68
Virginia	10.34	14.24

An examination of the figures for 1850 reveals that the states with the lowest percentages of mulattoes were Alabama, Georgia, Mississippi, North Carolina, and South Carolina, all predominantly slave-*using* states of the older South. The states with the highest percentages of mulattoes fell into two groups: Arkansas and Texas, predominantly slave-*using* states of the newer South; and Kentucky, Virginia, and Missouri, primarily slave-*selling* states. In 1860 the same group of states remained lowest in percentage of mulattoes, although all had shown increases. Of the high states in 1850, only two—Arkansas and Texas—had shown declines in percentages of mulattoes by 1860, while the group had been supplemented by Tennessee and Maryland, like the others primarily slave-exporting states.

The groupings and trends between 1850 and 1860 suggest these conclusions: (1) Slave-exporting states tended to have high and increasing percentages of mulattoes, because, as we have seen, black slaves sold more readily in the lower South, with mulattoes consequently being kept at home where they formed an increasingly large percentage of the slave population. (2) The slave-using states of the older South had low percentages of mulattoes since they for many years had been purchasing mostly black slaves. But the percentage of mulattoes was increasing as these states in turn exported black slaves to the newer South. (3) The slave-importing states of the newer South (Arkansas and Texas) had high percentages of mulattoes at first because

Census, *Negro Population, 1790-1915* (Washington, 1918), p. 207. Throughout this study the term "mulatto" has been used to mean a Negro of any degree of mixed blood.

when settlers entered they took with them the slaves they already owned, including, presumably, a high proportion of mulatto house-servants. The statistical importance of mulattoes was also enhanced by the relatively small numbers of slaves in Arkansas and Texas in 1850. But by 1860 the percentages of mulattoes had declined because slaves purchased to work on the rapidly growing plantations were mainly blacks rather than mulattoes. The fact that Arkansas and Texas had the largest increases in slave population in the 1850-1860 decade and yet were the only states in which the percentages of mulattoes decreased tends to verify the latter conclusion.

Most of the verifiable instances of slave women having children fathered by white men are found in the reports of cases which came before the Arkansas Supreme Court. Some of these cases have been referred to in other connections, and will be considered again in a later discussion of the free Negro. When Duncan Campbell of Chicot County died in 1845, he acknowledged in his will that he was the father of Viney, small daughter of one of his slaves.[17] An instance of openly and readily admitted paternity of a slave child concerns James H. Dunn, a merchant of Fulton, Hempstead County, and the slave woman Mourning. Mourning was hired by Dunn from the estate of James Moss to serve as cook and housekeeper, and in time she gave birth to a girl named Eliza. "At divers times, and to divers persons" Dunn admitted that he was the father of Eliza, and he publicly recognized her as his child. He attempted to purchase Eliza from the Moss estate in order that he might free her, but died before he was able to do so.[18]

Allen T. Wilkins of Lafayette County was the acknowledged father of the slave boy John, son of his slave woman Sarah Jane, and also of another child who had died in infancy. A few months before Wilkins died in Lewisville in November, 1851, he engaged in a conversation with William H. Dillard which throws interesting light on the frequency with which white men fathered children of slaves and then set them free, as Wilkins directed in his deathbed will. During the conversation Wilkins told Dillard that

[17] *Campbell et al* v. *Campbell*, 13 Ark. 513.
[18] *Moss* v. *Sandefur, Ex.*, 15 Ark. 381.

he was the father of the slave boy John, and Dillard advised him to set the boy free while he was still alive, since such manumissions were not always satisfactorily carried out after a man's death. Dillard cited "a number of cases in this county" to prove his point.[19]

In considering sexual relationships between white men and slave women, quite naturally this question arises: how willing were the slaves to enter into such relationships? This is another area within which there is practically no direct evidence, but common sense and a general knowledge of the operation of the slave system help to provide an answer. There is no evidence to support the folk belief that Negro women are by nature abnormally sensual and licentious, and that they therefore invited the attentions of white men. But, as was pointed out earlier, there was a general lack of social and legal restraint to sexual promiscuity among slaves themselves, so certainly this attitude must have carried over to some extent into the relations of slave women with white men. Living under a social order which deprived them of virtually all means of gaining personal preferment except the granting of sexual favors, there is little doubt that many slave women submitted willingly to the advances of their masters, sons of the family, or overseers, hoping thereby to receive favors in return. John Roles, who attempted to portray the slave girl in his account as an injured innocent, alluded to this practice when he spoke of the jealousy between the two slave girls, both of whom were involved in sexual affairs with their Fort Smith master. And even if a slave woman had moral scruples against sexual relations with her white master, she had no effective means of restraining him, for she was a mere chattel with whom the master, short of actual physical injury, could do as he chose. Legally, there was no such thing as the rape of a slave woman by a white man.

A final matter for speculation in the realm of sexual relationships between whites and slaves is that of voluntary relationships between white women and male Negro slaves. This is by far the most obscure of all aspects of the matter. No verified incidents of this type in Arkansas were encountered, as in some other

[19] *Abraham* v. *Wilkins*, 17 Ark. 292.

states,[20] although when the slave man Pleasant was being tried for the rape of a white woman, Sophia Fulmer, his defense counsel implied that the woman, who had a reputation for sexual promiscuity, had not really been raped, but had submitted to Pleasant willingly. In commenting on this in the verdict of the Arkansas Supreme Court, before which the case was eventually taken, Chief Justice Elbert H. English expressed the generally held attitude toward sexual relations between white women and slave men:

But surely, it may not be unsafe, or unjust to the prisoner, to say, that, in this State, where sexual intercourse between white women and negroes, is generally regarded with the utmost abhorrence, the presumption that a white woman yielded herself to the embraces of a negro, without force, arising from a want of chastity in her, would not be great, unless she had sunk to the lowest degree of prostitution.[21]

[20] Many accounts of voluntary sexual relationships between white women and slave men may be found in cases quoted in Helen Tunnicliff Catterall, *Judicial Cases Concerning American Slavery and the Negro* (5 vols.; Washington, 1926-1937). See, for example, *Armstrong* v. *Hodges*, I, 357; *Re Puckett*, II, 12; *Horton* v. *Reavis*, II, 35; *Scroggins* v. *Scroggins*, II, 63; *Lamb* v. *Pigford*, II, 183; *Midgett* v. *McBride*, II, 192.

[21] *Pleasant* v. *The State*, 15 Ark. 624.

"... a saucy set of negroes ...."

NOT ALL ARKANSAS SLAVES were like those described by one overseer as "a saucy set of negroes," but some of them did commit
offenses against their masters or the laws of Arkansas which
necessitated punishment. They were disobedient, or failed to perform their work properly, or were impudent, or misused property.
More rarely, they committed assaults and thefts, ran away, or
even committed rape and murder. In the great majority of
cases, punishment or discipline was administered by the master
or the overseer; only in extreme cases was there recourse to the
law. Owners did not usurp the privileges of law-enforcement
officials in punishing their slaves, but since they were more than
mere work-day employers, and were largely responsible for the
round-the-clock conduct of their slaves, many problems which
today would fall to the police or family control devolved upon
them.

Arkansas law did not specify precisely at what point a master's
prerogatives in disciplining his slaves ended and those of the law
enforcement officials began, nor did it place a specific limitation
upon the power of a man over his slave. Rather it was generally
understood that the master could use such disciplinary measures
as he saw fit, as long as they did not come into conflict with the
law. Problems of discipline had to be faced individually and
dealt with in the manner which seemed most appropriate or
effective at the time. Certainly it would have been impossible to
lay down a set of disciplinary regulations adequate for control of
all of the slaves in Arkansas, varied as they were in personality,

temperament, and skills, and in distribution between small house-holds and farms and larger plantations.

Although the power of a master over his slave was great, it was not unlimited. A historian of the South has aptly written:

Slavery, as it developed in the United States, did not give to the master absolute, arbitrary, despotic power over the slave. It was not the Roman type of slavery. . . . for violence against the person of the slave, the master was amenable to the State. For brutality or over-working his slaves, the owner met the disapproval of public opinion. Edward Bryan summed up the whole tangled relationship by saying: "Our slave property lies only incidently [*sic*] in the *person* of the slave; but essentially in his *labor*."[1]

On occasion some masters did assume "absolute, arbitrary, des-potic power" over their slaves, even to the point of killing them, but such cases were the exceptions and not the rule.[2]

Whipping was often used in punishing slaves for infractions of discipline. To contemporary critics of slavery the whip was the very symbol of the force inherent in the slavery system, and there is no doubt that it was used often, with no effort made to conceal the fact. Casual allusions to the practice of whipping appear throughout the sources of the period, and a substantial number of runaway slaves were described as bearing whip marks.[3] Since running away was proof in itself that the slave posed disciplinary problems, it is probable, however, that the incidence of whip marks was much greater among runaways than among the slave popula-tion as a whole. But while whipping was common, it is doubtful that it was usually as brutal as often alleged. A slave was an extremely valuable piece of property, and the very basis of the labor system for much of the state; when an owner had paid a large sum of money for a slave, had fed and clothed him, and had cared for his ills, all in an effort to secure and maintain a constant supply of labor, it hardly seems reasonable that he would deliber-ately have undermined his own efforts by whipping the slave severely enough to incapacitate him.

---

[1] Craven, *Coming of the Civil War*, p. 75.
[2] The *Arkansas Gazette*, March 11, 1829, contains an item concerning George C. Pervis, of Chicot County, who was tried for killing his slave.
[3] *Arkansas Gazette*, Oct. 18, 1831, Aug. 9, 1836; *True Democrat*, July 14, 1858.

In the heat of anger, however, some men forgot such consider-ations, and there are rare records of whippings brutal almost be-yond belief. The most extreme case found, which occurred in Washington County, involved a man named Spencer and his newly purchased slave woman.

A few days after Spencer bought the slave, he was found whip-ping her. He had her stripped, and staked down on the ground; her hands and feet extended, and fastened to stakes; and her face down-ward. He . . . was whipping her at intervals, using a cowhide, with a plaited buckskin lash about fifteen inches long. He asked what made her [run away], and she said that Bedford and Buchanan told her, that if she staid there, she would be whipped to death. The witness examined the negro, and found her to look wild. Spencer had drawn some blood, but not a great deal. He took salt and a cob, and salted her back.[4]

That whippings such as this were considered outside the bounds of normal conduct is evident from a statement of Justice Townsend Dickinson in rendering the decision of the Arkansas Supreme Court in the above case, not a criminal case involving the whipping, but a civil one concerning payment of the purchase price of the slave. Justice Dickinson wrote: "It is with pain and sensibility that the court feels itself constrained to remark that whatever seeming wildness and aberration of mind might be perceived in the slave, it is but reasonable to suppose, was caused by grief and the excessive cruelty of the owner."[5]

More common than instances of extreme brutality were such uses of the whip as two mentioned previously in other connec-tions. After James Sheppard's impudent and disobedient slave Nora refused to take quinine, reported the overseer, "I gave her about 15 or 20 cuts with my little cowhide & not wanting to whip her called in Aggy & Patsy & told her I'd gap her if it took the whole plantation she took it then & afterwards. . . ."[6] In the other incident the wielder of the whip was the overseer on the Ingham plantation, on which Henry M. Stanley was visiting. While supervising the slaves in felling timber, Stanley wrote, "he cried out his commands with a more imperious note. A young

[4] *Pyeatt* v. *Spencer,* 4 Ark. 563.
[5] *Ibid.*
[6] Robert W. Miller to James Sheppard, July 16, 1859, Sheppard Papers.

fellow named Jim was the first victim of his ire, . . . and he could not answer him as politely as expected. He flicked at his naked shoulders with his whip, and the lash, flying unexpectedly near me, caused us both to drop our spikes."[7]

Whipping of almost any degree of severity seems generally abhorrent today, but it should be remembered, as one writer on slavery has said, that "the penological practices of the age were not adverse to this kind of punishment."[8] White apprentices, soldiers and sailors, and school students were whipped as a matter of course, and as for children in the home, the maxim of "spare the rod and spoil the child" was still strongly in force.[9] White criminals were also flogged. Slaves were perhaps whipped more severely or more often than those in these categories, but the difference was not so great as the twentieth-century mind, conditioned by a generation or two of nonviolent punishment, might imagine.

But there were more subtle, and more effective, methods of enforcement of discipline than the indiscriminate use of the lash. Granting a special privilege to a slave, or withholding one he already enjoyed, did more in most cases to make him amenable to the wishes of his master than indiscriminate whipping. After a whipping, a slave's life went on much as before, but a privilege withheld accentuated an already humdrum existence, while one granted as a reward for good service could lend enrichment. The practice of granting and withholding privileges as a means of maintaining morale and discipline was widespread. John Brown mentioned it frequently in his diary. During the cotton-picking season in 1853, he wrote of an incentive plan he used: "I give the pickers a chance for all they pick over 100 lbs and chaps in proportion, best hands pick 170 or 180."[10] Like most planters, Brown permitted his well-behaved slaves freedom from work to celebrate the various holidays. One Christmas he commented:

This day which has for centuries been dedicated as a holyday is in our retired situation but little noticed. The family all at home spent

---

[7] Stanley, *Autobiography,* p. 149.   [8] Sydnor, *Slavery in Mississippi,* p. 94.
[9] For an especially graphic account of early whipping practices, see Joseph J. Thompson, "Early Corporal Punishments," *Illinois Law Quarterly,* VI (Dec., 1923), 37-49.
[10] Diary of John Brown, Nov. 16, 1853.

the day as usual. The only difference being amoung the servants. It is a human as well as a wise regulation to allow them a few days as a Jubilee, and they enjoy it. All are brushing up, putting on their best rigging, and with boisterous joy hailing the approach of the Holy days, while we are in some degree relieved of the particular oversight of them. So all are happy.[11]

But Brown did not hesitate to deprive his slaves of holidays if they had behaved badly. In July, 1853: "The negroes have holy-day . . . except two boys who disobeyed my order at their last holyday and went down to the river without permission."[12]

Brown also followed the common practice of paying his slaves if they chose to work during the holidays when they would otherwise be free. During the Christmas holiday period mentioned above, Brown paid several slaves fifty cents a day for splitting rails, hauling cotton and corn, and operating the plantation cotton gin. Thom, Brown's most valuable and trusted slave, earned small amounts of incentive pay at other times of the year as well.[13] Granting holidays to the slaves was customary on James Sheppard's Waterford Plantation, as was the practice of giving them some special treat, such as a beef, at the same time.[14]

Contemporary observers frequently commented on the participation of slaves in the holiday celebrations. The description of a Fourth of July "negro-ball" by Ida Pfeiffer, the English traveler, has already been mentioned.[15] At Christmas in 1859, Robert F. Kellam of Camden wrote, "Town full of Negroes Great Holliday for the Darkies & the Children."[16] Amusing insight into the relationship between whites and slaves, and evidence that the relationship could be anything but grim and impersonal, is found in a brief comment concerning holiday celebrations in Fayetteville in a letter from William Allen Martin, son of Jared Martin, to his sister Elizabeth: "Some of the boys blacked themselves and went

[11] *Ibid.*, Dec. 25, 1853. See also Jan. 4, 1858.
[12] *Ibid.*, July 23, 1853. See also June 18, 1853.
[13] *Ibid.*, Dec. 29, 1853, Jan. 30, 1855, July 12, 1856.
[14] Robert W. Miller to James Sheppard, July 16, 1859, Sheppard Papers. Masters were required by law to give their slaves freedom from work on Sunday, although slaves could work for themselves on that day if they chose. Josiah Gould, ed., *A Digest of the Statutes of Arkansas; Embracing All Laws of a General and Permanent Character, in Force at the Close of the Session of the General Assembly of 1856* (Little Rock, 1858), pp. 1032-1035.
[15] See p. 144 above.
[16] Diary of Robert F. Kellam, Dec. 26, 1859.

to a negro party for a christmas trick. And some of the negros said that it was funn to see negros with white years."[17] Certainly the mutually friendly feelings often prevalent must have done much to permit the two races to live and work together in harmony. A series of letters written by William Allen Martin to his family in Little Rock while he was absent at school in Fayetteville gives strong evidence of the respect and affection which so frequently marked the feelings of white people toward their slaves. Every letter during a two-year period contained some remark such as "Give my love to all the blacks" or "Give my respects to the Blacks and tell them to make that cotton patch look black."[18] In households where mutual respect and affection existed, there must have been very little harsh punishment.

Since the primary responsibility for the conduct of a slave lay with his master, the slave was expected to remain on his home plantation or premises unless he had legitimate business elsewhere. The law provided that a slave leaving the "premises or tenements" of his master without a pass or letter of permission could be apprehended by any person, taken before a justice of the peace, and, by order of the justice, punished with not more than twenty-five lashes. A slave who went to another plantation without permission in writing from his owner or overseer could also be given twenty-five lashes, in this instance by the owner of the plantation where he was found. An owner or overseer who permitted a slave not his own to remain for more than four hours on his plantation could be required to pay five dollars to the owner of the slave for each offense, and an owner or overseer who permitted more than five slaves, other than his own, to remain on his plantation for any length of time, with or without permission of the owner of the slaves, could be required to "pay to the informer

[17] William A. Martin to Elizabeth A. Martin, Jan. 6, 1855, Martin Papers.
[18] William A. Martin to Elizabeth A. Martin, Dec. 22, 1855, Oct. 7, 1856, Martin Papers. It is known that slaves on some plantations in the South assumed or were given a certain degree of responsibility for maintaining discipline among themselves. Obviously it was advantageous to the slaves to maintain order and obedience, since the irresponsible acts of a troublemaker might result in stricter control of the entire group. Such factors as pride in their own plantation and loyalty to the master also operated powerfully to preserve equanimity in the relations of slave to master. For a discussion of operation of these factors in the South generally, see Phillips, *American Negro Slavery*, pp. 306-308, and Sydnor, *Slavery in Mississippi*, p. 76.

one dollar for every slave above [five]." An exception was made in the case of Sunday worship services, work, and other "lawful occasions." All "riots, routs, unlawful speeches, and seditious assemblies" of slaves were to be punished by whipping the slaves involved, by order of a justice of the peace.

White men and free Negroes were also forbidden to gather in unlawful meetings with slaves, white men under a penalty of a fine of a hundred dollars and thirty to sixty days in jail, and free Negroes the same fine and thirty lashes. Only if white men or free Negroes were involved were cases of this sort to be tried in the circuit courts; all slaves were to be tried before a justice of the peace.[19] Since justices courts were usually very informal, and often kept the most rudimentary records, if any, there is little evidence of the degree to which police regulations such as these were enforced. In all probability, however, they were not enforced rigidly and consistently, but only when slaves seemed bent on creating real trouble. As sparse as the population of Arkansas was, even in 1860, most white people doubtless knew most of the slaves of the neighborhood, and could make individual judgments as to whether the law should be invoked.

Any person had the authority to apprehend a slave believed to have violated the police regulations mentioned, but the law provided for more formal surveillance of slave activities by township slave patrols. Patrols were organized on a local basis, and were not required by law, but merely authorized when "thought necessary." Prior to 1853, patrols, one for each township, were appointed by the county courts for a period of one year, and were composed of "one discreet person" who served as captain and not more than ten subordinate members. Thereafter the appointments were made by a justice of the peace upon request of three householders, the number of patrols per township was increased to a maximum of three, the size of the patrol was reduced to a captain and not more than five members, and the period of service was shortened to four months. The 1853 modification of the patrol law also reduced the frequency of patrolling; previously it was "as many hours in each night as the court shall direct, (not less than

[19] *Gould's Digest,* 1858, pp. 1032-1035.

twelve)," while afterward the requirement was only "once every two weeks, or oftener if necessary."

The duty of the patrol was to visit all places within the assigned area where it was believed slaves might be assembled unlawfully, and to look for slaves "strolling about from one house or plantation to another, without a pass from his master, employer, or overseer." Any slave apprehended and deemed guilty of these offenses could be given up to twenty lashes by the patrol immediately, no appearance before a justice of the peace with the culprit being necessary. Until 1853 white people and free Negroes found by patrols in company with slaves at unlawful meetings could be punished, upon conviction in circuit court, "with the like number of lashes as would have been inflicted on a slave," but later, as noted above, the punishment was changed to fine and imprisonment for white men, and fine and thirty lashes for free Negroes.

Apparently patrol duty, which amounted to a sort of military draft, was considered something of a burden, for the law prescribed a penalty of from $5.00 to $25.00 upon conviction before a justice of the peace of refusal to serve. Further evidence of the burdensome nature of the duty may be detected in the 1853 reduction of period of service, number of members, and frequency of patrolling. These changes perhaps also indicated a recognition of the relatively slight need of the patrol. That the system was considered a passive device is shown by a statement by the Arkansas Supreme Court: "The patrol system is a police regulation, which, being kept alive on the statute book, is a slumbering power, ready to be aroused and called into action, whenever there is an apparent necessity for it."[20] There were some rewards for patrol duty: the county courts could award such compensation to members as thought proper, and members were exempt from working on the roads, serving on juries, and performing military duty during the period of appointment.[21]

Since patrols were not required by law to make reports of their activities, it is only by chance or because of some unusual circumstance that any records of patrol activities have survived. The infrequent records which were found give bare evidence of actual

[20] *Hervey* v. *Armstrong*, 15 Ark. 162.
[21] *Revised Statutes, 1838*, pp. 604-605; *Gould's Digest, 1858*, pp. 822-823.

operation of the system, but no indication of the prevalence of its use. One of the few records found is that of appointment of a patrol in Franklin County. This brief statement appears in the county court records: "And now on this day the court appointed Samuel W. Cravens Captain of a patrol in lower township & R. E. Lambert, Wm. M. Woods, Wm. Fort & Wm. G. Titsworth his associates."[22]

The most detailed single account of patrol activities found is in the report of a case heard before the Arkansas Supreme Court in 1854. On a Sunday some time before, the patrol of Jefferson Township, Ouachita County, hearing of a reputedly unlawful assemblage of slaves in neighboring Marion Township, crossed the township line, arrested the slaves involved, tied them, and whipped them with not more than ten lashes each. A witness reported that the punishment did not seem to be cruel or excessive, although the cries of the slaves and the sound of the blows could be heard at some distance. Armstrong, owner of the slaves, sued the members of the patrol for damages, claiming that the slaves had been "so bruised and hurt by the beating, as to be unable to perform labor and service . . . for a long space of time thereafter," that the slaves had merely been on their way home from an orderly and well-conducted religious meeting at which white people had properly been present, and, finally, that the patrol had exceeded its jurisdiction by going out of its own township. The Supreme Court ruled that although the jurisdiction of a patrol was confined to the township for which it was appointed even when the patrol of another township was inoperative, as had been true in Marion Township, Armstrong could collect no damages, since he had not proved actual damage to his slaves. The court also upheld the statutory rights of slaves to gather peaceably for Sunday religious services.[23]

Disciplinary problems among slaves on the large Arkansas plantations, although differing little in nature from those in smaller holdings, could not always be handled in the same personal manner as in the small groups. For example, some large plantations

[22] Franklin County County Court Record, 1847-1854, p. 1.
[23] *Hervey v. Armstrong*, 15 Ark. 162.

had their own jails for confinement of slaves. A well-preserved slave jail still stands on Yellow Bayou Plantation in Chicot County, owned during slavery days by the Craig family. There are no contemporary references to the jail, but the building itself bears ample evidence of the purposes for which it was used. And it could only have been used as a plantation jail, for the nearest town, Lake Village, then a mere hamlet, is five miles away. The jail is about thirty-two feet long by twenty-four feet wide, constructed of six-inch-square rough-sawed oak timbers notched at the corners and fastened together at frequent intervals with large iron spikes. Interior partitions and ceilings are of the same construction. There are four compartments in the jail: two small cells at one end, a narrow entrance hall running the width of the building in the center, and a large cell at the other end. The interior subdivision evidently was to permit segregation of male and female slaves, and also to provide a place for the guard. Small square windows between the center hall and each of the cells permitted passage of food and water without opening the cell doors. Each cell has iron rings fastened to the walls for use in chaining prisoners. The few small exterior windows are double iron-barred, one set of bars recessed into the logs and the other bolted to the outside; the wooden-barred entrance door is also double, giving greater security. All of the hardware is made of heavy, hand-forged iron. The jail is so massive and well-constructed that breaking out of it would have been very difficult.[24]

The jail was doubtless used primarily for punishment of the slaves on Yellow Bayou and adjacent Bellevue plantations (more than two hundred altogether), but it might also have been used for slaves from other nearby plantations in that important slave section. It also could have been used for detention of runaways which had been "taken up," or even for confinement of slaves being sold, although it is much smaller than jails used for that purpose in other states, and jails of that type usually were located in urban centers of the slave trade. James Sheppard's Waterford Plantation had no jail, or at least there is no surviving record of one,

---

[24] This description of the Yellow Bayou slave jail is based upon personal observation by the author.

Slave Jail, Yellow Bayou Plantation, Chicot County
(Photographs by the author)

but it was equipped with stocks for confinement and punishment of slaves.[25]

Running away, of which some Arkansas slaves were guilty, was both a disciplinary and a criminal problem. The act was a violation of the law, of course, and yet prior to 1849 no provision was made for punishment of a runaway by the state; after 1849 the punishment prescribed—confinement in the penitentiary for life —applied only if the slave were not claimed by his owner. Clearly the state considered its function to be that of aiding in the return of the runaway, while punishment was left to the owner. A slave was judged to be a runaway when he was found more than twenty miles away from home without a written pass or "permission to that effect." Any person was empowered to seize a runaway and take him before a justice of the peace. Arkansas laws often used the term "any person" when "any white person" was actually meant, but in this instance slaves and free Negroes apparently were also included. Negroes were not only authorized to apprehend runaways but encouraged to do so. When James Sheppard's slave Austin ran away in 1858, he was caught by Jim, the slave of C. W. Knott. Knott wrote Sheppard, "I let Jim go over to see you to get pay for ketching your boy Oston if you will give him five Dollars I will be perfectly satisfied I all wayes like to incourage Negroes in betraying runaways and Jim informed me whose he was I am willing for him to have the pay. . . ."[26]

If a runaway slave was recognized by the apprehender or the justice before whom he was taken, he was to be taken home immediately; otherwise he was to be committed to the county jail. The exact procedure followed is shown in this entry from the records of Ashley County:

On the 7th day of June 1861 comes James G. Ross and brings in his custody a certain Negro boy calling himself Ferdinand charged with being a runaway slave. And it appearing to the satisfaction of the undersigned Justice that Said boy is a runaway Slave the Owner whereof is unknown, It is therefore ordered that Said James G. Ross

[25] D. T. Weeks to James Sheppard, Sept. 10, 1854, Sheppard Papers.
[26] C. W. Knott to James Sheppard, Dec. 5, 1858, Sheppard Papers. Another account of an absent slave being reported by other slaves is in the *Des Arc Weekly Citizen*, Aug. 24, 1859.

Convey and deliver Said Slave to the Sheriff or Jailor of Ashley County State of Arkansas to be kept according to law.   And the following fees are due To James G. Ross

for apprehending	25.00
Same for 20 mi. travel 10¢	2.00
Samson J. P. for committing	2.00

On the 10 day of May [June?] comes W. B. Miles and pays the fee for committing and reports the above runaway delivered to Samuel J. Williams of this county who proved his property according to law.
                              WM. S. SAMSON J. P.[27]

Prior to 1849 the procedure followed after a runaway was delivered to the jail was this: the sheriff posted an advertisement at the courthouse door, describing the runaway by name, wearing apparel, and the name and address of the supposed owner.   If the owner had not claimed his slave within two months, another advertisement was published in a newspaper for twelve months. Finally, if the slave remained unclaimed, the sheriff sold him at the courthouse door, first giving thirty days' notice of the time and place of the sale.   Proceeds of the sale, after deduction of expenses incurred in keeping the slave, were paid into the county treasury.   It was still possible for an owner to escape total financial loss, however, for if he appeared within three years of the sale and proved ownership, he could collect what remained of the proceeds.

In 1849 the procedure was changed somewhat.   After commitment to the county jail, the runaway was kept for six months while the usual newspaper advertisement was being published.[28]   If the slave was unclaimed at the end of the period, he was delivered to the state penitentiary, located then on the site of the present state capitol in Little Rock.   The penitentiary keeper then published for six months an advertisement such as this:

RECEIVED AT THE PENITENTIARY

From the Sheriff of Lafayette county, a negro slave who says his name is Alfred Gilmore, and belongs to V. N. T. Rogers, of Alexan-

[27] Ashley County County Court Record, 1861, p. 240.
[28] A copy of an advertisement of this type from the *Arkansas State Democrat,* Dec. 14, 1849, is given on p. 68 above.   A few of the many others published may be found in the *Arkansas Gazette,* June 17, 1829, and April 12, 1836; the *True Democrat,* Feb. 14, 1855, and April 14, 1857; and the *Southern Shield,* Feb. 23, 1856.   These advertisements were placed by the sheriffs of Greene, Phillips, Union, Chicot, Bradley, and Pulaski Counties.

dria, Louisiana. Said boy is 5 feet 8 inches high; dark complexion;
39 years of age. The middle finger of the left hand is crooked. He
had on a coat and pantaloons made of "hard times;" shirt of Lowell
cotton; and glazed oilcloth cap.

J. H. HAMMACK, *Contractor of*
State Penitentiary[29]

Little Rock, Jan. 12, 1850

If still unclaimed, the runaway was to remain in the penitentiary
for life or until the owner appeared, paid all expenses, and took
him away.[30]

These, then, were the formal procedures outlined by the law
for recovery of runaway slaves. Although there is ample evidence
in the newspaper advertisements and county records that the
procedures were often followed, it is probable that far more runaways were recovered without recourse to the legal procedures,
which were not mandatory if the owner could recover his slave
without use of them. Running away chiefly concerned the owner
and the slave involved, and was more a crime against the master
than against the state.

Slaves ran away for many different reasons, and not always
in attempts to gain permanent freedom, as has been popularly
supposed. Some examples, largely taken from newspaper notices placed by owners of runaway slaves, will illustrate the
diversity of motives. John Brown's young slave Thomas (not the
skilled and trusted Thom) ran away because he "took offense at
being slightly punished and put out," was hidden for several weeks
by slaves belonging to Hawes Coleman near Arkadelphia, and was
drowned while trying to swim across the Ouachita River.[31] Some
slaves fled to escape punishment for crimes they had committed.
Lewis Ball, the ginger-bread colored, goateed slave of Nathan Ross
of Chicot County, broke out of the plantation jail where he was being held on suspicion of having burned his master's gin, and ran
away "under the belief, no doubt, that he would be hung."[32]
After murdering his master, Colonel Reedy of Clarendon, one
slave took horse, "passed himself off on the ferryman" at White

[29] *Arkansas State Democrat*, Jan. 25, 1850.
[30] *Revised Statutes, 1838*, pp. 712-715; *Gould's Digest, 1858*, pp. 1026-1030.
[31] Diary of John Brown, March 6, 9, April 9, 1855.
[32] *True Democrat*, July 14, 1858.

River as an Indian, and galloped westward toward the Indian nations with "several gentlemen" in hot pursuit.[33]

Many slaves ran away to rejoin friends or members of their families from whom they had been separated by sales or other causes. Roswell Beebe's slave Peter, formerly a servant in the Anthony House, was expected to go to Dallas County, where his mother lived, when he ran away from Little Rock.[34] Jerry, who was "likely, artful, and cunning," might well have succeeded in getting from Little Rock to Kentucky, where he had been reared,[35] and his slowness of speech seemed to be no handicap to Peter, who, accompanied by his wife Susan, was attempting to return to his old home near Batesville; after escaping from their master near Arkansas Post, the pair was apprehended at Gray's Sulphur Spring, but ran away again.[36]

One member of a slave family already a fugitive sometimes influenced another to join him. In the late fall of 1831 Henry, a husky young man bearing scars from a burn and the stab of a dirk, ran away from Captain John D. Moseby of Little Rock, but remained in the general vicinity for several months. On January 26, 1832, his wife Ann and their three children, Peter, Allen, and Betts, all slaves of Thomas Massengill of the Maumelle settlement above Little Rock, joined him. Equipped with a feather bed and a "variety of clothing," the fugitive family paddled down the Arkansas River in a stolen canoe.[37] The charm of the free life enjoyed by his brother Sam evidently proved too strong for young Jess, the slave of Nancy Newland of Batesville, so he ran away to join him. Sam had run away two years before, but had continued to "prowl about" the vicinity.[38]

At times slaves displayed the most dogged persistence in trying to get back to members of their families. During the few months she was the property of the man Spencer, the slave woman who was beaten so brutally in the incident related previously ran away four times to see her children, but was recovered each time

[33] *Ibid.*, Oct. 21, 1856.
[34] *Arkansas State Democrat*, Nov. 13, 1849.
[35] *Arkansas Gazette*, Oct. 27, 1830.
[36] *Ibid.*, Feb. 20, 1839.
[37] *Ibid.*, Feb. 1, 1832. Two separate notices in this issue give information of this group of runaways.
[38] *Batesville Eagle*, June 27, 1848.

and beaten. One witness said that "she was obstinate and dis-
agreeable, because she wanted to go to her children. She seemed
much devoted to her children, and when her [former] mistress
gave her time, would make clothes, and knit for them." When
questioned about the possible insanity of the slave woman,
another witness conjectured that "strong attachment for her children, and grief at being separated from them, with severe chastise-
ment, would be . . . likely to cause it."[39] The unconventional
family relationships sometimes existing among slaves occasionally
complicated the search for slaves seeking to return to members of
their families: when Henry ran away, he was expected to go to
either of his two wives, one living in Tennessee and the other in
St. Louis.[40]

In territorial and early statehood days, and also occasionally
even later, a substantial number of slaves, some part Indian, ran
away in attempts to return to former Indian masters. Slaves
were believed to have run away to each of the Five Civilized
Tribes (Cherokee, Choctaw, Chickasaw, Creek, and Seminole) except the Seminoles, and doubtless some unrecorded slaves sought
them also. The "keen, likely" slave Austin, who ran away from
William Watson of Arkansas Post in 1821, had once lived in
the Tennessee part of the "old Cherokee nation," and was
expected to go either there or to the western band of Cherokees,
then living in western Arkansas.[41] In 1823 the slave woman
Celia broke out of the Pulaski County jail, where she had been
placed under an attachment, and supposedly started for the Cherokee Nation with two slaves of Walter Webber, her Cherokee
former master.[42] Tom, who was "supposed to be part Indian, as
his features resemble those of an Indian," was also believed to
be on his way to the Cherokees after he escaped from Rufus Stone
of New Port (the present Newport). This possibility was
strengthened by the disappearance of an Indian, Washington
Eaton, at the same time.[43]

While Ambrose H. Sevier, the Arkansas territorial delegate
to Congress, was in Washington attempting to get the state consti-

[39] Pyeatt v. Spencer, 4 Ark. 563.
[41] Arkansas Gazette, April 7, 1821.
[43] Batesville News, July 11, 1839.
[40] True Democrat, July 12, 1854.
[42] Ibid., Oct. 14, 1823.

tution adopted, one of his slaves, Tony, whose jaws "appear[ed] to be swelled from toothache," escaped from Chicot County along with two slaves belonging to Benjamin Johnson. All had been purchased in the Creek Nation in Indian Territory, but it was thought that they might go either there or to the Creeks in Alabama.[44] The slave Mitch was expected to try to get to the Chickasaw Nation, "where he [was] acquainted," but since he had been purchased in Crittenden County, it was possible that he was "lurking about there."[45] When his slave Ben ran away, Michael Bozeman of Arkadelphia advertised: "I have every reason to believe he is going to the Choctaw Nation or Texas."[46]

After the great forced migration of the Five Civilized Tribes from the southeastern states to Indian Territory in the mid-1830's, a number of slaves fled from their Indian masters to their old homes east of the Mississippi. Since Arkansas lay between the two areas, many of the runaways retraced the famous "Trail of Tears" over which they had journeyed with their masters across the state.[47] One of these was Simon, taken to Indian Territory by Winey, his Creek Indian mistress, and there sold to Captain B. L. E. Bonneville, immortalized by Washington Irving in *The Adventures of Captain Bonneville, U. S. A.* When last seen, Simon, wearing a fur cap and a "drab surtout" and astride a light cream-colored mare, was on the road to Little Rock, attempting "to make his way to Alabama or Georgia, by the route the immigrants came."[48]

There were slaveholders in all of the Civilized Tribes, and each tribe had laws concerning runaway slaves much like those of the slave states.[49] Hence it is improbable that many of the

[44] *Arkansas Gazette,* April 12, 1836.
[45] *Ibid.,* April 19, 1836.
[46] *Washington Telegraph,* Aug. 12, 1846.
[47] The best account of the removal of the Five Civilized Tribes is Grant Foreman, *Indian Removal* (Norman, Oklahoma, 1932). Opposite page 394 is a good map of the "Trail of Tears," a term applied collectively to the many different routes followed by the Indians, all crossing Arkansas at some point.
[48] *Arkansas Gazette,* Dec. 5, 1837.
[49] Annie H. Abel, *The American Indian as Slaveholder and Secessionist* (Cleveland, 1915), pp. 17-62; Foreman, *Indian Removal, passim; Census of 1860 (population),* p. xv; *Western Frontier Whig,* Dec. 9, 1845. The first statistics on slavery among the Five Civilized Tribes, given in the *Census of 1860,* show that 1,154 Indians owned a total of 7,369 slaves, or an average of 6.3 each. The largest single holding was 227, owned by a Choctaw. Slaves comprised approximately 12.5 per cent of the total population, and about one

runaway Arkansas slaves who attempted to go to the Indian country were motivated by a desire for permanent freedom. This is further borne out by the fact that many of the slaves evidently were returning to former Indian masters. In most of the tribes, however, the distinction between master and servant was less marked than among white people, and the Creeks, especially, had no aversion to marriage to Negroes, and even adopted them into the tribe.[50] No doubt the higher status attainable, even as slaves, attracted many runaways.[51]

But the possibilities of genuine freedom in the Indian country, even though of uncertain duration and under harsher living conditions, beckoned to some Arkansas slaves. After the 1830's Arkansas runaways along with those of Texas and Missouri enjoyed a unique advantage in this respect, for only they could get to Indian Territory without having to cross intervening slave states. Some runaway slaves in Indian Territory gathered in "Negro towns." One report published in 1850 told of the breaking up of one such town and the arrest of a hundred runaway slaves, including some from Arkansas, who had become involved in pending warfare between the Creeks and the Seminoles.[52] There were several small settlements of legitimately free Negroes in the vicinity of Wewoka, near where the town was located, and possibly some of them were included in the hundred, which appears unreasonably high to have been composed of runaways alone.[53]

Occasionally Arkansas slaves managed to join Indians as far away as Mexico. A third-hand account published in Arkansas in 1851 told of the existence of a Negro town in Mexico to which Arkansas runaways had gone. According to the tale, related by

---

Indian in fifty owned slaves. The census reported no slaves among the Seminoles in 1860, although they had owned them earlier. The relationship between Arkansas and Indian Territory was close in many ways other than geography. For example, from 1834 to the Civil War the territory was attached for judicial purposes to the western district of Arkansas, Indian families often sent their children to Arkansas schools, and the secretary of the Arkansas secession convention in 1861 was Elias Boudinot, a Cherokee. *Dictionary of American Biography*, II, 479.

[50] Abel, *American Indian as Slaveholder*, p. 23.

[51] See Foreman, *Indian Removal*, p. 325, for a discussion of the relationship between Indians and their slaves.

[52] *Southern Shield*, Aug. 17, 1850. Part of the report was reprinted from the *Arkansas Intelligencer*.

[53] A map on p. 26 of Abel, *American Indian as Slaveholder*, shows the location of the free Negro settlements.

one W. Secrest to the editor of the *Houston Telegraph* and copied by Arkansas newspapers, runaway slaves were crossing the Rio Grande at Laredo and Eagle Pass, Texas, at the rate of several hundred a year and gathering in the town, under control of an Indian named Wild Cat. Secrest reported not less than eighteen hundred runaways there, about five hundred from Texas and most of the remainder from Arkansas. Wild Cat had armed the slaves, and used them, along with Indians, in frequent forays against the Comanches across the American border.[54] The number of Arkansas runaways must actually have been only a fraction of the number reported; otherwise there doubtless would have been an international incident and great concern among Arkansas and Texas slaveowners.

Not all slaves who ran away did so of their own accord; some were stolen or enticed away by white men, free Negroes, or Indians. No reasonable estimate of the prevalence of Negro-stealing can be made; many owners alluded to this possibility in their newspaper notices of runaways, but only rarely is it possible to determine the conclusion of the runaway career of a given slave. Arkansas law placed a heavy penalty on Negro-stealing, and although there are verified accounts of such thefts, there was no large number of convictions.

After 1838 the penalty for stealing a slave was from five to twenty-five years imprisonment, and for enticing one to run away from two to five years imprisonment.[55] The law in effect previously carried no prison penalty, but a variety of other types: upon conviction the thief was required to restore the slave to his master and pay the owner double the value, pay a fine ranging from the value of to ten times the value of the slave, receive fifty lashes, stand in the pillory for two hours, and for two years thereafter wear a six-inch scarlet "T" in full view on his back "as a badge of his crime." This interesting and complex penalty, evidently devised because of the lack of facilities for confinement during the territorial period, also applied to horse and mule thieves.[56] No instance of the "T" actually being worn was found.

[54] *Southern Shield*, Sept. 27, 1851.
[55] *Gould's Digest, 1858*, pp. 341-342, 344.
[56] *Revised Statutes, 1838*, p. 252.

"Negro-running"—stealing slaves in connivance with the slaves themselves—usually operated in one of two ways, or a combination of the two. Under one system the thief influenced strange slaves to abscond with him by promise of freedom or money, and under the other the thief and the slave performed as a sort of team, the slave being alternately sold and stolen in various parts of the country. Part of a long and rambling confession made by Thomas Jefferson Jenkins, a Choctaw Indian, prior to his execution for murder at Paducah, Kentucky, in 1856 illustrates the use of the first system:

I went from [Fort Smith] to Van Buren, and stopped there with a man of color named Bush—he had a store there. I forged a note on a man by the name of Samson, of Shreveport; I sold it for one hundred dollars to Bush. I gambled and finally lost all my ill-gotten gains. Bush and myself had some conversation, he persuaded me to quit gaming and go out and stay with Mr. Hicks, a very fine man, that lived some thirty miles from Van Buren, I told them I had lost a pony off a boat and was looking for my pony, I asked for Mr. Hicks, made out I was well-acquainted with him, and told the people of Ozark I was going to farm it with Mr. Hicks, who lived in what is called McLane's Bottom. I fulfilled my word, I was employed by Mr. Hicks, but it was not my intention to stay with him; I stayed about nineteen days, and then hired myself to Spear Titsworth. During my stay in that neighborhood I became acquainted with all the negroes in the settlement and persuaded them to leave their masters—wrote many of them passes, and gave some of them free papers, the form of which I got from a free man by the name of Abraham, and he got them from a traveler who was trading in horses, and on his way to Texas. One night during the time the Masons held their meeting, I took three Negro men, one woman and the horses, and left. I went to Ozark, but thought it not safe to remain there; I went to Ft. Smith—told them they were my father's negroes, but I was detected by them knowing one of Spear Titsworth's negroes by the name of Abraham, a son of the free man I spoke of, I told them my father bought the negroes but was not believed. I endeavored to make my escape, but was overtaken and carried back to McLane's Bottom—had my trial, I was removed to Ozark jail. Hicks and Titsworth prosecuted me; during the time I was in jail to await my trial, a man by the name of Converse Crooks, was put in for committing rape. He and I broke jail, crossed the river [and left the state].[57]

[57] *True Democrat*, Feb. 3, 1857.

The second method was described by George W. Featherston-haugh, an Englishman who traveled through Arkansas in 1834 and later wrote a highly uncomplimentary description of the territory and the people. He wrote:

It seems that amongst other modes of getting a livelihood in the Southern States, that of "running negroes" is practiced by a class of fellows who are united in a fraternity for the purpose of carrying on the business, and for protecting each other in time of danger. If one of them falls under the notice of the law and is committed to take his trial, some of the fraternity benevolently contrive, "somehow or other," to get upon the jury, or kindly become his bail. To "run a negro" it is necessary to have a good understanding with an intelligent male slave on some plantation, and if he is a mechanic he is always the more valuable. At a time agreed upon the slave runs aways from his master's premises and joins the man who has instigated him to do it; they then proceed to some quarter where they are not known, and the negro is sold for seven or eight hundred dollars, or more, to a new master. A few days after the money has been paid, he runs away again, and is sold a second time, and as oft as the trick can be played with any hope of safety. The negro who does the harlequinade part of the manoeuvre has an agreement with his friend, in virtue of which he supposes he is to receive part of the money; but the poor devil in the end is sure to be cheated, and when he becomes dangerous to the fraternity is, as I have been well assured, first cajoled and put off his guard, and then, on crossing some river or reaching a secret place, shot before he suspects their intention, or otherwise made away with.[58]

James L. Ross of St. Francis County believed that this method was used in stealing his slave Robert in 1849. In a newspaper notice he wrote, "I purchased him, last November, from a stranger, (at a very reduced rate) who called himself John Watkins . . . . From many circumstances, I think the negro was run off from South Carolina, or Georgia, last fall, by this fellow Watkins, and sold to me, and that he has now taken him off for the same purpose."[59]

The "fraternity" to which Featherstonhaugh referred evidently was the infamous gang headed by John R. Murrell, the "Land Pirate," which was active at about the time he crossed Arkansas.

[58] George W. Featherstonhaugh, *Excursion through the Slave States* (2 vols.; London, 1844), I, 255-256.
[59] *Arkansas State Democrat*, June 22, 1849.

Briefly, this is known about Murrell's life and activities: He was born in Tennessee, began a criminal career early in life, and gradually progressed to Negro-stealing in the manner described by Featherstonhaugh. A young man named Virgil A. Stewart wormed his way into the confidences of Murrell, and eventually had him arrested for Negro-stealing. Murrell was convicted in 1834 at Jackson, Tennessee, and sentenced to ten years in the penetentiary, which he served. A few years after being released he died. During the trial at Jackson, Stewart, the chief prosecution witness, made a sensational assertion that for several years Murrell and his underlings has been planning a great Negro rebellion in the region. The headquarters of the "Mystic Clan," to which Stewart said he had been taken by Murrell, supposedly was deep in the swamps of eastern Arkansas. Stewart produced a list of several hundred secret members of the clan, including forty-six Arkansas men.

Stewart's testimony concerning the planned rebellion was never confirmed and was widely discredited at the time. Nevertheless, when several small slave outbreaks occurred the next year (none in Arkansas), with some of the instigators admitting they were members of the Murrell gang, many people became alarmed and "more than a score were hanged before the excitement was allayed."[60] So far as can be determined none of these hangings occurred in Arkansas, but throughout 1835 the newspapers of the state were filled with rumors of the activities of the Murrell gang, which reputedly continued its activities after the leader was imprisoned.[61]

The extent to which the Murrell gang actually operated in Arkansas cannot be determined. It was common knowledge that the swamps of eastern Arkansas were havens for frontier ruffians of various sorts, but there is no proof that Murrell planned a slave rebellion from a headquarters there. No organized attempts were made to break up the conspiracy, and after 1836 little was

[60] *Dictionary of American Biography,* XIII, 369-370; H. R. Howard, comp., *The History of Virgil A. Stewart, and His Adventure in Capturing and Exposing the Great "Western Land Pirate" and His Gang, in Connexion With the Evidence* (New York, 1836).
[61] *Arkansas Gazette,* March 31, April 7, 21, May 19, July 7, 14, Aug. 18, Sept. 1, 8, 29, Oct. 27, Nov. 24, Dec. 22, 1835.

heard of it. Probably the most tangible effect of the rumors was that during the period they were current a large proportion of owners of runaway slaves claimed that they had been enticed away by white men. One man advertised as late as 1837 for his slave Will, carried off, he asserted, by one of Murrell's men in April, 1834.[62]

No actual mass slave rebellions ever occurred in Arkansas, although there were rumors, in addition to those concerning the Murrell gang, that they were being planned. But in each case the rumors were unconfirmed. In 1856 the Little Rock *True Democrat* published an item from the Columbia, Missouri, *Union Democrat* reporting purported conspiracies in Arkansas, prefaced by this editorial comment: "The subjoined article we clip . . . and give it to our readers as an item of news. Until we read it in the Democrat, we were not aware that such a state of things existed in our midst!"[63] Part of the article follows:

NEGRO INSURRECTION

It appears that insurrections among the negroes are becoming very common in Arkansas and Texas. A conspiracy was recently detected at Little Rock, in Arkansas, with their signs and passwords. There was considerable alarm among the citizens of the city in consequence of the disclosures. It appears from the facts gathered from the conspirators, that the plot at Little Rock was a part of the same conspiracy which was recently detected in Texas and in Union County, Arkansas. Their schemes were deeper laid—their intentions being to take the United States Arsenal at Little Rock. White men are at the head of the affair, no doubt, and we need not be surprised if something of the kind should take place in Missouri, ere long.[64]

A careful search of the Arkansas newspapers and other contemporary sources fails to reveal any information at all about the supposed Little Rock and Union County plots. Evidently they were complete fabrications. The previous year the *Gazette and Democrat* published a third-hand report of a planned insurrection in

[62] *Ibid.,* July 4, 1837.
[63] *True Democrat,* Dec. 16, 1856.
[64] Columbia (Missouri) *Union Democrat,* quoted in *True Democrat,* Dec. 16, 1856.

Ouachita County, but there is no other contemporary evidence that a plot existed there.[65]

The motives of runaway slaves, in the great majority of cases, cannot be determined. The newspaper notices, chief source of information concerning runaways, usually only named and described the fugitive, speculated on his possible destination, and offered a reward ranging from ten to six hundred dollars, the larger amounts only when there were several runaways or when apprehension of a Negro-thief was required. A hundred dollars was about the maximum reward offered for a single slave who had run away of his own accord. It is probable, although no direct evidence of this was found in Arkansas sources, that a large percentage of Arkansas slaves who ran away did so in a simple attempt to escape work for as long as possible. Charles S. Sydnor concluded that in Mississippi an increase in number of runaways coincided with the periods of most intensive labor in spring and fall;[66] no doubt this was also true in Arkansas.

The advertisements for runaway slaves contain a wealth of information, not only about the circumstances of the escapes, but also about the individual slaves involved. They show, among other things, that slaves were as individualistic as white people, despite the regimentation of slavery. It seems worthwhile, therefore, to present a number of the advertisements in entirety.

RANAWAY

From my residence, distant one and a half miles south of Hot Springs, State of Arkansas, a negro man named Peter, aged about forty years; about five feet eight or nine inches high, decayed teeth, with one or two teeth out in front; yellow complexion, with rather an indian and negro face. He is a good house carpenter, plays the fiddle, and speaks Spanish. His English is broken. Ever ready to force a *rude* politeness. I will give ten dollars if taken in Hot Spring County; thirty if taken more than one hundred miles from my residence; and seventy dollars if taken out of the state of Arkansas. His ears

[65] *Gazette and Democrat,* Nov. 2, 1855. Assertions that there were slave revolts in Arkansas are found in Herbert Aptheker, *Negro Slave Revolts in the United States, 1526-1860* (New York, 1939), pp. 56-57, 72, and Joseph C. Carroll, *Slave Insurrections in the United States, 1800-1860* (Boston, 1938), pp. 191-192. Both writers, however, used the same unreliable "evidence" referred to here.

[66] Sydnor, *Slavery in Mississippi,* pp. 103-104.

have been bored, and he sometimes wears ear rings.   He had on
when he left, bluish cottonade pantaloons, and I believe, a round
jacket.   The above reward I will give if the said boy Peter is taken
and delivered to me, or placed in some jail so that I safely get him.

A letter addressed to me here, at Hot Springs, Arks., will be
promptly noticed.

This fellows eyes are red or bloodshot, and film slightly growing
over one of them; and a new scar under the left eye, which looks
whitish—Any man is at liberty to whip this fellow, as I myself have
never done it.

Hot Springs, May 29, 1849   JOHN H. WARD[67]

$200 REWARD

Will be paid for the delivery to me, of the following described
mulatto boy, and the Thief who stole him, if alive—but, if dead,
nothing, for the villain of a white man; or One Hundred Dollars for
the delivery to me of my Negro Boy Edmond, or for securing him
in Jail, so that I get him.

Said boy is a bright mulatto, about 24 years old, his hair straight,
face considerably freckled, which can only be seen on close examination, high cheek bones, round face, is quite talkative, but has rather
a down look when spoken to, stout made, and rather under the common height of Negroes.   I think it more than likely that he has a free
pass and will try to pass himself off as a white man; but, if he has
been sold by the villain who conveyed him off, or the one who had
him conveyed away, he perhaps has none.

I have dreamed, with both eyes open, that he went toward the
Spanish country; but as dreams are like some would-be-thought-hon-
est men—quite uncertain—he may have gone some other direction.

Jeff. Co., near Pine Bluffs, Ark., Dec. 3, 1836   THOMAS BAYLISS[68]

$150 REWARD

RANAWAY from my farm, on Thursday last, a negro man
named MOSES, about 33 years of age, 5 feet 6 or 8 inches high, black
complexion, very fleshy and heavy built, weighs about 200 pounds, is
fond of liquor, and is a notorious liar, and quite boisterous when in-
toxicated.—He had a variety of good clothing and bedding, and it is
probable that he is still lurking around Little Rock.   If apprehended in
this county, and brought back to me, I will pay a reward of $10; $20,
if apprehended in an adjoining county; $30 if taken in any other part
of the state, and secured in any jail so that I can get him again; and
in either case, reasonable expenses, if brought to me; and, if stolen,

[67] *Arkansas State Democrat,* June 1, 1849.
[68] *Arkansas Gazette,* Dec. 6, 1836.

or seduced away by any white man or free negro or mulatto, I will pay an additional reward of $100, on the apprehension and conviction of the thief.

Little Rock, August 21, 1844   WM. E. WOODRUFF[69]

FIFTY DOLLARS REWARD

RAN AWAY from the plantation of the subscriber, in Lafayette County, Arkansas, the following described Negro Men, viz.:

Henry, Peter, and Barnaby

The two first named left on the 13th August, and the other on the 3d Sept. (inst.)

HENRY is about 6 feet high, well formed, very black, has a fine countenance, usually laughs when spoken to, is about 35 years of age, and, in his upper jaw, there is a wide space or gap between his front teeth.

PETER is about 4 feet 6 inches high, rather bad countenance, and is about 21 years of age.

BARNABY is about 30 years of age, about 4 feet 6 inches high, heavy set, and has a very bushy head of hair.

Lafayette County, September 16, 1850   PHEBE NASH[70]

20 DOLLARS REWARD

RANAWAY from the subscriber, the 30th day of November last, a dark yellow girl, aged about 25 years, named JINNY. She is about 5 feet 4 inches high, very bold, speaks and laughs loud. On her right hand middle finger is a bad nail, the finger is much larger at the end than the others. She is said to be harbored in town.—The above reward will be given, if found in this county, and a liberal addition made, if found in other counties, and lodged in jail, so I can get her.

Little Rock, January 24, 1850   JAMES VANCE[71]

$150 Reward
WAS STOLEN

On or about the 1st of June last, from my plantation, near Rankin, Yazoo county, Mississippi, an African Negro Man, by the name of JOE—5 feet 10 or 11 inches high, rather slender made, black complexion, about 23 years of age, speaks very broken English, quick spoken, fond of spirits, went off in company with two other Africans,

[69] *Arkansas Banner,* Aug. 28, 1844.
[70] *Gazette and Democrat,* Sept. 27, 1850.
[71] *Arkansas State Democrat,* Jan. 25, 1850.

by the name of *Sam* and *John*. Sam is very large, upwards of six feet high, speaks tolerably good English, though broad and brash, about 30 years of age. John is about 25 years of age, near the size of Joe, with some scars of his native marks, does not speak any English to be understood. They say they are brothers. They were brought to Mobile and sold out by the Custom House Officer and brought here. Sam and John belong to a man by the name of Robuck, of this county. I will give *Fifty Dollars* for the delivery of Joe in any jail in this state, and all reasonable expenses paid, provided I get him again, and One Hundred Dollars for the thief. Any information from any gentleman, by letter or otherwise, will be thankfully received by
Rankin., Miss., Dec. 29, 1831.   WILEY DAVIS[72]

Little is known of what slaves did while they were fugitives. The items stolen by many slaves when they ran away give some indication of their plans, at least. Frequently taken were horses, guns, bedding, canoes, and extra clothing.[73] In such instances there is little doubt that the thefts were merely incidental to the runaway and were for the purpose of making life in the broad world a bit easier and more comfortable. But runaway slaves who had stolen large sums of money or other valuables might have run away to escape punishment for the crimes. Lewis stole five or six hundred dollars—a hundred and fifty in five dollar gold pieces—from his master in Lewisburg before he fled. An unusually liberal reward was offered: a hundred dollars plus half of the stolen money found in Lewis's possession.[74] One slave carried off "two silver and one gilt watches" when he ran away in 1820.[75]

Owners often believed that their slaves were "lurking about" the vicinity from which they had escaped; obviously these were simply trying to avoid work as long as they could.[76] One runaway slave who remained in the woods for several weeks returned

[72] *Arkansas Gazette,* Feb. 22, 1832. This notice, although applying to Mississippi slaves, is given because of the rarity of mention of "African" (a term applied only to those born in Africa) slaves. Since the slave trade had been outlawed in 1808, it is obvious that these slaves had been smuggled into the United States, unless they had been brought in as very small children shortly before 1808.

[73] *Arkansas Gazette,* Sept. 8, 1821, Feb. 1, 1832, April 19, 1836, Dec. 5, 1837; *Batesville News,* July 11, 1839; *Arkansas State Democrat,* June 22, 1849. See also pp. 143-144 above for information on clothing worn and taken by runaways.

[74] *Gazette and Democrat,* Oct. 11, 1850.

[75] *Arkansas Gazette,* Aug. 12, 1820.

[76] *Arkansas Banner,* Aug. 28, 1844; *Batesville Eagle,* June 27, 1848; *Arkansas State Democrat,* Jan. 25, 1850; *Southern Shield,* July 9, 1853.

Jefferson county, June 9, 1851.   6—5w.

Runaway Negro in Jail.

WAS committed to the Jail of Saline county, as a runaway, on the 8th day of June, 1851, a negro man, who says his name is JOHN, and that he belongs to *Henry Johnson*, of Desha county, Ark. He is aged about 24 or 25 years, straight in stature, quick spoken, looks very fierce out of his eyes, and plays on the fiddle. Had on, when apprehended, white cotton pants, coarse cotton shirt, and black hat. The owner is hereby notified to come forward, prove property, and pay the expenses of committal and advertisement, otherwise the said negro will be dealt with according to law.   THOMAS PACK, *Sheriff*
and Jailor of Saline county.
Benton, June 21, 1851.   7—26w.

Pay up! Pay up!!

ALL persons indebted to the undersigned, whose notes and accounts are *now due*, are requested to call and *pay up*, by the 1st day of July next.   JOHN D. ADAMS.
June 13, 1851.   5—

Thirty Dollars Reward.

LEFT my plantation, in Arkansas county, near Post of Arkansas, on the 26th May (ult.), two Negro Men, viz:

GEORGE, a dark copper-colored man, about 30 years of age, 5 ft. 8 or 10 inches high, forehead rather low, some beard on his chin, stutters considerably and has a habit of winking his eyes when talking. He was recently purchased from Mr. Wm. E. Woodruff, at Little Rock, and has a wife at Dr. Watkins', near that city.

Also, HARRISON, about the same age, as the other, and belongs to Mr. W. R. Perry, of the same county.

The above slaves left in company, and it is supposed will make for Little Rock.

The above reward will be paid for arresting and securing said negroes, so that their owners may get them, or one-half the amount for either of them. Letters will reach me if addressed to Arkansas Post, Ark's.   J. FLOYD SMITH.
Arkansas co., June 6, 1851.   4—tf.

Military Land Warrants,

ISSUED in the names of the following soldiers
in the late

home "much reduced in flesh, and [looking] feeble and ema-
ciated," a condition judged to have been caused by "exposure,
alternate hunger and excessive eating, [and] anxiety of mind."
He died a few weeks later.[77] Swamps along the rivers of the state
provided hiding places for some escaped slaves;[78] one, reminiscent
of Mark Twain's Jim in *Huckleberry Finn,* took refuge on an
island in the Mississippi.[79] Another was believed to be working
as a waiter or a steward on a Mississippi River steamboat.[80]

A good many runaway slaves were known to possess forged
passes or "free papers," or were expected to try to forge them.[81]
The possibility of a genuine break for freedom was much greater
in such cases. As we have seen, some slaves fled to the Indian
country or to Mexico; others managed to get to free states.
Many years after the end of slavery, Calvin Fairbank, a member
of the famous Cincinnati Underground Railroad ring led by Levi
Coffin, wrote an account of the dramatic escape to freedom made
by the slave boy William Minnis in 1842. It is quite possible, of
course, that the details of the story became more dramatic as the
author grew older. Originally a slave near Lexington, Kentucky,
William was supposed to have been freed on the authority of his
master's will, but instead he was sold by the son and executor to
a Lexington slave-dealer named Pullum, who took him to Memphis and resold him to a Little Rock man named Brennan. Upon
hearing of these events, the Underground Railroad ring sent
Fairbank to rescue the boy.

Eventually Fairbank found William hired out at a Little Rock
hotel, revealed his identity to him, and with the aid of a French
barber and a New England school teacher concocted and carried
out a plot for smuggling the boy northward. The barber supplied a wig and false beard and mustache, and the school teacher
disguised William to resemble a white man who lived in the area.
As "Mr. Young," accompanied by Fairbank, William went aboard
a steamboat at Little Rock and without difficulty made the trip
to Cincinnati. Since he had no proof of freedom, William went to

[77] *Lindsay* v. *Wayland,* 17 Ark. 385.
[78] *Batesville News,* Jan. 30, 1840; *Southern Shield,* July 9, 1853.
[79] *Arkansas Gazette,* Nov. 2, 1831.
[80] *Ibid.,* July 4, 1837.
[81] *Ibid.,* Oct. 27, 1830, July 4, 1837, May 31, Dec. 13, 1850.

Canada, and later served in the Union army during the Civil War.[82]

Although there are records of the capture or return of many runaway slaves, only a few of the accounts explain in detail just how the recoveries were accomplished. The Waterford Plantation overseer D. T. Weeks wrote James Sheppard of the runaway career of Cornelius:

I am in some trouble just Now on last friday Morning Cornelius left the field & went off & has been dodging around ever since to night About half hour since he came to the door and reported himself I took my light and started with him to the stocks with intention of lodging him there till morning and before we got down he run off again and you know thats provoking I bear it as patient as possible.[83]

The attitude displayed by Weeks here, a sort of long-suffering resignation, can often be detected in contemporary comments of white people concerning their slaves. Ten days later Cornelius "come in" again, to what punishment we are not told.[84] While on the way from Washington (Arkansas) to Fort Smith with his master to attend a Fourth of July horse race in 1854, the slave James ran away, but was taken into custody in Indian Territory a few days later when he rode too trustingly into the camp of a Mr. Holliday, an emigrant bound for California.[85] Mike, a twenty-two-year-old midget or dwarf only three feet, nine inches tall, was seized at Grand Lake, Chicot County, shortly after he had debarked from the steamboat *Kimble* in company with an Irishman who had "decoyed [him] off" from New Orleans.[86] Certainly Mike would have had difficulty in prolonging his freedom. Eleven-year-old Harry, the youngest runaway of whom information was found, also escaped from New Orleans by steamboat, but was taken into custody by the captain and turned over to a justice of the peace at Cypress Bend on the Arkansas River.[87] Ambrose Sevier's slave Tony fled to the Creek Nation as expected, but was "taken up" there, jaws still swollen with the toothache. While

[82] Calvin Fairbank, *Rev. Calvin Fairbank during Slavery Times* (Chicago, 1890), pp. 34-44.
[83] D. T. Weeks to James Sheppard, Sept. 10, 1854, Sheppard Papers.
[84] Weeks to Sheppard, Sept. 20, 1854, Sheppard Papers.
[85] *Washington Telegraph*, Sept. 27, 1854.
[86] *True Democrat*, Feb. 14, 1855.
[87] *Arkansas Gazette*, Oct. 24, 1832.

being returned to Chicot County by steamboat, however, he again made his escape.[88]

Occasionally a slave's runaway career ended in death. In 1836 the runaway slave Jefferson camped near the home of David Tramel in Hot Spring County. Tramel and several other men attempted to capture him, but, Tramel reported,

> he drew his knife, declared he would not be taken, and commenced battle. In the scuffle that ensued, he made several passes with the knife at the company, in one of which he cut the hunting shirt of one of the young men and seized hold of the gun held by the latter, and in endeavoring to wrest it from him, it was discharged and its contents lodged in his (the negro's) body. He even then resisted, and continued to make battle until he was again shot. He was then subdued, but his wounds proved mortal, and he died shortly afterward.[89]

One recaptured runaway slave committed suicide as he was being returned to his home. Suicides among slaves were extremely rare, and this is the only such instance encountered. The slave had escaped from Coahoma County, Mississippi, but was captured across the Mississippi River near Helena. While being taken back across the Mississippi on a ferry, he leaped over the side with thirty pounds of iron tied to his body and drowned without coming to the surface. How he managed to fasten the iron to his body while in custody was not explained.[90]

It is impossible to make an even reasonably accurate estimate of the number or proportion of slaves who ran away in Arkansas. According to the federal census of 1850, twenty-one slaves who had run away in the previous year were still at large, but without doubt many more than that had been recovered. The 1860 census is of even less value; it gives no breakdown by states, merely stating that 803 slaves had escaped the previous year from all of the slave states, as compared to 1,011 in 1850. Individual state figures would be of little value, however, for only "Fugitives from the State" were enumerated, and certainly few owners could have given that information correctly.[91] In 1848 two newspapers, the

[88] *Ibid.*, June 7, 1836.   [89] *Ibid.*, Feb. 2, 1836.
[90] *Southern Shield*, July 30, 1853.
[91] *Census of 1850*, p. xxiii; *Census of 1860 (Population)*, pp. xv-xvi; J. B. D. De Bow, *The Industrial Resources of the Southern and Western States* (3 vols.; New Orleans, 1852-1853), III, 426; Sydnor, *Slavery in Mississippi*, p. 129.

Woodville Republican (Mississippi) and the Concordia, Louisiana, *Intelligencer,* began publication of a register of runaway slaves held in jails in Arkansas, Louisiana, and Mississippi, which, if continued, would have provided interesting and significant data on runaways.   Of the forty-four runaways reported in the first (and only) issue of the register, only three were in Arkansas jails.[92]

The number of newspaper notices of runaways also gives little indication of the number of runaways, for most owners found it unnecessary to use this method of finding their absent slaves.   In the forty-one years of its existence before the Civil War, the *Arkansas Gazette* published advertisements concerning no more than three hundred different runaways, and all other newspapers far fewer.   As we have seen, comparatively few runaways are mentioned in legal records.   Published and other tangible evidence would seem, then, to imply that relatively few slaves ran away from their masters.   Compared to the total number of slaves in the state at any one time, that was doubtless true, but since many, and probably most, runaways were recovered without recourse to any formal or established procedure, the number was not insignificant.   It probably would be safe to say, in the absence of complete and positive evidence, that running away was a fairly common slave offense, but one which was considered a normal hazard of slaveholding and did not disturb most owners greatly.

The Arkansas constitution guaranteed slaves equality with white people in criminal matters in some respects—notably the rights of trial by jury and assignment of counsel—and there is no evidence that the courts of the state ever deprived them of those equalities.   But there were some crimes for which a slave could be punished more severely than a white person—rape, for example. The statute applying to white men specified the death penalty only when an actual rape had been committed, but the slave statute decreed the death penalty for attempted as well as successful rape.[93]

---

[92] *Woodville Republican,* Nov. 21, 1848, cited in Sydnor, *Slavery in Mississippi,* pp. 128-129.

[93] *Gould's Digest, 1858,* pp. 334-335.   From Dec. 17, 1838, to Dec. 14, 1842, white men convicted of rape were given prison terms rather than the death sentence.   *Dennis, a Slave* v. *The State,* 5 Ark. 233.   In this case the Arkansas

Constitutionality of this law was challenged in 1847 by the attorney defending the slave Joe Sullivant, who had been convicted in Dallas County Circuit Court for attempted rape. The attorney appealed the conviction to the Arkansas Supreme Court, asserting that the death penalty for attempted rape was in conflict with the clause in the constitution which said that "any slave who shall be convicted of a capital offense, shall suffer the same degree of punishment as would be inflicted on a white person, and no other." The lower court decision was reversed, but on the basis of a defective indictment, and the constitutionality of the law was not ruled upon at this time.[94]

Three years later the same question was taken before the Supreme Court, this time in the significant case of *Charles* v. *The State*. Charles was convicted in Hempstead County Circuit Court for assault to commit rape upon Almyra Summeron, a fourteen-year-old white girl, and sentenced to be hanged. His attorney appealed, claiming the law was unconstitutional. The Supreme Court again reversed the decision of the lower court, this time because the prosecution had not proved use of force, a fact necessary for conviction. The court did, however, uphold the constitutionality of the double-standard statute. Chief Justice Elbert M. English wrote:

> We think it clear, therefore, that all that was designed to be understood by the provision in the constitution was that, in case a negro should be convicted of a capital crime, he should not undergo other or greater punishment than that which should be inflicted upon a white man for an offense which would subject him to capital punishment. [It was] doubtless inserted from a feeling of humanity . . . to secure them against that barbarous treatment and excessive cruelty . . . practiced upon them in the earlier years of our colonial history. . . .[95]

Five cases involving rape by slaves came before the Arkansas Supreme Court during the slavery period, and, interestingly enough, in four instances the convictions by the lower courts were reversed. Two were referred to immediately above; the other two were in successive cases involving a single offense by the slave

---

Supreme Court upheld the conviction of two slaves and a white man who had been convicted of rape of a white woman.
[94] *Joe Sullivant, a Slave* v. *The State,* 8 Ark. 400.
[95] *Charles* v. *The State,* 11 Ark. 390.

Pleasant of Ouachita County. All of the reversals were because of defective procedures or improperly admitted evidence in the lower courts.[96] It is evident, then, that cases concerning slaves were considered as carefully by the Supreme Court as those involving white people.

The double standard also applied, if not so markedly, to slaves charged with killing a person. While first and second degree murder, voluntary and involuntary manslaughter, and justifiable homicide were recognized for white people and free Negroes, only a single degree of murder and a single degree of manslaughter were recognized for slaves. Punishment for these crimes was the same for slaves as for whites—hanging for murder and a maximum of seven years imprisonment for manslaughter.[97]

In punishment for most of the other serious crimes, the double standard reacted in favor of the slaves. Following are examples of punishments stipulated for slaves and for whites. Arson: slave, one year's imprisonment and three hours in the pillory; white, two to ten years' imprisonment. Burglary: slave, six months' imprisonment and thirty-nine lashes; white, one to fifteen years' imprisonment. Larceny: slave, thirty-nine lashes and one hour in the pillory; white, one to five years' imprisonment. For the first offense of stealing slaves or livestock, the punishment for a slave was fifty lashes and an hour in the pillory, as compared to five to twenty-one years' imprisonment for a white man, but a slave was to suffer death upon a second conviction.[98] No records of actual use of the pillory in Arkansas were found. The types of punishment meted out to slaves, rarely including extended imprisonment, show that Arkansas law-makers were averse to depriving slaveowners of the services of their slaves for long periods of time. Actually, of course, imprisonment would not have served as useful a penal purpose as in the case of white men, for slaves had little freedom of which they could be deprived.

When slaves committed crimes of a lesser degree than felony (defined in Arkansas law as a crime which could be punished with

<hr>

[96] *Joe Sullivant, a Slave* v. *The State,* 8 Ark. 400; *Charles* v. *The State,* 11 Ark. 390; *Pleasant* v. *State,* 13 Ark. 360; *Pleasant* v. *State,* 15 Ark. 624. Conviction was upheld in the case of *Dennis, a Slave* v. *The State,* 5 Ark. 233.
[97] *Gould's Digest, 1858,* pp. 327-333, 384-385.
[98] *Ibid.,* pp. 338-342, 357, 385-386.

execution or imprisonment), such as trespass or larceny, they could not be indicted until the master had been given an opportunity to "compound with the injured party, and punish his own slave." Any damages were always paid by the master.[99] This provision of the law accounted for the rare appearance in court of slaves charged with minor crimes.

Court procedure in the trial of slaves was much the same as in trial of white people. As we have seen, slaves were guaranteed juries and defense counsel, and the same rules of evidence were observed. The only difference in trial procedure was that testimony by slaves or free Negroes was admissible, while it was not in the trial of white people.[100]

Although a slave charged with serious crime was assured of fair treatment once he appeared before a court, sometimes white men, living in an era when the use of "lynch law"—against both white and black—was far more frequent than today, took matters into their own hands and meted out their own punishment. Only a few such incidents involving slaves were reported in the newspapers or were recorded elsewhere, but there doubtless were more. Following are newspaper accounts of several lynchings:

A revolting rape and murder has occurred near Palmyra. A negro, belonging to Glascock, committed violence on, and murdered Miss Bright, aged 14 years, and killed her brother, aged 11 years. The negro was to be burned.[101]

We learn from the Helena Shield that Mr. Henry Yerby an old resident of Phillips county was murdered a few days since by two of his negroes. The negroes were arrested, and their guilt being evident they were burnt to death.[102]

A grisly murder culminating in a lynching was committed in Hot Spring County in 1836. A slave who was a member of a group migrating to Texas murdered his master, another white man, and five fellow-slaves with an axe, and then attempted to burn the bodies in a campfire. He returned to his old home near Memphis and reported that his master and the other slaves had been murdered by Indians, but, informed of the circumstances of

[99] *Ibid.*, p. 385.   [100] *Ibid.*
[101] *Arkansas State Democrat,* Nov. 16, 1849.
[102] *Ibid.,* Nov. 23, 1849.

the case by a special proclamation of the governor of Arkansas, Tennessee law-enforcement officials arrested the slave and returned him to Hot Spring County.[103] A few weeks later the *Arkansas Gazette* reported the conclusion of the episode.

'On Horror's head, let horrors accumulate'—We have been informed that the slave William, who murdered his master some weeks since, (Huskey), and several negroes, was taken by a party, a few days since, from the sheriff of Hot Spring, and burned alive! Yes, tied up to the limb of a tree, a fire built under him, and consumed in slow and lingering torture!

The attitude of law-abiding citizens to this sort of punishment of slaves was shown by the editor's further comment.

We have mentioned this disgraceful and barbarous outrage, that the ministers of the law may take steps to bring those implicated in the guilt of so black a crime, to punishment. The circumstances of this criminal outrage are aggravated by the fact, that the evidence against the negro was of such a character, that there was no chance of his escape from a just expiation of his crime by law—his condemnation was next to certain.[104]

A question concerning crime among slaves which arises is this: were slaves more criminal than white people? If only the testimony of the records is considered, the answer would be that slaves committed fewer crimes. But, as we have seen, a great many offenses punished as crimes among the free population were, under the system of slavery, merely subject to disciplinary action by the master, with no record kept. In other words, the crime rate among slaves was largely dependent upon the definition of crime during that period. But in all probability slaves did commit proportionately fewer crimes than white people, not because their basic tendencies were different, but simply because the regimented nature of slavery permitted less freedom for commission of crimes.

[103] *Arkansas Gazette*, Nov. 1, 1836.
[104] *Ibid.*, Nov. 29, 1836.

XIII

"... hereby manumitted and set free."

It was always recognized that some Arkansas slaveowners, for various reasons, might want to free, or manumit, their slaves. Therefore the laws governing slavery in Arkansas, from the earliest French days until near the end of the slavery period, provided for manumission of slaves by their owners. The earliest of these, it will be recalled, was found in the Black Code, which governed slavery for seventy-nine years while Arkansas was a part of Louisiana. To manumit a slave, an owner was required to be twenty-five years of age and to obtain a decree of permission from the Superior Council. An exception was that if a slave were appointed tutor of his master's children he automatically became free.[1] No records of manumission of slaves in Arkansas under the provisions of the Black Code have been found; it is not likely that many were freed, since the number of slaves was small and the number of free Negroes even smaller.

During the remaining years prior to statehood, manumission of slaves in Arkansas was regulated by the law of October 1, 1804, passed by the legislature of Louisiana Territory but re-enacted by the legislatures of the various governmental bodies controlling Arkansas subsequently. Under this law, slaves could be emancipated by will or other written instrument, but to prevent the master from avoiding payment of his debts, they were made subject to seizure to satisfy debts contracted prior to emancipation.[2]

Manumission of slaves first assumed political importance at the

[1] Black Code, Sections L and LI, French, *Historical Collections of Louisiana*, III, 94.
[2] Steele and M'Campbell, *Laws of Arkansas Territory*, p. 526.

time Arkansas presented its constitution to Congress with an application for statehood in 1836. The chief objection to the constitution by the anti-slavery forces, it will be remembered, was to the provision that "The General Assembly shall have no power to pass laws for the emancipation of slaves, without the consent of their owners." While mass emancipation was thus prohibited, the legislature was given the right to permit individual emancipation: "They shall have power to pass laws to permit owners to emancipate them, saving the rights of creditors, and preventing them from becoming a public charge."[3]

Objections in Congress to prohibition of legislative emancipation of slaves were overcome, and at its first session the Arkansas General Assembly enacted a law, effective March 20, 1839, providing for individual emancipation. The law was basically the same as that in force previously, but in somewhat greater detail. A slave could be emancipated by last will and testament, or by any other written instrument attested by two witnesses and proved in the circuit court or acknowledged by the emancipator in the same court. An emancipated slave could be taken in execution to satisfy a debt made by his owner prior to the emancipation, and the owner was held liable for the freed slave if he were not of sound mind or was above the age of forty-five, under the age of twenty-one if male, or under the age of eighteen if female. A freed slave was required to keep in his possession a copy of the document by which he had been set free.[4]

The emancipation law was challenged in the courts only once: in the early 1850's there was an unsuccessful attempt to prove that it had been repealed, by implication, by a law passed on January 20, 1843, prohibiting further emigration of free Negroes to Arkansas.[5] This attempt will be discussed later in connection with the free Negro. The courts of the state insisted upon close compliance with the state emancipation law and with local ordinances based upon it. On two occasions the Arkansas Supreme

---

[3] See p. 43 above. The terms "manumit" and "emancipate" were used almost synonymously during the slavery period. But since "emancipate" is ordinarily associated with the mass freeing of the slaves by President Lincoln, "manumit" will be used in most cases when referring to freeing of small numbers of slaves.

[4] *Revised Statutes, 1838,* pp. 359-360.

[5] *Campbell et al.* v. *Campbell,* 13 Ark. 513.

Court ruled against Negroes who claimed freedom by virtue of wills or deeds on grounds that proper procedures had not been followed. The slaves Isaac and Harriet and their five children were denied emancipation, despite a deed made by their master Gilbert Barden, because the deed had not been proved or acknowledged in court.[6] Aramynta and her children failed to secure their freedom, at least for the moment, because they had obtained their decree of freedom from the probate court, rather than from the circuit court as provided in the law.[7] In at least one instance local permission for continuing residence of a free Negro was denied temporarily because he did not have in his possession evidence of freedom.[8]

The motives prompting Arkansas owners to free their slaves were chiefly these: genuine antipathy toward the institution of slavery, gratitude for services rendered by the slaves, and affection or consideration for slaves who were mistresses or children of the owner. Many owners, of course, gave no reasons when manumitting their slaves. The least amount of evidence exists concerning the first reason—antipathy toward slavery. Only two instances of this, both rather inconclusive, were found:

John Latta of Vineyard township, Washington County . . . died a bachelor, September 23, 1834, in his forty-fourth year. He had imbibed many of the Henry Clay notions about slavery and was a great believer in the colonization of Negroes to Africa. Not to be inconsistent he emancipated his slaves at his death, and not to be inhumane provided for them by a bequest of $2,500 in gold in his will. The hills of northwest Arkansas had no charms for these dusky freedmen and when they got their money they went back to Kentucky to live as freedmen in the old haunts where they had been born.[9]

When Abel Knowlton of Desha County manumitted his slave Jack by deed, he wrote of "motives of benevolence and humanity," but it is impossible to tell whether he disapproved of slavery as a whole, or only had kindly feelings for Jack.[10]

[6] *Harriet et al.* v. *Swan,* 18 Ark. 495.
[7] *Aramynta et al.* v. *Woodruff as Exec.,* 7 Ark. 422.
[8] Little Rock City Council Record, 1835-1842, p. 359.
[9] Josiah H. Shinn, *Pioneers and Makers of Arkansas* (Little Rock, 1908), pp. 342-343. The American Colonization Society, founded in 1816 to promote colonization of freed slaves to Africa, was never active in an organized manner in Arkansas, but did receive some support from individuals in the state.
[10] Desha County Deed Record "C," 1847-1850, p. 358.

Gratitude for services of the slaves was clearly given as the reason for manumission by many owners. In providing for the freeing of her slave Aramynta and children, Cynthia Robinson of Pulaski County wrote, "As my female slave Aramynta hath generally served me with great diligence and integrity, . . . it is my will and greatest desire that at my decease the said Aramynta, for her faithful services to me while living be and hereby is manumitted and set free together with her three children. . . ."[11] Francis Roycroft of Chicot County provided for the manumission of his "old and faithful slave Nancy" upon his death,[12] and Eli Crow of Yell County made the same provision for his nine slaves "in consideration of faithful services and attention rendered. . . ."[13]

It was not uncommon for white men to father children by their slave women, as we have seen, and the consequent ties of affection and blood understandably prompted some manumissions.[14] Only a few may be determined from the records to have been motivated by this reason, but since men rarely wrote or spoke of such matters, it is probably that many others were also. The bare fact that mulattoes made up a much larger percentage of the free Negro population than of the slave is strong indication of the prevalence of freeing children of white fathers, although, of course, all mulattoes among free Negroes could not be attributed to this, since presumably free Negroes tended to marry or cohabit among themselves more than with slaves. In 1850, 66.94 per cent of the free Negroes in Arkansas were of mixed blood, compared to only 15.61 per cent of the slaves. By 1860 the proportion of mulattoes among each class had declined slightly, to 60.42 for free Negroes and 12.64 for slaves, but the decline was less among free Negroes than among slaves.[15]

In some Southern states slaves had an additional means of securing their freedom—purchasing themselves. But since Arkansas slaves were not legally permitted to hire their own time, it would have been extremely difficult, if not impossible, for a slave

---

[11] Pulaski County Will Book "A," p. 77.
[12] Chicot County Will Record "C," p. 23.
[13] *Bob alias Robert Crow* v. *Powers,* 19 Ark. 424.
[14] See pp. 200-201 above.
[15] *Compendium of the Seventh Census,* p. 83; *Census of 1860 (Population),* p. xiii. Censuses prior to 1850 contain no data on color of Negroes.

to save enough money to purchase himself. There was no Arkansas law prohibiting self-purchase, but the Arkansas Supreme Court, while not eliminating the possibility of such action, ruled in 1857 that a slave had no legal means of forcing his master to carry out an agreement for self-purchase, either outright or by working for a given period of time.

> If the master contract with the slave, or any one for him, that the slave shall be emancipated upon his paying to his master a sum of money, or rendering him some stipulated amount of labor, although the slave may pay the money, or tender it, or perform the labor, yet he cannot compel his master to execute the contract, because both the money and the labor of the slave belong to the master and could constitute no legal consideration for the contract.[16]

By no means all slaves whose manumission was provided for by will or by deed received their freedom immediately. Masters often stipulated that freedom was to take effect at some later time. If the slaves were children, it was sometimes deferred until they were grown to prevent them from becoming an economic burden to the estate, since the law required guarantee of their support until that time.[17] One Pulaski County slaveholder, John M. Maclin, provided that six of his slaves be manumitted immediately after his death and the remaining four after a period of three years, during which they were to work for his sister.[18] The nineteen slaves of Joshua Averett of Union County received their freedom by virtue of their master's will seven years after his death.[19] James Kuykendall of Pulaski County stipulated a sort of conditional immediate freedom for his four slaves: they were required to pay eight hundred dollars to two of Kuykendall's relatives within a period of five years, and were given the use of a farm on which to earn the money; if they failed to pay the money within the specified time, they were to revert to the relatives.[20]

[16] *Jackson* v. *Bob,* 18 Ark. 399.
[17] *Abraham* v. *Wilkins,* 17 Ark. 292; Will of Charlotte Bardon, Oct. 29, 1850, Pulaski County Will Book "B," p. 23; Will of Richard S. Parker, March 4, 1840, Pulaski County Will Book "A," p. 69.
[18] Will of John M. Maclin, July 22, 1853, Pulaski County Will Book "B," p. 53.
[19] Union County Executors, Administrators, and Guardians Bonds, Book "E," p. 72; *Phebe et al.* v. *Quillin et al.,* 21 Ark. 490.
[20] Will of Joseph Kuykendall, Feb. 23, 1828, Pulaski County Will Book "A," p. 24.

The freed slaves were able to pay the money and receive absolute freedom, for eleven years later two of them, bearing the surname of their deceased master, appeared before the Little Rock City Council, filed bonds, and received certificates of residence as provided for in the "Ordinance of the City relative to Free Negroes and Mulattoes."[21]

Many owners bequeathed money to the slaves they freed. The most liberal gift encountered was the five thousand dollars willed by Duncan Campbell of Chicot County to Viney, his small slave (and daughter), when she received her freedom at the age of fifteen.[22] Five of the slaves of Elisha North of Chicot County received a thousand dollars each upon being taken to a free state and given their freedom; the remaining slaves, although not freed, were permitted to choose their own masters.[23] The gift of $2,500 to the freed slaves of John Latta of Washington County has already been mentioned. When providing for the manumission of her slave children when they reached twenty-one, Charlotte Bardon of Pulaski County directed that they be hired out in the interim, and that the proceeds of their hire, after payment of expenses, be divided equally between "the Methodist church . . . for the benefit of said church, and the spread of the Gospel of Christ," and each of the slaves upon being freed.[24] Eliza, the slave of John Peake of Clark County, was permitted to take her choice of a thousand dollars in cash or a deed to the tract of land upon which her master had resided when she received her freedom in 1858.[25]

Other freed slaves were given property, or both property and money. John M. Maclin's six freed slaves were to "enjoy the use of" a house and lots four, five, and six in block nineteen of the original city of Little Rock along with Maclin's sister, and upon her death the title was to pass to them.[26] Mary Dickson of Clark

[21] Little Rock City Council Record, 1835-1842, p. 161. Although the amount the slaves were required to pay was considerably less than their actual value, it is obvious that this was a thinly concealed case of self-purchase. Note, however, that it occurred many years before the Supreme Court ruling on self-purchase.
[22] Chicot County Will Record "C," p. 25.
[23] *Ibid.*, pp. 176-177.
[24] Pulaski County Will Book "B," p. 23.
[25] Clark County Will Book "B," pp. 63-64.
[26] Pulaski County Will Book "B," p. 53.

County was much more generous with her manumitted slaves than with her daughter. The daughter received only one half of the cattle, while the four slaves, along with York, a Negro man freed previously, got all of the "land with all the tenements and Hereditaments thereon situated and thereunto belonging all the stock of horses and horse beasts of every description all of the Hogs and one-half of the stock of cattle of every description. . . ." Apparently the previously freed York was the husband of Leah, one of the slaves being freed, for in addition to the grants of land and stock they received the "farming utensils and kitchen furniture . . . to be enjoyed equally between them."[27]

Some owners, less well-endowed with property than those mentioned above, merely gave their slaves household goods or small numbers of livestock. Francis Roycroft's Nancy got the household furniture and "two horse creatures which she has always claimed from their foalding as well as two cows & calves,"[28] and the legacy of Aramynta, the manumitted slave of Cynthia Robinson, consisted of "One Tea Kettle, two dutch ovens, one Pine table, two bedsteads, one cow and her calf—the cow of a Red color with a star in her face—One Sow with her litter of six pigs—and the only bureau now in my house with her apparel."[29]

No reasonable estimate of the number or frequency of manumissions in Arkansas can be made, although without doubt they comprised only a minute proportion of the number of slaves in the state at any one time. They were common enough, however, that records of them may be found readily in county will and deed registers. The number of free Negroes in the state was never large, but even their number is no accurate indication of the frequency of manumission, for some freed slaves were sent out of the state immediately by the manumitter or were given their freedom in a free state, while many others left of their own accord because of the generally unfriendly attitude toward free Negroes in Arkansas. The federal censuses contain statistics on numbers of slaves manumitted, but their correctness is unlikely; even the compilers of the 1860 census admitted that "great irregularity, as

[27] Clark County Will Book "A," p. 20.
[28] Chicot County Will Record "C," p. 23.
[29] Pulaski County Will Book "A," p. 77.

might naturally be expected, appears to exist for the two periods whereof we have returns on this subject." The number of slaves reported manumitted in 1850 was only one, and in 1860 forty-one, certainly a more nearly correct figure than the first.[30]

While manumission of slaves was prompted, in general, by the kindly feelings of the owners, the prevalent attitude of the white people of Arkansas toward the inevitable products of manumission —the free Negroes—was anything but kindly.   That attitude ranged from bare tolerance at the time of achievement of state-hood in 1836 to bitter animosity by 1858.   Consequently the number of free Negroes was always small, reaching a maximum of only 608 in 1850,[31] but the continuing controversy they caused was all out of proportion to their number.   It will be recalled that the Black Code of Louisiana contained relatively liberal provisions concerning free Negroes; partly because of this, and partly because of the natural proclivities of the predominantly French population, free Negroes became quite numerous in Louisiana—18,647 in 1860—[32] and were not generally discriminated against.   But Arkansas had only a handful of free Negroes while it was a part of Louisiana, and the Anglo-Americans who came to make up the great majority of the population of the territory and state did not share the French tolerance.

Immediately after Arkansas became a state, the legislature indicated clearly the dominant Arkansas attitude toward free Negroes by passing a law designed to discourage them from entering.

No free negro or mulatto shall hereafter be permitted to emigrate or settle in this state unless he shall produce to the clerk of the county court of the county in which he wishes to settle, within twenty days after his arrival therein, a certificate of his freedom, and enter into bond to the State of Arkansas for the use of any county that may be damnified by such negro or mulatto, with good and sufficient security in any sum not less than five hundred dollars, before the clerk of the county court, conditioned for the good behavior of such

[30] U. S. Bureau of the Census, *Preliminary Report on the Eighth Census* (Washington, 1862), pp. 11, 137.
[31] *Census of 1850,* p. 535.
[32] *Census of 1860 (Population),* p. 194.

negro or mulatto and to pay for the support of such negro or mulatto in case he shall at any time thereafter be unable to support himself and become chargeable to any county of this State.[33]

A free Negro who failed to comply with the law could be fined from ten to a hundred dollars, and if he still had not complied by the next term of the county court he could be given not more than twenty-five lashes and ordered out of the state, and could also be hired out long enough to earn money to pay his fine, court costs, and expenses of imprisonment. Free Negroes between the ages of seven and twenty-one were to be bound out as apprentices until they had reached the age of twenty-one.[34]

There were only 59 free Negroes in Arkansas in 1820 and 141 in 1830; it is somewhat surprising, in view of the unfavorable conditions, that the number grew to 465 in 1840.[35] But without doubt most of the increased number had entered Arkansas before the restrictive statute became effective only the year before.

The state law requiring registration and bond evidently applied only to those free Negroes entering the state after its enactment, but local ordinances in some towns made similar requirements for all free Negroes. On June 22, 1839, twenty free Negroes appeared before the Little Rock City Council, produced satisfactory evidence of their freedom, and having previously filed bonds with the city recorder, were issued certificates of residence as provided for in the city ordinance.[36] Several months earlier, the bond of the free Negro Nace Waring, with Chester Ashley, the wealthy Little Rock slaveowner, as security, had been approved by the city council.[37]

Nace Waring was the best known of all Little Rock free Negroes, and, quite unlike most of his class, was held in high regard by the white population. His real name was Nathan Warren, but "Nace Waring" was so commonly used that it even appears in legal records. Born a slave in Maryland in 1812 and reared in the District of Columbia, Warren was brought to Little Rock about 1834 as a slave of Robert Crittenden. After the

[33] *Revised Statutes, 1838,* pp. 584-585.
[34] *Ibid.,* pp. 586-587.
[35] *Negro Population, 1790-1915,* p. 57.
[36] Little Rock City Council Record, 1835-1842, p. 161.
[37] *Ibid.,* p. 141.

death of Crittenden, he passed to the estate of Daniel Greathouse and in 1837 was given his freedom. At some time during these years he married Chester Ashley's slave cook, Anne, like himself a mulatto. They had a number of children, and Nathan had others by later marriages. Several of the children were members of the famous "Ashley Band," and some of them became prominent in post-Civil War Little Rock affairs.

Warren was a jack-of-all-trades, working at one time or another as barber, carriage driver, cook, and general handyman, but he eventually settled down in the bakery and confectionery business, operating, at various times, shops on Markham Street near the corner of Louisiana Street and on the west side of Main Street near Markham. His services as caterer were constantly in demand for parties, weddings, and other social events of the town.[88] Many years later, two Little Rock women who had known Warren as they were growing up reminisced:

Uncle Nace Warren was the first confectioner we remember in Little Rock. He was a free Negro, but had married Mr. Ashley's cook, so, of course, he was adopted by the community as kinfolks. He was an expert in making cakes and was patronized by the best people in town. He was smart enough to keep the secret of his success in his own possession, saying, "If I lets you white ladies have my receipts, I gives away my trade." He was always ready to supply them on short notice.[39]

There is evidence that the Little Rock ordinance requiring free Negroes to register and make bond was not promptly and consistently enforced: as late as 1849, several years after further emigration of free Negroes to Arkansas had been banned by state law, bonds were still being accepted by the Little Rock City Council. Frequently security for the bonds was furnished by prominent white citizens, in some cases, judging by the names of the Negroes, the same men who had freed them. On January 30,

---

[88] Mary P. Fletcher, "Susan Bricelin Fletcher," *Arkansas Pioneers*, I (Sept., 1912), 10; Margaret S. Ross, "Nathan Warren, Free Negro Confectioner," *Pulaski County Historical Review*, III (March, 1955), 10; Margaret S. Ross, "Nathan Warren, a Free Negro of the Old South," *Arkansas Historical Quarterly*, XV (Spring, 1956), 53-61. The latter two articles, by the research associate of the Arkansas History Commission, are based upon manuscript census records and other original sources.

[39] Mrs. Sue Crease Peay and Miss Sophia Crease, "Good Cheer of Early Days," *Arkansas Pioneers*, I (Jan., 1913), 11.

1840, bond for Sarah Jones was furnished by Nicholas Peay, a former alderman and member of a famous early family of the city, and that of Peter L. Randolph by R. C. Byrd, owner of a plantation adjacent to the city on the east and the man for whom the present day Byrd Street was named. Jesse Brown, mayor of Little Rock, made bond for Matilda Stokes on January 15, 1841, and Samuel Hobson for Jane Hobson on June 2, 1849. These are only a few of the numerous instances which are found in the Little Rock City Council records.[40]

But on occasion court action was taken to enforce the registration ordinance: on February 10, 1842, Jane Menser was fined ten dollars and costs (a total of $23.82½) upon conviction in the Little Rock Corporation Court of having come into the city without filing bond and security and was ordered to "depart immediately beyond the limits of the City of Little Rock." At the same time her husband, Edward Menser, was fined twenty-five dollars and costs (a total of $39.07½) after conviction on charges of employing and harboring a free Negro—evidently his wife. Edward was also convicted of assault and battery, victim unspecified in the court records; one wonders if it were also his wife. During the month of April, 1842, ten free Negroes were tried for failure to make bond, nine being convicted.[41]

The period during which free Negroes were permitted to continue entering Arkansas was very brief, for on January 20, 1843, the legislature passed a law, effective March 1, 1843, which prohibited further entrance of free Negroes, but permitted those already in the state to remain if, prior to July 1, 1843, they produced satisfactory evidence of freedom, proved that they had entered before March 1, and posted bond of five hundred dollars. Punishment for unlawful entry into Arkansas was to be a fine of not more than two hundred dollars and a jail term of not more than six months, followed by immediate expulsion from the state. Free Negroes already in Arkansas who failed to comply with the law within the specified time were to be treated the same as those illegally entering.[42]

---

[40] Little Rock City Council Record, 1835-1842, 1841-1852, *passim*.
[41] Little Rock Corporation Court Record "A," Feb. 10, April 23, 28, 1842.
[42] Elbert H. English, ed., *A Digest of the Statutes of Arkansas; Embracing*

For several years the newspapers of the state had been agitating for a law such as this one, or one even more restrictive. In 1836 William E. Woodruff, as editor of the *Arkansas Gazette* one of the chief moulders of public opinion in the state, wrote sarcastically of "this valuable class of citizens," and advocated that they be barred from the state.[43] Woodruff's successor, Edward Cole, continued the paper's policy of opposition to the free Negro. In 1839 he noted editorially the passage of a law in Alabama barring further entrance of free Negroes and requiring all within the state to leave within twenty days under penalty of flogging, and commented, "A wholesome law."[44]

Not long after passage, constitutionality of the 1843 law was tested in the courts. John Pendleton, a free Negro already in the state, was tried and convicted in Crawford County Circuit Court on charges of failure to register and post bond. He maintained that the law was unconstitutional and appealed the conviction to the Arkansas Supreme Court, which in 1846 upheld the decision of the lower court. Speaking for the court, Justice James Cross stated that if the law was in conflict with either the state or the federal constitution, it was with that part of Article IV, Section II, of the federal constitution which guarantees that "The citizens of each State shall be entitled to all privileges and immunities of citizens in the several states." But, continued Justice Cross, in the opinion of the court a free Negro was not a citizen within the meaning of the privileges and immunities clause. Justice Cross's elaboration of this belief is such a clear expression of a view widely held in the South during the period that an extended transcription is given:

In recurring to the past history of the [United States] constitution, and prior to its formation . . . it will be found that nothing beyond a kind of quasi citizenship has ever been recognized in the case of colored persons. The protection of their persons and the right of property is provided for to a just and humane extent. To assault, to maim, or to murder a free person of color is as fully prohibited by our

All Laws of a General and Permanent Character, in Force at the Close of the Session of the General Assembly of 1846 (Little Rock, 1848), pp. 546-551.
[43] *Arkansas Gazette,* Feb. 9, 1836. For other *Gazette* editorial opinion on the subject, see the issues of July 7 and Nov. 17, 1835.
[44] *Ibid.,* April 10, 1839.

constitution and laws as the like offense against one of the white race, and so as to depredations on their property or habitations. If citizens in a full and constitutional sense, why were they not permitted to participate in its formation? They certainly were not. The constitution was the work of the white race; the government, for which it provides, and of which it is the fundamental law, is in their hands and under their control, and it would not have intended to place a different race of people in all things upon terms of equality with themselves. Indeed, if such had been the desire, its utter impracticability is too evident to admit of doubt. The two races, differing as they do in complexion, habits, conformations, and intellectual endowments, could not nor ever will live together upon terms of social or political equality. A higher than human power has so ordered it, and a greater than human agency must change the decree. Those who framed the constitution were aware of this, and hence their intention to exclude them as citizens within the meaning of the clause to which we have referred .... In our state constitution there is nothing either express or implied with which, in our judgment, the act in question conflicts. We entertain no doubt, therefore, as to the constitutionality of the act upon which the prosecution is based.[45]

At least one attempt was made to prove that the 1843 law barring further entry of free Negroes had repealed, by implication, the earlier statute authorizing manumission of slaves. Shortly before he died in 1845, Duncan Campbell of Chicot County made a will giving his three-year-old slave daughter Viney her freedom and five thousand dollars when she reached fifteen, the remainder of the estate to go to brother and sisters. One brother, Cornelius Campbell, named executor of the estate, took Viney to Missouri and sold her, and was soon sentenced to six months in prison for contempt of court upon failure to deliver her to chancery court as a ward. Another brother, then appointed executor by the court, finally found Viney in Missouri and recovered possession of her by a writ of *habeas corpus*. A legal quarrel between the brothers arose, with Cornelius maintaining that he had been justified in selling Viney, since the 1843 law had invalidated the law permitting manumission. Eight years after Duncan Campbell's death the case reached the Arkansas Supreme Court, which awarded Viney her freedom and the five thousand dollars. Con-

---

[45] *Pendleton* v. *State*, 6 Ark. 509.

cerning the assertion of Cornelius Campbell that the manumission law was void, the court said:

> . . . though the act of 1843 implies a change of policy, as to the increase of free Negroes, . . . it is not a repeal by implication of the law authorizing emancipation . . . . Our statutes contain no . . . prohibition [against emancipated negroes remaining in the state] . . . . The act of 1843 was . . . but a measure of self-defense, declaring that while this State will not be infested with the free negroes of other States, we will tolerate the evils resulting from the emancipation of our own slaves, until . . . the sense of the people may require an avowed change of policy.[46]

Why were free Negroes so thoroughly disliked and resented? There appear to have been three chief reasons: a belief that they were immoral, criminal, and generally troublesome in the community; a belief that they were likely to cause—either overtly or merely by their presence—discontent, unrest, and possibly open rebellion among the slaves; and fear of their economic competition, especially by the white artisans and mechanics of the towns. The first two reasons were clearly summed up in a portion of a circular published in 1858: " . . . with few exceptions, [free Negroes] are a lazy, worthless, immoral, impudent and unprincipled population, intentionally exerting the worst influence on the slaves, encouraging them in all their evil habits and inclinations, hating us who deny them equal privileges with ourselves; ever ready to receive stolen wares and to harbor the fugitive; and wholly *unfit* to be free."[47]

The fact that many free Negroes had received their freedom, either directly or indirectly, as a result of sexual immorality contributed further to the popular belief. It was commonly believed during the period that people of mixed race had a natural inclination to immorality; the superintendent of the federal census wrote at the close of the slavery period: "That corruption of morals progresses with greater admixture of races, and that the product of vice stimulates the propensity to immorality, is as evident to observation as it is natural to circumstances."[48]

The economic jealousy of the free Negroes felt by white skilled

[46] *Campbell et al.* v. *Campbell*, 13 Ark. 573.
[47] *Washington Telegraph*, Aug. 4, 1858.
[48] *Census of 1860 (Population)*, p. xi.

workers in Arkansas was demonstrated by the organized protest movement against them mentioned earlier in another connection.[49] It will be recalled that two white artisans led the movement which resulted in passage of resolutions protesting the use of free Negroes (and also slaves) as mechanics and the teaching of any Negroes the skilled trades and urging the passage of laws to accomplish the desired ends.

The opposition to free Negroes in Arkansas was not unique, but only a segment of a movement which had been growing in intensity in the entire South since the 1820's, set off largely by the discovery in 1820 of a rebellious conspiracy among the slaves of Charleston, South Carolina, organized by Denmark Vesey, a free Negro, and by circulation in the South of an inflammatory pamphlet, *Walker's Appeal to the Colored Citizens of the World,* published in 1829 by David Walker, a North Carolina free Negro who had moved to Boston. As a result, practically all Southern states enacted more stringent laws concerning free Negroes, many of them more harsh and restrictive than those in Arkansas.[50] Most of the people of Arkansas had migrated from the older slave states, and quite naturally they brought with them the ideas and prejudices prevalent there.

It is doubtful that the 1843 law prohibiting further entrance of free Negroes and requiring bond of those already in the state was uniformly and rigidly enforced. County records contain very few references to free Negroes, except in connection with manumission; they must therefore have complied closely with the law or have been permitted to evade it. And the fact that some free Negroes were permitted to file bonds for years after the deadline set by the state law suggests laxity in enforcement. In Little Rock, as we have seen, bonds were being filed as late as 1849, and at the July, 1848, term of the Franklin County Court Elijah Williams appeared and filed bond of five hundred dollars with William Hail and William Cureton as securities.[51] It is possible, of

---

[49] See p. 111 above.

[50] Carter G. Woodson, *Free Negro Heads of Families in the United States in 1830 together with a Brief Treatment of the Free Negro* (Washington, 1925), pp. xxviii-xxx. Although not entirely objective at times, this is one of the best brief historical accounts of the free Negro available.

[51] Franklin County County Court Record, 1847-1854, p. 23.

course, that the free Negroes who filed bonds after 1843 had recently been manumitted. With the exception of the case of William Pendleton previously mentioned, no instances of conviction under the 1843 law were found.

Whether carefully enforced or not, the 1843 law did check the migration of free Negroes to Arkansas. By 1850 the number grew to 608 (from 465 in 1840), but the gain represented little more than the normal increase to be expected from reproduction, while, of course, slaves were constantly being freed, with at least some of them remaining within the state. In 1850 there were free Negroes in all counties except Drew, Izard, Lafayette, Madison, Pike, Polk, Pope, Searcy, and Van Buren, most of these counties also having few slaves. A majority—373—lived in six counties, Crawford, Desha, Hempstead, Marion, Pulaski, and Sevier, while the remaining 235 were distributed in numbers of from one to sixteen in the thirty-six other counties having free Negroes. There were 129 in Marion, 92 in Crawford, 57 in Desha, 32 each in Hempstead and Pulaski, and 31 in Sevier.

Free Negroes in Arkansas lived predominantly in the rural areas, while in the South as a whole they were found mainly in the towns and cities. The only Arkansas towns which had significant concentrations were Little Rock in Pulaski County, with twenty-one, and Fort Smith in Crawford County, with thirty. Even in the counties with the largest numbers listed above, with the exception of Pulaski, the free Negroes lived mainly in the rural townships. The greatest single concentration of free Negroes in the state was in North Fork Township, Marion County, along the Missouri line. The eighty living there comprised almost a third of the total township population and formed a sort of agricultural colony on the North Fork of the White River.[52]

The small number of free Negroes in the state (smaller at every census than in any other slave state) and the fact that they lived chiefly in the rural areas rather than in the towns suggests strongly that the fears of rivalry with the whites in the skilled trades were largely unfounded. And there is little evidence to support the other charges against free Negroes—that they were criminal

[52] *Census of 1850*, pp. 534-547.

and degenerate, and that they caused unrest among the slaves. Doubtless the white people of the 1840's and 1850's had more evidence in support of their views than has survived down to the present; nevertheless, there are few court records of crime by free Negroes. For example, in the Little Rock Corporation Court in the entire pre-Civil War period there were, with the exception of cases involving failure to make bond, only three criminal convictions of free Negroes: two for harboring free Negroes (in both instances the wives of the men charged), and one for assault and battery. In addition, one charge against a free Negro of being in company with slaves at an unlawful meeting was nol-prossed.[53] The influence of free Negroes upon the slaves would be very difficult to determine, but it is not likely that it was as dangerous as asserted. In the absence of much evidence to the contrary, it seems reasonable to conclude that most free Negroes earned their living as best they could in the midst of an officially hostile (but probably often actually otherwise) atmosphere and did little to upset the established relationship between the white masters and the Negro slaves.

In his position intermediate between the white man and the slave, the Arkansas free Negro was subject to legal regulations and restrictions which must have been confusing and troublesome. In some respects he was treated like a white person, and in others like a slave. He had perfect freedom to own real estate and personal property, but he was discouraged from owning slaves. There was no Arkansas law forbidding free Negroes to own slaves, but the Arkansas Supreme Court ruled in 1859 that it was contrary to public policy for them to do so. The court decision gives further insight into the prevalent white attitude:

. . . slavery . . . has its foundation in an inferiority of race. There is a striking difference between the black and white man, in intellect, feelings, and principles. In the order of providence, the former was made inferior to the latter; and hence the bondage of the one to the other. It is upon this principle alone, that slavery can be maintained as an institution. The bondage of one Negro to another, has not this solid foundation to rest upon. The free negro finds in the slave

[53] Little Rock Corporation Court Record "A," Feb. 10, April 23, 28, 1842; Little Rock City Council Record, 1835-1842, pp. 414, 419.

his brother in blood, in color, feelings, education and principle. He has but few civil rights, nor can have, consistent with the good order of society; and is almost as dependent on the white race as the slave himself. He is, therefore, civilly and morally disqualified to extend protection, and exercise dominion over the slave.

So, it may be laid down as a rule, that the ownership of slaves by free negroes, is directly opposed to the principles upon which slavery exists among us, is subversive of all police regulations for the good government of our slave population, and is, therefore, contrary to public policy.[54]

In the case cited a free Negro had not actually owned slaves but was attempting to get possession of some willed to him by his master at the time he was freed. There are only two known instances of free Negroes owning slaves in Arkansas: in 1830 "Free Bob" of Lafayette County owned three,[55] and in 1844 Nathan Warren and a brother, Henry, jointly purchased another brother, James, from Timothy Crittenden. Henry sold his interest in James to Nathan for the token sum of ten dollars in 1850, and a few weeks later Nathan manumitted James.[56] Although there may have been a few other isolated cases, the practice of free Negroes owning slaves was much less prevalent in Arkansas than in other slave states.[57]

Free Negroes were fully liable for "trespasses and felonies, to the same extent and manner that white persons [were] and [were] tried in like manner," but, like slaves, they were not permitted to testify in court against white people, while at the same time slaves were permitted to testify against them. The right of keeping guns was withheld from free Negroes just as from slaves.[58] And while free Negroes had to fulfil such obligations of a citizen as working on the roads and paying taxes, they were not permitted to vote.[59] Even the fact of being free was considered an abnormal

[54] *Ewell et al.* v. *Tidwell Exr.*, 20 Ark. 136.
[55] Carter G. Woodson, ed., *Free Negro Owners of Slaves in the United States in 1830 together with Absentee Ownership of Slaves in the United States in 1830* (Washington, 1924), p. 1.
[56] Ross, "Nathan Warren. . . ," *Arkansas Historical Quarterly*, XV (Spring, 1956), 55.
[57] Woodson, *Free Negro Owners of Slaves, passim;* David Y. Thomas, "The Free Negro in Florida before 1865," *South Atlantic Quarterly*, X (Oct., 1911), 343-344; Andrew Forest Muir, "The Free Negro in Jefferson and Orange Counties, Texas," *Journal of Negro History*, XXXV (April, 1950), 195.
[58] *Gould's Digest, 1858*, pp. 384, 557.
[59] *Ibid.*, pp. 28, 964.

status for a Negro. The Arkansas Supreme Court, in a case in which a Negro was suing for freedom, ruled in 1857:

. . . we think the following would be safe rules of evidence.

1. Where a person held as a slave, sues for freedom, and it manifestly appears that he belongs to the *negro race,* whether of full or mixed blood, he is presumed to be a slave, that being the condition generally of such people in this State.

2. If it appears that he belongs to the white race, he is presumed to be free.

3. If it be doubtful, whether he belong to the white or the negro race, there is no basis for legal presumption, one way or another, but it is safest to give him the benefit of the doubt, as the courts should be careful that a person of the white race be not deprived of his liberty.[60]

Passage of the 1843 law did not satisfy the extremists in Arkansas, and there was continuing agitation to expel free Negroes entirely. The newspapers kept up their propaganda in favor of such action. In 1849 William E. Woodruff wrote, "We believe if a general edict was promulgated for [the expulsion of free Negroes] from the South, it would tend more toward silencing the clamor of Northern abolitionists, than any other movement that could be made. We hope the next Legislature of Arkansas will take measures to rid us of this worse than useless population."[61] An editorial in the *Gazette and Democrat* the next year said:

In glancing over the proceedings of the house, on yesterday, we are pleased to find a notice, by Mr. STEWART, of Crawford, that he will, on Monday next, introduce a bill for the removal of all free negroes beyond the limits of the State. This ought to be done, and the sooner the better. They are the greatest curse our state labors under, and are ruinous to our slave population.[62]

A bill was introduced in the 1850 session of the legislature to expel all free Negroes, but it met with defeat, as did similar bills in succeeding sessions, chiefly because a majority of the legislators believed that free Negroes were citizens of the United States, and therefore had a right to remain in Arkansas.[63]

[60] *Daniel* v. *Guy,* 19 Ark. 121.   [61] *Arkansas State Democrat,* Oct. 5, 1849.
[62] *Gazette and Democrat,* Nov. 8, 1850.
[63] Elsie M. Lewis, "From Nationalism to Disunion: A Study in the Seces-

But the Dred Scott decision of the United States Supreme Court in 1856 eliminated the final barrier to expulsion of free Negroes from Arkansas. The court's opinion, written by Chief Justice Roger B. Taney, said, in part:

The question before us is, whether [free Negroes] compose a portion of this [sovereign] people, and are constituent members of this sovreignty? We think they are not, and that they are not included, and were not intended to be included, under the word "citizens" in the Constitution, and can therefore claim none of the rights and privileges which that instrument provides for and secures to citizens of the United States.[64]

With this as justification, there was a renewed attempt to influence the Arkansas legislature to pass an expulsion law. The movement centered in Little Rock, where a public meeting in the summer of 1858 resulted in appointment of a committee charged with preparing and publishing a circular "calling your attention to a serious evil that afflicts the State, expressing their opinions upon it, and inviting your cooperation to effect its removal. The evil is the presence among us of a class of free colored persons."[65]

The circular was signed by twelve citizens of Little Rock and Pulaski County, including such prominent men as T. J. Churchill, later Confederate general and governor; Benjamin F. Danley, former Pulaski County sheriff; Henry M. Rector, Supreme Court justice who would be elected governor the next year; and Albert Pike. The circular was a long and bitter attack upon free Negroes, containing such terms as "immorality, filth, and laziness," "the free Negro so worthless and depraved an animal," and "the laziness and bestiality of a degraded race." It concluded by pointing out that in the Dred Scott decision the United States Supreme Court had ruled that the free Negro had no constitutional rights, and by issuing a plea to the people "to require of those who desire

sion Movement in Arkansas, 1850-1860" (Unpublished Ph. D. dissertation, Department of History, University of Chicago, 1947), p. 78. By an Arkansas Negro historian, this is an excellent study of the political aspects of the decade prior to the Civil War.

[64] *A Report of the Decisions of the Supreme Court of the United States and the Opinions of the Judges Thereof in the Case of Dred Scott, versus John F. A. Sandford* (New York, 1857), p. 404.

[65] "Circular to the People of the State of Arkansas," *Washington Telegraph*, Aug. 4, 1858.

to represent you in the Legislature of the State a pledge that they will help to enact a law that shall remove beyond the borders of Arkansas *every* free negro and mulatto within its limits, and forbid them for the future to enter into or remain in the state."[66]

In his message to the legislature which convened in December, 1858, Governor Elias N. Conway called for passage of a law expelling free Negroes and providing money for transporting them out of the state and supporting them for a short time in their new homes.[67] The legislature complied promptly, although the law was less liberal than suggested by the governor. It provided that after January 1, 1860, free Negroes over the age of twenty-one were barred from living within the state, and that all found there after that date would be seized and hired out for a year, after which they would be given the choice of leaving the state within thirty days or being sold into slavery. Children under the age of seven could leave the state with their parents, but those between the ages of seven and twenty-one were to be taken into custody and hired out to the highest bidder until they reached the age of twenty-one, when they were to be paid the proceeds of their hire and required to leave the state under provisions of the law.

Free Negroes who desired to remain in the state could do so by enslaving themselves to masters or mistresses who were required to make bond as a guarantee that the slaves would not be permitted to act as free persons or to hire their own time. The only humane provision in the otherwise harsh law was a requirement that the county courts care for the orphans under the age of seven and the aged and infirm who were physically incapable of leaving the state or who could not be sold. Further manumission of slaves within the state was prohibited.[68]

The extent to which this law was enforced cannot be ascertained readily. No instances of free Negroes being sold involuntarily into slavery or voluntarily enslaving themselves were found, and the census of 1860, taken several months after the law went into effect, shows 144 free Negroes still in Arkansas. Forty-

[66] *Ibid.*
[67] Fay Hempstead, *Historical Review of Arkansas* (3 vols.; Chicago, 1911), I, 198.
[68] *Acts Passed at the Twelfth Session of the General Assembly of the State of Arkansas, . . . 1858-1859* (Little Rock, 1859), pp. 69, 175-178.

seven of them were in Washington County, where there had been only fourteen in 1850, twenty were in Desha, and twelve in Jefferson, while the remainder were scattered in smaller numbers through eighteen counties.[69] It is possible that the 144 consisted entirely of orphans, the aged and infirm, those between seven and twenty-one, and those who had been hired out for the one-year period, but this is hardly likely, since the number in the state when the law was passed was doubtless little larger as a result of the increasingly harsh attitude toward free Negroes. It is more probable that there was the usual laxity in enforcement of laws pertaining to free Negroes.

Early in 1861 the Arkansas legislature recognized the injustice, or at least the impracticability, of the expulsion law by suspending its further operation until January 1, 1863.[70] But when that day came Arkansas was in the midst of the Civil War, President Lincoln's Emancipation Proclamation was being placed in effect, and soon all Arkansas Negroes were to be free.

[69] *Census of 1860 (Population)*, p. 15.
[70] *Acts Passed at the Thirteenth Session of the General Assembly of the State of Arkansas, . . . 1860-1861* (Little Rock, 1861), p. 206.

Selected Bibliography

I. PRIMARY SOURCES

A. Manuscripts

1. NATIONAL ARCHIVES, WASHINGTON, D. C.

Original returns of the federal censuses of 1850 and 1860, free and slave population. Microfilm copies of the original returns in the Arkansas History Commission, Little Rock, were also used.

2. ARKANSAS HISTORY COMMISSION, LITTLE ROCK

Minutes of the Arkansas Annual Conference, Methodist Episcopal Church, 1836-1881.

Account Book of Henry Pernot, M. D., Van Buren, Arkansas, 1852-1856.

Tax assessment lists: Arkansas County, 1850 and 1855; Crawford County, 1835; Phillips County, 1855 and 1859; Pulaski County, 1853; Union County, 1853; Washington County, 1835.

These are a part of a collection of several hundred bound volumes of annual assessment lists embracing the period from 1818 to 1861. Practically all Arkansas counties in existence during the period are represented. Although only the volumes listed were cited specifically, practically all were consulted.

3. ARKANSAS MANUSCRIPTS COLLECTION, UNIVERSITY OF ARKANSAS LIBRARY, FAYETTEVILLE

Letter from John C. Luttig, Polk Bayou [Batesville], to Christian Wilt, April 16, 1815.

4. MANUSCRIPT COLLECTION, DUKE UNIVERSITY LIBRARY, DURHAM, N. C.

James Sheppard Papers, 1830-1889. 1,538 items.

James Sheppard (ca. 1816-1870) had large holdings of land and slaves in Jefferson County, Arkansas, Copiah County, Mississippi and New Hanover County, Virginia. Approximately one-fourth of the papers pertain to his plantation operations in Jefferson County. Included are letters and invoices from merchants and factors in New Orleans and other cities, letters from overseers and family members, plantation records, bills of sale for slaves, tax records, and many other types of records. Much of the material deals directly or indirectly with slavery.

5. ARCHIVES OF THE EPISCOPAL DIOCESE OF ARKANSAS, LITTLE ROCK
Baptismal Record, Grace Episcopal Church, Washington, Arkansas, 1860-1867.

6. ARKANSAS MANUSCRIPTS COLLECTION, JOHN A. LARSON MEMORIAL LIBRARY, LITTLE ROCK UNIVERSITY, LITTLE ROCK, ARKANSAS
Roy Stephenson Papers, 1813-1913. 123 items.
This collection was assembled by Mr. Roy Stephenson of Hope, Arkansas. It includes bills of sale for slaves, inventories of estates giving values of slaves, letters, statements, and legal papers of various types. Practically all items pertain to Arkansas.

7. DEPARTMENT OF ARCHIVES, LOUISIANA STATE UNIVERSITY, BATON ROUGE.
Ledger of J. E. Hawkins, M. D., Stephens, Columbia County, Arkansas, 1860-1865.
Daybook of J. E. Hawkins, M. D., Stephens, Columbia County, Arkansas, 1860-1862.
These two volumes are in the J. E. Hawkins Papers, 1859-1912, (4,464 items and 184 volumes). They contain a number of references to medical treatment of slaves.

8. OUACHITA COLLEGE LIBRARY, ARKADELPHIA, ARKANSAS
Minutes of New Hope Baptist Church, Clark County, Arkansas, 1850-1860.

9. IN PRIVATE HANDS
Minutes of the First Baptist Church, Arkadelphia, Arkansas, 1851 to present.
In custody of the church clerk.
Diary of John Brown, Princeton and Camden, Arkansas, 1852-1865.
In possession of a granddaughter, Mrs. Van Manning, Little Rock. Brown operated a plantation near Princeton, then moved to Camden, where he practiced law, operated an insurance business, and hired his slaves out by the day, week, month, or year. The diary consists of one large ledger. The daily entries cover the broad range of Brown's farming, business, social, political, and family activities. There are hundreds of references to various aspects of slave life and work.
Appraisement of the Personal Property of the Estate of Junius W.

Craig, as made on the 14th day of July, A. D., 1860, Exhibit C-No. 3, of Bill of Complaints in case of Joshua M. Craig and John A. Craig vs. Emma J. Wright and others, in Circuit Court, County of Chicot, State of Arkansas, April Term, A. D., 1861.

    In possession of Mr. Robert Chotard, Lake Village, Arkansas, a descendant of the Craig family. Drawn up in connection with a court suit involving possession of Yellow Bayou and Bellevue plantations—worth, with their equipment, supplies, and 211 slaves, more than $300,000—, this document gives names and values of the slaves, and lists and gives the value of all plantation supplies and equipment.

Hanks Family Papers, Helena, Arkansas, 1805-1865. Approximately 100 items.

    In possession of Mrs. Harry Stephens, Sr., Helena, a member of the Hanks family. Most of the papers pertain to Fleetwood Hanks, one of the earliest settlers of Helena. Included are tax receipts, bills of sale, notes, and other business records, many of them dealing with slaves.

Diary of Robert F. Kellam, Camden, Arkansas, 1859-1861.

    In possession of a grandson, Mr. Charles Gee, Camden, Arkansas. A Camden merchant, Kellam occasionally owned a few slaves and at times hired slaves as house servants. He commented on social, economic, and political activities of the community, state, and nation. The diary was kept in one small notebook.

Bible of Robert Isaac Lemon, Pine Bluff, Arkansas.

    In possession of a granddaughter, Mrs. Walter Combs, Pine Bluff. This was the Lemon family Bible. Names and dates of birth of the slave children owned by the family are listed along with those of the white children.

Martin Family Papers, Little Rock, Arkansas, 1798-1875. Approximately 150 items.

    In possession of Miss Blanche Martin, Little Rock, Arkansas. The papers are largely those of Jared C. Martin, Little Rock planter and businessman, although the earlier and later ones are those of ancestors and descendants. There are letters from members of the family in other states and other parts of Arkansas, many bills of sale for slaves, business records, and papers of other types. This collection especially gives insight into methods and practices involved in buying and selling slaves.

Minutes of Point Remove Baptist Church, Atkins, Arkansas, 1833 to present.

    In possession of Elder J. H. O'Neal, Atkins, Arkansas. One of the oldest in continuous existence in Arkansas, the church was originally located on Point Remove Creek, a few miles north of its present location.

Baptismal Record, St. Joseph's Catholic Church, Pine Bluff, Arkansas.

Located in the church.

Baptismal Record, St. Mary's Catholic Church, New Gascony, Arkansas.

Located in the church.

Bill of Sale, Simon Vanarsdale to Louis Fletcher, August 18, 1817.

In possession of Miss Mary P. Fletcher, Little Rock, Arkansas, a descendant of Louis Fletcher, early member of a prominent Arkansas family.

10. COUNTY AND CITY RECORDS (All located in county courthouses and city halls.)

Ashley County (Hamburg).

County Court Record, 1861.

Chicot County (Lake Village).

Circuit Court Records "A" through "F."

Deed Records "A" through "K."

Probate Court Records "A" through "C."

Will Records "A" through "D."

Clark County (Arkadelphia).

Probate Court Records "A" and "B."

Will Books "A" and "B."

Desha County (Arkansas City).

Deed Records "A" through "C."

Probate Court Record, 1852-1857.

Franklin County (Ozark).

Administrators' Record, 1840-1866.

County Court Record, 1847-1854.

County Court Record, 1854-1860.

Probate Record, 1840-1849.

Probate Court Record, 1852-1859.

Jefferson County (Pine Bluff).

Chattel Mortgage Record, 1841-1868.

Record of Settlements "A."

Phillips County (Helena).

Circuit Court Record 1, 1821-1831.

Pulaski County (Little Rock).

Will Books "A" through "C."

Union County (El Dorado).

Executors', Administrators', and Guardians' Bonds, Book "E."

Probate Court Record "A."

City of Little Rock
City Council Records, 1835-1842, 1842-1852, 1852-1861.
Corporation Court Record "A."

B. *Printed Works*

1. STATE AND FEDERAL DOCUMENTS
Acts Passed at the Twelfth Session of the General Assembly of the State of Arkansas, . . . 1858-1859. Little Rock, 1859.
Acts Passed at the Thirteenth Session of the General Assembly of the State of Arkansas, . . . 1860-1861. Little Rock, 1861.
BALL, WILLIAM McK., and SAM C. ROANE, compilers. *Revised Statutes of the State of Arkansas, Adopted at the October Session of the General Assembly of Said State, A. D., 1837.* Boston, 1838.
Consolidated Index of Claims Reported by the Commissioners of Claims to the House of Representatives from 1871 to 1880. Washington, 1892.
ENGLISH, ELBERT H., ed. *A Digest of the Statutes of Arkansas; Embracing All Laws of a General and Permanent Character in Force at the Close of the Session of the General Assembly of 1846.* Little Rock, 1848.
GOULD, JOSIAH, ed. *A Digest of the Statutes of Arkansas; Embracing All Laws of a General and Permanent Character in Force at the Close of the Session of the General Assembly of 1856.* Little Rock, 1858.
Journal of the Constitutional Convention of 1836. Little Rock, 1836.
A Report of the Decisions of the Supreme Court of the United States and the Opinions of the Judges Thereof in the Case of Dred Scott, versus John F. A. Sandford. New York, 1857.
Reports of Cases Argued and Determined in the Supreme Court of the State of Arkansas in Law and Equity. 227 vols. Little Rock, 1840 to present. Cited throughout this work in this manner: "13 Ark. 263."
The Statutes at Large of the United States of America. 71 vols. Boston and Washington, 1855——.
STEELE, J. and J. M'CAMPBELL, eds. *Laws of Arkansas Territory.* Little Rock, 1835.
THORPE, FRANCIS N., ed. *The Federal and State Constitutions, Colonial Charters, and Other Organic Laws of the States, Territories, and Colonies now or Heretofore Forming the United States of America.* House Document No. 357, 59th Congress, 2nd Session. 7 vols. Washington, 1909.
U. S. Bureau of the Census. *Negro Population, 1790-1915.* Washington, 1918.

———— *Census of 1810.* Washington, 1811.

———— *Census of 1820.* Washington, 1821.

———— *Census of 1830.* Washington, 1830.

———— *Census of 1840.* Washington, 1841.

———— *Census of 1850.* Washington, 1853.

———— *Compendium of the Seventh Census, 1850.* Washington, 1854.

———— *Mortality Statistics of the Seventh Census of the United States, 1850.* Washington, 1855.

———— *Preliminary Report on the Eighth Census, 1860.* Washington, 1862.

———— *Census of 1860 (Population).* Washington, 1864.

———— *Census of 1860 (Agriculture).* Washington, 1864.

U. S. Congress. *American State Papers; Documents, Legislative and Executive, of the Congress of the United States.* 38 vols. Washington, 1832-1861.

———— *Annals of the Congress of the United States, 1789-1824.* 42 vols. Washington, 1834-1856.

———— *Register of Debates in Congress, 1824-1837.* 14 vols. Washington, 1825-1837.

———— *The Congressional Globe, 1833-1873.* 46 vols. Washington, 1834-1873.

U. S. Congress, House of Representatives. *Ninth General Report of the Commissioners of Claims.* House Miscellaneous Document No. 10, 46th Congress, 2nd Session. Washington, 1892.

U. S. Congress, Senate. *Indian Affairs, Laws and Treaties.* Senate Document No. 452, 57th Congress, 1st Session. 5 vols. Washington, 1903-1941.

2. SOURCE COLLECTIONS

CARTER, CLARENCE E., ed. *The Territorial Papers of the United States.* 20 vols. Washington, 1934-.

CATTERALL, HELEN TUNNICLIFF, ed. *Judicial Cases Concerning Slavery and the Negro.* 5 vols. Washington, 1926-1937.

FRENCH, B. F., ed. *Historical Collections of Louisiana.* 7 vols. New York, 1846-1875.

KINNAIRD, LAWRENCE, ed. *Spain in the Mississippi Valley,* Vols. II-IV of *Annual Report of the American Historical Association, 1945.* 4 vols. Washington, 1949.

THWAITES, REUBEN GOLD, ed. *The Jesuit Relations and Allied Documents; Travels and Explorations of the Jesuit Missionaries in New France, 1610-1791.* 73 vols. Cleveland, 1896-1901.

3. MISCELLANEOUS PRINTED WORKS

BOND, SCOTT. *Life of Scott Bond.* Little Rock, 1917.

CARTWRIGHT, SAMUEL A. *The Pathology and Treatment of Cholera.* New Orleans, 1849.

CHARLEVOIX, FATHER. A *Voyage to North America: Undertaken by Command of the present King of France. Containing the Geograhical Description and Natural History of Canada and Louisiana.* 2 vols. Dublin, 1766.

CHESTER, SAMUEL. *Pioneer Days in Arkansas.* Richmond, 1927.

CONNELL, ROBERT. *Arkansas.* New York, 1947.

DUMONT DE MONTIGNY. *Mémoires Historiques sur la Louisiane, Contenant ce qui est arrivé l'année 1687.* 3 vols. Paris, 1753.

DUPRATZ, ANTOINE SIMON LE PAGE. *The History of Louisiana, or of the Western Parts of Virginia and Carolina, Containing a Description of the Countries That Lie on Both Sides of the River Mississippi.* 2 vols. London, 1763.

FAIRBANK, CALVIN. *Rev. Calvin Fairbank During Slavery Times.* Chicago, 1890.

FEATHERSTONHAUGH, GEORGE W. *Excursion Through the Slave States.* 2 vols. London, 1844.

A Full and Impartial Account of the Company of Mississippi, otherwise called the French East-India-Company, Projected and Settled by Mr. Law. London, 1720.

GUINN, NANCY COOPER. "Rural Arkansas in the '20's," *Arkansas Pioneers,* I (September, 1912), 11-12.

HOWARD, R. H., compiler. *The History of Virgil A. Stewart, and His Adventures in Capturing and Exposing the Great "Western Land Pirate" and His Gang, in Connexion with the Evidence.* New York, 1836.

"Journal of Bishop Henry C. Lay, 1862-1863," *Historical Magazine of the Protestant Episcopal Church,* VIII (March, 1939), 67-90.

Journal of the General Convention of the Episcopal Church, 1847. N.p., n.d.

KNIGHT, HANNAH D. "Hospitality of Early Days," *Arkansas Pioneers,* I (September, 1912), 10-11.

A Letter to a Member of the P--------t of G---t B------n, Occasion'd by the Privilege Granted by the French King to Mr. Crozat. London, 1713.

MARSHALL, MRS. A. J. *The Autobiography of Mrs. A. J. Marshall.* Pine Bluff, Arkansas, 1897.

Minutes of the Thirteenth Annual Session of the Liberty Baptist Association, Held With Salem Church, Columbia County, Arkansas, September 11th-14th, 1858. Mount Lebanon, Louisiana, 1858.

PEAY, SUE CREASE, and SOPHIA CREASE. "Good Cheer of Early Days," *Arkansas Pioneers,* I (January, 1913), 11.

PFEIFFER, IDA. *A Lady's Second Journey Round the World: from*

London to the Cape of Good Hope, Borneo, Java, Sumatra, Celebes, Ceram, the Moluccas, etc., California, Panama, Peru, Ecuador, and the United States. New York, 1856.

ROLES, JOHN. *Inside Views of Slavery on Southern Plantations.* New York, 1864.

STANLEY, HENRY M. *The Autobiography of Sir Henry Morton Stanley.* New York, 1909.

DE TONTI, HENRI. *An Account of Monsieur de la Salle's Last Expedition and Discoveries in North America.* London, 1698.

WOODSON, CARTER G., ed. *Free Negro Owners of Slaves in the United States in 1830 together with Absentee Ownership of Slaves in the United States in 1830.* Washington, 1924.

C. Newspapers

Arkansas Advocate, Little Rock. 1833-1837.
Arkansas Banner, Little Rock. 1843-1846.
Arkansas Gazette, Little Rock. 1819-1860.
  Variant titles: *Arkansas State Gazette, Arkansas State Gazette and Democrat, Gazette and Democrat.*
Arkansas Intelligencer, Van Buren. 1843-1849.
Arkansas State Democrat, Little Rock. 1846-1850.
  Variant title: *Arkansas Democrat.*
Arkansas True Democrat, Little Rock. 1855-1860.
Batesville Eagle, Batesville. 1848-1850.
Batesville News, Batesville. 1838-1842.
Des Arc Weekly Citizen, Des Arc. 1855-1859.
Hope Star, Hope. Centennial Edition, June 26, 1936.
Memphis Daily Eagle, Memphis, Tennessee. 1850.
Ouachita Herald, Camden. 1856-1860.
Southern Shield, Helena. 1840-1860.
Southern Standard, Arkadelphia. 1896.
The Times, Little Rock. 1835-1836.
Washington Telegraph, Washington, Arkansas. 1843-1859.
Western Frontier Whig, Van Buren. 1844-1846.

II. SECONDARY SOURCES

A. Books and Articles

ABEL, ANNIE H. *The American Indian as Slaveholder and Secessionist.* Cleveland, 1915.

ACUFF, E. H. *Bartholomew Baptist Association of Arkansas, 1850-1950.* n.p., 1950.

APTHEKER, HERBERT. *Negro Slave Revolts in the United States, 1526-1860.* New York, 1939.

ARMSTRONG, ORLAND K. *Old Massa's People.* Indianapolis, 1931.

BANCROFT, FREDERIC. *Slave-Trading in the Old South.* Baltimore, 1931.

BOTKIN, B. A., ed. *Lay My Burden Down.* New York, 1946.

CARROLL, JOSEPH C. *Slave Insurrections in the United States, 1800-1865.* Boston, 1938.

CHAMBERS, J. S. *The Conquest of Cholera, America's Greatest Scourge.* New York, 1938.

COBB, THOMAS R. R. *An Inquiry into the Law of Negro Slavery in the United States of America. To Which is Prefixed, an Historical Sketch of Slavery.* Philadelphia, 1858.

COLEMAN, J. WINSTON. *Slavery Times in Kentucky.* Chapel Hill, 1940.

CRAVEN, AVERY O. *The Coming of the Civil War.* New York, 1942.

DALTON, LAWRENCE. *History of Randolph County.* Little Rock, 1946.

DAVIS, CHARLES S. *The Cotton Kingdom in Alabama.* Montgomery, 1939.

DE BOW, J. D. B. *The Industrial Resources of the Southern and Western States.* 3 vols. New Orleans, 1852-1853.

DEILER, J. HANNO. *The Settlement of the German Coast of Louisiana and the Creoles of German Descent.* Philadelphia, 1909.

EATON, CLEMENT. *A History of the Old South.* New York, 1949.

FLANDERS, RALPH BETTS. *Plantation Slavery in Georgia.* Chapel Hill, 1933.

FLETCHER, MARY P. "Susan Bricelin Fletcher," *Arkansas Pioneers,* I (September, 1912), 10.

FOREMAN, GRANT. *Indian Removal.* Norman, Oklahoma, 1932.

GAYARRÉ, CHARLES. *History of Louisiana.* (3rd ed.) 4 vols. New Orleans, 1885.

GOODELL, WILLIAM. *The American Slave Code in Theory and Practice: Its Distinctive Features Shown by Its Statutes, Judicial Decisions, and Illustrative Facts.* New York, 1853.

GOODSPEED, WESTON A., ed. *The Province and the States, a History of the Province of Louisiana under France and Spain, and of the Territories and States of the United States Formed Therefrom.* 7 vols. Madison, Wisconsin, 1904.

GOVAN, THOMAS P. "Was Plantation Slavery Profitable?," *Journal of Southern History,* VIII (November, 1942), 513-535.

GRAY, LEWIS C. *History of Agriculture in the Southern United States to 1860.* 2 vols. Washington, 1933.

HAMMOND, MATTHEW B. *The Cotton Industry*. Ithaca, New York, 1897.

HEMPSTEAD, FAY. *Historical Review of Arkansas*. 3 vols. Chicago, 1911.

HERNDON, DALLAS T., ed. *The Arkansas Handbook, 1949-1950*. Little Rock, 1950.

———— *Why Little Rock Was Born*. Little Rock, 1933.

JEWELL, HORACE. *A History of Methodism in Arkansas*. Little Rock, 1923.

JOHNSON, FANNY ASHLEY. "The Ashley Mansion and the Ashley Band—the Johnson Residence," *Arkansas Pioneers,* I (September, 1912), 10-11.

Journal of the Eighty-First Annual Convention of the Protestant Episcopal Church in the Diocese of Arkansas, 1953. Little Rock, 1953.

McLEOD, WALTER E. *Centennial Memorial History of Lawrence County*. Russellville, Arkansas, 1936.

MEDARIS, R. C. *Historical Sketch of the Mt. Zion Baptist Church, Greene County, Arkansas, also a Short Historical Sketch of Mt. Zion Baptist Association*. Jonesboro, Arkansas, 1927.

MILLER, S. G. *The History of Presbyterianism in Arkansas, 1828-1902*. Little Rock, n.d.

MOFFATT, WALTER. "Medicine and Dentistry in Pioneer Arkansas," *Arkansas Historical Quarterly,* X (Summer, 1951), 89-94.

MOORE, GLOVER. *The Missouri Controversy*. Lexington, Kentucky, 1953.

MUIR, ANDREW F. "The Free Negro in Jefferson and Orange Counties, Texas," *Journal of Negro History,* XXXV (April, 1950), 183-206.

PHILLIPS, ULRICH B. *American Negro Slavery*. New York, 1918.

POSTELL, WILLIAM D. *The Health of Slaves on Southern Plantations*. Baton Rouge, 1951.

Publications of the Arkansas Historical Association. 4 vols. Fayetteville and Conway, 1906-1917.

QUICK, HERBERT and EDWARD. *Mississippi Steamboatin': A History of Steamboating on the Mississippi and Its Tributaries*. New York, 1926.

RANDALL, JAMES G. *The Civil War and Reconstruction*. New York, 1937.

REYNOLDS, JOHN HUGH. *Makers of Arkansas History*. New York, 1905.

ROGERS, J. S. *History of Arkansas Baptists*. Conway, 1948.

ROSS, MARGARET S. "Early Little Rock Doctors," *Pulaski County Historical Review,* I (June, 1953), 32.

—— "Nathan Warren, Free Negro Confectioner," *ibid.,* III (March, 1955), 10-11.

—— "Nathan Warren, a Free Negro of the Old South," *Arkansas Historical Quarterly,* XV (Spring, 1956), 53-61.

RYLAND, EDWIN, and ANNA FLOURNOY BASSETT. *History of the First Baptist Church, Pine Bluff, Arkansas.* Pine Bluff, 1936.

SELLERS, JAMES B. *Slavery in Alabama.* University, Alabama, 1950.

SHERRARD, THOMAS JOHNSON. *The Sherrard Family of Steubenville, Together with Letters, Records, and Genealogies of Related Families.* Philadelphia, 1890.

SHINN, JOSIAH H. *Pioneers and Makers of Arkansas.* Little Rock, 1908.

SMITH, ROBERT W. "Was Slavery Profitable in the Ante-Bellum South?" *Agricultural History,* XX (January, 1946), 62-64.

St. John's Church, 1850-1950. n.p., n.d.

SYDNOR, CHARLES S. *Slavery in Mississippi.* New York, 1933.

THIERS, ADOLPHE. *The Mississippi Bubble: A Memoir of John Law.* New York, 1859.

THOMAS, DAVID Y. *Arkansas and its People, a History, 1541-1930.* 4 vols. New York, 1930.

—— "The Free Negro in Florida Before 1865," *South Atlantic Quarterly,* X (October, 1911), 335-345.

THOMPSON, JOSEPH J. "Early Corporal Punishments," *Illinois Law Quarterly,* VI (December, 1923), 37-49.

U. S. CONGRESS, SENATE. *Arkansas 1836-1936: A Study of its Growth and Characteristics in Observance of its Centennial Year, 1936.* Senate Document No. 191, 74th Congress, 2nd Session, Washington, 1936.

WILLIAMS, CHARLEAN MOSS. *The Old Town Speaks.* Houston, 1951.

WOODSON, CARTER G. *Free Negro Heads of Families in the United States in 1830 together with a Brief Treatment of the Free Negro.* Washington, 1925.

WORLEY, TED R., ed. "Story of an Early Settlement in Central Arkansas," *Arkansas Historical Quarterly,* X (Summer, 1951), 117-137.

B. *Theses and Other Unpublished Papers*

BROWN, MATTIE. "A History of River Transportation in Arkansas from 1819-1880." Unpublished Master's thesis, Department of History, University of Arkansas, 1934.

CATHEY, CLYDE W. "Slavery in Arkansas." Unpublished Master's thesis, Department of History, University of Arkansas, 1936.

HENDERSON, J. H. "The Negro in Arkansas County." Unpublished paper in possession of the author, De Witt, Arkansas.

LEWIS, ELSIE M. "From Nationalism to Disunion: A Study in the Secession Movement in Arkansas, 1850-1861." Unpublished Ph. D. dissertation, Department of History, University of Chicago, 1947.

PIPKIN, JOHN G. "Slavery in Arkansas." Unpublished Master's thesis, Department of History, University of Chicago, 1923.

STINSON, MRS. GEORGE H. "Mrs. Mary Washington Graham." Unpublished paper in possession of John Stinson, Sr., Camden, Arkansas.

Index